I0893183

KENTUCKY CONFEDERATES

KENTUCKY CONFEDERATES

Secession, Civil War, and the Jackson Purchase

BERRY CRAIG

UNIVERSITY PRESS OF KENTUCKY

Copyright © 2014 by The University Press of Kentucky
Paperback edition 2018

Scholarly publisher for the Commonwealth,
serving Bellarmine University, Berea College, Centre College of Kentucky, Eastern Kentucky University, The Filson Historical Society, Georgetown College, Kentucky Historical Society, Kentucky State University, Morehead State University, Murray State University, Northern Kentucky University, Transylvania University, University of Kentucky, University of Louisville, and Western Kentucky University.
All rights reserved.

Editorial and Sales Offices: The University Press of Kentucky
663 South Limestone Street, Lexington, Kentucky 40508-4008
www.kentuckypress.com

Library of Congress Cataloging-in-Publication Data

Craig, Berry.
Kentucky Confederates : secession, Civil War, and the Jackson Purchase / Berry Craig.
pages cm
Includes bibliographical references and index.
ISBN 978-0-8131-4692-8 (hardcover : alk. paper)—ISBN 978-0-8131-4693-5 (pdf)—ISBN 978-0-8131-4694-2 (epub)
1. Jackson Purchase (Ky.)—History—19th century. 2. Kentucky—History—Civil War, 1861–1865. I. Title.
F457.J23C73 2014
976.9'03—dc23 2014019

ISBN 978-0-8131-7439-6 (pbk. : alk. paper)

This book is printed on acid-free paper meeting
the requirements of the American National Standard
for Permanence in Paper for Printed Library Materials.
∞

Manufactured in the United States of America.

Member of the Association of
American University Presses

To the late Professor Roy O. Hatton of Murray State University,
my mentor and a student of T. Harry Williams,
and to his late wife, Marjorie Hatton,
who always laughed at my jokes

Contents

Introduction

"The South Carolina of Kentucky"

During the Civil War, unionism prevailed to one degree or another in every region of Kentucky except one: the Jackson Purchase, the 2,396-square-mile territory west of the Tennessee River. The Purchase, comprising Ballard, Calloway, Carlisle, Fulton, Graves, Hickman, Marshall, and McCracken Counties, is the Bluegrass State's westernmost region, though during the Civil War, the territory was often called "Southern Kentucky" or "Southwestern Kentucky." The Purchase was also Kentucky's last frontier, Chickasaw country until 1818, when a treaty added the area to the Bluegrass State.[1]

All states have distinct regions. The Civil War made the Purchase unique to Kentucky. Dubbed "the South Carolina of Kentucky," the area was pro-Confederate from the start of America's bloodiest conflict in 1861 and remained Rebel until the war ended in southern defeat in 1865. The Purchase was so intensely secessionist that several of its political leaders and other influential citizens met in Mayfield, the Graves County seat, in May 1861 and debated joining Tennessee in a military alliance or possibly merging with West Tennessee as a Confederate state. Evidently, no other section of a loyal slave state contemplated secession on its own.[2]

"The Jackson Purchase was as southern as catfish and hushpuppies and hominy grits," writes Purchase historian-journalist Hall Allen of Paducah. "Its sympathies were with the South, most of its men going into the Confederate army by the simple process of stepping across the Tennessee line and enlisting." Allen claims the proposed separation of the Purchase from the rest of Kentucky in 1861 was the culmination of many years of alienation the citizens had felt toward the state.[3]

Allen argues that the first Purchase settlers discovered that while the Tennessee and Cumberland Rivers furnished them "such a broad highway of travel," the two wide, deep waterways "could also serve as barriers to shut them out from the rest of the state. The Purchase, it was said, became the stepchild of Kentucky politics, and there was from the beginning, some agitation to pull away from Kentucky and form a separate state of the Jackson Purchase area of Kentucky and Tennessee. Early settlers who came to this Garden of Eden soon found themselves reluctant Kentuckians." Allen concludes that left on their own, "the people of the Jackson Purchase became isolationists. If they could get no help from the state, they would lead their own lives apart from it."[4]

Allen's argument that Purchase dwellers were "reluctant Kentuckians" was not new. "The Jackson Purchase is substantially an annex to the state of Kentucky," J. H. Battle, W. H. Perrin, and G. C. Kniffen write in the Purchase edition of their 1885 book *Kentucky: A History of the State.* "Many of its people feel that they are placed at a serious disadvantage in respect to their proper rights and privileges under the State government." Thus, the authors add, the citizens "have hoped for years that they might join with the remainder of the Purchase in Tennessee, and thus form a State whose government would be more immediately identified with their interests." Battle, Perrin, and Kniffen conclude that the Mayfield convention was "a strong proof of the growth of this sentiment."[5]

Other than the convention, neither Allen nor the authors of the old history book offer any evidence to prove that the region's inhabitants were especially unhappy to live in Kentucky. However, for many years, Purchase Democrats grumbled that the state party took them for granted, especially when the Purchase became such a reliably Democratic region. Before the Civil War, the Democrats never put up a Purchase man for governor or for the US Senate, though Linn Boyd of Paducah, a former speaker of the US House of Representatives, was elected lieutenant governor on the Democratic ticket in 1859.

On the other hand, one important aspect of the Mayfield convention would seem to prove Purchase fealty to the Bluegrass State, or at least to fellow Kentucky secessionists. That is, the delegates opted against separation, apparently because they did not want to harm the Confederate cause statewide. They believed, erroneously, that all of Kentucky was bound to exit the Union sooner or later. Hence, they decided there was no reason for the Purchase to separate on its own.

In any event, the Mayfield convention is all but forgotten. Few history books even mention the gathering. Nonetheless, the conclave greatly alarmed Kentucky Unionists. It grabbed headlines in New York newspapers. President Abraham Lincoln heard about the meeting from a worried Major General George B. McClellan. When it ultimately became plain that Kentucky would not abandon the Stars and Stripes, some Purchase secessionists again threatened regional separation. But military developments in the region thwarted them.[6]

The Purchase was the first part of Kentucky where neutrality was breached. In early September 1861, Confederate forces led by Brigadier General Gideon J. Pillow and Major General Leonidas Polk occupied Hickman and Columbus. Soon afterward, Union troops under Brigadier General Ulysses S. Grant captured Paducah and Smithland, the latter just beyond the Purchase. With Paducah, the region's principal town, and its environs under Yankee control, regional secession would have been unlikely, if not impossible. Confederate sympathizers who lived in territory controlled by the Rebel army might have considered Purchase disunion unnecessary. After all, they were confident, or at least hopeful, that their gray-clad "saviors" were among them to stay.

While not ignoring military matters in the Purchase, this study will focus on the political side of the war in the region. It will emphasize the period from President Abraham Lincoln's election in November 1860 through early 1862, when the Confederates retreated from the region. After Lincoln issued the Emancipation Proclamation in September 1862, most of the rest of Kentucky began to swing toward the Purchase in sentiment. Nonetheless, the balance of the state, with the exception of a few scattered counties, was never out-and-out secessionist like Kentucky's westernmost region.

To the end of the war, most Kentucky Unionists believed their secessionist fellow citizens were traitors to their state and country. Yet almost all pro-Union Kentuckians were proslavery white supremacists, like the Confederate sympathizers they so vehemently disdained. Though the Emancipation Proclamation did not apply to Kentucky, almost every white Kentuckian hated it, just as they despised the idea of making soldiers of slaves. From the beginning, secessionists in Kentucky and everywhere else claimed that Lincoln and his "Black Republican" party aimed ultimately to sound slavery's death knell. Thus, they argued, secession was necessary to save slavery. Even so, when Kentucky forsook neutrality for outright support for the northern war effort, most of its citizens still saw the conflict as a fight to preserve the Union they revered, not to end slavery. Despite the Emancipation Proclamation, which obviously put slavery on the road to extinction, most Kentucky Unionists continued to stand for the Union *and* slavery and apparently saw no contradiction in their position.

In any event, the Purchase and the rest of Kentucky began to tread different paths when Lincoln won. The coming split was not so evident before the election. Lincoln had almost no support anywhere in his native state. Virtually every white Kentuckian believed that Lincoln and the Republicans were willing to sacrifice the Union to end slavery. At the same time, many of them suspected that southern Democrat John C. Breckinridge, though from Lexington, would be a pawn of rabidly proslavery southern "Fire Eaters," who seemed just as willing to destroy the Union to save slavery. Those Kentuckians believed that John Bell, the conservative Constitutional Unionist, or northern Democrat Stephen A. Douglas, was the candidate most likely to safeguard their idea of a perfect union—a union with slavery. Kentucky went for Bell, while Breckinridge pocketed the Purchase. Statewide, Bell came in first, followed by Breckinridge, then Douglas. Lincoln finished last with a mere 1,364 votes. It was Breckinridge, Bell, Douglas, and Lincoln in the Purchase, where the Great Emancipator received only 10 votes.[7]

Fearing president-elect Lincoln and his party soon would end slavery, South Carolina seceded in December 1860. Kentucky governor Beriah Magoffin, a Breckinridge Democrat, ordered the General Assembly to meet in January 1861 to determine the state's future. Friends of the Union cobbled together majorities in the Kentucky house and senate and were able to thwart secession. All five Purchase representatives and two of the region's three senators were secessionists; the other waffled. State representative William D. Lannom was perhaps the most outspoken secessionist in the legislature. From Clinton, the Hickman County seat, Lannom would become a Confederate lieutenant colonel.[8]

Lannom's local newspaper was the *Crescent,* published at nearby Columbus. In 1861, it and the region's three other journals, the *Paducah Tri-Weekly Herald,* the *Mayfield Southern Yeoman,* and the *Hickman Courier,* all supported secession. But in 1860, the *Courier* came out for Douglas, while the *Crescent, Herald,* and *Yeoman* boosted Breckinridge. Elsewhere in Kentucky, most Bell and Douglas supporters formed the core of the Union Party, while Breckinridge voters comprised the base of the Southern Rights or secessionist party. After the firing on Fort Sumter and the start of the war in April 1861, almost every leading Bell and Douglas partisan in the Purchase closed ranks with the pro-secession Breckinridge men. The same was true in the Confederate states. For example, Bell embraced the Confederate cause. Georgian Herschel V. Johnson, Douglas's running mate, became a Confederate senator.

On the other hand, Fort Sumter could not shake Kentucky's historic unionism. Yet Union party leaders worried that the popular excitement over war between the slave and free states might stampede slave state Kentucky into the Confederacy. So the Unionists embraced neutrality within the Union in hopes of staving off secession. They also got behind a May 27 border slave state convention in Frankfort, Kentucky's capital. An election for delegates was held on May 4. The Southern Rights candidates pulled out in late April; the party leadership urged Kentuckians to boycott the canvas.

Of course, the Unionists won all of the delegate slots. Beyond the Purchase, turnout was significant, strongly suggesting that most Kentuckians were happy with neutrality under the Stars and Stripes. Later in May, the legislature and Magoffin made neutrality official state policy. No Purchase lawmaker voted for neutrality.

Less than a month after the Mayfield convention came another statewide test vote on Union or secession. President Lincoln summoned Congress to meet in special session on July 4. On June 20, election day, Union candidates swept to easy victories in nine of the state's ten congressional districts. First District representative Henry C. Burnett, an erstwhile Democrat nominated on the Southern Rights ticket at the Mayfield convention, won another term. But the Purchase carried him to victory. Beyond the region, he captured only Trigg, his home county, and barely.

Meanwhile, neutrality could not stop several Kentuckians from leaving the state and donning Yankee blue or Rebel gray. A number of Purchase volunteers opted for the latter hue. Many of them had served under future Confederate general Lloyd Tilghman of Paducah in the Kentucky State Guard, or state militia. In July, some Purchase secessionists decided to help the Confederate war effort by stealing muskets and cannons belonging to the guard and sending the ordnance south.

The results of the crucial August 1861 elections for the state legislature cemented Kentucky's ties to the Union. The Unionists won their greatest victory yet, enhancing their majorities in both houses. The Purchase sent six secessionists to the house; at least five of them ran unopposed. A month later, both armies advanced into Kentucky. With every Purchase lawmaker voting no, the legislature ordered only the Rebels to leave and authorized the raising of troops for the Union side. Thus, neutrality was finished. So was the tenure of all but two Purchase lawmakers in Frankfort. The rest decamped from the capital and ended up at the Russellville convention of November 1861, which created a rump Confederate government for Kentucky. Evidence of who chose the delegates and how is sketchy. Yet there is no doubt that the convention represented minority opinion in every region except the Purchase. Only the Purchase could claim any degree of legitimate representation.

While most citizens of the Purchase and the rest of Kentucky parted company in 1861, the story of "the South Carolina of Kentucky" is not well known beyond the region. Nor is much else of the region's history. The story of the eastern Kentucky mountains and the Bluegrass is well chronicled, and rightly so. Both are considerably larger areas than the Purchase. The mountains are part of Appalachia, a multistate region that is historically and culturally distinctive. The Bluegrass is Kentucky's heartland and encompasses Frankfort, the state capital, and Lexington, early Kentucky's principal town. Louisville, the state's largest city, is on what is commonly considered the western edge of the region.[9]

To be sure, some history books and scholarly articles document military operations in the Purchase in 1861–65. Many such accounts are well done and comprehensive. Therefore, it would serve no purpose for this study to rehash them. Hopefully, by concentrating on politics, this work will reveal to readers why the Purchase was unique to Kentucky in the Civil War.[10]

At any rate, it is understandable that historians have concentrated on military matters in the Purchase. After all, early in the war, Union and Confederate brass believed the region was one of the most strategic spots in the country because of its big rivers. The Ohio bounds the region on the north, the Tennessee on the east. The Mississippi is the region's western border. Wresting control of the Father of Waters from Cairo, Illinois, south to the Gulf of Mexico was a key feature of the 1861 "Anaconda Plan" that Lieutenant General Winfield Scott, the Union army's general-in-chief, devised for squeezing the Confederacy into submission.

The Ohio merges with the Mississippi at Cairo, across from Ballard County. Illinois authorities quickly recognized Cairo's military value; state troops occupied and fortified the town only days after the war started. Militarily, Paducah was hardly less important than Cairo. Paducah is about forty-five miles up the Ohio; here, the Tennessee merges with the Ohio after flowing south past Knoxville and Chattanooga, Tennessee, before bending west and finally north in a great arc. The junction of the Cumberland and Ohio is at Smithland, another twelve miles up the Ohio from Paducah. Nashville, the Volunteer State capital, is a little less than two hundred miles up the Cumberland from Smithland.

As militarily important as Paducah and Smithland were, Yankee and Rebel brass considered Columbus the grand military prize. The little port clung to mosquito-plagued Mississippi River bottomland below steep-sided dirt bluffs said to be two hundred feet tall, or close to it. An army could plant long-range cannons on the high ground and command the river for miles upstream or down. Soon after the war started, Columbus citizens hoisted a big Rebel flag over the town and begged the Confederates to come. Town leaders trekked south several times seeking weapons to defend themselves against Cairo.

When the Rebels finally showed up, they lost no time in bolstering Columbus with massive earthworks and multiple long-range artillery batteries. They dragged a massive chain across the Mississippi to block the river to Yankee shipping. Most citizens cheered their arrival; the editor of the *Crescent* renamed his paper the *Daily Confederate News.* The Rebels boasted that the town was their "Gibraltar of the West." On November 7, 1861, Grant decided to see if the strongpoint was as rock solid as the Rebels believed it was. Advancing downriver from Cairo, he attacked and captured the Rebels' small outpost at Belmont. The Rebels fired their big guns across the river, rushed more troops to the Missouri side, and counterattacked. Grant and his soldiers retreated, fighting their way through the enemy to reach their transport boats, which carried them safely back to Cairo.

In the end, Grant used the Tennessee and Cumberland for attack routes into the Confederacy's heartland. On February 6, 1862, his gunboats captured Fort Henry, Tennessee, and Brigadier General Tilghman, the bastion's luckless commander. On February 16, Grant's soldiers and sailors bagged Fort Donelson, on the Cumberland near Dover, Tennessee, and about twelve thousand prisoners, several of them Purchase Rebels. The fall of Henry and Donelson forced the Confederates to pull out of Kentucky. Before the end of the month, blue-clad troops marched into Nashville, the first capital of a Confederate state to fall to Union forces. Grant's success played a major role in the South's ultimate defeat. Indeed, Grant's military star rose the minute he stepped off a transport boat at the Paducah waterfront. He would, of course, journey on to the White House after the war.[11]

Paducah and the rest of the Purchase chafed under Union occupation. Most citizens longed for the Rebels to return in force. They had to wait until 1864, when Major General Nathan Bedford Forrest raided northward with his cavalry army, which included many men from the region. On March 25, the Rebels attacked Fort Anderson, whose defenders included white and African American soldiers from the Purchase. The battle of Paducah, tiny in size and significance compared to major Civil War battles such as Shiloh, Vicksburg, and Gettysburg, was the only sizeable clash of arms on Purchase soil.

Meanwhile, the advance of Union armies and the retreat of the Rebels did not bring peace to the Purchase or, for that matter, to the rest of the state. Guerrilla fighting ensued. In the Purchase, Union commanders suspected, correctly, that many civilians sustained the guerrillas, supplying them with food, shelter, smuggled weapons and ammunition, and intelligence on Yankee military movements. Indeed, history instructs that guerrillas succeed when they have the support, active or tacit, of most of the people in the areas where they operate. "The guerrilla must move amongst the people as a fish swims in the sea," Mao Zedong reputedly said. The Purchase "sea" teemed with many schools of such "fish," leading local Union commanders, notably Brigadier General Eleazer A. Paine, to deal harshly with the Purchase.

From the start, Grant and other Union commanders tried to suppress widespread illicit trading between the Purchase and the Confederacy. Grant became convinced that the leading suppliers of the contraband were Jews, and in December 1862, he ordered them expelled "as a class" from Paducah and the rest of the area he commanded. After Cesar Kaskel of Paducah protested the order in person to Lincoln, the president promptly countermanded it, thus forestalling any massive removal. Grant spent the rest of his life deeply sorry for the order and trying to atone for it.

As unwelcome as Grant was in Paducah in 1861, Paine, who took command in the Purchase in 1864, went down in history as the region's greatest villain. He was accused of heading "a fifty-one days' reign of violence, terror, rapine, extortion, oppression, bribery, and military murders." The state's conservative Unionist political powers-that-be ultimately demanded that Paine be removed and prosecuted. He was dismissed and tried by court-martial, but exonerated on all but a minor charge and given a reprimand in general orders.[12]

Hard evidence does not substantiate charges that Paine was a heartless fiend and a wholesale murderer. The general claimed he had no choice but to rule the region with an iron hand because it was filled with unrepentant Rebel spies and smugglers, as well as many citizens who aided and abetted guerrillas. At any rate, Paine's reputation seems to stem more from his politics than from his military policies. To Purchase secessionists—and conservative Unionists in the region and statewide—he was the worst sort of Yankee officer: Paine was a staunch Republican, a warm friend of Lincoln, and an outspoken foe of slavery.

In any event, Paine and every other Union commander in the region failed to make good Unionists of the majority of Purchase citizens. Throughout the war, volunteering for the Union forces lagged far behind the rest of the state. Indeed, the best proof of the Purchase's enduring southern sympathy is the number of troops the region furnished to each side, compared to the remainder of the state. Yankees outnumbered Rebels in every region save the Purchase. Nearly 5,000 Purchase men donned Confederate gray in 1861–65, and approximately 850 men—about 600 white and 250 African American—put on Union blue. Statewide, between 90,000 and 100,000 Kentuckians—white and African American—fought for the Union, and between 25,000 and 40,000 took up arms for the Confederacy.[13]

Election results from 1862, when all of the Purchase fell under Union army control, to the end of the war are more proof that the Purchase was ever cool toward the Union cause. State law, enforced by Union soldiers, kept known or suspected secessionists from voting on the grounds that they were disloyal. Voter turnout was tiny in the Purchase—albeit also small in the rest of the state—compared to the presidential election of 1860 and elections in 1861.

So why did the Purchase and "upper Kentucky" diverge in the Civil War? There were several reasons. To begin with, the region was always more southern in temperament than the rest of the Bluegrass State. Geography was an important factor as well. The region was a natural land extension of West Tennessee, cut off from the balance of Kentucky by the Cumberland and Tennessee. A narrow neck of rugged, thickly timbered hill-and-hollow country known as "Between the Rivers" separated the waterways. Both streams were bridgeless until the early twentieth century. As a result, many of the early Purchase settlers came overland from West Tennessee, some journeying from as far away as Virginia and the Carolinas.[14]

Trade linked the Purchase more tightly to the South than to the rest of Kentucky. Commercially—and geographically—the region was closer to Memphis than to Louisville or Cincinnati. Paducah, Hickman, and Columbus, the region's three most significant river towns, not only were busy ports but were also at the ends of railroads that ran to New Orleans, Mobile, and Nashville.

Politics and religion, too, helped shaped the Purchase's southern outlook. The region's political hero was a Tennessean, Andrew Jackson, the region's namesake and coacquirer. Elsewhere in antebellum Kentucky, most voters idolized Henry Clay. Indeed, from the 1830s to the 1850s, Clay made Kentucky a bulwark of the Whig Party. Yet the Purchase, with the exception of Whiggish McCracken County and Paducah, its seat, remained steadfastly loyal to the Democrats, the party of "Old Hickory." The Purchase was dubbed Kentucky's "Gibraltar of Democracy."

The Democratic Party was, by and large, the party of slavery; its base was the slave state South. A few northern Democrats opposed slavery, but most of them supported slavery or were indifferent to human bondage. Southern Democrats doggedly defended slavery against its Yankee detractors—mostly northern Whigs and later Republicans—claiming slavery was essential to their "civilization." Southerners—Democrats and southern Whigs—demanded the right to have slaves and to extend their peculiar institution into the western territories.

While Purchase politics was proslavery, so was its predominant faith. Historian Alan Bearman says that religion played a significant, if overlooked, role in shaping the region's intensely proslavery and pro-Confederate views. He points out that most Purchase whites belonged to southern white evangelical Protestant churches, many of whose pastors came from the South. Almost all evangelical ministers and church officials declared that slavery was heaven ordained or at least was of the secular world and, hence, none of the church's business.[15]

Kentucky was not a large slaveholding state compared to the cotton states. Indeed, slavery declined in Kentucky after 1830, the year it peaked at 24 percent of the total population. In 1860, slaves comprised less than 20 percent of the state's population and about 16 percent in the Purchase. The Purchase was not Kentucky's largest slave-owning region; the Bluegrass was. Even so, Unionism prevailed in the Bluegrass. On the other hand, the percentage of slaves significantly increased in the Purchase between its early settlement period and 1860. Historian Patricia Ann Hoskins convincingly argues that the growth of a slave-based economy was the most important factor in shaping the region's intense Confederate sympathy. In other words, while slavery was waning statewide, it was waxing in the Purchase.[16]

At any rate, when secessionists, including those in Kentucky, cried "states' rights," they meant the right of states to have slaves. When Kentucky Unionists cried "Union," they meant a union with slavery. Geography, settlement patterns, trade ties, and Democratic politics only partially explain why the Purchase was "the South Carolina of Kentucky." But Hoskins makes a solid case that, more than anything else, a growing economy and a consequent expansion of slavery caused the region to veer sharply from the rest of Kentucky in the Civil War. She writes that the number of slaves in the Purchase increased by 41 percent between 1850 and 1860.[17]

1

Kentucky's South Carolina

Geography, early settlement patterns, trade ties, proslavery Democratic politics, and evangelical Christian religion all helped make the Jackson Purchase Kentucky's only Confederate region. But the most crucial factor was the growth of an economy rooted in slavery. Statewide, slavery declined in Kentucky after 1830, but it grew in the Purchase. To be sure, the difference between the Purchase and the rest of the state was not readily apparent until the Civil War, when the territory west of the Tennessee River was nicknamed "the South Carolina of Kentucky" for the first state to leave the Union. Likewise, Paducah, the region's principal town, was "the Charleston of Kentucky," a comparison to the Palmetto State's largest and most ardently secessionist city.

Just as Kentucky led the nation west, the Jackson Purchase led Kentucky west. In 1792, Kentucky became the first state admitted to the Union from beyond the Appalachian Mountains. The Purchase was the last part of the state opened to white settlement and slavery. The region was Chickasaw country until 1818, when President James Monroe authorized future president Andrew Jackson of Tennessee and past Kentucky governor Isaac Shelby to buy the land on behalf of the US government. Ironically, both men were well known for battling Native Americans.[1]

Kentucky's section of the deal apparently did not become the Jackson Purchase because Old Hickory was more famous than Shelby. The Chickasaws reputedly harbored "some ill-will" toward Shelby and thus "were loth to treat with him." On the other hand, "they had learned both to fear and respect" Jackson. At the same time, it has been claimed that Shelby was ailing during most of the negotiations, and thus "the treaty became known as the Jackson Purchase since it was Andrew Jackson and the land speculators in Tennessee who were the driving force behind the effort to break the 1805 treaty with the Chickasaws that had assured them that the United States would never again ask them for land 'as long as the sun shines and the grass grows.'"[2]

In the pact, signed on October 19, 1818, the Native Americans relinquished their land for $300,000, payable in $20,000 annual installments over fifteen years. The approximately 8,100-square-mile region encompassed Chickasaw territory between the Tennessee and Mississippi Rivers, north to the Ohio River, and south to the Tennessee-Mississippi border. In 1819, the US Senate ratified the agreement, and Monroe signed it.[3]

Kentucky and Tennessee agreed to divide the Jackson Purchase at thirty-six degrees, thirty minutes latitude, which was thought to be the boundary between the two states. However, surveyors discovered that the state line east of the Purchase was about ten miles north of true thirty-six thirty. The two states wrangled over the line, delaying settlement until 1821. In the end, the old border stayed the same west to the Tennessee River, and Kentucky and Tennessee assented to split the Purchase at the actual thirty-six thirty.[4]

Many Purchase residents probably think the region's pioneers—like most Kentucky pioneers—chopped their towns and farms from giant forests primeval. Parts of Kentucky, notably the eastern mountains, were heavily forested. But much of the Purchase's interior, mainly Graves County, was a prairie that Native Americans had created to attract game. "The greater part of the county was almost entirely devoid of timber" and blanketed "with a tall grass in which but few shrubs of any kind were to be seen, except along the streams." Whites called such grasslands "barrens," a misnomer because the soil was fertile. Indeed, the prairie sustained a bounty of buffalo, elk, and deer, which Native Americans hunted for food and for hides. The Indians maintained the barrens by burning the grass every spring for many years.[5]

Woodlands, mostly oak and hickory, returned after white settlement. But for a long time, trees remained scarce in large areas. It was said that along the road between Mayfield, the Graves County seat, and Murray, the seat of Calloway County, there was insufficient timber to cut even a switch.[6]

The other striking feature of the Purchase was, of course, the three mighty rivers—the Mississippi, Ohio, and Tennessee—that bounded the territory on three sides. Otherwise, the terrain might have appeared unremarkable to most early settlers. The land varied from cottonwood- and sycamore-studded floodplains along the big rivers to low, rolling hills and little valleys bisected by small, shallow, meandering creeks that all but dried up in summer.[7]

Just as the Purchase is the western end of Kentucky, Kentucky was the westernmost section of Virginia. As the Old Dominion expanded westward, the legislature created large counties, then, as population increased, subdivided them into smaller ones. When Kentucky became a state, its lawmakers continued Virginia's method of county formation.

Thus, in 1821, Kentucky's entire share of the Jackson Purchase became

Hickman County. Geography determined that many, if not most, of the region's pioneer settlers were from southern states, not Kentucky. The region was a land bridge from the Tennessee portion of the Purchase, orphaned from "upper Kentucky" by the Cumberland and Tennessee and the land "Between the Rivers." No bridges spanned either stream until the early twentieth century. Consequently, many of the early Purchase settlers were southerners, not Kentuckians, who traveled "from and through Tennessee."[8]

Prior to the treaty, some whites—including Revolutionary War veterans with Virginia land grants for their military service —lived in the Purchase. How many is difficult, if not impossible, to say with accuracy. Columbus, where dirt bluffs called the Iron Banks towered above the Mississippi River, was settled in 1804. Ultimately, the issue of the land grants was solved, and in 1822, the state opened a land office at Wadesboro, a village in the eastern Purchase named for Banester Wade, an early arrival. Wadesboro became the seat of Calloway County, which the legislature struck off from the southeastern section of Hickman County, also in 1822. The settlement "was much frequented by emigrants and land speculators," attracted in large numbers by well-advertised land sales, which created "great interest and excitement." Settlers, including "goodly aggregations from Virginia and the Carolinas . . . arrived in overland conveyances ranging from ox wagons to surreys led by spirited horses, not to mention those who came horseback. Prospective buyers would bring with them the silver and gold coins of several national identities, including English, Spanish and French, but for the most part U.S. coins." The flood of land purchasers "taxed the capacity of the little town against the log-walled accommodations during these festive intervals to the point of overflowing into wagon bed sleeping quarters." Wadesboro grew to include several houses, fourteen large stores, and a brick courthouse. But Wadesboro was doomed, mainly by the shifting of the county seat to Murray in 1842; the town was incorporated two years later. Wadesboro was gone by about 1910.[9]

Though spelled "Calloway," the county was named for Colonel Richard Callaway, the famous Virginia-born Kentucky pioneer. Hickman, too, was named for a Kentucky hero, Captain Paschal Hickman. It was the first of three Purchase counties whose names commemorate Kentuckians slain in the War of 1812 Battle of the River Raisin, near what is now Monroe, Michigan. The others are Graves and McCracken; Ballard County was named for a survivor of the battle.[10]

As immigration into the Purchase increased, the legislature continued to create additional counties out of Hickman County, whose original seat was Columbus, the oldest permanent white settlement in the Purchase. While no part of Kentucky was ever a federal territory, the Purchase was the only part of the state where land was surveyed and mapped for sale using the township and range grid system that the Land Ordinance of 1785 established for the Old Northwest Territory—the future states of Ohio, Indiana, Illinois, Michigan, and Wisconsin.

As a result, county lines in the Purchase—except where the counties are bounded by the rivers—are generally straighter than county boundaries elsewhere in Kentucky. Graves County, the largest Purchase county, area wise, is an almost perfect rectangle.[11]

The legislature created Graves in 1823; the county seat is Mayfield, evidently settled in 1819. McCracken (1824) memorialized Captain Virgil McCracken. Paducah became the county seat in 1831. Ballard County (1842) commemorated Captain Bland Ballard, who was captured in the Battle of the River Raisin. Blandville, the first county seat, was superseded by Wickliffe after the Civil War. Marshall County (1842) saluted Chief Justice John Marshall of the US Supreme Court. Benton, the county seat, was named for Senator Thomas Hart Benton of Missouri. In naming Fulton County (1845), the legislature paid homage to Robert Fulton, who built the first practical steamboat. Hickman is the county seat.[12]

While the Purchase was the last territory added to Kentucky, the region was evidently the first part of the future Bluegrass State that Europeans visited. In 1673, Father Jacques Marquette and Louis Joliet, the famous French explorers, briefly stopped at the site of Wickliffe and at Columbus, where the duo saw great potential in the rust-streaked bluffs the Confederates would fortify in the Civil War, almost two centuries later. Mining, not military matters, was on their minds. They marked the high ground on their map as the *mine de fer,* or iron mine. The two figured it was a rich deposit of iron ore. They were wrong, but the high ground is still called the "Iron Banks."[13]

Marquette, a Jesuit priest and missionary, and Joliet, a fur trader, were the first Europeans to traverse and map much of the Mississippi River. They left French-claimed Lake Michigan in May 1673, with five men aboard two birch-bark canoes. Exploring down the Mississippi, they found the *mine de fer* almost twenty miles downriver from its juncture with the Ohio River. Marquette's account of his historic journey is in *The Jesuit Relations,* a series of books about the travels of French Jesuit missionaries in America in the seventeenth and eighteenth centuries. He credited a boatman with spying the "iron mine" in earthen "cliffs" beside the river's edge. "There are several veins of ore, and a bed a foot thick, and one sees large masses of it united with Pebbles," Marquette wrote. He added that the bluffs were made of "a sticky earth . . . of three different colors—purple, violet, and Red. The water in which the latter is washed assumes a bloody tinge. There is also very heavy, red sand."

Marquette tested the iron content in the sand by rubbing a handful of grains on his canoe paddle. The paddle, he noted, "was dyed with its color—so deeply that the water could not wash it away during the 15 days while I used it for paddling." Even today, the bluffs contain bits of iron ore, reddish sand, and pudding stone, Marquette's masses of ore "united with Pebbles."[14]

Except for a metal state historical marker in Columbus that says the Iron Banks were "so named by early French explorers," there are no other memorials linking Columbus to the voyage of Marquette and Joliet, who reached the mouth of the Arkansas River before returning to Canada. However, at Wickliffe another historical marker on busy US Highway 51 says the Frenchmen "stopped on this bank in 1673, according to the 'Jesuit Relations.'" The marker, just south of where the Mississippi and Ohio merge, says the Europeans "were feasted by the Indians." Marquette wrote that the explorers indeed encountered Native Americans, who seemed to be spoiling for a fight. He confessed he was mistaken. "They were as frightened as we were; and what we took for a signal for battle was an Invitation that they gave us to draw near, that they might give us food," he wrote. "We therefore landed, and entered their Cabins, where they offered us meat from wild cattle and bear's grease, with white plums, which are very good."[15]

A little more than a century after Marquette and Joliet stopped at the site of Wickliffe, Clarksville, the first white settlement in the Purchase, sprouted near Revolutionary War Fort Jefferson. The community was named for Brigadier General George Rogers Clark, who had the wooden-walled fort built against the British and their Chickasaw allies in the spring of 1780. The Chickasaws attacked in August but were repulsed. More than 565 people—soldiers and civilians—lived at the bastion and settlement, both of which were abandoned in June 1781.[16]

Clark was hardly the first person to recognize the strategic importance of the nearby Ohio-Mississippi river junction. Wickliffe Mounds State Historic Site preserves the remains of a village occupied by Native Americans of the Mississippian culture from 1000 to 1300 C.E. The settlement encompassed earthen mounds as well as houses, all overlooking the Mississippi about three miles south of its confluence with the Ohio.[17]

Virtually all traces of Fort Jefferson and Clarksville, about three miles south of Wickliffe Mounds, disappeared long ago. According to a local legend, the heroism of a teenage girl, Nancy Ann Hunter, saved the fort and the settlement from Chickasaw warriors. In their 1928 *History of Kentucky,* Temple Bodley and Samuel M. Wilson suggest that had the youth lived in New England, with its plentiful printing presses and book publishers, she "would be celebrated in history, romance and song, and known to every school girl in the land."[18]

Louisville lawyer and editor Reuben T. Durrett told her story in an 1883 speech in Falls City. While the Native Americans besieged Fort Jefferson, Hunter, fifteen, supposedly ran a gauntlet of gunfire to retrieve a cow and a calf. "In the fort were many infants, likely to die for want of nourishment; while outside, but within range of Indian guns, was a cow and calf," Bodley and Wilson explain. "Bringing that cow into the fort meant the saving of young lives." Durrett, who founded the Louisville-based Filson Historical Society, claimed that while the men parleyed over what to do, Nancy Ann Hunter dashed out and hustled the baby bovine back to the fort, "the cow following, while shots whistled by and cut her clothing, herself unharmed."[19]

State Historical Society markers on US 51 at the entrance to the Fort Jefferson Cross, a ninety-foot metal crucifix, show where the old fort stood. The signs do not mention Hunter, and little else is known of the young woman. It seems possible that Durrett stretched the truth. Besides, one would assume that breast feeding would have provided adequate nourishment for the infants. No matter, his tale is not as tall as another one told about the heroine. According to that old yarn, Hunter went buffalo hunting to bring sustenance to the starving soldiers and settlers. Allegedly, she swam the Mississippi, fully clad, with a musket strapped on her back, slew the buffalo on the opposite shore, and returned, using the carcass as a personal flotation device.[20]

The Fort Jefferson fight was apparently the last significant battle between Native Americans and whites in the Purchase. But early nineteenth-century settlers faced unseen and often deadly foes—diseases eradicated long ago. John Anderson, who is considered the founder of Mayfield, lost six of his children to various maladies. He, his wife, Nancy Davenport Anderson, their offspring, and their descendants are buried in the old brick-walled Anderson family cemetery in town. Though they migrated to Graves County from Caldwell County in 1819, the Andersons, like so many early Purchase settlers, were not Kentucky natives. He was born in South Carolina; Virginia was her birthplace. Their son, Rollin Lee Anderson, succumbed to "typhus fever" in 1838 at age nineteen. In a little leather-bound journal, John Anderson scrupulously detailed Rollin's agonizing death. The journal documents standard nineteenth-century medical treatments for typhus that modern physicians would dismiss as deadly quackery.[21]

Anderson began his story by describing the family's trek "to the district . . . West of the Tennessee river." They "settled on Mayfield Creek in the woods two & half miles north of the town of Mayfield (or where the town now stands for it was then in the woods)." Anderson recalled that the family was "three days on the route encamping in the woods of night and threading our way through the thickets by day." They arrived "at the place of our future residence" on October 27, 1819, "my family then consisting of myself & wife one Negro girl named Felicia and my three sons that are now dead towit Vincent Wadsworth Anderson and John Davenport Anderson and Rollin Lee Anderson the subject of this sketch."[22]

John Anderson said he "built cabins and cleared land and resided at this place until December 1824." His appointment as county clerk necessitated the move to Mayfield, where "Rollin was raised and educated amidst great difficulties." John Anderson opened a store and became one of the community's leading citizens. He was circuit court clerk when he died in 1842.[23]

He and Nancy mourned the death of John Davenport on May 3, 1837. Vincent Wadsworth was in Clinton, which became the Hickman County seat in 1829, when he perished on December 26, 1837. He was working in the clerk's office, and on his deathbed, the recently wedded Vincent asked Rollin to take his job and provide for his widow.[24]

"Alas!" John Anderson penned, "cruel relentless death was there aiming a deadly shaft at [Rollin's] vitals." Rollin fell ill on June 3, 1838, suffering violent headaches. He summoned a local doctor; typhus was the dreaded diagnosis. The doctor prescribed "pills" and "copious bleeding," after which Rollin rallied. John rushed to his son, expecting to witness his recovery. But relapse followed. Rollin's fever soared; he drifted into delirium, shocking his father with outbursts of "vulgar or profane language." Desperate to save his patient, the physician "blistered him severely . . . right upon the region of the lung, and in the course of the next 24 hours he cut all his hair from his head and caused it to be rubbed profusely with tincture of Canthardy which reduced his whole head to a solid blister."[25]

Anderson poured out his anguish: "I never shall forget his agonies he begged most piteously for a knife to put an end to his sufferings Oh! God am I destined to see all my children die in the order of nature to be reversed in my case and instead of my sons being spared to comfort me in my old age and commit my body to the tomb am I to witness the destruction of my whole race? Save me Oh! God from this melancholy fate."[26]

Rollin's life ended on June 12. John paid the doctor for his services, bought a coffin, and arranged for a wagon and driver to carry Rollin's corpse home. He also "dispatched a messenger to Mayfield to advise my family of the melancholy event." Rollin was buried just before sundown on June 13. "My family cemetery is situated about 400 yards north of the court house . . . on a narrow ledge of land on the right side and overlooking the western road to Paducah," Anderson wrote of the burial plot around which the town has grown. "Here now I have six children buried & have only 5 left and here I intend to be buried myself." When Anderson watched the burial of his son, he "was forcibly struck with the great truth that 'there is nothing firm and enduring but heaven.'"[27]

Paducah lay at the terminus of "the western road" from Mayfield, about twenty-five miles distant. Clark, the town's progenitor, chose the confluence of the Ohio and Tennessee Rivers for a settlement site two years before he had Fort Jefferson erected. In 1778, Clark and his little army paddled down the Ohio in canoes to start his famous western campaign against the British outposts at Kaskaskia and Cahokia, Illinois, and Vincennes, Indiana. They landed on Barataria Island in the mouth of the Tennessee before crossing over to Illinois, a short way downstream, and beginning their 120-mile northwesterly march to Kaskaskia, their first objective.[28]

Clark staked a claim to the site of Paducah in 1795, but settlement could not proceed because the land belonged to the Chickasaws. Clark died in February 1818, eight months before the Jackson Purchase treaty. Deeply in debt, Clark had passed his claim to his younger brother, William, one-half of the storied Lewis and Clark Expedition of 1804–6. The courts disallowed the transfer, claiming it was "fraudulent as to the creditors of George Rogers Clark." Undaunted, William Clark tried to buy the Paducah site. But a court ruling held his purchase defective and corrected the record to show that George Woolfolk of Shelbyville, Kentucky, bought the land. The court ordered the Clark heirs to deed the land to Woolfolk; if they refused, Samuel Dickenson, as court-appointed commissioner, was "to do it for them." The Clarks did not budge, and in June 1827, Dickenson gave the deed to Woolfolk. But four months later, he sold the land to William Clark "for the sum of five dollars in hand paid," a transaction commemorated by a state historical marker in Paducah. Nonetheless, Clark still had competition for the right to found the town. The family of a Virginia officer killed in the Revolutionary War alleged that his claim to the tract predated Clark's. Not until 1844 did the US Supreme Court rule in favor of Clark, who had died in 1838.[29]

Paducah grew rapidly. Between 1830 and 1847, the population increased from 105 to nearly 2,000. According to pioneer Kentucky historian Lewis Collins, Clark, who lived in St. Louis, named his new town "after the celebrated Indian chief *Paducah,*" thus giving birth to a myth that would persist for many years.[30]

The tale grew taller in an 1859 Paducah city directory, which claimed that "the name of Paducah is derived from that of an Indian Chief who died about the year 1819, and was buried, in what is now called Jersey City, by being laid on top of the ground and surrounded by a rude wooden pen, constructed by warriors of his tribe." The chief "was of Herculean size, a great favorite among his people who were in the habit of visiting the place of his remains for several years after his death." Collins and the directory author apparently were unaware of an April 27, 1827, letter Clark wrote to his son, Meriwether Lewis Clark, explaining how Paducah got its name. "I expect to go to the mouth of Tennessee the 26th of next month and be absent about two weeks," he penned. "I have laid out a town there and intend to sell some lots in it, the name is Pa du cah once the largest nation of Indians known in this country, and now almost forgotten." The Padoucas lived near the Red River in what is now Texas when Clark learned of them: "Once numerous, they had been debased by Europeans to the point of slavery and extermination." To ensure his town's name would be correctly pronounced, Clark dropped the French spelling—"Padouca"—for "Paducah," which is Kentucky's only major city that has an Indian name.[31]

For years, locals believed Paduke was chief of the Paducah Indians, a supposed subtribe of the Chickasaws. Reputedly, they had lived where the town sprouted. In any event, grade school children wrote on "Chief Paduke" tablets emblazoned with his face, framed by a multifeathered war bonnet. A similar image appeared larger than life on the back of the screen at the old Paducah Drive In. The latter likeness might have been appropriate, because city historian Fred G. Neuman one-upped the old city directory, claiming that the chief loomed "Atlas-like above the common range" and "towered above his braves as the pyramid of Ghizah above the desert." After the Purchase treaty, Paduke and the Paducahas left to join other Chickasaws in Mississippi, according to Neuman. Nonetheless, Paduke pined to meet Clark and pay him "personal homage." The chief heard that Clark was coming to "Pekin," the name of the tribe's old camping grounds, on which Paducah began, in the summer of 1819. Paduke and ninety warriors paddled to Pekin only to find Clark was not there. Disappointed, they headed for home, but Paduke became ill and died on the way. The warriors returned his body to Pekin for burial on "the old camping site" where "his wigwam had stood under a large sycamore tree in a royal grove on the hill." Clark did name the city for Paduke, but too late for the chief to know about it, declares Neuman, who provides readers not a shred of evidence for what he writes.[32]

No matter, a Native American is still part of the city's official logo, and Paduke is the subject of a statue. In 1909, the Paducah Chapter of the Daughters of the American Revolution raised money and commissioned celebrated Chicago sculptor Loredo Taft to chisel a supposed likeness of Paduke. Unveiled at the corner of Fifth and Broadway, the stonework was removed to its present location, Nineteenth and Jefferson, after the great Ohio River flood of 1937.

Paducah's location at the convergence of the two rivers helped make it the largest town in the Purchase. Steamboats hauled away tons of Purchase produce, especially tobacco. By 1860, Paducah included 4,590 inhabitants. Besides a wharf boat and a riverboat repair and refitting facility, pre–Civil War Paducah boasted a multitude of stores and shops, three banks, twenty-one lawyers, two carriage makers, a trio of bakeries, a brewery, a distillery, twenty-one coffee houses, four hotels, four schools, and two seminaries. Fair's cornet band was available for entertainment, and thirsts could be slaked by beer, wine, and spirits, all of which flowed freely at Louis Mueller's Pleasure Garden.[33]

Nowhere in the Mississippi Valley "have enterprise and the mechanic arts been more amply rewarded than at Paducah," the city directory advised. Riverboat building and the shipping trade "have both increased in a ratio without any parallel in western towns—the result of all which is, that nothing is wanted to build up a great city at said place but the regular process of events—permanency of our free institutions, and the continuance of industry, virtue and intelligence of the people." The directory confidently predicted that the city's new railroad would "within the next eighteen months" put Paducah "in direct communication with all the cities and markets of the South." The booklet added that combined with the town's lively river trade, the shiny steel rails "will give her, beyond all doubt, a monopoly of every description of article which can be manufactured with coal, iron and wood."[34]

Paducah became the northern end the New Orleans & Ohio Railroad. Lloyd Tilghman, a West Point graduate and experienced railroad construction engineer, came to town to build the line. Work began in the winter of 1853–54 under the watchful eye of Tilghman, a goateed Maryland native who would become the Purchase's only Civil War general. He was a Confederate, like most other men from the region, who marched away to fight.

Tilghman's railroad brought great excitement to Paducah. By Independence Day, 1854, tracks stretched southward seven miles to Florence Station. The city celebrated with an excursion and barbecue. "People drove in carriages and ox-teams and came on foot and horse and on mule-back from miles to witness for the first time in their lives the thrilling spectacle of a roaring 'iron horse' consuming wood and water and belching forth smoke, fire, and steam as it pulled a train of cars at the amazing speed of 15 miles per hour." The Paducah railroad's original equipment consisted of a single locomotive, "about as big as a thresher," and a pair of small flat cars. Passengers worried about the train's speed, fearing they would be unable to breathe at such a rapid clip.[35]

By the end of 1854, workers had laid tracks all the way to Mayfield; the trip took two hours. In 1859, mechanics at the Paducah railroad shop built a locomotive and named it the "James Campbell," in honor of circuit judge James Campbell, who was also president of the line. By 1860, the rails stretched another twenty-three miles, to the Kentucky-Tennessee state line. The station, just inside Kentucky, was named Fulton for Fulton County, which surrounded it. Between Paducah and Fulton, the tracks bisected Graves County, leading John C. Noble's *Paducah Herald* newspaper to claim that the line provided the county "an unparalleled increase in wealth and energy almost impossible to realize." At the same time, Paducah, according to the hometown paper, had enjoyed "as much, if not more, prosperity and growth in everything that makes a city great." The railroad transformed Mayfield from "a dull, sluggish, uninteresting little village that only lacked a pair of tombstones to announce her decease" into "an active, prosperous, commercial town." Shortly before the Civil War began, track crews pushed the railroad twenty more miles to Rives, Tennessee, where it joined the Mobile and Ohio Railroad, whose northern terminus was Columbus: "For the first time Paducah and Mayfield were linked by rail with Jackson, Memphis, Vicksburg, Mobile, New Orleans, and many other cities."[36]

Columbus is about forty-five miles southwest of Paducah. Though the town eventually lost county-seat status to Clinton, Columbus remained the largest and most important county town for many years. The railroad was completed all the way from Mobile to Columbus shortly after the Civil War began. A ferry shuttled passengers and freight approximately twenty miles between Columbus and Cairo, the southern terminus of the Chicago-based Illinois Central Railroad. A brisk river and rail trade helped boost the population of Columbus to 963 souls in 1860, when Clinton had but 264 inhabitants.[37]

Evidently, soldiers from Fort Jefferson visited the site of Columbus, named for Christopher Columbus, in 1780. Though the area west of the Tennessee River was Chickasaw land until 1818, the Virginia legislature envisioned a town on the site as early as 1783–84, when lawmakers approved the "laying of land warrants" along the Mississippi, Ohio, and other rivers for the benefit of the Old Dominion's Revolutionary War veterans. But surveyors got no further than "establishing corners"; Chickasaw attacks forced them to flee. The town of Columbus sprouted from a blockhouse built in 1804 and used as a fort while ex–vice president Aaron Burr was allegedly conspiring against the federal government. In 1822, the first county and circuit courts in the Purchase convened in the old log strongpoint. "It was the cherished dream of the projectors of the enterprise to found here a large city, which should not only become the commercial center of the United States, but eventually the seat of national government as well."[38]

Legend has it that President Thomas Jefferson wanted Columbus to be the capital of the United States. "The old folks said that he stood on the bluff overlooking the Mississippi River and declared that the capital should be built here," declared the late Lucille Owings, a Columbus historian. "I've also heard it was James Madison. Anyway, for years, they called the spot 'Capitol Hill.'"[39]

An old historical marker in town claims "COLUMBUS WAS PROPOSED AS THE NATION'S CAPITAL AFTER THE WAR OF 1812." But historians doubt it. Even so, some Hickman County residents have had fun with the capital legend. The late Virginia Jewell of Clinton, a local newspaper columnist, once illustrated a story on the subject with a doctored photo showing the US Capitol perched on a Columbus bluff top. "It's a good story, the kind of folklore that makes history interesting," Owings said. "But it ought to be taken with a grain of salt." Perhaps a boulder would be more like it.[40]

While Columbus was the third-largest Purchase town in 1860, Hickman, first called Mills' Point, was number two, with 1,006 inhabitants. The Nashville & Northwestern Railroad wedded Hickman and Union City, Tennessee, which was also a junction town for the New Orleans & Ohio and the Mobile & Ohio. As at Columbus, tall dirt bluffs towered over the town, which survived pestilence and fire in its early years. In 1827, the Kentucky side of the Mississippi suffered "the great plague of squirrels." The furry rodents "swarmed over the country like the locusts of Egypt, utterly destroying the corn, and doing severe damage generally." Reputedly, they swam the Mississippi and stayed for several months: "There was a lady washing clothes on the bank of the river at Mills' Point . . . on the day the little pests crossed, and with her clothes paddle she killed over seventy of them." Just as the Civil War was starting, a blaze swept through Hickman, burning $200,000 worth of property. The fire destroyed the *Hickman Courier* office.[41]

Owned by Ed K. Warren, George Warren, and Tim Willis, the paper reflected the intensely Democratic views of the town, the county, and almost all of the Purchase region. Yet in 1860, the *Courier* departed from the region's three other papers and endorsed northern Democrat Stephen A. Douglas of Illinois for president. Noble's *Herald,* Len G. Faxon's *Columbus Crescent,* and C. C. Coulter's *Mayfield Southern Yeoman* backed southern Democrat John C. Breckinridge, a Kentuckian. All four papers would become intensely secessionist, reflecting the region's uniqueness to Kentucky during the Civil War.

But the Purchase had always gone its own way, especially in politics. When the region became part of Kentucky, the nationalist-minded Henry Clay of Lexington was the hero of the Bluegrass State. Elected speaker of the House in 1811, he would go on to become secretary of state, a US senator, and a three-time presidential candidate. But he is most famous for helping broker three compromises to save the Union. Thus dubbed "the Great Pacificator," Clay, along with Senator John J. Crittenden, later "put the Union first and the state second; or to put it more accurately, had thought of the state in terms of the Union."[42]

Clay made his first run for the presidency in 1824, battling Jackson, William Crawford of Georgia, and John Quincy Adams of Massachusetts, the ultimate winner. Only Clay and Jackson were on the ballot in Kentucky. Bluegrass State voters cast almost 73 percent of their ballots for their favorite son, who nonetheless finished last in the four-man race.[43]

Clay won every Kentucky region except the Purchase, which gave Jackson nearly 72 percent of its ballots. Jackson beat Adams in the 1828 presidential election and even carried Kentucky. Statewide, Jackson received 55.5 percent of the vote. The Purchase was Old Hickory's best region, furnishing him more than 87 percent of its ballots.[44]

Under Clay's guiding hand, the nationalistic Whig Party dominated Kentucky politics from the 1830s to the 1850s. Between 1834 and 1851, state voters elected seven straight Whig governors. After Jackson, a Democrat did not win Kentucky in a presidential contest until James Buchanan carried the state in 1856. On the other hand, the Purchase, except for Paducah and McCracken County, a Whig enclave, remained true to the Democrats. In presidential elections from 1832 to 1856, the region's Democratic vote was 70 percent of all votes cast.[45]

Dr. George Beeler of Clinton was part of the Whig minority, or at least he voted for General Winfield Scott, the party standard bearer, in 1852. "Old Fuss and Feathers" carried Kentucky, but Democrat Franklin Pierce won the election and topped Scott in Hickman County, 379–155. "I had to talk a good deal before I could get to vote," the physician recorded in his diary on November 2, election day. "Squire Clark bought a barrel of whiskey and knocked out the head and told them to 'ruff' in. The Democrats drank more than the Whigs." Eight days later, he was "up in town" where "some of the boys wanted me to help illuminate the town in honor of Mr. Pierce's triumph. If it was customary for a man to rejoice after being whipped I might accede to the proposition but as it is I don't think I would be treating my conscience with due respect."[46]

Beeler might have felt more at home politically in Paducah. In the 1830s, a strong Whig party developed in McCracken County, probably because of the growing commercial importance of the county seat. The county voted Whig in presidential elections in 1836, 1840, 1844, and 1848; in 1856, it went for ex-president Millard Fillmore, candidate of the American or "Know-

Nothing" Party. Nationally, the Whigs were divided over slavery. Northern Whigs wanted human bondage ended, at least gradually. Slave state Whigs, including those in the Purchase, were proslavery.[47]

More than anything else, a growing economy that went hand in hand with a significant expansion of slavery made the Purchase "the South Carolina of Kentucky," according to historian Patricia Ann Hoskins. She likens the region to parts of the South that experienced similar simultaneous and significant growth in their economies and enslaved populations. There, slave owners were outspoken secessionists, and nonslaveholders supported secession to preserve white supremacy. Thus, secession represented white solidarity. Hoskins concludes that, "flush with material progress and long overlooked by the rest of the state, the Purchase during the secession crisis revealed itself as never before to be different from the Commonwealth."[48]

Despite the growth of slavery, the Purchase did not surpass the Bluegrass as the state's major slave-owning region. In 1860 in Woodford County, for example, slaves outnumbered whites; in Bourbon County, the white population exceeded slaves by only 727. In Fayette County, which encompassed Lexington, and Bourbon County, slaves made up approximately 46 percent of the total population. In 1860, the seven-county Purchase was home to 53,847 whites, 10,471 slaves, and 189 free African Americans. Slaves comprised about 19.5 percent of Kentucky's population but approximately 16 percent in the Purchase. Yet slavery was growing in the Purchase, while shrinking statewide. Between 1790 and 1830—the year of the first Purchase census—the slave percentage in Kentucky increased from 16.2 to 24 percent, the highest-ever percentage. Between 1850 and 1860, the slave population in the Purchase increased by 41 percent. The percentage of slaves was greatest in Fulton—20.3—followed by Ballard (19.8) and Hickman (17.8). Slaves comprised 17.5 percent of the population of Graves County, 15.9 percent in McCracken, and 15 percent in Calloway. In Marshall County, slaves made up only 5 percent of the population.[49]

To be sure, slavery was not a wedge issue in Kentucky. Most Bluegrass State Unionists rejected abolitionism as firmly as all "states' rightist" Democrats did. By "states' rights," the Democrats meant the right of states to have slavery. By "Union," the Unionists meant a union with slavery. In border slave states Kentucky and Missouri, white supremacy was at the heart of universal white values, "or, more specifically, a belief that Western civilization was a product of characteristics unique to the white race and that all interracial relationships must protect the white race from subjugation and degradation by the black race," historian Aaron Astor writes. Most Kentuckians were conservative Unionists. Astor adds that as such they believed that "the 'twin heresies' of abolitionism and secession equally threatened the very fabric of border South society by abrogating the tradition of practical decision making and compromise threatening to destabilize the slave-based social order." In short, almost all white Kentuckians—including nearly every Unionist—supported slavery to one degree or another. The presidential election of 1860 would prove that; Lincoln, the candidate of what almost every white Kentuckian scorned as the "Black Republican" party, would receive a mere 1,364 votes in his native state and just 10 votes in the Purchase. The eleven slave states that seceded in 1860–61 did so because they feared Lincoln and the Republicans would abolish the South's peculiar institution.[50]

While cotton was king in the Deep South, tobacco boosted the Purchase economy. Between 1850 and 1860, regional production of the leaf rose from three million to twelve million pounds. Landholdings and farm values also grew. Improved acreage in the Purchase increased from approximately two hundred thousand acres in 1850 to three hundred thousand in 1860. The cash value of farms went up from approximately three million dollars to more than twelve million dollars.[51]

Reminiscences of Purchase slaves are rare. But an account of slavery in Ballard County published in *Kentucky Slave Narratives: A Folk History of Slavery in Kentucky from Interviews with Former Slaves* would probably be typical of the region: "Buying and selling of slaves was carried on at irregular intervals. The trading usually took place at the home of the slave owner. The prices paid for slaves was dependent upon certain conditions. In case of a full grown, robust negro boy the price was sometimes as high as one thousand dollars. The prices paid was varied according to age, the general health and other conditions of the individual." The narrative continues: "At times pathetic scenes prevailed in the selling of slaves; namely, the separation of mother and child. Often, a boy or girl would be sold and taken away from his or her mother. In many cases the parting would be permanent and the child and its mother would never see each other again."[52]

Ballard County, like the rest of the Purchase, was not plantation country. Real Taras were elsewhere. Besides tobacco, Purchase farmers raised corn, wheat, hay, hogs, horses, and mules. The Purchase was just north of the cotton belt, which extended upward to northwestern Tennessee. Yet at least some cotton was grown in the southern Purchase. Hickman exported two thousand bales in 1845.[53]

Though tobacco, not cotton, was the big moneymaker for Purchase whites, cotton-state-style evangelical Protestant Christianity dominated in matters of faith. Indeed, historian Alan Bearman convincingly argues that religion was also crucial in shaping Purchase support for slavery and secession: "Repeatedly, historians have recognized how religious belief caused the South to view its cause as just. This was the case in the Purchase; its inhabitants believed they were on the side of God, and therefore chose secession with great confidence. . . . Purchase residents determined their identity as Southerners, in part, through their evangelicalism. Therefore, as the secession dispute became a religious battle they could, ultimately, only choose to support one side—the Confederacy."[54]

The Purchase's largest denominations were the proslavery Southern Baptist Church and the Methodist Episcopal Church, South. Both denominations had many adherents across Kentucky. Yet Purchase Methodist and Baptist orientation was toward Tennessee. In 1828, the Methodist Church permanently put the Purchase in the Memphis-based Tennessee conference. Hence, Methodists in Kentucky's westernmost region looked to Memphis for leadership. Also, affiliation with the Tennessee Conference meant Purchase pastors would be southerners. At the same time, Purchase Baptists were heavily influenced by Landmarkism, debates that were centered in Nashville and its environs. Landmarkists claimed John the Baptist founded the Baptist Church. According to Bearman, "the geographical and cultural distance of Purchase Baptists from most of Kentucky made a fertile ground for Landmarkist ideology and further helped to tie them to Baptists in the South." Therefore, Bearman concludes, "the dominant intellectual and spiritual ethos of the Purchase came not from the Bluegrass region of Kentucky but from the South."[55]

Bearman adds that the exclusivist nature of Landmarkists caused them to view antislavery agitation as unjustified and, even more significantly, as an outside threat to their cultural identity: "Their honor and sense of distinctiveness meant that they were predisposed to defending their sense of being southern when such attacks began. The Purchase culture was southern and to attack slavery would have meant, for evangelical churches, running the risk of becoming outsiders in their own communities." Faith in Landmarkism caused Baptists to believe they were always right theologically, according to Bearman: "The evangelical leadership of the region was Southern in culture and could hardly contemplate a South without slavery; it was certainly unacceptable to have even suggested such a possibility publicly." Southern pastors used the Bible to claim slavery was heaven-blessed. They argued that the obvious presence of Christian slaves proved that human bondage was how God chose to bring Jesus to Africans.[56]

White southern evangelicals also argued that slavery was a render-unto-Caesar issue. Not wishing to confront the theological aspects of slavery, Purchase Methodists insisted it was a secular matter. Bearman quoted Wadesboro and Murray District Methodists: "We believe that slavery is a civil institution, subject to the control of the civil powers alone, and whereas we believe that any interference of our Ecclesiastical tribunal with our civil rights and privileges is to be deprecated." He says the statement represents a distinctly sectional approach in defense of slavery. The Methodists were "arguing that if slavery were legal within a particular state, then outside agitators should respect the rights of the residents of that region." He concludes, "the Southern tint to their argument is telling because it was a territory that profited in substantial fashion from slavery." According to Bearman, "this attempt to declare slavery a civil institution, in all ways outside of the moral responsibility of the church, was a common Southern tactic."[57]

Like Purchase Methodists, Baptists in the region entertained "no thought of confronting the evils of slavery; to them it was a Biblically ordained and natural system. Their sole concern was to ensure ongoing efforts of proselytizing among the African-Americans of the region. The Southern belief structure that claimed that God had ordained slavery meant that the people of the Purchase became defenders of the right to own slaves."[58]

The expansion of slavery into the national territories became the most important issue in the presidential election of 1860. This was the most crucial vote in American history because the fate of the Union hung in the balance. Four candidates sought the presidency: Abraham Lincoln of Illinois, Vice President John C. Breckinridge of Kentucky, Senator Stephen A. Douglas of Illinois, and John Bell of Tennessee.

In April, the Democratic national convention met in Charleston, South Carolina. Douglas was the favorite for the nomination. He had long championed "popular sovereignty," or letting citizens of the territories vote slavery in or out. In 1857, a proslavery Supreme Court ruled in *Dred Scott v. Sandford* that Congress could not bar slavery from the territories. When Douglas and his supporters stuck to popular sovereignty at the convention, fifty militant southern, proslavery "Fire Eaters" decamped. Kentucky's delegation, including circuit judge Rufus King Williams of Mayfield, stayed put and proposed James Guthrie of Louisville as a unity candidate. President of the Louisville and Nashville Railroad, he had been President Franklin Pierce's treasury secretary. Guthrie's nomination went nowhere, but Douglas could not muster enough support to get the nod either. Hopelessly deadlocked, the convention adjourned and reconvened in Baltimore in June.[59]

When Douglas partisans refused to admit the "Fire Eaters," 105 more delegates departed; most of them, including nine Kentuckians, were from slave states. Fifteen Kentucky delegates, Williams among them, kept their seats. Nine endorsed Douglas, who won the nomination; Williams and five others declined to vote for "the Little Giant." Meanwhile, the Baltimore bolters, having joined the "Fire Eaters," nominated Breckinridge. He supported *Dred Scott* and demanded strict enforcement of the federal fugitive slave law. The most contentious part of Clay's Compromise of 1850, it compelled state and local officials and private citizens in the free states to help slave owners recover slaves who escaped to the North.[60]

Conservatives, most of them ex-Whigs and former members of the defunct semisecret, anti-Catholic, and anti-foreign American or "Know-Nothing" Party, formed the Constitutional Union Party. John Bell was their candidate. He sidestepped the issue of slavery's expansion and called only for "the Constitution of the Country, the Union of the States and the enforcement of the laws." Republican Abraham Lincoln's platform demanded that slavery be excluded from the territories.[61]

Lincoln had no chance in Kentucky, though he was born near Hodgenville in 1809. Almost all white Kentuckians despised the Republicans, some of whom wanted more than a ban on slavery's expansion. Republican abolitionists, whose ranks did not include Lincoln, demanded an immediate and unconditional end to slavery in Kentucky and the other fourteen slave states. Douglas also looked like a long shot in Kentucky. Most Kentuckians viewed "popular sovereignty" as an equivocation on slavery's spread. Besides, southern Democrat Breckinridge was the state's rising political star. In 1859, the General Assembly elected him to the US Senate, where he was to begin serving in 1861 after his vice presidency ended.

In 1860, the Democrats controlled both houses of the Kentucky General Assembly. Elected in 1859, Governor Beriah Magoffin was a Breckinridge Democrat. Even so, Kentucky became Democratic by default. The Bluegrass State was faithfully Whig until the Kansas-Nebraska Act of 1854 shattered the party. While most northern Whigs became Republicans and most southern Whigs joined the Democrats, the majority of Kentucky Whigs embraced the "Know-Nothing" Party, in part, at least, because it downplayed the explosive slavery controversy, which Kentuckians in the Clay mold feared would destroy the Union. The Democrats gained the ascendancy only after the Know-Nothings faded away. Bell had been a Whig, Clay ally, and "Know-Nothing." He reflected the Constitutional Unionist base, which was comprised largely of older, conservative men.[62]

The election of 1860 was really two elections: Lincoln versus Douglas in the free states and Bell versus Breckinridge in the slave states. Breckinridge was almost certain to sweep the Deep South. It seemed like the border states could swing to Bell or to Breckinridge. In Kentucky, the question was whether the state would return to its Whig roots or go with its southern Democratic son. Purchase politics was more like Deep South politics than Kentucky politics. The region leaned decidedly toward Breckinridge, though Bell seemed to have significant support in traditionally Whig McCracken County, or at least in Paducah. Douglas looked like an also-ran, and Lincoln partisans could be counted on one hand, maybe two.

Nonetheless, the four parties named First District electors. As it turned out, they were Paducah lawyers. Albert P. Thompson, who was also the local commonwealth attorney, stood for Breckinridge. Lawrence S. Trimble was Douglas's man. Quintus Quincy Quigley was Bell's elector, and Samuel McCann was Lincoln's. In his diary, Quigley predicted that Lincoln, the nominee "of the Black Republican Convention," had the best chance to win. He "has obtained a considerable reputation by the political conflict with Douglass [*sic*] in Illinois and has the farther popular hip and hurrah always following a self made man and is styled Honest Abe."[63]

Quigley said nothing of McCann. But the Bell booster wrote that he got along famously with Thompson and Trimble. Sometimes, they stumped the district together. Quigley said Trimble "took the position that Douglas was the regular nominee of the Democratic Party both at Charleston and at the adjourned convention in Baltimore" and "that the doctrine of popular sovereignty was the only correct and sensible way to settle the question of slavery and that it was in all of their platforms since 1847." Thompson "took the position that the Republican Party had avowed that there should be no more slave states or territories and that it was the duty of the people of the South to meet that issue and that because of the failure to do that the Breckenridge [*sic*] party had seceded from the convention and adopted the [slavery] protection plank of their platform." In addition, Thompson maintained that Douglas had been "nominated by a minority or rather less than two thirds of the convention which was the universal rule of the party." Additionally, Thompson charged that Douglas "got many of the votes he got through fraud and deceit." Quigley added that his stance was "that the Democratic Party had verified any conceivable position upon the slavery question," including popular sovereignty. He admitted "our canvass was altogether a very pleasant one and no ungentlemanly language or advantage sought."[64]

On July 2, "the Democracy of Hickman county" met in Clinton and passed resolutions lauding the Kentucky Democrats who exited the Baltimore convention and nominated Breckinridge, *"Kentucky's favorite son."* The gathering expressed "unfeigned satisfaction" with the Breckinridge-Lane ticket—"our gallant standard bearers" who represented "the 'Constitutional' Democracy of the nation." Former state representative Edward Crossland of

Clinton presided over the conclave, which also pledged Hickman County would "give them the largest vote she has ever cast for any candidate in a Presidential race." In addition, the crowd approved a resolution offered by attorney George W. Silvertooth lauding "the constitutional States' rights doctrine advocated by Col. John C. Noble, editor of the Paducah Herald." The *Herald* would become the region's principal secessionist newspaper. Rally-goers recommended that the *Herald* was "worthy of Democratic patronage," promising "we will use our best exertions to extend its circulation." Further, the assemblage approved a series of proslavery resolutions, including one endorsing the *Dred Scott* decision: "Congress has no power to prohibit the introduction of, or to abolish slavery in, any of the Territories of the United States." The resolution asserted that territorial legislatures had no "right by direct legislation to prohibit or abolish" slavery or "by direct or unfriendly legislation to render slave property valueless." Too, the convention agreed "it is the duty of the Territorial legislatures to protect all citizens of the various Territories in the enjoyment of their rights in and to property of every description and character, (slave property included)."[65]

The Breckinridge backers agreed that if territorial legislatures failed to safeguard slavery and if the courts ruled that the constitution and laws were inadequate to guarantee slavery, then Congress should provide slave owners "adequate legal remedies for the protection of their constitutional rights." Further, the Democrats named State Representative W. D. Lannom of Clinton, Silvertooth, and seventeen other men as delegates to a state Democratic unity convention in Frankfort on July 18. The meeting was also to nominate a candidate to succeed recently deceased Rankin R. Revill, clerk of the court of appeals and a Democrat. Voting would take place on August 6. The Hickman County gathering favored Thomas G. Poore, a county lawyer, to replace Revill. "The First Congressional District is entitled to have an incumbent in one of the State offices," the Democrats argued. It was a complaint heard from Purchase Democrats for years before and after the Civil War: the state party took the region for granted, and the Purchase was woefully underrepresented in high offices.[66]

Also on July 2, "Jefferson" echoed the Purchase-deserves-its-share-of-offices sentiment in a letter to the pro-Breckinridge *Louisville Daily Courier* from Shiloh in Calloway County. But first he advised readers of the paper that "the most humble man in Southern Kentucky is lifting his voice in support of Breckinridge and Lane; and you may be assured that the First Congressional District, the Gibraltar of Democracy, will present an unbroken phalanx in favor of this ticket." He predicted that the district "will roll up a majority for Breckinridge, unprecedented in the history of the party in this State—say six to eight thousand." "Jefferson" boasted, "Were every Congressional District in this State as largely in the ascendancy as the glorious old First, Kentucky alone would give the Constitutional Democracy a majority of sixty thousand." He hastened to add, "this district has done more hard Democratic labor, thereby contributing more to the success of the Democracy of the State than any other district in it."[67]

Having bragged on western Kentucky's fealty to the party of Tom Jefferson and Andy Jackson, "Jefferson" suggested that western Kentucky "is entitled to her *pro rata* of state officers as a remuneration for her fidelity to the party, and ardent support of its nominees in times past." He had a fellow Calloway countian in mind for Revill's job—veteran circuit clerk Paris M. Ellison. According to "Jefferson," Ellison was an "affable and courteous" gent, a "zealous and vigilant" officer of the court, and "a Democrat . . . unwavering in his devotion to States' Rights Democracy."[68]

On the same day as the Clinton meeting, a Democratic gathering in Benton endorsed Ellison, approved "the course pursued by the Southern States and Seceders in the Baltimore Convention," and boosted the Breckinridge and Lane ticket. State representative Thomas L. Goheen Sr., a former county judge, was chairman. Another resolution cheered the principles in the Breckinridge-Lane platform as "the only true and wholesome ones upon which we can stand, under the Constitution."[69]

The *Herald* hopped on the Ellison bandwagon, too, claiming it was time for a Purchase Democrat to shine in Frankfort. Noble pointed out that the First was the only congressional district "which has no son in a State office." Thus, the paper appealed "to the justice, fairness, and sense of comity on the part of the balance of the State, to say whether the old Democratic First is not entitled to the position of Clerk of the Court of Appeals." The editor challenged, "What say our friends of the newspaper press of upper Kentucky?"[70]

Meanwhile, after helping run the Clinton Breckinridge-Lane meeting, Silvertooth journeyed to Paducah to evangelize for his candidates at a Democratic rally on July 5. He reportedly delivered an oration "replete with stirring eloquence, sound argument, and Democratic truth, which elicited the most enthusiastic applause." Alfred Boyd, brother of the late lieutenant governor Linn Boyd, chaired the gathering at the Market House. The Democrats offered "zealous support" for Breckinridge and Lane. The gathering passed proslavery resolutions similar to those approved in the Clinton and Benton rallies. Others affirmed a plank hammered into the party platform in Baltimore and reaffirmed the party platform from 1856: "The government of a Territory organized by Congress is provisional and temporary; and during its existence, all citizens of the United States have an equal right to settle with their property in the Territory without their rights, either of persons or property, being destroyed or impaired by Congressional legislation." Further, the meeting resolved, "it is the duty of the Federal Government, in all its departments, to protect, when necessary, the rights of persons and property in the Territories, and wherever else its constitutional authority exists." The Democrats also resolved that if citizens of a territory voted to create a slave state, then they should be admitted to the Union "on an equal footing with people of other states." At the same time, the meeting declared support for the annexation of Cuba, which proslavery Southerners had long wanted to grab and turn into a slave state, and claimed "the enactments of state legislatures to defeat the faithful execution of the fugitive slave law are hostile in character, subversive to the constitution, and revolutionary in their effect."[71]

Ed K. Warren of the *Hickman Courier* was also proslavery, but he was a Douglas man in the summer of 1860. He called a meeting for the night of July 7 to endorse Douglas. Warren's efforts did not impress "Snap Jack," who dashed off a letter to the *Louisville Courier* claiming that nobody came to the editor's meeting. But the Douglas supporters turned up on July 9, county court day, when the Democrats planned to choose their delegates to the state convention. The ever-present Silvertooth arrived, "and such another scoring as he gave the Douglasites, men never received before." When the Douglas backers proposed endorsing their candidate, enough Breckinridge men were present to pass a resolution favoring their man. "In the voting, it was discovered that the Bell-Everetts were voting with the Douglasites, which was objected to by the Breckinridge side," according to "Snap Jack." Thus rebuffed, the Douglas men "went home cursing, swearing, and making lager fly." Undaunted, Warren quickly printed handbills advertising that the meeting was rescheduled for that night. "The Douglasites led off in two set speeches, after which a Breckinridge and Lane man arose to answer, but was promptly told that that was a Douglas ratification meeting, so of course he gave way." Consequently, the Douglas faithful—"not over twelve or fifteen"—apparently endorsed their candidate, "Snap Jack" wrote, predicting, "Douglas cannot get one hundred votes in this county." Nonetheless, the Douglas devotees "got out an old anvil and fired it three times." "Snap Jack" scoffed that the triple explosions equaled "the votes that he will get in this precinct at the election in November next."[72]

Meanwhile, the *Louisville Courier* was happy to report that another Breckinridge organ had started up in the Purchase—the *Mayfield Southern Yeoman*. C. C. Coulter's new paper hooted, "In this portion of the State it is altogether a one-sided business. Only a few political croakers are heard to raise the Douglas note, and that sounds more like the dying wail of intriguing but thwarted demagoguery, than the clear notes of whole souled Democracy."

The *Courier* also reported that "an intelligent gentleman, in Paducah," claimed the Breckinridge-Lane ticket was faring well in the McCracken County seat with elector Thompson set to open "the ball with a speech, at the Court House." Even so, the correspondent said Paducah was home to "some hot Douglas men . . . more than in all the balance of the district." But he assured the *Courier* that all but one or two of the leading district Democrats were for Breckinridge. Further, "many sensible men, who were for Bell before the Baltimore convention, are now for Kentucky's noble son."[73]

Judge Williams raised eyebrows and hackles when he tried to talk against the *Yeoman*'s candidate at a July 16 meeting in Mayfield of Democrats who "turned out in droves to ratify" his nomination, according to a letter from J. E. Anderson to Graves County judge A. R. Boone.

"It leaked out that [Williams] would not support the seceder's candidate," Anderson wrote. "Immediately the secession wing took fright, and determined that Williams should not speak lest they could not ratify for as well you know the Democracy have ever opposed investigation, it being their true policy to keep the rank and file in ignorance." After the county candidates spoke, "Lush," apparently Mayfield attorney and former state representative Lucian Anderson, told "the unwashed that the Judge wanted to give an account of the [Democratic National] Convention." J. E. Anderson, a Bell backer, claimed "the Douglas wing (though as you well know are not a whit more honest than the Breckenridge [*sic*] wing) were anxious for Williams to speak, believing it would make Douglas capital." The crowd wanted to hear Williams, but the "Breck leaders" would have none of it, according to Anderson: "Then commenced a scene, the like of which old Mayfield's Court House never saw. Each Breck leader cried 'have let loose the dogs of war.' Bedlam seemed turned loose amongst us. Coats were flung in every direction, while 'he shall not speak' 'he shall not speak' 'take him out' etc. resounded from every side." Williams retreated to the Market House, trailed by two-thirds of the crowd. The Breckinridge boosters, according to Anderson, stayed put and "listened to a drunken speech from a Mr. Winn from Calloway—full of sound and fury, signifying nothing." Anderson said Williams delivered "a very lengthy speech, in which he informed us, what we all knew before, that neighter [*sic*] Breck nor Dug was worthy of our support." Anderson said as proof of the difference between Democrats and Bell men, "we (ie), the Union loving men had a ratification meeting here yesterday which was largely attended and passed off harmoniously. . . . It would have done your heart good to have seen the enthusiasm here exhibited for Bell & Everett." He added that J. T. Bolinger and Dick Hardin had gotten into a fight with "politics the cause—lie given and returned. Effect—Dick got a very black eye."[74]

While Hardin was willing to take a punch for his candidate, whoever he was, Columbus attorney Edward I. Bullock, who was a part owner in the *Crescent,* was wont to wear out traveling shoes for his man. On July 23, he stumped for Breckinridge in Blandville, the Ballard County seat, according to another *Courier* correspondent. It was county court day, and a large crowd had gathered to hear pro-Breckinridge First District congressman Henry C. Burnett of Cadiz. Burnett failed to appear, but Bullock spoke "for more than two hours" and "held his audience enchained." Bullock maintained that the *Dred Scott* case had decided the issue of slavery's expansion once and for all. Bullock "by clear and undeniable logic . . . exposed the mischief, the danger, and the absurdity" of popular sovereignty and "showed, most satisfactorily, that the question was already adjudged in our favor." Meanwhile, the state convention had spurned the two Purchase favorites and nominated Clinton McClarty, a Breckinridge Democrat from Louisville, for court of appeals clerk. The Hickman County Democrats fell in line behind McClarty, according to the *Courier* correspondent, who promised "nearly the entire vote will be given for him.[75]

On August 2, the *Courier* claimed there was no question how westernmost Kentucky would vote. "The needle is not truer to the pole than are the Democracy of Jackson's purchase to their principles. They will come up now, in the hour of need, with a majority that will confound our enemies and astonish our friends." The Louisville paper quoted the *Herald:* "We are asked how the First District will vote in November. We answer that it will give Breckinridge and Lane from three to four thousand majority—we think four thousand—over Bell. Mr. Douglas is not in the fight; he is an outsider, and will poll but a small vote in the District."[76]

But the August 6 election results doubtless disappointed the *Herald.* The winner was Leslie Combs, an old-line Lexington Whig and former state house speaker, who ran as the Bell candidate. He collected 68,165 votes. McClarty finished second with 44,942 ballots, and Robert R. Bolling, the Douglas Democrat, trailed with 10,971 votes. Other candidates received a scattering of ballots. The Purchase went for McClarty, who won Graves, Hickman, and Marshall Counties; Combs pocketed Ballard, Fulton, and McCracken Counties.[77]

A Ballard Breckinridge backer waxed philosophic in defeat, confessing in a letter to the *Courier,* "we feel that we have not done our duty." He promised, "We shall take a lesson from the past, and awake to a double diligence in battling for Breckinridge and Lane, 'the Constitution and the equality of the States.'" Writing from Blandville, the correspondent assured the *Courier* that twenty-five hundred voters had skipped the election and that at least "two thousand of them" would vote the Breckinridge-Lane ticket. "We intend to make a bold fight for our standard-bearers, and if every Democrat in other districts will but resolve to do his duty, 'To be a hero in the strife,' there is no longer a doubt but what old Kentucky will rebuke Squatter Sovereignty and hold up her gallant Breckinridge to the world and say, 'Lo! my choice for the Presidency.'" The letter-writer also decried Douglas supporters who wanted to make common cause with the Breckinridge men. "We do not wish to unite with the Squattors [*sic*]," he declared. "They thought in June that they could win by themselves; we accepted the fight; and now we say again, 'Lay on Macduff, And damned be he who first cries hold, enough.'"[78]

The next day, the *Courier* published a letter from Fulton County, describing a debate at Sassafras Ridge, about as far west as Kentucky goes, between Lannom the Breckinridge man and attorney A. D. Kingman of Hickman, who was for Bell. "Spectator," the letter's author, who favored Breckinridge, claimed that Kingman would not say "how Bell and his friends propose to settle the questions raised by the Black Republicans." Kingman denounced Breckinridge and William L. Yancey of Alabama, a leader of the extreme proslavery and secessionist-minded southern "Fire Eaters," and praised Bell. But the letter writer suspected Douglas was really his first choice for president. "This was the tenor of his speech, but he was careful to correct himself once or twice by saying he was for Bell, and would be for Douglas next to him." In any event, after Kingman was through with "his 'no point' harangue," Lannom "gave him a scathing, withering rebuke—just such a one as he deserved." He said Kingman had diagnosed "the patient," meaning the country, as "very sick, 'nigh unto death,' and had advised them to call in Dr. Bell." Kingman charged "that neither Dr. Bell nor his friend Kingman would attempt to describe the disease nor prescribe a remedy." Lannom wanted "very much . . . to know whether Dr. Bell proposes Moffett's pills, Fahnestock's vermifuge, or some other patent medicine, or does he propose a scientific course of treatment?" Lannom "showed conclusively the inconsistencies and self-contradictions of Kingman's speech."[79]

Nonetheless, the court of appeals election suggested that most Kentucky voters might see "Dr. Bell" as the cure for the nation's ills on November 6. No matter, a Graves County Breckinridge supporter wrote the *Courier* on September 2, claiming that state representative George B. Hodge of Newport, a Breckinridge elector, had vanquished Bell elector W. H. Wadsworth of Mason County at a political rally in Feliciana in southern Graves County. Hodge, according to the letter writer, "met and refuted the charge of disunion against the Breckinridge party, passed a high eulogy on our glorious candidates, and took his seat amidst loud cheers and enthusiastic shouts for Breckinridge and

Lane." Hodge was "a glorious, eloquent speaker, logical, and ponderous in his vindication of truth, fearless and terrible in exposing error."[80]

As it turned out, Wadsworth and Quigley got to cast two of Kentucky's dozen electoral votes for Bell. The secret ballot had yet to come to the Bluegrass State; voice voting was the constitutionally mandated method of electing candidates. Typically, voting "right" earned a citizen at least a swig of whiskey from a grateful candidate or his aides. Liquor-fueled fisticuffs, stabbings, and shootings were common on election days. But the balloting on November 6 was uneventful in Paducah, according to Quigley. "It has come and gone with all its hopes and anxieties and like many other days predicted by the wise and knowing it has not yet been disastrous," he penned on November 7. "When the day of election came there was no excitement, no pulling, and hauling to the polls, no fights, no drunkenness. Those who voted went quietly away after voting." Deadly fighting would come soon enough.[81]

The "Fire-Eaters" and like-minded white Southerners had warned that if Lincoln was elected, then the South would secede. Lincoln won the White House by sweeping the free state North. Breckinridge won the Deep South, plus border slave states Maryland and Delaware. Douglas managed only slave state Missouri, though he shared free state New Jersey's electoral vote with Lincoln. Bell carried a trio of slave states: Virginia, Kentucky, and Tennessee. In the Bluegrass State, Bell garnered 66,051 votes to 53,143 for Breckinridge. Douglas received 25,638 votes and Lincoln 1,364. The court of appeals contest indeed proved to be a harbinger of the outcome of the presidential race.[82] William George Pirtle of Water Valley in southern Graves County said Bell, Douglas, and Breckinridge beat themselves. "If the parties opposed to the Lincoln platform would have agreed on one man, they could have elected him easily, as the three parties poled [*sic*] more than three fourths of a million more votes than Lincoln did," he wrote in his memoirs. "But every man would go for his man, or rather his own way. So when the returns of the election . . . was heard from Lincoln was elected by a safe plurality." He added that after the election, "excitement became intence, and increased every day in the south as the idea of the loss of their property in slaved did not set well."[83]

Another Graves countian, Eliza Gregory, said Lincoln's victory caused a great stir in Dublin, where she lived and ran a store. "Nothing but uproar . . . and talk of fighting in the Union," she wrote in a letter. "But I think the storm will so be over and scarcely anybody hurt." The Civil War would be America's bloodiest war, claiming approximately 752,000 lives on both sides.[84]

The man who became commander in chief of the Union military forces managed a mere ten votes in the Purchase—eight in McCracken County, one in Ballard County, and one in Hickman County. Breckinridge carried the region, but not by the 4,000-vote majority Noble predicted. He took Calloway, Fulton, Graves, Hickman, and Marshall Counties, piling up 4,547 votes Purchase-wide. Bell attracted 2,885 votes and captured Ballard and McCracken Counties. Douglas collected 1,089.[85]

The vote of Kentucky in the presidential election was a mandate for the Union in that most Bluegrass State voters believed Bell or Douglas was safest on the Union question. Together, they polled almost 63 percent of the vote. The majority of Kentuckians feared that Lincoln, whose share of the vote was less than 1 percent, was an out-and-out abolitionist willing to destroy the Union to end slavery. Likewise, they worried that Breckinridge might be a tool of southern "Fire Eaters" like Yancey, who was willing to sacrifice the Union to save slavery. Breckinridge vehemently denied he was a disunionist, but he managed just a little over 36 percent of ballots cast in his home state, where Bell and Douglas men would form the nucleus of the Union Party. Yet in the Purchase, Lincoln's election would turn most Bell and Douglas voters into secessionists, including Quigley.[86]

On December 4, he was in Frankfort to cast his electoral vote for Bell and Everett. They voted the next day. He recalled sadly that the Bell electors parted "with no hope that we or others would ever meet to cast the vote of Kentucky for President and Vice President of the United States as it now is."[87]

When the steamboat that carried Quigley home arrived at the Paducah wharf boat on December 10, he debarked "with heart high to see my wife and children, who are above all friends and pleasures in my affections. Found them all well and with bright laughing faces that flew to me. How sweet and holy the charms of a peaceful and happy home." Peace would end on April 12, 1861, when Confederate cannons opened fire on Fort Sumter in the harbor at Charleston, South Carolina. The Palmetto State would secede ten days after Quigley was reunited with his family.[88]

The day before Quigley got home, Governor Magoffin sent letters to the other fourteen slave state governors seeking their support for a half-dozen proposals to preserve the Union on southern proslavery terms. They included a constitutional amendment that would strictly enforce the federal fugitive slave law and federal legislation that would force free states to compensate slave owners for slaves not returned to them and require free state governors to extradite anyone indicted in a slave state "for stealing or enticing away a slave." Magoffin, too, called for another three constitutional amendments dividing the territories into slave and free sections along the thirty-seventh parallel, guaranteeing all states free access to the Mississippi River and empowering the South to protect itself in the US Senate against "unconstitutional or oppressive" legislation against slavery.[89]

Most Kentuckians shared Magoffin's deep disappointment at Lincoln's election. Even so, beyond the Purchase, only a minority of Kentuckians seemed ready to forsake the Union over Lincoln's victory. Throughout November, Union meetings, usually without party distinction, were held in Frankfort and other towns.[90]

December meetings in Benton and in Hickman County expressed only conditional support for the Union. The Marshall men loved the Union and hated any "separation and dissolution of this Confederacy." But they refused to "defend a Union that is made an engine of oppression and injustice to any member of this Confederacy." Additionally, the gathering, chaired by state representative Goheen, hoped Kentucky's "sister States of the South" would not rush to secede but agreed disunion was justified if "the North refuses to recede from her acts of aggression upon the rights of the South"; in that event, Kentucky ought to depart, too. The meeting agreed "that we should stand side by side with our sister States in preventing the employment of force to coerce any of the Southern States into an unjust submission," arguing "that a compulsory Union of these States would be worthless." The Marshall countians called on Governor Magoffin to convene the state legislature so lawmakers could raise, arm, and equip "a sufficient force for the defense of the State" and enact legislation "taxing all Northern goods, and all goods imported through Northern ports, to the extent of *prohibition.*" Their last resolution expressed hearty sympathy "with the movements of South Carolina and other Southern States in regard to secession, unless the Northern States repeal their Personal Liberty bills, and restore to us our rights under the Constitution."[91]

The Hickman meeting was probably in Columbus; the city's W. R. Vance, who had been mayor of Louisville, chaired the gathering. Their first resolution defined the United States not as a federal republic, but as "a confederacy of sovereign States" whose basis was "the perfect equality of all the confederate parties." Thus, they said, the central government had to guarantee "the inalienable rights of the citizens of every State . . . alike in their person and property," the latter including slaves. The citizens hoped the Union might be preserved but condemned the northern states for their "open and premeditated resistance to the Fugitive Slave Law" and for their personal liberty laws. They resolved, "If the people of the North desire to preserve the Union, we call upon them to show their good faith by ceasing their mob violence, repealing their unconstitutional enactments [personal liberty laws] . . . and giving additional security for the future." The men also declared that Kentucky's "people, interests, institutions, and destiny are irrevocably identified with the South." In addition, the meeting urged that in the wake of "the election of Lincoln, and the impending annihilation of the Republic," Bell, Breckinridge, and Douglas supporters should unite "as brothers and Kentuckians" and "as national men anxious to preserve the Union, and as Southern men determined to maintain our rights." The gathering advised Magoffin to convene the legislature "and if necessary to call for a State [sovereignty] Convention."[92]

Quigley thought he was going to a Union meeting in Paducah on December 22, but when he showed up at Gardner Hall, he "at once discovered antagonistic elements had assembled." R. B. J. Twyman proposed conservative unionist resolutions, but Judge Campbell, an erstwhile Douglas man, countered with "ultra-Southern" resolutions. Quigley said he had heard Campbell "was fast going over to dissolution" but confessed he was not prepared for the "defiance breathed by the resolutions." John Quincy Adams King challenged Campbell. He proposed resolutions that "were a mere recapitulation of the glory of our institutions panegyrics in their own language upon Washington and Jefferson and closing with no manly, bold and clear line of policy set forth in them." After the gathering spurned Quigley's "compromise motion," he left. The crowd passed King's resolutions "by 2 or 3 to 1." But Quigley added, "It has stirred up instead of settled the public mind. [Secessionist] Cockades are mounted upon the hats of a few and the excitement is fully organized. What will be the end? None can certainly predict."[93]

Meanwhile, on December 18, Senator John J. Crittenden of Kentucky, in true Clay fashion, had proposed a series of constitutional amendments that protected slavery where it existed and extended the old Missouri Compromise line (thirty-six degrees, thirty minutes latitude) to California. The Crittenden Compromise generated little support beyond Kentucky and the other border slave states, and consequently, it failed. South Carolina left the Union on December 20, and invited the fourteen other slave states "to join us, in forming a Confederacy of Slaveholding States." The lower South prepared to accept South Carolina's call. Before the end of December, commissioners from Mississippi and Alabama arrived in Frankfort and urged Magoffin to press for Kentucky's secession. They argued that only an independent southern nation could preserve slavery and white supremacy. Their argument would be repeated countless times by secessionists everywhere. The Alabama commissioner was a Kentucky native, Stephen Fowler Hale. Born in Crittenden County, just east of the Purchase, in 1816, he wrote Magoffin a long letter on December 27. Hale accused the North of "waging an unrelenting and fanatical war" against slavery "for the last quarter of a century." He praised the "peculiar institution" for binding up "not only the wealth and prosperity of the Southern people, but their very existence as a political community." Lincoln, he added, "stands forth as the representative of the fanaticism of the

North" and of the Republican Party, whose claims to popularity rested "upon the one dogma—the equality of the races, white and black." He predicted that if the Republicans abolished slavery, "the slave-holder and non-slave-holder must ultimately share the same fate; all be degraded to a position of equality with free negroes, stand side by side with them at the polls, and fraternize in all the social relations of life, or else there will be an eternal war of races, desolating the land with blood, and utterly wasting and destroying all the resources of the country." Hale asked, "What Southern man, be he slave-holder or non-slave-holder, can without indignation and horror contemplate the triumph of negro equality, and see his own sons and daughters in the not distant future associating with free negroes upon terms of political and social equality, and the white man stripped by the heaven-daring hand of fanaticism of that title to superiority over the black race which God himself has bestowed?" The proslavery Magoffin's reply was sympathetic, but he did not embrace state-by-state secession. Instead, he proposed a convention of all fifteen slave states, where common action could be agreed upon and a plan presented to Lincoln. If the president rejected the plan, then the slave states could exit the Union with the power of a united section. When nothing came of his proposal, the governor, on December 27, called for a special session of the legislature to convene on January 17.[94]

On December 29, McCracken County judge G. A. Flournoy chaired a public meeting in Paducah that endorsed Magoffin's slave state convention plan as the right response to "the crisis forced upon the slaveholding States." Attendees were for preserving the Union, but not if that meant sacrificing "our rights to the domination of the Black Republican party, or to the fanaticism of Abolitionists." The gathering was "unwilling to be drawn into a Southern Confederacy by the hasty or precipitate action of any Southern State" yet agreed that "when all just efforts . . . to maintain our rights and honor and perfect equality in the present Union . . . fail, we will then seek a Southern Confederation." Another resolution urged "Kentucky as a border State" to make one more appeal to the northern states "to abandon, at once, their aggressive policy" and to simultaneously entreat the southern states "not to destroy, by hasty action, the last hope of preserving this great Confederacy of States." In addition, the meeting called on the northern states to repeal their personal liberty laws, demanded that Lincoln enforce the fugitive slave law, and asserted that slavery must not be abolished in the District of Columbia without the consent of Virginia, Maryland, and the other slave states and without compensation to slave owners. Too, Congress ought to "abstain from all legislation on the subject of slavery except for its protection, enumeration, and representation." At the same time, the citizens warned that the North and

Congress must not interfere with the slave trade or prevent masters from traveling with their slaves through the North "for lawful purposes." The gathering claimed that "the right of revolution against tyranny and oppression, is as inherent in the masses as the right of self-defense in individual man." The meeting also resolved "that the right to meet revolution already begun, with force of arms, cannot be questioned, nor stigmatized in turn as treason." Finally, the McCracken countians endorsed Magoffin's call for the General Assembly to meet.[95]

Worried that the legislature might put Kentucky out of the Union, the Unionists got organized. On January 8, 1861, leading supporters of Bell and Douglas met in separate conventions in Louisville. The groups jointly resolved that Lincoln's election was an affront to the South, but not cause for disunion. They endorsed the Crittenden Compromise and formed a ten-member Union State Central Committee to organize and coordinate Union sentiment across Kentucky.[96]

The committee found little support among Bell and Douglas men in the Purchase. The *Hickman Courier* was one of the first—if not the first—newspapers in the state to endorse secession:

> We have waited patiently and with anxious hearts to hear what our representatives in Congress would or could do to restore peace and confidence to our distracted country. Our hope has been in vain. Our representatives have been denied everything they demanded. The Republicans have been firm and unwilling to make any concessions or compromise. The South, therefore, who has considered herself aggrieved, who has been denied her rights in the Union, is bound, in order to have her rights, in order to maintain her honor, and the honor of her citizens, *to secede.* Therefore, we say, all honor to the Southern Confederacy.[97]

Later, the Hickman paper dismissed the Bell and Douglas conventions as "the expiring effort of defunct political organizations, whose great object can only be the spoils of office." The paper claimed "the convention was a grand congregation—from all accounts—of Fourth of July, Hail Columbia, Yankee Doodle orators, who delivered themselves of speeches red with blood *spilt* by their patriotic forefathers. All such Conventions are fustian, bombast and nonsense." The *Courier* challenged, "Why in the first place did they not look the issue in the face, whether Kentucky would remain as the tail of a Northern Black Republican Union, or would join a Confederacy of her Southern sisters, upon the principles of State equality." The paper charged, "this is the living, vital issue, and all who attempt to impede or retard the triumphant march of the people—determined to assert and maintain their own honor will be crushed and trampled to death beneath their feet." The paper concluded, "It would be a blot upon the escutcheon of the proud old Commonwealth of Kentucky to doubt her loyalty to the South and her institutions, which no time could wipe out."[98]

Still, it was the Purchase Breckinridge backers who clamored loudest for disunion. "Kentucky ought to act at once, in imitation of the example set by the gallant, glorious little state of South Carolina," Crossland wrote to the *Louisville Courier* on January 5. "(Would to God that Kentucky had led the van—had made the start in advance of any State.)" He conceded that "a great many insist that we ought to delay—that we ought to withhold any action, but to wait and see if the Northern people will not recede from their aggressive policy and thus give quiet to the country and save the Union." He also opposed Magoffin's call for a border slave state convention. He said those who favored a wait-and-see approach and supported a convention "agree that the Northern people will not recede." Crossland dismissed hesitancy to secede as "dangerous" and "a needless or senseless waste of precious time." He added, "this delay on the part of Kentucky is calculated to embarrass the South and is fraught with peril to the honor of our State." Crossland hoped the legislature would call a sovereignty convention that would "take immediate steps to cut Kentucky loose from the Union." He demanded, "Conscious of the rectitude of our motives, let us act like men who feel a lively interest in maintaining the honor of the State and that confidence of our Southern brethren so necessary to our safety." The *Herald* gleefully predicted that the "First District will indorse his views by 10,000 majority."[99]

Two days later, Burnett expressed similar sentiments in a long letter to the *Herald* that the *Louisville Courier* saw fit to publish. "There is not the slightest hope of any settlement or adjustment of existing troubles," Burnett wrote. "The Republicans have rejected with scorn and ridicule every proposition which has been submitted to them in the Senate and House committees." He denounced attempts at compromise by "certain Representatives from the Border States." The congressman confessed he had "felt humiliated and degraded by seeing men claiming to represent the South, begging their Abolitionist leaders to adopt, as a basis of settlement, propositions which would degrade the South, and which ought to be spurned by every true man in our borders." Burnett argued that if Congress agreed to divide the territories at thirty-six degrees, thirty minutes latitude and forbade slavery north of the line, "*then we should exact that South of the line slavery must be recognized and protected, both by the Territorial, and Federal governments, in the present territory, and all future acquisitions.* The latter part of the proposition is a *sine qua non* with me. I will take nothing that does not cover it." Burnett also demanded that Congress must never abolish slavery in the District of Columbia without the blessing of Maryland and Virginia and that northern states must repeal their personal liberty laws. Further, he proposed that the fugitive slave law be amended to include punishment for free state governors "and all others who obstruct or prevent its execution." Too, the western Kentuckian maintained that slave owners should have the right "to travel through the Free States with their property, and to be protected while in transitu." He declared that "these provisions must be incorporated in the Constitution by amendment, and property in slaves must be clearly and expressly recognized." Turning to Kentucky matters, Burnett said he hoped the legislature would quickly approve "a joint resolution strongly denouncing force against the Southern States." However, he warned that if the Republicans tried "to carry out their threats of 'whipping in,'" he would stand with those "who are for repelling force by force, and my voice shall be heard urging Kentuckians to stand by our brethren." He also wanted the legislature to call for "a state convention so that the sovereign voice of Kentucky can be heard in this momentous crisis." Burnett promised that his voice was not raised in favor of Noble's removal as Paducah postmaster. Burnett blamed the editor's ouster on Postmaster General Joseph Holt, a fellow Kentuckian, who would become a staunch Unionist. "The truth is, you are too much devoted to Southern rights to suit the taste of [Holt]," Burnett confided in Noble. The lawmaker could not resist a lengthy postscript to his epistle. He vowed he "would go as far as the farthest to preserve the Union upon just and constitutional principles." But he believed that with Lincoln's advent, "we can only preserve the Union at the price of our constitutional equality. In other words, if we will agree that our four thousand millions of dollars invested in slaves shall be outlawed in the common Territories, and consent to the aggressive warfare made upon the institution in the Slave States, then the Republicans will permit us to remain in the Union and not use against us the rod of coercion. The price is too dear for me." Even so, Burnett said if he were in the state legislature, he would vote to spend money to enroll and arm the state militia "upon the principle of self-preservation." Burnett said he would not be surprised if fighting broke out in Washington "between hostile forces within ten days."[100]

Meanwhile, the *Crescent* maintained that "the Rubicon is crossed, and Kentucky may as well prepare immediately to go with the Southern states into a separate confederacy—the sooner she does so the better it will be for her." The paper was disgusted with Republicans on a Senate committee who "promptly and contemptuously voted down" Mississippi senator Jefferson

Davis's resolution, "which simply declared that the Constitution recognized the right of property in negroes." The *Crescent* concluded that the Republicans thus showed "their determination to make no concessions whatever, but to have their own way, and carry out, if possible, their own odious and infamous doctrines."[101]

While the *Crescent, Courier,* and *Herald* editorialized in favor of secession, meetings in Ballard, Calloway, Fulton, Hickman, Marshall, and other First District counties "passed sterling State Rights resolutions with great unanimity." The Ballard gathering approved resolutions insisting that "unless the North will secure the South by additional constitutional guarantees, the political ties that connect us with the North should be severed." The meeting also resolved that "in the event of dissolution," Kentucky must "form a part of the Southern Confederacy." At the same time, the meeting endorsed the Crittenden Compromise and urged the legislature to declaim "the doctrine of coercion in the strongest terms" and "call a convention to take into consideration the political crisis, and to co-operate with our sister Southern States to protect our constitutional rights and give to us that security and peace which has been denied us by the North."[102]

Richard D. Gholson, the third governor of Washington Territory, may have been at the gathering. Gholson returned to his Ballard County home in May 1860, on a six-month leave of absence. The governor could not resist inserting his proslavery views into his only message to the legislature, which the acting governor read for him. Fearing the "awful catastrophe" of disunion, Gholson urged his fellow citizens to "stand upon the watch tower of liberty" and emulate the nation's founders by "leaving, as they did, unfettered and unmolested, to each political division of the Confederacy (who alone are responsible for them) the management of its own domestic affairs." Gholson meant, of course, that the Republicans should leave the slave states alone. In any event, Lincoln's election was too much for Gholson. He resigned the governorship, explaining in a February 14, 1861, letter to Washington's secretary of state that "he was 'unwilling, even for a day, to hold office under a Republican president.'" Never mind that Democrat James Buchanan was still president and that Lincoln would not be sworn in until March 4.[103]

In any event, the *Louisville Courier* said Gholson, a Kentucky state senator in 1851–55, had penned "a letter urging the Legislature to call a Convention to take into consideration the political crisis, and appoint Commissioners to the Southern Congress, who shall pledge Kentucky to stand by and share the fate of the South, whatever it may be." News of the letter reached the Pacific Northwest, where the *Oregon Statesman* told its readers about it on March 11, 1861.[104]

Some Purchase citizens still linked their fate to the Union, at least on Kentucky terms. Unionists dominated mass meetings in Feliciana, Mayfield, and Murray. Dr. S. P. Cope addressed the Feliciana gathering on January 18 at the Odd Fellows hall. The physician had "left the quietude of his rural home to canvass the county in defence of the Union," according to a letter in the pro-Bell *Louisville Daily Journal.* Cope claimed disunion would bring "bankruptcy, war, rapine, and misery." The meeting, chaired by E. Crutchfield, with W. A. Pirtle as secretary, evidently agreed. The citizens endorsed the pro-Union Bell and Douglas convention resolutions by voting with their feet. Crutchfield had the "ayes" go to one side of the house, the "nays" to the other. "To the surprise of all, a very large majority . . . indorsed them," the correspondent wrote. "The Secessionists, seeing themselves in a slim minority, took to their heels." Interestingly, he characterized the Union that Cope wanted to preserve as "our blood-bought Confederacy."[105]

Cope, Judge Williams, and Reverend W. W. Dugger spoke at a January 21 meeting in the Graves County courthouse in Mayfield. John Eaker chaired the gathering; William M. Cargill was secretary. On January 23, Eaker wrote Crittenden and Lazarus W. Powell, Kentucky's other senator, telling them about the meeting and including a report he and Cargill wrote. The meeting, according to the report, attracted "from 800 to 1000 voters . . . without distinction of party." The Graves countians backed Crittenden's proposed amendments "as a fair and honorable compromise" solution to "the present unhappy and perilous condition of the American Republic." They wanted the amendments to be put to a vote in Kentucky and nationwide. Also, they supported a convention to determine the state's future but agreed that nothing the convention decided "shall go into effect until it is submitted to the voters . . . and approved by a majority of them, tested by the last general election." Too, they resolved that the convention should meet around the time similar gatherings were scheduled for North Carolina, Virginia, Tennessee, and Missouri. Kentucky could thus "act in concert with those states." Another resolution called for a convention of the fifteen slave states, or at least the border slave states, to take united action "to preserve their constitutional rights" and to submit "an ultimatum to the people of the North." The crowd, by voice vote, approved the resolutions "with only five or six" against them. Before everybody left, Williams asked those who favored the resolutions and the Union to "file to the right and those against the cause" to go leftward. "The entire mass save some six to ten persons moved to the right." Finally, the meeting wanted Magoffin and members of the General Assembly "to use their joint influence with the President of the United States and seceding states to stay the hand of War until the people have had time to act upon the amendments proposed by Senator J.J. Crittenden."[106]

In his letter, Eaker said he thought the gathering represented "the feeling of the people of the entire county of Graves." Eaker hoped Crittenden's resolutions would be adopted and that the two senators' "patriotic actions, will ultimately prove successful, in averting the danger with which our beloved & once happy country is threatened." Also on January 23, Williams wrote Crittenden about the gathering, which he said was "one of the largest and most interesting meetings ever held in this County." He praised the senator's "patriotic and wise counsel and conduct in this darkest hour of our country's peril." Williams said, "The hearts of our people of all parties are for the preservation of the Union." But he wondered, "Is it possible that the Republicans can act so stubborn and unwise as to drive true, loyal Kentucky from the Union?" Williams hoped "that some honorable compromise may yet be made that will save the further disintegration of the Union." Turning to local politics, Williams said that "many of the Breckinridge leaders are now for the Southern Confederation and while they profess to be for your amendments 'they have no hopes of their adoption.'" He added, "we have no party here among the patriotic masses, and like myself the great majority having in times past been Democratic." Even so, he and his fellow Unionists were "now willing to cooperate with any patriotic party to save our Constitutional rights and the Union." He claimed the media was not helping the cause: "Every news paper we now have in this Congressional District I believe are for disunion and their statements are all directed to that end." He added that the papers were "making quite a false impression abroad" because "a very large majority of the common masses are for securing our rights and the preservation of the Union, the action of the Cotton States to the contrary notwithstanding." Williams told Crittenden that "steps are being taken to get up some conservative Union papers for securing and not destroying our Rights."[107]

On January 28, Williams's friend Dugger traveled to Murray to speak to a Union meeting at the Calloway County courthouse, where "a large number of the citizens . . . men of all parties" gathered. After Dugger's address, somebody proposed that the meeting endorse the Bell and Douglas convention resolutions and Crittenden's constitutional amendments. "Thereupon the Disunionists in the assembly raised as a big a yell as they could for one of their speakers to take the stand." Trouble was brewing, so "for the sake of peace, four fifths of those present repaired to the large Baptist Church that was too small to contain them, and adopted the resolutions without a dissenting voice, and an adjournment took place amid the most enthusiastic cheers." Captain H. W. Harding chaired the meeting, and J. B. England served as secretary.

Besides Dugger, Harding "and others made eloquent Union speeches, interrupted with loud and frequent applause."[108]

Eleven days before the Murray meeting, the most important session of the General Assembly in Bluegrass State history opened in the capitol, an impressive Greek Revival–style edifice built of local limestone and finished in 1830. Twenty years later, in the same building, lawmakers voted to donate a block of Kentucky marble for the new Washington Monument. "Under the auspices of Heaven, and the precepts of Washington, Kentucky will be the last to give up the Union," the inscription read. Would Kentucky, a slave state, honor that pledge now? Or would Kentucky accept South Carolina's invitation "to join us, in forming a confederacy of Slaveholding States"?[109]

Everyone knew that Breckinridge Democrats were leading the secession movement in the South. From Magoffin down, most Kentucky Democrats were Breckinridge men. In the legislature, the Democrats commanded a fifty-nine to forty-one House majority. They enjoyed a twenty-four to fourteen edge in the Senate. The minority, ex-Whigs and former "Know-Nothings," called itself the "Opposition." Magoffin, the entire house, and twenty-one senators were elected in 1859. The other half of the senate was elected in 1857.[110]

Naturally, friends of the Union feared that Magoffin and the legislature would instigate secession. South Carolina had exited the Union via a sovereignty convention. Unionists worried Kentucky might do likewise. Hence, their strategy was simple: stop Magoffin and the legislature from calling a convention. Pro-Confederate Kentuckians rightly suspected that the secession fever gripping the South would abate sooner or later. So they hoped for a quick convention. On the other hand, the Unionists correctly believed that the longer Kentucky stayed under the Stars and Stripes, the less likely the state would be to exit the Union.[111]

By January 17, Mississippi, Florida, and Alabama had seceded. Was Magoffin now ready to lead the state out of the Union? In his opening address to the legislature, the governor declared that "a political organization based upon the one idea of hostility to the institution of African slavery, and embodying as one of its material elements of strength, an intolerant sectional fanaticism, has been for years steadily gathering power in the non-slaveholding States, and has at last exhibited national ascendancy in the election of Abraham Lincoln, its faithful proponent, to the Presidency of the United States." As much as Magoffin deplored the president and his party, he did not call for Kentucky's immediate secession. He said that while the Crittenden Compromise did not "secure to the slave States the full measure of their constitutional equality, " he preferred it to "dissolution." But the governor blamed the Republicans for rejecting it. Magoffin also claimed "no power on earth" could "coerce . . . unwilling allegiance to the Federal Government" and repeated his call for a border slave state convention; he suggested Baltimore in February. To the disdain of disunion's foes—and the delight of secessionists—the governor called for "the election of delegates to a convention, to be assembled at an early day, to whom shall be referred, for full and final determination, the future Federal and inter-State relations of Kentucky."[112]

Already, legislators had dropped the old party labels. They were "Union" or "Southern Rights." Even so, "there were some half-dozen waverers who always opposed any decisive step toward secession but were equally unwilling to give any active support to the Government."[113] Wafflers aside, the Southern Rightists found themselves a minority in the house and senate. In only one region did they represent majority opinion: the Purchase, which sent a trio of senators and five representatives to Frankfort. All but one Purchase lawmaker had been a Democrat. The exception was Senator John M. Johnson of Paducah, a physician who had been an "Opposition" man.[114]

Johnson, who represented McCracken and Marshall Counties, joined the Southern Rights ranks, as did Senator John L. Irvan of Calloway County, whose constituents lived in Calloway and Trigg Counties. Senator Samuel H. Jenkins, from Ballard County, was apparently one of the "waverers." Besides Ballard, his district encompassed Fulton, Graves, and Hickman Counties.[115]

Representatives Virgil Coleman, who lived near Murray, John Cook of Graves County, Thomas L. Goheen of Marshall County, Lawrence Husbands of Paducah, and William D. Lannom of Clinton, were Southern Rights men. The Tennessee-born Lannom, whose constituency was Hickman and Fulton Counties, was perhaps the most vehement secessionist in the house. He officially listed his occupation as "Lawyer, advocate of Southern Rights." Goheen, also a Tennessee native, sat for Marshall and Livingston Counties. Husbands represented McCracken and Ballard Counties.[116]

The Purchase lawmakers, save perhaps Jenkins, went home disappointed after the session ended. House and senate Unionists blocked every move toward a convention. Yet no house member tried harder than Lannom to create a Confederate Kentucky. On January 18, he introduced resolutions denouncing the use of federal force to bring the seceded states back in the union, recognizing the right of secession, and declaring "that in any case of conflict between the constituted authorities of the General Government and those of a State, the first and paramount allegiance is, and of right ought to be, to his own state." Lannom's proposals got nowhere.[117]

Senator Johnson fared no better with resolutions he proposed on January 22. His package was similar to what Magoffin wanted. Johnson called for a convention of the southern states in "Nashville, or at such other suitable place as may be agreed upon, for consultation, and the adoption of such measures as will give full and complete protection of Southern institutions, having for their basis justice to every portion of the confederacy, and promising in their result peace and quiet upon the distracting subject of slavery, thereby strengthening and perpetuating the bonds of fraternal union." If the convention reached an agreement, according to Johnson's proposals, it would be submitted to the northern state legislatures for approval and eventually would be "ingrafted into the constitution of the United States as a part thereof." He also resolved that if the southern state convention failed or if the northern states rejected its "propositions for settlement" of the sectional dispute, then Magoffin "at the earliest practicable moment" should order the election of delegates to a state sovereignty convention.[118]

Having successfully fought off a state convention, the Unionists proposed a national convention that would make the Crittenden Compromise a constitutional amendment. Like the compromise, the plan failed.[119]

Still hopeful that the Union could be restored, the Unionist majority welcomed an invitation from the Virginia legislature to send representatives to a peace conference in Washington on February 4. The legislature took up Virginia's proffer rather than follow Magoffin's plan. On January 26, the senate voted unanimously to send a delegation; on the same day, the house concurred, eighty-one to five.[120]

The Kentucky delegation, which consisted of five Unionists and one Southern Rights man, was to propose the Crittenden Compromise as the basis for heading off disunion. Attended by delegates from only twenty-one states, the conference failed. Before the end of February, disunion was a fait accompli. South Carolina, Mississippi, Florida, Alabama, Georgia, Louisiana, and Texas were out of the old Union and calling themselves the new Confederate States of America. Montgomery, Alabama's capital, doubled as the Confederate capital. Meanwhile, on the day the Peace Conference met, Senator Irvan introduced resolutions directing Magoffin to announce an election for February 22 to decide whether to have a sovereignty convention and to elect delegates to such a convention, which Irvan wanted Magoffin to call for March 4. Further, the resolutions authorized the convention "to take such action in regard to the position, interests, duty and honor of Kentucky, as the circumstances may require" but recommended that whatever the convention decided "shall be ratified by the majority of the votes . . . at an election . . . to be held . . . not less than thirty days from the adjournment of the convention." Irvan's resolution stalled. Seven days later, the General Assembly adjourned until March 20. The Unionists had won the first round. Instead of calling a convention, the legislature chose compromise and conciliation under the old flag.[121]

Statewide, the Unionists were obviously relieved that the legislature had spurned secession. Yet there was predictable outrage in the Purchase. The *Hickman Courier* went so far as to threaten regional secession if Kentucky stayed in the Union. On February 6, the *Louisville Courier,* which had become the state's leading pro-Confederate newspaper, published an editorial from the Hickman newspaper under the headline, "What is thought of the Legislature—Threatened Secession of Southern Kentucky." The *Hickman Courier* argued that "the Kentucky Legislature has not, and is not, doing a thing towards the adjustment of our national difficulties." The *Courier* claimed, "better, far better for the State, that this Legislature had never been convened, than that it should thus mock the pride and wishes of the citizens of Kentucky. We know not what are the feelings of the citizens of the upper portion of Kentucky, but we can not believe that their representatives are reflecting their feelings in the present Legislature." The Hickman paper was sure "that Southern Kentucky feels humiliated at the present proceedings, and if the State does not afford some redress, and that too quickly, Southern Kentucky will per force link her destiny with that of chivalrous Tennessee." The editorial concluded, "Wild as the assertion may appear, thousands of hearts have long anxiously favored such a transfer. Only a state pride separates us now, when that is wantonly abused by those who adorn it, where is the link that binds us?"[122]

On February 22, Alfred Johnston of Marshall County penned a long letter to the *Herald* denouncing Union lawmakers in Frankfort. "Why in God's name, should Kentucky hesitate to come forward and place herself side by side with her sister States of the South, to whom she is allied by every consideration of interest and patriotism?" he challenged. "Judging from the action of our Legislature up to this time, I take it for granted that the people are to be denied at the ballot-box what they would have Kentucky do." Johnson did "not believe the sovereign people will feel very much flattered by this action of those who should be our servants instead of dictators." He presumed "that none of our worthy law-makers would have the hardihood to say that the voters of Kentucky are not capable and worthy to be trusted with the direction of their own important affairs." Johnson demanded a convention he hoped would put the state into the Confederacy. "It is too late to argue against a dissolution of the Union. The thing is done.—The question now is, where will Kentucky go?" His answer was "go with the South; and in my judgment she should go now. . . . A Southern Confederacy is now forming. Kentucky should meet with them, assist them in forming the Government, and then abide by its destiny." Johnson concluded: "I would to God that the Northern people would return to their duty—that all the States might live together as equals and in peace; but since equality is denied us . . . *I am for a Southern Confederacy, come what may.*"[123]

Also on February 22, the *Courier* published the *Herald*'s fulsome praise of the newly inaugurated Confederate leaders, President Jefferson Davis and Vice President Alexander H. Stephens of Georgia. "These are familiar names, and represent the two parties into which the people of the Southern States were recently divided—Immediate Secessionists and Co-operationists." The Paducah paper noted that Davis had supported Breckinridge for president and Stephens was a Douglas man. The *Herald* claimed Davis and Stephens were "two of the wisest, calmest, firmest, and bravest men in the South," adding that "Heaven must have inspired . . . with wisdom" those who chose the duo. The paper added, "May God continue to be with them, and to inspire them with like wisdom and the same moderation that has so far characterized their action."[124]

The *Hickman Courier* claimed there was no moderation among "the Black Republicans of the North" even when they might sound conciliatory to some people. The paper cited a speech by Senator William H. Seward, a New York Republican, that was "moderate in tone and redolent in its love for the Union." But his remarks, according to the paper, did not concede "a single cherished principle of the Black Republican party," notably its opposition to the spread of slavery into the federal territories and support for the abolition of slavery in the District of Columbia. The *Courier* said Seward's address served to arouse "the radicals and no compromisers of his party," and charged that his real motivation was to delay border state secession by hinting at compromise, but not really meaning it. The paper said his policy was based to some extent on calls by several northern delegates to the Washington Peace Conference for a national convention, but in three years. "They too, like Seward, want delay until they rivet the chains of tyranny upon the Border States." The *Courier* asked, "What protection will Lincoln's government give to a citizen of Kentucky in the enjoyment of slave property in the Territories, when the creed of his faith, the Chicago [Republican presidential] Platform [of 1860], has denounced the institution of slavery as a 'relic of barbarism.' They will afford that protection which the lion gives to the lamb, or the jackal to his prey." The paper predicted that "the people of Kentucky will not be cheated or duped any longer. They have exhausted the argument, and will assert their honor and independence regardless of consequences."[125]

Likewise, the *Crescent* urged Kentuckians to eschew moderation in their response to the General Assembly's refusal to put the state on the path to secession, challenging, "Are the people of Kentucky to be bullied by a few men, who represent them in our legislative halls—men who were elected before there was a thought that the present state of affairs would exist?" The editorial was in response to a *Louisville Daily Journal* correspondent who argued that Kentucky should stay in the Union even if every other slave state seceded. He was "no doubt a true blue Abolitionist," according to the *Crescent*, which also jabbed the *Journal* for not rebuking him and seeming to agree with him: "Such a thing is to be expected from a sheet which has for years past been exhibiting the cloven foot of Abolitionism." The *Crescent* demanded, "Are [Kentuckians'] . . . almost unanimous requests that the Legislature should call a Convention of the people, to decide as to what Kentucky should do in the present crisis, to be shouted at and treated with contempt, and their rights to be trampled under foot by these traitors to the Commonwealth?" Were the people "to be told that they are a parcel of idiots, and do not know how to manage their own business? Are they to be considered as a lot of cattle, to be driven here and there at the will of a few men who imagine they possess all the brains in the State? Or, are they to be considered a lot of children, who these very gracious legislators have assumed the task of speaking and thinking for?" In concluding, the *Crescent* thundered against Unionist efforts to thwart a sovereignty convention: "Treason for a majority of the people of the State to express their opinion, and announce their determination to stand up in defense of their rights! Preposterous! What think you of that, Kentuckians? Will you still shriek 'Union!' when Abolitionists and traitors are stalking abroad in your land in open daylight? Will you not, can you not, see the dangerous ground upon which you are standing?"[126]

Though down, the Southern Rights side was not quite out. The secessionists began circulating petitions across Kentucky urging the legislature to approve a convention. The secessionists also called a Southern Rights convention for Frankfort on March 20. The gathering was supposed to be a show of strength to influence the legislature.[127]

Three days before the convention met, Columbus mayor B. W. Sharp sought to sway the Confederate president. "I am prompted by many of your friends in this portion of Ky. to address you for the purpose of being advised how can a battalion of volunteer soldiers from this vicinity be received by the authorities of your Government, or can we after organization here, be received by you provided we rendavous [*sic*] at *Holly Springs*, Miss." Sharp added, "We wish to tender you our Services, in advance of the '*Old Fogger*' movements of our State, for in truth it seems that we are sold to the abolition dinasty [*sic*] of the North, and we will not submit to it."[128]

On the appointed day, Sharp's friend Crossland was among the Southern

Rights men who congregated in Frankfort and established a state central committee and committees in each of Kentucky's ten congressional districts. The convention central committee's Purchase delegation consisted of Crossland of Hickman County, Charles Wickliffe of Ballard County, Thomas Jones of Calloway County, C. T. Randle of Fulton County, Ervin Anderson of Graves County, Frank Stone of Marshall County, and McCracken countians J. S. Byers, W. F. Norton, and J. G. Fisher. Senator Johnson and Crossland were named convention vice presidents. Representative Lannom was named to a committee charged with "preparing some thorough and effective plan of organization of a Southern Rights party in the state."[129]

But when Johnson was "loudly called for" to speak, the *Courier* reported, "the genial Senator from McCracken" declined, protesting that "he was incapacitated on various grounds." The doctor "had been sitting up for several successive nights, and yesterday had eaten a hearty dinner, during which he had drank a great deal of—water, and did not feel brilliant." Yet he summoned enough energy to assure the faithful "that he was a true Southern man." He said "the only means by which anarchy could be prevented in our unfortunate country would be by a prompt, fearless, and firm demand on the part of the Border States for the recognition of Southern rights by the Federal Government." He condemned "the Black Republican party" for opposing further expansion of slavery into the territories. Johnson also predicted that if the Republicans got their way "many of those now on this floor would live to see eight or ten millions of slaves confined within a narrow compass, when the only question will be starvation, or one between the master and the slave as to which shall first cut the other's throat. Slavery must have room to expand."[130]

Meanwhile, the Southern Rightists apparently knew they were licked before the General Assembly reconvened. They did not even bother submitting more legislation calling for a sovereignty convention. Instead, they joined the Unionists in favor of a border slave state convention. The motives of the two groups were, of course, opposite. The Unionists hoped the convention would somehow lead to the restoration of the old Union. The Southern Rights men wanted to use the convention as a forum in which to present the Crittenden resolutions as an ultimatum to Lincoln and his party. The Republicans had opposed them in no uncertain terms. There was no reason to assume they were ready to change their minds. The Southern Rights Party was prepared to use another rejection as grounds for secession.[131]

On April 2, a bill calling for a border slave state convention passed the senate unanimously and passed by eighty-two to two in the house. Elections for Kentucky's twelve delegates were announced for May 4. On April 4, the legislature adjourned. A Union tide was rising everywhere except in the Purchase.

That tide began to flow with the presidential election of 1860. While Kentucky went for Bell, Breckinridge carried the Purchase. The Breckinridge Democrats formed the nucleus of the secessionist or Southern Rights Party in the region and the state. On the other hand, the Bell and Douglas men became the backbone of the Union Party everywhere except the Purchase. Here, most Bell and Douglas partisans became Southern Rightists. In the General Assembly, all but one Purchase lawmaker was an outright secessionist. The majority of senators and representatives from every other region were pro-Union. Even some Breckinridge men ebbed into the Union camp.

2

Armies on the Border

On April 12, Confederate troops fired on Fort Sumter, and suddenly the nation was at war. President Lincoln called for seventy-five thousand volunteers to put down the rebellion, and the free states quickly responded with an outpouring of eager enlistees. Kentuckians, ever ready to fight in wars, were loath to spill the blood of fellow Americans. So the state declared itself neutral within the Union. Neutrality represented majority sentiment in every Bluegrass State region except the Purchase. War made the Purchase even more solidly secessionist.

News of the Fort Sumter attack reached Paducah via telegraph on April 13, throwing the city "into a state of great excitement," Quigley wrote in his diary the next day. The dispatch, he added, "exposed fully the perfidy of Old Abe and convinced many of our people who had been urging that his policy was peace." Quigley added that during a performance of Don Rice's Circus later that night, the owner appeared before "an immense crowd in the canvas" and shared more news: Fort Sumter had capitulated. Rice's revelation triggered "a loud and deafening shout which was food for my very soul," Quigley penned. He confessed that "through the day from the reception of the first news I had been so full of anxiety for the South that the least excitement would have made me wild." Yet Quigley was also "much chagrined and mortified to hear many of our citizens express no preference for either side which to my mind amounts to a very decided preference to the North." Kentucky secessionists would echo Quigley's sentiments in their denunciations of neutrality, which was about to become the official policy of the state. Meanwhile, Quigley recalled that on the morning of April 14, Paducah was "alive . . . with enquiry upon every face and dejection upon that of many both Union and Southern men." The Unionists "fear that all hopes of peace are at an end and to many it is the announcement of the destruction of their party." The secessionists believed "that in all probability much blood and treasure will be expended before the difficulties here are settled." He prayed that the "giver of all things" would "avert the calamities of Civil War and incline the hearts and minds of men to settle this matter without blood." However, "if in his unfortunate ordering conflict must come then my prayers are for the noble and gallant sons of the South."[1]

Governor Magoffin sharply rebuked the president's call for troops to fight Quigley's "gallant sons of the South." "I say, *emphatically,* Kentucky will furnish no troops for the wicked purpose of subduing her sister Southern states," he replied on April 15, two days after Fort Sumter surrendered to the Confederates who let the Union garrison leave.[2]

Quigley said Lincoln's request for soldiers amounted to a declaration of war against the South. He noted Magoffin's refusal, adding that "Tennessee follows and last night Virginia seceded." Quigley denounced Thomas Hicks, the governor of Maryland, for agreeing to furnish troops, claiming he "is entitled to the just condemnation and scorn of all men." While Missouri, North Carolina, and Delaware had "not yet spoken," Paducah was "all united in rejecting [Lincoln] . . . and his government and for the support of the South." Quigley said the city had grown "wild and paraded out formations of companies and hallowing have filled up the town." The court adjourned, and most businesses had shut. "Flags with 15 stars [representing the slave states] were raised and now float over our city." Thus, he concluded, "we have inaugurated a war of secession, the end and finale of which to reach we will probably be compelled to travel through blood upon soil once common to us all, through scenes and acts which makes the heart sicken to contemplate." Again, he sought supplication: "May the spirit of him who holds the destinies of nations in his fist control this terrible storm, so that it may result in no great harm. But if it must come, then I, as well as every man in the South, must be prepared to defend our homes, our rights, our honors, and no cheap satisfaction."[3]

Heretofore, Kentuckians had enthusiastically rushed to the colors in wartime. They had fought the British and their Native American allies in the Revolutionary War and the War of 1812. They had battled in the Mexican-American War. But fighting fellow white Americans was different to them. So Kentucky hesitated. Unionists pleaded for calm. They feared that war between North and South might propel Kentucky into the Confederacy; after all, Kentucky had been a slave state since it came into the Union in 1792. In a Lexington speech on April 17, Senator Crittenden begged the state to keep out of the "fratricidal war impending between the North and the South." He wanted his state to act "as a peaceful mediator, remonstrating with both sections against involving the nation in civil war, the fatal consequences of which no wisdom nor foresight could foretell."[4]

The next day, James Guthrie, John Young Brown, Archibald Dixon, and William F. Bullock, all well-known Union men, spoke to a large gathering in Louisville, declaring that Kentucky would not take up arms for either the North or the South and warning both sides to keep out of the state. As a result of the meeting, the Union State Central Committee, in an "Address to the people of the Commonwealth," said much the same thing.[5]

Thus, the Unionists were sowing the seeds of neutrality, but neutrality within the Union. Down the Ohio at Paducah, editor John C. Noble was predictably unimpressed. The *Herald* scoffed that the Union men merely "resolved that it was foolish to risk Dixon's one hundred and fifty negroes and Guthrie's houses in Louisville for such things as the property, rights, liberty, and lives of the Southern people; and that they did not care who went under, so that *their* dumplings boiled peacefully in the pot." Noble likened the secessionists to the patriots of the American Revolution, a common comparison throughout the Confederacy. He concluded by quoting Patrick Henry's famous "reply to the dumpling men of that day . . . 'give me Liberty or give me death!'"[6]

Meanwhile, Magoffin's rebuff of Lincoln's request for troops might have prompted a swift military response from a less temperate president. Indeed, Magoffin's rebuke sounded treasonous, but the president wisely let it pass. Lincoln believed, or hoped, that in the end, Kentucky would stay in the Union fold. So he opted for patience over precipitate action toward the state of his birth, a prudent course that did much to help keep Kentucky under the Stars and Stripes.

On the other hand, Magoffin's scorning of Lincoln naturally cheered the Rebels. "Your patriotic response . . . justifies the belief that your people are prepared to unite with us in repelling the common enemy of the South," a hopeful Confederate secretary of war Leroy Pope Walker wrote Magoffin on April 22. Thus emboldened, he asked Magoffin to furnish an infantry regiment and send it post haste to Harper's Ferry, Virginia. Yet Magoffin "promptly, and in the fewest words, declined to comply with the request." Though ardently proslavery, he was not willing to lead a Kentucky charge into the Confederacy.[7]

Even so, about one thousand Kentuckians, led by Blanton Duncan and Thomas H. Taylor, both of Louisville, answered Walker on their own. They led ten companies, which would become the First Kentucky Infantry Regiment, to Harper's Ferry via Nashville. The contingent included the war's first Purchase volunteers. Crossland departed with approximately one hundred Hickman and Fulton County men. C. C. Bowman raised a like number of recruits in Calloway County. Crossland's outfit, the "Alexander Guards," formed Company E, and Bowman's band was Company F. Crossland and Bowman were elected captains of their companies; Crossland subsequently made major. Before they left, Crossland and his men paused at Moscow in Hickman County to accept a Confederate flag from "the accomplished and beautiful Miss Nannie Wilson." She presented the banner "in behalf of the ladies of Fulton County," according to the *Louisville Daily Courier.* A correspondent for the paper declared of the belle: "I have often been dazzled by the blaze of beauty, but never before beheld perfect loveliness. All the harmony of form and of soul was personified in this fair creature." She possessed "sweet patriotic lips, whose color mocks the rose, / Rich, ripe, and teeming with the dews of / bliss." Captain Crossland reportedly made "an elegant and patriotic speech" upon accepting the flag. The First Kentucky, raised for one year's service, fought in only two significant battles, both in Virginia—Dranesville on December, 20, 1861, and Yorktown on April 5–May 4, 1862. The regiment mustered out in May 1862.[8]

Meanwhile, Purchase secessionists might have wished Crossland and Bowman had stayed home with their men-at-arms. On April 23, Illinois state soldiers began trooping into strategic Cairo, where the Ohio and Mississippi merge. The Yankees were just a river's width away from Kentucky's "South Carolina."[9]

The day before, four local secessionists had written Davis, inviting the Confederate army to take their town and Cairo. "We acknowledge no Union but that of the Confederate States," they vowed. "We recognize no President but Your Excellency." They claimed that Cairo was strategically and militarily "one of the most important places in the West." They warned that, "if held by an abolition army, it will enable our enemies to cut off effectually all supplies from the above sources to the South." They promised "the citizens of Cairo are favorably disposed toward the Southern cause, and would lend a helping hand. . . . You will also find active and willing co-operation in Southern Kentucky, Southeastern Missouri, and West Tennessee. We are all with you heart and hand—your friends to the death!" The Columbus "friends" also advised that their community was "a very important place" where the Mississippi was "only half a mile wide. . . . To the north of the town are the iron banks—immense bluffs which rise 200 feet above the river. An efficient battery planted there would effectually command the channel." They also recommended nearby Wolf Island "as a naval station." The authors sought to reassure Davis "that Kentucky is still true to the holy cause of Southern rights, and we trust our confederated brethren will not place an uncharitable construction upon her long silence and seeming indifference." They vowed that Kentucky was determined "to link her destiny with her sisters of the Confederate States, but her voice has been stifled by politicians, who 'clothed in a little brief authority,' have basely used it to serve their own selfish ends."

They predicted "the secession of Kentucky is now a fixed fact" and added, "the war has commenced, and we desire to play our part in it. We long to take our stand in arms by the side of our friends and brothers, to show to the world what Kentuckians can dare in defense of Southern rights and Southern honor."[10]

The letter would prove typical of the misplaced faith most Purchase Confederates had in Kentucky's ultimate secession. They clung to it even after the firing on Fort Sumter failed to dislodge Kentucky from the Union. They kept the faith through Kentucky's neutrality period. They considered and rejected the Purchase allying itself with Tennessee or seceding on its own, evidently because they were sure the Southern Rights Party would win a majority in the legislature in the August state elections and put all of Kentucky in the Confederacy. They were wrong on every count.

Meanwhile, Columbus had other appeals to the military minded. South of the town, somewhat lower white clay cliffs—known as the Chalk Bluffs—rose up from the river's edge. In addition, the town's well-established port would provide easy access for soldiers and military equipment. The Mobile & Ohio Railroad connected Columbus with points south, adding another supply line for troops and war materiel.

More Columbus citizens tried to coax the Confederates to show up, especially after the Yankees arrived in Cairo. On April 24, John Tyler Jr., assistant secretary of war and son of the ninth president, replied to Sharp's offer to raise a battalion of Confederate troops. "You are doubtless aware by this time of the co-operation of Kentucky with this Government in our military movements. The Secretary, therefore, begs leave respectfully to refer you to His Excellency Governor Magoffin." There was no such cooperation.[11]

Also on April 24, a Columbus committee headed by W. R. Vance arrived in Memphis, "consulting with our military and civil authorities," the *Memphis Daily Appeal* reported the next day. In the same issue, the paper accused the Yankees of scheming to grab Columbus. Reportedly, Union officers boarded the *P. B. Cheney,* the boat that transferred railroad passengers and freight between Cairo and Columbus, and made a special trip to Columbus to survey the town. "This is corroborated by the fact that when the next train from this section reached Columbus the Cheeney [*sic*] was not waiting as usual, and the passengers had to go forward on a transient boat."[12]

On April 26, the paper claimed "a gentleman who came down from Columbus" on April 25 brought word "that preparations of defense will soon be commenced at the place with the view of establishing there a strong military post." The man said he was told that five hundred state guards "had already arrived and others were expected." The troops had two large cannons

"—one twenty-four and one thirty-two pounder—and design constructing a suitable battery so soon as a location can be selected and a survey made." The *Appeal* was "pleased to observe the alacrity with which the gallant people of our neighboring Commonwealth are responding to the urgent necessities of the occasion, and would assure them that no time can be lost in completing their works of defense with dispatch. Columbus is one of the most important military points on southern territory, and must be held against the enemy at all hazards."[13]

While their numbers were likely overstated, the state troops were apparently from the guard's Southwest Battalion, headquartered in Paducah and commanded by Major Tilghman, the "uncommonly athletic and muscular" railroad builder. Astride his horse, the dark-eyed, auburn-haired, six-foot, one-hundred-seventy-pound Tilghman reputedly "impressed one as powerful and even majestic, and often upon seeing him there flashed through the mind a remembrance of Byron's Moorish king as he rode benignly through the streets of Granada." Almost every officer and man under Tilghman was pro-southern. Statewide, too, the guard titled sharply toward the Confederates. Tilghman's force consisted of infantry, cavalry, and artillery troops.[14]

Also on April 26, the *Appeal* said more troops were coming to Columbus. The paper again advised its readers about the two big guns but added that "a secession banner was flying" over the town. The clerk of the steamboat *D. A. January* provided confirmation; he spied "a large piece of ordnance at the landing when the boat was at Columbus" and spotted the Confederate flag. From whence the thirty-two and twenty-four pounders came is a mystery; Tilghman's battery consisted of field guns. In any event, on April 28, Sharp wrote Walker, reminding the secretary of his offer to raise Rebel recruits and advising that he was drawing up a map of the country from Columbus to Cairo, which he claimed would "show fully and accurately the commanding position of this place as a bassis [*sic*] of military operations for the Southern Confederacy." The mayor suggested, "should it be deemed by you expedient to send hither a corps of *Topographical Engineers* and [if] my services shall be required in that department I am at your service." Sharp said he was a quartermaster of Missouri volunteers in New Mexico. He told Walker he was forty years old, "temperate in habits, and by birth and education a Southern man. My references are filed with President Davis."[15]

Meanwhile, a gathering in Mayfield on April 22 suggested that secessionist sentiment was growing in the Purchase. Pro-southern citizens turned out to hear a speech by Senator Breckinridge, according to the *Courier*. When he failed to appear, the locals, "having organized some military companies, and formed the old men into a Home Guard . . . resolved themselves into a public meeting with Col. W. Y. McNeely in the chair and J. M. Culbertson, secretary." The crowd approved "strong Southern resolutions . . . and stirring speeches were made by Col. [probably James T.] Lockridge, A. R. Brown [probably county judge A. R. Boone], A. T. Wright and others. The county is a unit."[16]

On July 19, 1862, the *Louisville Journal* published a letter signed "GRAVES," which was evidently written to editor Noble at the *Herald,* giving a fuller account of the meeting. The *Journal* cited it and another letter, apparently from the *Herald,* telling of a May 10, 1861, meeting in Mayfield that called for a May 30 "Convention of all the counties in the First Congressional District, to take action in forming a military league with Tennessee, provided Kentucky does not secede from the Union." Such was more proof of the Purchase's disloyalty, according to the *Journal.*[17]

"GRAVES" said that at the April 22 conclave the locals organized "military companies and a home guard" and enjoyed "a stirring, patriotic Southern Rights speech" by Lockridge and "a military exhortation" from Boone. With McNeely—the story identified him as "W. T. NcNeely" —presiding, "the spontaneous mass meeting" approved a series of resolutions. The secessionists aimed their first barb at Lincoln, condemning "the perfidy of a sectional President" and blaming him for starting the war and "mustering the myrmidions of his policy, preparing a mercenary crusade of Jim Lanes and John Browns against the institutions of an injured South under the guise of enforcing the law." The policy of Lincoln, they resolved, was "damnable" because he had "dealt the fatal blow for the union of our once united and glorious Government, and has foisted upon us his 'irrepressible conflict.'"[18]

In addition, the meeting called on Kentucky to "unite her destiny with the Confederate States of America." Meanwhile, the crowd "most heartily" agreed with "the refusal of our gallant Governor to aid an abolition government in its unholy war against our common South" and urged "immediate action in thoroughly arming and equipping the State against our Northern enemies." The meeting dismissed the border slave state convention as useless and declared "that each Southern State should immediately withdraw its allegiance from Lincoln's government of usurpation and tyranny" and start organizing troops "for the defence of Southern firesides." Too, since northern banks were helping pay for the war against the Confederacy, Kentucky banks should help fund the Confederate forces, the crowd also resolved. The letter writer identified Wright as "Dr. A. F. Wright." The correspondent said Wright had been "an ardent Union man" but "gave us a stirring appeal for the constitutional rights of the South in her patriotic position, declaring his final and uncompromising devotion to her united destiny." "GRAVES" concluded his epistle by reporting, "After rounds of deafening plaudits for the Southern Confederacy, Magoffin, Old Virginia, and Jeff Davis, the crowd dispersed to swell the ranks of the Southern volunteers."[19]

The Mayfield meeting suggested that Fort Sumter and the Union occupation of Cairo were sweeping away most Union sentiment in Graves County. There were other signs of fading unionism elsewhere in the Purchase. "Went with A. P. Thompson to Lovelaceville [in Ballard County] to make speeches in favor of going with the Southern government," Quigley put down in his journal on March 30. Thompson led off, speaking to a crowd of about forty, which "increased to 70 after an hour in which he made a fair argument." Quigley followed. "We were patiently listened to," he added. The Constitutional Unionist Bell carried Ballard County, but Quigley found sentiment in the Lovelaceville neighborhood "about equal as far as I could learn."[20]

Twyman, a Paducah Unionist, said the firing on Fort Sumter was the death blow to the Union cause in the Purchase's largest town. He claimed that when South Carolina seceded, "there were not half a dozen out-spoken secessionists in Paducah, but as State after State went out and took their stand by the side of South Carolina, the secession element gained strength, and one by one the people turned over to the side of the Confederacy." Twyman probably underestimated secessionist strength in Paducah, but he insisted that the Union cause had prevailed until the Fort Sumter attack, news of which made the townsfolk "wild with excitement. Men and women seemed really to go mad." Lincoln's call for seventy-five thousand Union volunteers to quell the rebellion "increased the excitement and madness of the hour," he said, adding that "few, very few were able to withstand the tempest of excited public sentiment. The weak and wavering were irresistibly borne down and along with the great flood of secession fanaticism, scarcely knowing how or wherefore, and, taking advantage of the trepidation they had strategically produced in the public mind, the leaders and managers of the Revolution pressed on the issue of resistance to the Federal Government."[21]

Likewise, the *Louisville Journal,* edited by fiercely Unionist George D. Prentice, regretted to see Paducah, "a thriving young city fast rising into commercial importance, once distinguished for the law and order that prevailed and the morality of its citizens, . . . seized with this full spirit of secessionism." The Louisville paper recalled that following "their disgraceful defeat in November," southern Democratic luminaries, including lawyer Thompson, had "exerted every influence . . . to inaugurate a revolution and to chain Kentucky to the car of South Carolina." The *Journal* said Unionism "seemed to be largely in the ascendant" until Fort Sumter, after which "many of the Bell and Douglas leaders succumbed to the passion of the hour, and, in their new-found, revolutionary zeal, determined to outstrip the Breckinridge men." The paper cited as secessionist converts Judge James Campbell, John Quincy Adams King, and A. F. Williams of Paducah, plus A. D. Kingman and Josiah Parker of Fulton County and W. R. Bradley and other Hickman countians.[22]

The Yankees at Cairo also worried southern sympathizers at Paducah. The steamer *Grey Eagle* was in town when news of Cairo's occupation arrived. "The people were intensely excited about the proceedings at Cairo," one of the vessel's officers said. But excitement begat action, he added: "Eight companies have been formed; they have sent Major Tilghman to St. Louis to procure arms. They state that they have intelligence that some of the southern counties of Illinois will aid them in an attack upon Cairo, and as a beginning they will tear down the trestle work on the railroad beyond Cairo, thus putting a stop to the entrance of any more troops by that avenue."[23]

Meanwhile, Noble did his part to fire up the secessionist faithful, headlining a *Herald* story, "Ready for a Fight." "From every part of the Purchase, and from the adjacent counties of Tennessee, the feeling of resistance to Lincoln and his unholy war is intense and deep-seated," the *Herald* bragged. "It only needs the signal to be given, and thousands of true men, from every direction around us, will rush to the standard of independence, and clean the pirates and plunderers out of Cairo." The paper claimed the task would be easy: "In God's name, let it be done. It is disgraceful to Kentucky and the South to suffer these Vandals to quietly plunder our commerce. To arms! To arms!" Cairo might have been a tough nut even for "thousands of true men" to crack. The *Herald* reported that Union forces in Illinois's southernmost city included "about twenty pieces of cannon . . . some of them very heavy, and from five to six thousand troops." Formidable firepower notwithstanding, several Purchase communities offered volunteers for Paducah's defense. Nearby Fowler's Landing pledged "two or three companies." Feliciana, in Graves County, offered a company. State Line, in Fulton County, agreed to furnish "a company to help defend the city or to drive the plunderers from Cairo." Colonel Jimmy Brien, a War of 1812 veteran, promised three hundred men from Marshall County. The old soldier boasted that he could "take one thousand men, armed with dog-wood cudgels, and swim the Ohio with them at high-tide and clean Cairo of the scum that now infests it." The *Herald*'s Cairo correspondent claimed the Yankees were "a lot of robbers, and nothing more. The men are generally dressed in stolen shirts, pants, and shoes, and wear side arms, cutlasses &c, taken by violence from their neighbors."[24]

The threat from Cairo also prompted Purchase citizens to look southward again for military assistance. On April 29, Oscar Turner of Ballard County wrote Secretary Walker from Memphis, explaining, "I am here for the purpose of procuring arms for defense of counties in Kentucky bordering on the Mississippi and mouth of Ohio. We are without means of defense and depend upon sister States for aid." Turner claimed to "have a letter from J. C. Breckinridge on the subject, asking [for] this aid." He pleaded, "Can you sell or loan us 5,000 stand, or how many? It is of greatest importance that we should have them for immediate protection. No arms can be had here."[25]

Also on April 29, Mississippi governor John J. Pettus wrote Walker that A. D. Bright of western Tennessee "visits Montgomery" in search of weapons for his region and the Purchase. "I think it a matter of vital importance to put arms in the hands of the people of West Tennessee and West Kentucky," the governor advised.[26]

It is uncertain if the western Kentuckians who traveled to Memphis met with Gideon J. Pillow, who was soon to be appointed head of the Provisional Army of Tennessee. At any rate, on May 1, Pillow wrote Secretary Walker from Memphis: "Could you assist Kentucky with artillery and small-arms, and to what extent? I speak not without authority."[27]

Seven days later, Sharp was in Montgomery, seeking a personal audience with Walker. The mayor carried a letter of introduction from former congressman Percy Walker, the secretary's brother. Sharp sought "arms for the defense of Columbus and the adjacent section," Percy wrote his sibling. "He informs me that he has already had some official correspondence with your Department on the subject, and his representations of things in his locality, the importance of Columbus in a military point of view, will, I have no doubt, indicate the propriety of a compliance with the object of his visit, if within the policy of our Government."[28]

On May 9, William W. Lee of Trenton in northwest Tennessee wrote Walker, urging Confederate forces to seize Sharp's town. "There are now at Cairo . . . 7,000 men, well armed, having field artillery and plenty of heavy guns, and everything indicates that it is being made a strong point-d'appui, or basis of operations, for an extensive invasion of the country below," he said. Lee, who explained that he had just moved back home to Trenton from his plantation in Noxubee County, Mississippi, added that "it is quite probable that in a few days a force of 20,000 to 30,000 men will be concentrated at Cairo, and in all this section there are only a few half-formed companies of volunteers and home guards, mostly without arms of any kind, to meet and repel any attempt at invasion." Lee claimed "the best defense of Memphis, as well as all points below, on and off the river, may be made at Columbus, Ky. Below the mouth of the Ohio River there is no strategic point of half so much importance, and it should be immediately occupied by a strong force, notwithstanding the neutral position of Kentucky. Self-preservation demands it." It was obvious Lee knew the territory around Columbus. While proposing "a strong fort at" Columbus, he suggested "an auxiliary" strongpoint on the site of old Fort Jefferson, "at the mouth of Mayfield Creek, eight miles above Columbus." He said a "sufficient garrison in each, would protect the terminus of the Mobile and Ohio Railroad and prevent passage of any but an overwhelming force." But if Rebel troops were not sent to Columbus and the old Fort Jefferson site, then they should at least be concentrated in and around Union City, Tennessee, where the Mobile & Ohio converged with the Nashville & Northwestern Railroad, whose terminus was Hickman.[29]

Though Tennessee authorities declined to send troops to Columbus, a group of Hickman countians decided to join them. Drew Outlaw led some volunteers to Union City, where they enlisted in the Twelfth Tennessee Infantry.[30]

Too, Albert P. Thompson eventually went to Tennessee and joined the Confederate army. But he was yet at home. On May 11, he wrote Walker from Murray, where he had lived, seeking weapons for his region. He decried the majority Unionists in the state legislature, who had "so far disgraced themselves and to the extent of their power sullied the fair fame of Kentucky in not arousing our people and calling a convention." Thompson said the legislature was "now in session, and I fear [lawmakers] will not prove themselves equal to the occasion." He promised Walker that the Purchase was "entirely Southern," adding that he had "advocated secession ever since gallant South Carolina led off." Even though the Purchase was relatively poor and "unarmed, comparatively speaking," Thompson promised "we, with arms in our hands, would resist to the death" an invasion from Cairo. Thompson told Walker he expected the Yankees would wait until autumn, "owing to the Southern climate." Meanwhile, he had "spent both time and money in endeavoring to procure arms for this end of the State, and . . . have so far only succeeded to a very partial extent. . . . Should we be disappointed in our cherished hope to take both men and arms? Southern Kentucky is my birthplace, and I should be pained to be exiled from her while there remains a hope of her yet being true to her former character." As an afterthought, Thompson suggested that a likeness of George Washington should be placed on the Confederate flag. "I believe it would have an untold influence with the masses."[31]

Tennessee governor Isham G. Harris worried that the attack Thompson pledged to resist was imminent. He wrote Walker on May 12, declaring, "there is very little doubt upon my mind that the settled purpose of the troops at Cairo is at a very early day to take possession of and fortify Columbus, Ky., and make that the base of their operations south." He said Purchase citizens were "determined to resist, but unfortunately . . . have no arms." Tennessee, he added, could not spare weapons to help them. In addition, Harris said he was concentrating troops at Union City, about ten miles south of the Kentucky state line, so that he could assist the Purchase "at any moment it may be necessary." Harris said he had "not arms sufficient for the general purpose of defense." He concluded by requesting any surplus arms be sent to Tennessee for his soldiers.[32]

Newly minted major general Pillow, now commander of the Tennessee army, sent a brief message to Walker on May 15, warning, "I must have support in assuming a position on the new line at Union City or Columbus. Have applied for permission to occupy and fortify Columbus. No answer yet." Pillow said he could have two regiments of Mississippi volunteers at Corinth by an order from Walker, but not otherwise. "Must move without loss of time, else will be too late," he pressed the secretary. "Say at once."[33]

Also on May 15, Pillow sent a longer message to Walker, telling the secretary he had sent a special messenger to Magoffin, seeking the governor's blessing to take Columbus. "If he should withhold his consent, my present impression is that I shall go forward and occupy the work upon the ground of its necessity for protecting Tennessee," he explained. "I have serious apprehension that the enemy will seize the place before I can possibly get in hand a sufficient force to occupy it." Pillow said that with the secretary's permission he could bring those eighteen hundred Mississippi volunteers from Corinth. The general also predicted that when his fortifications on the Mississippi above Memphis were complete, Union forces would make an end run around them. He said the federal soldiers would capture Columbus, fortify the town, "and with a strong invading column turn my works, attack them in reverse, crush my supporting force, capture the guns and open the river." Next, Union forces would drive southward to New Orleans, thus hewing Arkansas, part of Louisiana, and Texas from the rest of the Confederacy, according to Pillow. "Such an amputation will require all the surgical skill of President Davis to restore the patient," he warned, but he assured Walker that "with arms I could roll back the invading column."[34]

The next day, Pillow wrote to Davis, lamenting, "I cannot resist the forces of the enemy rapidly preparing to advance upon us through the interior of Western Kentucky and Tennessee without I can get more small-arms." He repeated that he must occupy Columbus, and he also told Davis about the courier he dispatched to Magoffin. However, Pillow expected that the governor "will withhold his consent." Thus, Pillow said, "I know no alternative but to take the responsibility of acting on my own judgment. Tennessee is for all practical purposes in the Confederate States. With arms I can protect the West; without them it is impossible." As expected, Magoffin did not give Pillow leave to take Columbus. Instead, he sought assurances from Davis that Pillow would stay in Tennessee. Pillow steered clear of Kentucky until September.[35]

Meanwhile, Kentucky authorities wanted guarantees from Colonel Benjamin Prentiss, the Union commander at Cairo, that he had no designs on the Bluegrass State either. On April 29, Inspector General Simon Bolivar Buckner, the state guard chief, and Senator Johnson went to Cairo to confer with Prentiss. Buckner was a thirty-eight-year-old West Point graduate and Mexican-American War veteran whose job was to keep both armies out of the state. Prentiss had established a river blockade, and Buckner wanted to know about "the seizure and detention at Cairo of private property" by Union troops. The colonel explained that he had not captured any "boats or property except under special instructions." He said his instructions did not include the confiscation of "arms and ammunition belong to the State of Kentucky, in passing from a United States arsenal." Prentiss told his visitors that the governor of Illinois had sent him to Cairo but that he and his men soon would be under federal authority. Prentiss also warned the Kentuckians that he would not let arms destined for Columbus pass Cairo because Columbus citizens "and persons from other States cooperating with them" had menaced his post. Too, he charged that Columbus residents had threatened to stop the *Cheney*'s trips to and from Cairo. Nonetheless, Prentiss said he did not intend to occupy points in Kentucky. Buckner promised to visit Columbus and investigate. The state guard commander indeed went to Columbus, and on April 30 he wrote Prentiss that he had found nothing to support the colonel's charges. Prentiss refused to budge. On May 3, he wrote Buckner that he still intended to halt all shipments of arms and ammunition bound for Columbus unless it could be proved that the consignee was a Unionist. The colonel warned he intended to examine all cargoes.[36]

Soon afterward, Tilghman and Charles Wickliffe, a state guard captain and leading Ballard County secessionist, met with Prentiss at Cairo. Tilghman reassured the colonel that Cairo was not in danger from Columbus, Paducah, or Tennessee. However, the major protested Prentiss's attitude on arms shipments and complained that Kentuckians "feel that they cannot ship a barrel of flour without being subjected to this system of *espionage*, which is entirely inadmissible." Prentiss was unyielding but explained he was "instructed to seize no property unless I have information that such property consists of munitions of war, destined to the enemies of the United States Government."[37]

Meanwhile, Kentucky Unionists were anxious to discover Lincoln's intentions toward Kentucky. Accordingly, in late April, Unionists Garrett

Davis and Warner L. Underwood went to Washington to confer with the president. On April 26, Lincoln told Davis he hoped Kentucky would furnish the troops he asked for, but he would not compel the state to do so. Lincoln promised that "he had no intention of invading any state that obeyed the laws of the United States" and that he contemplated no military moves that would require him to send troops into Kentucky. The president added that if Kentucky "made no military move against the Federal government, he would not molest her." The next day, Lincoln confided to Underwood that he hoped Kentucky "would stand by the Government, in the present difficulties; but, if she would not do that, let her stand still and take no hostile part against it; and that no hostile step should tread her soil." Thus assured that Lincoln would accept a neutral Kentucky, the Unionists in the legislature got busy making neutrality Kentucky's official policy. At the same time, the dozen Unionist candidates for the border slave state convention, including Judge Williams, called for neutrality and the Crittenden Compromise. Facing almost certain defeat, the Southern Rights candidates withdrew on April 29.[38]

Though the Southern Rights candidates exited the election, the Unionists had plenty to cheer over the results, however inevitable they were. Statewide, the Union candidates polled 107,334 votes, or more than 73 percent of the total vote in the 1860 presidential election. The Unionist total in the border slave state convention balloting exceeded the Bell, Douglas, and Lincoln vote by 14,281. The numbers added up decidedly differently in the Purchase. No returns were reported from Ballard, Graves, Hickman, Marshall, and McCracken Counties. Only 133 Unionist votes were recorded in Calloway County. Fulton County ended up in the Southern Rights column, 181–92.[39]

"In several of the counties of the First District no poll was opened, in others none at a majority of the precincts," the *Journal* complained later. "Union men at various places, who were determined to vote at all hazards, had to do so in the face of the insults and outrages of the revolutionists." The state's leading Unionist paper charged that "at one precinct in Graves County, there was but one Union man who dared to vote; after doing so, he was forcibly led up to the polls, and, amid sneers, derisions, and the threats of the crowd, made to *look at his vote;* then, after being otherwise brutally insulted, he was *driven home.*"[40]

In the last analysis, the border slave state convention election proved that Fort Sumter had a decidedly different effect on the Purchase than it did on the rest of Kentucky. Beyond the region, the significant voter turnout indicated that war had turned Kentucky toward neutrality, not disunion. On the other hand, the fact that the Purchase barely participated in the election suggested that the Unionist minority in the region was shrinking.

Despite the election results, the *Herald* believed Unionism was on the wane statewide. "It is our solemn conviction that if the vote could be taken today as to whether Kentucky would join the Southern Confederacy, it would carry by fifty thousand majority," the paper editorialized.[41]

Editor Noble was whistling in the dark. Union power was holding firm, also notably in the legislature, which Magoffin called back into session. When lawmakers met on May 6, Magoffin again recommended "the passage of a law providing for the submission to the people of the question of a Convention, and the election of delegates."[42]

Two days later, Johnson introduced a petition from Paducah asking the state to build a fort in the city. The supplication went nowhere. Unionist senator Lovell H. Rousseau of Louisville suspected "the assumed preparation for defense was, in fact, a preparation to fight our own government."[43]

The *Herald* bragged that Paducah was well armed anyway and ready to fight. The paper vowed if the "order were given to drive the pirates and plunderers from Cairo, who have been depredating upon our commerce . . . the Kentucky Purchase would turn out thousands of brave and true men, who would march as to a jubilee to the conflict." The *Herald* admitted "Illinois has a right to occupy Cairo with her troops" but claimed that stopping boats and seizing cargoes was "an act of war, and the people of the Purchase will march to avenge the wrong."[44]

Several more Purchase men joined the state guard in May. Additional companies turned the Southwest Battalion into the Fourth Regiment and earned Tilghman promotion to colonel. The new companies, all infantry, were the "Boyd Grays," "Dukedom Rifles," "Tilghman Grays," and "Feliciana Invincibles," all of Graves County, plus the "Ballard Grays."[45]

On May 16, the house moved to fight neither the Union nor the Confederate government. Lawmakers voted sixty-nine to twenty-six to approve a resolution declaring that "this state and the citizens thereof should not take part in the civil war now being waged, except as mediators and friends of the belligerent parties; and that Kentucky should, during the contest, occupy the position of strict neutrality." All five Purchase representatives sided with the minority. Also, by a vote of eighty-nine to four, the house approved Magoffin's refusal to furnish troops to the Union army. On May 20, Magoffin issued a proclamation of neutrality that warned both sides to keep out of Kentucky.[46]

Four days later, the senate approved its own version of neutrality by a vote of thirteen to nine, resolving that "Kentucky will not sever her connection with the National Government, nor will she take up arms for either of the belligerent parties, but will arm herself for the one purpose of preserving peace and tranquility within her own borders." Irvan voted "nay," and Jenkins and Johnson did not vote.[47]

The Unionist lawmakers were elated at blocking a convention again and at making neutrality within the Union the state's official policy. Yet they worried that Magoffin might use the state guard to force Kentucky into the Confederacy. Under the state constitution, the governor was commander-in-chief of the state's armed forces. The Unionists wanted to strip him of that power and disband the state guard. The plan stalled amid much wrangling, but a compromise was finally reached. On May 21, the senate passed a measure creating a five-member Military Board of Kentucky. Magoffin was to be president, but the majority would be Unionists. The board was authorized to borrow money, buy arms and ammunition, build powder mills—though not in any border counties—and have total control over the arming of the state. The state guard remained, but the bill created a pro-Union home guard as a counterweight to the mostly pro-Confederate militia. The two organizations were to be placed on the same footing and could draw equally from an initial military fund totaling $750,000. The vote for the bill was thirty-four to four, with the opposition coming from uncompromising Unionists. Two days later, the House concurred, seventy-six to fourteen, again with the nay votes coming from the staunchest Union men.[48]

On May 24, the General Assembly adjourned and would not meet again until after the August 5 elections for a new legislature. Meanwhile, official neutrality was welcome news to the great majority of Kentuckians in every part of the state save the Purchase, where most citizens were dismayed. They would accept nothing short of secession. Some of the most zealous Confederate sympathizers seemed determined that if the state would not go into the new Confederacy, then the Purchase, and perhaps all of Kentucky south of the Green River, would secede or would become a military ally of Confederate Tennessee.

3

The Mayfield Convention

While the weather warmed in the Purchase, the people grew even cooler toward neutrality. The firing on Fort Sumter caused four more slave states to exit the Union: Virginia, Arkansas, North Carolina, and Tennessee. By joining South Carolina, Mississippi, Florida, Alabama, Georgia, Louisiana, and Texas, they expanded the Confederacy to eleven states. The Confederate capital ultimately switched to Richmond, the capital of Virginia, Kentucky's parent state. Meanwhile, some leading Purchase secessionists even talked of the region forming a military alliance with Tennessee or separating from the rest of Kentucky and forming a Confederate state with West Tennessee shortly before the Volunteer State seceded. Word of such Purchase perfidy spread far beyond the Bluegrass State, to New York and even to President Lincoln in Washington.

If Tennessee had not seceded, the Purchase might have—as part of a new Confederate state, according to a state historical marker on the courthouse lawn in Mayfield. The metal plaque, painted olive green with gold letters, says that in May 1861, representatives from the Purchase and twenty West Tennessee counties gathered in town. According to the marker, they expressed "belief in Southern cause, [and] dissatisfaction with Kentucky adherence to Union and Tennessee delay in joining South," and thus voted "to secede and form a Confederate State." The inscription also says that "with Tennessee's vote to secede, June 8, 1861, proposal abandoned." The convention is largely unknown, though the conclave was apparently unprecedented. The Purchase was evidently the only section of a loyal state that considered secession.[1]

The Mayfield convention alarmed Kentucky Unionists and made news in New York. Even President Lincoln heard about it. But Prentice's *Journal* gave the story the most play, denouncing the convention as a treasonous conspiracy and warning its perpetrators that their disloyalty would lead to dire consequences.

Apparently, minutes of the convention do not survive. Ironically, J. N. Beadles, a local Unionist, provided the most detailed account of the meeting. Somehow, he managed to view the proceedings. Beadles claimed the western Kentuckians rejected regional secession because they believed the entire state would ultimately leave the Union. He also reported that Tennessee representatives, who apparently came on their own, were cool to the idea; they, too, thought Kentucky's ultimate destiny was Confederate. Before they went home, the Kentuckians took the unlikely step of renominating Burnett for Congress on the pro-Confederate Southern Rights ticket. On April 14, Lincoln had called a special session of Congress to convene on Independence Day. In Kentucky, elections for the US House were set for June 20. So was the Mayfield meeting really just a convention to tap Burnett or somebody else to run?

A short article in the pro-Confederate *Lexington Kentucky Statesman* of June 7, 1861, suggested that the goal of the gathering was to name a congressional candidate. The paper printed resolutions from a McCracken County Southern Rights meeting that authorized its delegates to "vote for a known and reliable Southern man, one who is in favor of the success of the Confederate States, and in favor of Kentucky, when the opportunity presents, of allying her destiny with the Confederate States."[2]

Was the *Statesman* unfamiliar with the "preliminary" May 10 meeting in Mayfield? Did the Lexington paper know about it and deliberately fail to publicize it for fear of jeopardizing the secession cause statewide? In any event, supporting an avowed secessionist for the US Congress seems strange enough. Perhaps stranger still, in a 1907 speech, Judge Herbert Carr of Fulton County vowed that the convention did vote to secede and carve a Confederate state from the Purchase and West Tennessee. Presumably, the text of the historical marker was based on his address.[3]

Oscar Turner, who sat in Burnett's House seat after the war, was apparently the prime mover for the Purchase-Tennessee alliance. Born in New Orleans in 1825, he was Ballard County attorney in 1851–55. The idea of military cooperation may have come from the April trips that Purchase secessionists, including Turner, made to Memphis, seeking arms. The alliance proposal was supposed to have been considered at the May 10 meeting in Mayfield. However, because the *Paducah Herald* failed to announce the conclave, only representatives from Ballard, Fulton, Graves, and Hickman Counties showed up, an anonymous Mayfield Unionist told the *Journal* in a letter dated May 10. Signed "N," the missive appeared in the paper eleven days later.[4]

Though the delegates represented just four counties, the meeting went ahead, chaired by A. D. Kingman, the erstwhile Douglas Democrat; "a Mr. Warren" was secretary. Kingman claimed the Purchase was "threatened with invasion by an army of abolitionists now stationed at Cairo" and that the region was "wholly unarmed and not likely to get any arms soon." He said that "some ten days since a proposition from Memphis, had been sent up, proposing a military league with this portion of Kentucky and to furnish arms and munitions of war and garrison the banks of the Mississippi and Ohio rivers, and make common cause with us." The correspondent did not say if Kingman revealed who had "sent up" the alliance proposal, but he admitted that Tennessee "acknowledged selfishness in the case by desiring to move the site of war off her soil to that of Kentucky, thereby saving her of all the desecrating and devastating influences attending the scene of war." Nonetheless, because the Purchase was unarmed, Kingman was for the proposal. He ended the gathering by calling it a "primary meeting" and announced another meeting for Mayfield on May 30, unless in the meantime Kentucky "armed itself and furnished this part of the State with the necessary means of defense." Resolutions were drafted and plans made to publicize the May 30 meeting districtwide. Turner "made a double and twisted blood and thunder war speech, denouncing armed neutrality immeasurably, as being mean and cowardly," the Unionist wrote. Turner said "no such thing could exist, and that the issue was pro-slavery or abolitionism; that the North was bent on a war of extermination, that it was perfectly mad with enthusiasm." In concluding his communiqué, the Unionist observed: "What is to be the programme here is hard to tell. From the proceeding some of the parties seemed to regard the move as a move of the seven counties west of the Tennessee river. Turner seemed to regard it as a Congressional district move. I think he wants to go to Congress; indeed he is already a candidate and thinks a division of the district would destroy his hopes. Of course, he expects to go to Montgomery and not to Washington." The correspondent added that "Bradley, Lockridge, and Beckham made rampant, uproarious, inflammatory speeches, denouncing the Legislature as abolitionized, &c., &c. But these are the ordinary kind of speeches made here of late."[5]

The *Journal* was certain a fiendish conspiracy was afoot. The paper warned, "the object [of the Mayfield convention], though not officially explained, is believed to be the separation of the First District from Kentucky if Kentucky remains in the Union, and its annexation to Tennessee." The paper demanded that Magoffin stop any such move and challenged the *Courier* to condemn it. Mum was the word from the governor and the Louisville paper.[6]

The *Journal*'s July 26, 1862, retrospective on the April 22 and May 10, 1861, Mayfield meetings provided the allegedly incriminating details of both gatherings, evidently all gleaned from the *Herald*. *Hickman Courier* editor Ed

K. Warren was secretary of the April 22 meeting, and speechmakers included Kingman, Mayfield attorneys P. H. Beckham and W. R Bradley, and James T. Lockridge, also of Mayfield. Others also spoke, but the story does not name them. Turner, Bradley, J. Moss of Hickman County, and R. B. Alexander and A. S. Tyler of Fulton County were named to draft resolutions. Turner, Bradley, and Graves circuit court clerk Ervin Anderson were named to a committee charged with publishing "an address to the citizens of this Congressional District, urging upon them the propriety and importance of taking action in this matter." In addition, the group approved another resolution calling on each of the counties in the district "to hold their preliminary meetings and appoint delegates" for the May 30 gathering.[7]

The *Journal* also included an appeal *"To the People of the First Congressional District of Kentucky"* and signed by "that trio of traitors," Turner, Bradley, and Anderson. The three congratulated Magoffin for convening the legislature against "the imminent danger to the State from the invasion of the abolition hordes of the North." But they chastised the majority Unionists for adjourning "without even providing arms for our self-defense, and this, too, in defiance of the overwhelming sentiment of the people." Either the trio genuinely misunderstood the sentiment of most Kentuckians beyond the Purchase—even in the other First District counties—or they were just posturing about the legislature frustrating the general will of the people. In any event, Turner, Anderson, and Bradley also condemned the federal troops at Cairo for invading "the jurisdiction of Kentucky by stopping boats within our limits, seizing our arms and powder, breaking open boxes shipped to Kentucky and Tennessee, and [for having] . . . an armed boat cruising in our waters, interfering with our commerce—all in violation of law." The three denounced Lincoln and the "despotic" Republicans for converting Washington "into a military camp" and turning "the Government which was formed by our forefathers, which guarantees to us freedom and equality of rights . . . into a military despotism" whose "mandates . . . are being carried out by destroying and burning millions of dollars' worth of public property in which we have a common interest."[8]

In addition, Turner, Anderson, and Bradley cited a St. Louis incident in which Union troops, many of them antislavery German immigrants, captured a force of secessionist Missouri militia who were evidently planning to seize the city's federal arsenal. Southern sympathizers rioted, and the Union soldiers, according to the Purchase trio, "ruthlessly fired upon and murdered some seventy or eighty . . . unarmed men, women and children." The western Kentuckians bent the truth; the soldiers fired after somebody shot one of their officers. Twenty-eight civilians and two soldiers ended up dead or dying, and many more were wounded; other civilians and soldiers died in subsequent clashes. Turner, Anderson, and Bradley claimed that after the bloodshed, the Union commander at St. Louis asserted his determination to permit no militia organizations "and to set aside the whole State authority of the sovereign State of Missouri." Of course, their implication was that the same fate awaited the Purchase. Too, the trio disparaged neutrality as "a doctrine . . . condemned and despised by the North" and "futile for our protection, even if we were cowardly and base enough to rely on it for protection." They concluded by rhetorically asking, "Now what are the freemen of Kentucky, and particularly of this District, to do?" They supplied the answer: "However much we may regret it, we are thrown upon the first principle of the law of Nature—that of SELF DEFENCE. We must act for ourselves, and adopt such measures as will result in the protection of the lives, liberty, and property of our citizens from invading forces now upon our borders."[9]

They asked all fifteen First District counties to send delegates to the convention. But they also invited other Kentucky counties "as may feel inclined to act with us." They urged "all the counties by all they hold sacred and dear, by their love of freedom, of their wives and children, and by their love and respect for the past historic fame of Kentucky" to lose no time in holding their county meetings and appointing their representatives so "that we may counsel together and secure the wisdom and best judgment of the District."[10]

Meanwhile, on May 18, 1861, Unionism flickered in Hickman when N. N. Cowgill chaired a meeting that resolved "the Government of the United States is our Government, its triumphs belong to us, its glories are shed upon our heads." The Union men, whose numbers included Mayor E. Case, also resolved "that while we explicitly disclaim to be creatures of Northern fanaticism, we profess to be equally untrammeled by the influence of Southern recklessness."[11]

On the day of the Union gathering in Hickman, the *Journal* printed another letter—this one from "A UNION MAN" in Paducah—that warned western Kentucky Rebels were out to spill Yankee blood: "Some of the leading and most influential secessionists are using every means in their power to get the populace enraged to such a pitch that they will at once, in connection with the Tennesseans, attack the United States troops at Cairo, which they know would be a signal for a general collision." The author denounced "these wily incendiaries" for "performing all their evil deeds in secret." Such machinations reportedly included scheming "towards dividing the State if the whole will not secede. They boldly assert that the territory south of Green river must secede." He added, "There is scarcely a secessionist in the whole of this country who does not affirm that Southern Kentucky will go out of the Union under any circumstances." He said the secessionists agreed "that Northern Kentucky is thoroughly abolitionized, and they have now about given up all hope of the whole State uniting its destiny with the Southern Confederacy." He lamented that "to gratify the ambition of these political demagogues, these traitors and rebels, devoid alike of conscience and soul, we must submit to a revolution in our own State." "A UNION MAN" charged they were "travelling night and day, despatching messengers to every point for the expressed purpose of accomplishing the end I have indicated." The correspondent said that some citizens of Paducah and the surrounding area had just returned home "very much disappointed" and empty-handed from a search for weapons "for companies destined no doubt for Jeff Davis's land." Since they had failed to get any arms, "there is but one hope remaining, and that is to coerce the State into secession by committing a flagrant outrage at Cairo, thereby bringing upon the citizens of this immediate vicinity instant ruin of property and loss of life." An attack on Cairo, he predicted, would lead to the murder of "our wives and children," the pillage of "our towns and villages," and the loss of "our negroes." He added that the secessionists had become "so daring that it is a common talk among them of hanging men of Union sentiments." Even so, he believed that secessionism was on the wane: "I think there are five men here for the Union now to where there was only one ten days ago, though I am indeed sorry to know that in this region, our flag, the flag of our country, is at the present not allowed to unfurl to the breeze the stars and stripes. But we should not be surprised to see it again, and that speedily." There was no evidence that local ardor for the stars and bars was flagging in the spring of 1861. Indeed, the Stars and Stripes would not fly conspicuously from Paducah poles until Union troops arrived in Kentucky's "Charleston" in September.[12]

Four days later, the *Journal* ran a letter from "SENTINEL," a Paducah Unionist, which seemed to confirm what "A UNION MAN" had written. He cited the May 30 convention and declared that Purchase secessionists were determined that the region "shall go out whether the State does or not." He said the secessionists "are now concentrating a force . . . at Union City, the terminus of our railroad." He claimed two hundred barrels of flour were at the Paducah depot awaiting transport by train to Union City and that "the arms furnished by the State are being shipped there also." He said a company of twenty-five men had left Paducah, presumably for Union City, and complained that city Unionists "are all firm but have no arms," while "the arms are all in the hands of traitors," meaning state guards. The writer was sure "a deep scheme is being laid here for some purpose. The secessionists here say that Jackson's purchase *shall revolutionize,* and all who oppose it should have a dagger run through them." The letter concluded with a plea for help: "We need some protection here. The lives of our best citizens are in danger. This city is yet strong for the Union, but we have been overawed by the disunionists from the fact that they have all the arms belonging to the State. Some active measures should be taken immediately, or else this portion of Kentucky will be in a state of excitement. Then the Union men will have to flee for their lives. Cannot something be done for us in the end of the State by the Government?" It seems doubtful that Paducah was still "strong for the Union." Indeed, the *Journal* agreed that treason was brewing in the city and throughout the Purchase. "We have no doubt that the impressions entertained by the writer of this letter in regard to an infernal plot are true and will soon prove so."[13]

Also on May 22, the *Journal* alleged that it had uncovered in Fulton County another dastardly scheme that stretched all the way to the governor's office in Frankfort. The paper noted that the day before, the rival *Courier* had reported that Captain John A. Lauderdale and "the Magoffin Guards," a company of Fulton County volunteers, had "mustered into the Tennessee service." The *Journal* charged that when Lauderdale was in Louisville "a few weeks ago," the western Kentuckian "stated explicitly that he had received arms for his company from Governor Magoffin." The paper claimed that Lauderdale also admitted "*his company had never been mustered into the State Guard.*" The *Journal* demanded to know "what authority had the Governor to let out those arms? Were they granted to a company for the Southern Confederacy? If not, have they been returned?" The Unionist paper challenged the *Courier* and the pro-southern *Kentucky Yeoman,* each an "organ . . . of His Excellency," to answer. Apparently, neither paper nor the governor responded. In any event, Lauderdale and his band, which included some Confederate sympathizers from southern Illinois, became Company L of the Fifth Tennessee Infantry Regiment.[14]

On May 28, the *Journal,* fed up with the Purchase provocateurs, real or imagined, aimed its sharpest yet barb at the region:

> A secession convention in the First District is soon to be held. Probably the reckless spirits comprising it will undertake to inaugurate the secession of the District. We warn them, however, that, if their people attempt anything of the kind, they may look out for that terrible thing "coercion." If they have the power to carry out a successful rebellion or revolution, well and good; but at any rate they will have to fight for it. They may think to call in the aid of Tennessee, but we

can assure them that they wouldn't find this a paying business. Kentucky is too proud of her fair proportions to be hacked up.[15]

On May 29 came another letter from Paducah, disputing "SENTINEL." The author, "Union," was "convinced that the Mayfield convention will turn out an abortion." He said the state arms were still in Kentucky, though he did not tell where. He said the twenty-five Paducah volunteers went to Florence, Alabama, "in the hope of getting in the Southern army" and that a Columbus resident bought the flour. "Union" warned that "the fire-eaters can bluster, but they have never yet overawed the Union men, nor will they ever attempt it, for I can never believe that the people of Kentucky here or in any other portion of the State will ever so far forget themselves as to imbrue their hands in a brother's blood for merely an honest difference of opinion." "Union" conceded "there are some young hot-heads who are boiling over for a fight, and at times may be guilty of some improprieties, but certainly what a few wild boys may do should not be laid at the door of every good citizen of Paducah, for they do not countenance immoderate action."[16]

Nonetheless, on the day the convention was to meet, the *Journal* published more correspondence from unnamed Purchase Unionists that did not square with the epistle from "Union." Dated May 21, a letter from Paducah claimed that "forty-eight boxes containing Minnie rifles, muskets, &c.; six pieces artillery; one hundred and fifty soldiers," had just left by train, "destination Union City." The writer advised that Pillow had been seen scouting Cairo from the Kentucky side of the Ohio on May 25 and had spent that night in Columbus. The man "stated to me that Pillow would have 4,000 troops in Columbus in less than four days." The *Journal* insisted the letter came from a trustworthy source. "We don't deal in sensational items," the paper explained, then concluded that "all the events enumerated certainly appear to indicate very strongly indeed, that on this very day . . . or as soon as the District Convention which meets to-day can hurry through a secession ordinance, the disunionists of that District, with a strong Kentucky military force at Mayfield, backed by a far stronger Tennessee military force at Union city in Tennessee, will strike for disunion." The *Journal* also demanded that Magoffin enforce his recent neutrality proclamation against the state guards purportedly heading to Tennessee for the purpose of fighting "troops of the United States." The governor "knows, unless evil counsels and counsellors have made a madman of him, that if, either through his cooperation, his connivance, or his supinness, a war shall be inaugurated at the mouth of the [Ohio River] . . . or in the Southern portion or any portion of our State, an ocean of blood will rest upon his soul, and a mountain of curses upon his name."[17]

The *Journal,* too, printed a May 24 letter without the name of the author or where it came from, which said that "six pieces of brass cannon" and "one thousand stand of small arms" belonging to the state guard were sent to Mayfield on the night of May 21. He claimed that some people "who professed to know" said the weapons were removed in anticipation of a Yankee invasion from Cairo. The letter writer was skeptical. *"Why should the arms be carried off from the point expected to be attacked?"* he asked. He said he had learned from a solid source that the arms were dispatched to Mayfield "to be ready on the 30th inst., when a secession ordinance would be adopted by the seven counties west of the Tennessee river, revolution inaugurated, and the arms handed over to the district soldiers." The troops at Union City would "be ready at once to move upon this part of the State and Federal and State authority at once defied." The correspondent claimed that one of the guard officers in on the arms transfer from Paducah bragged "that Kentucky, or this portion, would secede, and snapping his fingers together, he said, 'When it is done, it will be done as quick as that.'" The officer added that in a few weeks, Mayfield would be a training camp with six to ten thousand soldiers. Judge Boone, who was also a state guard captain, declared "that in ten days," the local guard units "would be entirely broken up," and, presumably, be part of the camp, or serving elsewhere in the Confederate army. "It is evident some revolutionary movement is in contemplation," the letter writer warned. "Whether it is to be confined in the Purchase or not, I cannot say. I am apprehensive it is concerted all over the State, if not, it is evidently contemplated here."[18]

On June 1, the *New York Times* quoted a story from the May 24 *Cairo Camp Register,* an army paper, which said three hundred guards had decamped from Paducah. Reportedly, the militia men were to join Colonel Benjamin Cheatham's force "near the Tennessee line." The Kentuckians took "1,300 stand of muskets, six pieces of artillery, with all munitions of war in the city." The guards allegedly left because they believed three thousand soldiers from Cairo would be ordered to Paducah to seize the weapons and the town. City residents were "said to be in the constant expectation of the arrival of Northern forces, and many of them are preparing to leave, so confident are they that this expectation will speedily be realized." Cheatham's command, including the guards, reportedly would combine with other Tennessee troops at Jackson to block a Yankee invasion via the Mobile & Ohio Railroad. Pillow's division was expected to be divided between Union City and Jackson to help forestall an attack from Cairo. "Business of all kinds is perfectly stagnant in Paducah, and many houses are said to be closed from one week's end to another," the *Times* story said, adding that Noble, in anticipation of invasion, had stopped publishing the *Herald.*[19]

Meanwhile, news of the convention even reached the White House. On May 30, McClellan wrote Lincoln from Cincinnati that "a very delicate question is arising as to Western Ky—that portion west of the Tenna. River." McClellan said that navy lieutenant William O. Nelson, a leading Kentucky Unionist, "will explain to you that a convention is now being held at Mayfield which may declare the 'Jackson position' separate from Ky, its annexation to [T]enna, & that this will be followed by an advance of Tenna. troops upon Columbus & Paducah."[20]

The best-known account of the Mayfield convention is a long letter from Beadles, which the *Journal* published on June 6. The *New York Daily Tribune* reprinted Beadles's epistle four days later. The *Courier,* the *Kentucky Yeoman,* and the *Kentucky Statesman* also ran stories on the meeting. Whether Purchase papers published anything about the convention is unknown because no 1861 copies of the papers are believed to exist. Evidently, neither Memphis nor Nashville papers reported on the gathering, though whatever the Kentuckians did surely would have been newsworthy to Tennesseans.

In any event, Beadles wrote that on May 29 several delegates arrived in Mayfield "from Trigg, Caldwell, and other counties, headed by Burnett and other aspirants to Congress." He added, "Such a scene of juggling and wire-working and private caucusing I never witnessed before." Late that evening, he learned that a majority of delegates likely would reject "Turner's project for forming a military alliance with Tennessee, and that he and his pet would be crushed together." That night at the courthouse, R. D. Gholson gave a ninety-minute speech by candlelight "which was designed to kill the monster effectually." He was "against any attempt to take any portion of the State out without the whole. It was contrary to State rights and State sovereignty—the very thing for which the South was fighting—Jeff. Davis could not accept it." Gholson warned that the secession of western Kentucky "would destroy the friends in upper Kentucky, and possibly defeat the ultimate secession of the State." He argued that the fighting in Virginia would compel Lincoln to order into Kentucky Yankee troops, "against whom the State was committed to use force." Thus, when fighting began in the Bluegrass State, "Kentucky would be ready to go." The secessionists would win majorities in the state house and senate in the August election. In turn, the Southern Rights lawmakers would call a sovereignty convention or pass a secession ordinance, "and, with a true Governor at the head of affairs, by fall the State would be in the Southern Confederacy," according to Gholson's scenario.[21]

Meanwhile, Gholson, who had been a captain in the Mexican-American War, urged the organization and training of local military companies, "thoroughly drilled, ready for service." He said state guards who wanted "to be in more active duty" should resign, go to Tennessee, and join the Rebel army. Gholson, who was captain of the "Woodville Cavalry," a state guard company, said he planned to take his outfit to the Volunteer State "or elsewhere that their services may be needed." When Kentucky refused to secede, he moved his family and slaves to Troy, Tennessee, near Union City. He died in an accident in late August 1861. After Gholson finished speaking, the convention adjourned until the next day, Beadles wrote.[22]

When the delegates came back together, they named a chairman "and appoint[ed] sundry secretaries," Beadles wrote. He called the chairman "G. W. Bosher"; the *Statesman* and *Yeoman* said "George W. Barber" of Princeton served as "president" of the gathering. More than likely he was George W. Barbour of Trigg County; he was a former state senator and representative.[23]

At the same time, a number of committees were formed, but they had to gather outdoors because the courthouse was full. As many as thirty-five hundred people may have attended the convention. Henry Clay King of Memphis, formerly of Paducah, made a speech asking for Confederate volunteers. Next, a Colonel Austin of Memphis told the gathering that "Kentucky was bound to belong to the Southern Confederacy—destiny had fixed it; she was a little more tardy than some other States, but she was moving as rapidly as he expected her." He praised Magoffin and said neutrality was "equal to secession." Austin promised he "was prepared to furnish every man in Western Kentucky in twenty-four hours with a gun of any size and character that might be desired." Austin added that the weapons "were now within twenty-five miles of this place." He merely asked that the weapons not be used against the Confederacy. Austin also called on the crowd to name "some reliable gentleman" whom he could trust to hand out the weapons. He requested that a resolution be passed but not printed "in regard to the matter." A. R. Boone and Ervin Anderson were named to distribute the arms. Austin further proposed that a military training camp be opened at Columbus and that the town be fortified with cannons. "He said any size or character of arms or implements needed would be sent up any day." Officers would be available "to drill and instruct in all the arts of war," Beadles wrote. "Men for that purpose were now on the ground." Austin said the Columbus facility would only be a school for soldiers, but he promised that "whenever the Administration attempted to move troops on the soil of Kentucky or down the river, [men at the school] would be ready to strike a blow, and from their camp in Union City as many men as might be needed could be furnished at Columbus in a few hours." Austin's remarks were "applauded greatly."[24]

Tilghman followed Austin to the speaker's stand and emphatically denied the accusation "he was for the North." He said "the author was a d—n liar."

The major also "denounced The Louisville Journal and Prentice," vowing "that the moment Lincoln's forces put a foot upon Kentucky he should attack them if he had but 500 men to do it with." But he cautioned against an assault on Cairo "because he and the soldiers of this end of the State had no arms, and it would have been contrary to the orders of those under whose command he was placed." Tilghman said "he was willing to fight, but did not wish to do it rashly or unwisely."[25]

Also on June 6, the *Journal* published another letter from a Unionist who claimed Tilghman also played the mystery man at the convention, advising "the young men not to leave the State" because "all who wanted to fight would soon have an opportunity to do so, and would be needed at home." He added that the major advised that "a '*movement was now on foot which it was not proper for him to divulge at this time.*'" Tilghman predicted Kentucky would secede, according to the letter's author, whom the *Journal* characterized as "one of the most respectable gentlemen in this State, a gentleman trusted and honored by all who know him." In any event, the correspondent wrote that Tilghman said if Kentucky "had 50,000 stands of arms it would be equal to 70,000 votes." The Unionist concluded, "What does this mean? It is evident to my mind that something wrong is in embryo." The *Journal* described Tilghman as "a very vehement secessionist," adding, "his whole heart is in the secession cause, and he is necessarily cognizant of the secret designs of the secession party." The *Journal* linked Tilghman's cryptic remarks to a letter the paper had received in abstract form from "a highly respectable and intelligent gentleman in one of the interior counties of this State." The man's "friend and neighbor" had just received the letter "from a strong secessionist in Tennessee." The "letter stated that Kentucky would certainly secede very soon from the United States—that a plan was on foot and in operation by which the result would inevitably be accomplished." The *Journal* was about to publish the letter when another missive from the "highly respectable and intelligent gentleman" arrived, "informing us that his friend and neighbor had withdrawn his consent to the use of the letter of the Tennessee secessionist." As a result, the paper published "only this brief exposition of the fact." Yet the *Journal* made no bones about what it saw as a conspiracy of Kentucky and Tennessee secessionists "to hurry Kentucky out of the Union by a process almost as sudden as the explosion of a mine beneath our feet." Tilghman, according to the *Journal,* was hinting at "a movement looking, as is clearly and distinctly implied, to Kentucky's secession and the inauguration of a terrible war upon Kentucky soil." The paper claimed "all the energies of the leading secessionists of Kentucky and Tennessee are evidently directed to the consummation of that secret plan." The *Journal* declined to speculate on the nature of the scheme but proposed "the best thing our people can do is await calmly the progress of events, keeping their eyes open and their nerves steady."[26]

Beadles wrote that after Tilghman's remarks, two sets of resolutions were reported by the majority committee, headed by Judge Campbell, and the minority committee, which Turner chaired. However, Beadles said the delegates argued the resolutions until two a.m. on May 31 and then approved "several resolutions . . . in lieu of both sets offered by the Committees." He added that "as they are to be published in the Courier," he would not give the details.[27]

But the *Courier* never printed an account of the resolutions or of the convention. It ran an article on June 5, 1861, devoid of details. The *Courier* admitted it had "not received the report of what was done." But the paper had heard from "an intelligent gentleman who had participated in its proceedings." Based on what he said, the *Courier* reported that the convention denounced the "usurpations" of the Lincoln administration and declaimed federal war measures "as illegal, unconstitutional, and revolutionary, tending to the establishment of a military despotism, on the ruins of, our republican system." While the convention opposed neutrality, the delegates agreed to abide by it "in good faith" until Kentucky voters decided otherwise. The *Courier* also claimed "a proposition in favor of uniting the . . . First District to Tennessee . . . in the event that this State should finally decide to go with Free States was rejected by a vote of 130 to 30, being deemed inexpedient and improper, and conflicting with their expressed determination to stand by the State in whatever position a majority of her people shall place her." The article concluded by reporting that delegates unanimously renominated Burnett for Congress.[28]

Meanwhile, Beadles said that Turner favored "immediate action towards uniting with the Southern Confederacy, as it is our ultimate destination and now our interest." He added that Turner could not honestly swear the oath of allegiance required for service in the legislature or Congress. Turner said he would not anyway. But Burnett, former state representative Willis B. Machen of Lyon County, and state senator Benjamin Cissell of Union County said they could swear the oath. The trio promised that if elected to Congress they would "do all they could to promote the interests of the South," thereby upholding the constitution against "the infamous, hell-deserving Administration that now resided at Washington" and was doing all it could to subvert the constitution and establish "a military despotism." Cissell also urged state guards to swear "the necessary oath" so they could get state arms. After Burnett received the nomination "by a pretty large majority as the State rights candidate," the convention adjourned.[29]

Beadles also said, "a respectable gentleman, who stood very near Col. Austin" and was able to better hear him, claimed the Tennessean boasted "that in sixty days Tennessee and other Southern States would have 6,000 to 10,000 men at Columbus, not as soldiers but as individuals under train, at a military school, and that a branch would be established at Paducah, and probably at other points in Kentucky." Austin said such facilities would be lawful because "individuals had a right to form for their own benefit as many military schools and accumulate arms and practice the arts of war as much as they desire." He said Paducah and Columbus were well suited as school sites. Beadles also said a Confederate colonel was present. He wrote that he forgot the officer's name but that the man was recruiting Rebel soldiers. Gholson told Beadles the colonel "was an excellent man—an old associate of his in the Mexican war." Beadles concluded by admitting that he had furnished the *Journal* "an imperfect account of events." But he promised he had "endeavored to make it strictly correct." The *Journal* was "free to use it in any way you desire."[30]

The *Kentucky Yeoman* also published a long story about the meeting because "imputations had been freely made in the sensation newspapers in the interest virtually of Lincoln's usurpation, to the effect that the State Rights Convention for the First District to nominate a candidate for Congress, was called with a view of cutting off that district from Kentucky and annexing it to Tennessee." The Frankfort paper also said its story was "condensed from the Uniontown News."[31]

According to the *Yeoman*, about thirty-five hundred citizens attended. The paper said that "Col. George W. Barber of Princeton" was named convention president and that a resolutions committee was organized. The panel's members included B. F. Stone of Marshall County, Daniel Matthewson of Calloway County, state senator Benjamin P. Cissell of Union County, W. H. Martin of Trigg County, Judge John Edwards of Caldwell County, Willis B. Machen of Lyon County, P. E. Barnett of Crittenden County, Dr. J. W. Singleton of Livingston County, R. J. [R. B.] Alexander of Fulton County, E. J. [I.] Bullock of Hickman County, Oscar Turner of Ballard County, Judge James Campbell of McCracken County, and John Aker [Eaker] of Graves County. The *Yeoman* said several men from Kentucky and Tennessee made speeches while the committees were at work. The Tennesseans solemnly declared "that neither the authorities nor the people of their State, entertained any wish or design to violate Kentucky's chosen attitude of neutrality in this wicked war." Rather, the Volunteer State "would scrupulously respect the attitude of Kentucky, and never cross our boundary, unless invited by our lawful authorities."[32]

Campbell, chair of the resolutions committee, presented a lengthy report that included seven resolutions. The report's preamble said that Southern Kentucky had always wished "to do all in its power, (not inconsistent with its honor and integrity) to bring to a speedy conclusion the unholy, suicidal, and fratricidal war, now being so waged; and to show its allegiance to Kentucky, even when we may believe her position to be fallacious and impracticable." The first resolution said the region would "for the present" accept neutrality and abide by it "so long as our territory is respected, and until by a course of aggression upon our interests—civil and commercial—honor shall demand a change of policy." Thus, the panel's support for neutrality was at best qualified. Obviously, too, the committee saw the Yankees at Cairo as potential, if not likely, aggressors against their interests. If the committee members did not hear the Tennesseans' speeches, it seems almost certain they went into their meeting with assurances from the Tennessee representatives that the Volunteer State would respect Kentucky's neutrality.[33]

The second resolution warned that if the region were invaded, "we pledge ourselves and all that we have and are, to the expulsion of the invader, and for its accomplishment will avail ourselves of all the means within our reach—striving therein to observe, on all occasions, a due regard to constituted authorities." Did "all means within our reach" mean Tilghman and the state guard? Or did "all means" include the Confederate troops just over the state line? And what was meant by "constituted authorities"? Were they the governor and the legislature or local elected officials? It seems likely that the framers of the resolution carefully chose their words to make it vague.[34]

The third resolution was a stock condemnation of Lincoln and the war, denouncing the conflict as "in violation of all law, Constitutional and Legislative, and of every principle which ought to govern in a free country, and tends to the entire subversion of republicanism and the establishment of despotism." The fourth resolution was also anti-Lincoln, castigating the president for introducing "arms into this State . . . with a view of arming the so-called 'Union men' of the State, against those sympathizing with the South." In sending the weapons to Kentucky, Lincoln had evinced "a depravity of heart so damnable, as to demand the universal condemnation of the civilized world; and those in Kentucky who have co-operated therein, are unworthy the names of Kentuckians, and ought to receive universal execration."[35]

The fifth resolution elaborated on the first. While the region acquiesced in neutrality "for the present . . . we proclaim to the world our entire sympathy with the South; and whenever the final adjustment takes place between the North and South, we shall claim our natural position with that Government." The sixth resolution endorsed Magoffin's rebuff of Lincoln's request for troops. The last resolution said that the presence of Union and Confederate troops along the borders of the Purchase "cannot fail to impress every thinking man, that there does now exist such a case of public danger as was contemplated by the Legislature in the passage of the military laws, and we then respectfully request that our Governor shall call into the field the military force of Kentucky, and hold them prepared to resist any invasion of Kentucky soil—from what quarter soever it may come." By "military force of Kentucky," the resolution writers obviously meant the state guard, though in May, the legislature had created a pro-Union home guard, the recipients of the "Lincoln guns" they denounced in the fourth resolution. Too, they doubtless foresaw the invaders as men in blue uniforms, having been assured that the Tennessee troops would stay put.[36]

Before the resolutions were put to a vote of the convention, Turner presented the minority report, a package of six resolutions that were clear in their meaning. The first one declared "that all our sympathies are with the South" and denounced Lincoln for "calling the troops in the field" to invade the Confederacy. The resolution also maintained that "the concentration of troops at Cairo to interfere with the free navigation of the Ohio and Mississippi" was "illegal and unconstitutional." The second resolution said "the invasion of the jurisdiction of Kentucky by the troops at Cairo, in firing upon boats in the Ohio river, and the stoppage and the searching of our boats, and the detention of articles of our commerce" were all "flagrant outrages upon the rights of Kentucky." The third resolution put no trust "in the professions of the present administration as they have falsified them by the acts of their agents in every instance." The fourth one dismissed Kentucky's neutrality as "futile, as protection [from invasion] is concerned." The fifth resolution proclaimed that "the course of the South is our course, and we are determined to share the same fate with the gallant men who are fighting for their constitutional rights, guaranteed by our forefathers, which are attempted to be trampled underfoot by a Black Republican despotism." The last resolution said Kentucky's government was duty-bound to repel a Union invasion with all of its power and not permit the North "to make a lodgment of troops on Kentucky soil, under any pretext whatever and that the aid of Tennessee, or the Confederate States should be invited to accomplish this purpose." If Kentucky troops could not drive the Yankees out, "it is the determination of the people to co-operate with the Tennessee troops and troops of the Confederate States to repel any invasion of this district, and to fortify such points in this district as they deem necessary."[37]

According to the *Yeoman*, "a very animated debate" began over the majority and minority reports. Burnett, Cissell, and Machen sided with Campbell against Turner. "The main point of discussion was upon the last resolution in the minority report, which seemed to imply not only a contingent design to take the First District out of Kentucky, but to carry a hypothetical censure against Governor Magoffin," the paper said. "The champions of the majority report, however, with overwhelming eloquence of argument maintained the loyalty of the First District to the State, avowing their purpose as good citizens to share whatever destiny the sovereign people of Kentucky decreed."[38]

Burnett then proposed four resolutions. The first one decried Lincoln for "waging a bloody and cruel war against eleven of our sister slave States" militarily and economically in violation of the Constitution "and substituting a wicked military despotism to rule over the rights and liberty of the people." The second resolution declared that if federal troops occupied any part of a neutral Kentucky, then the move "would be regarded as a menace against the sovereignty of the State, and a coercion upon the freedom of opinion and action of the citizens, and the Governor should expel such troops, using all the force at his command, and such other as the Governor of Kentucky may be able to procure." By "other" force, did Burnett mean Tennessee or Confederate soldiers? In any event, the third and fourth resolutions also denounced the "Lincoln guns" and praised Magoffin for spurning Lincoln's call for Kentucky troops.[39]

Afterward, Turner again touted his minority report, but Campbell headed him off. Then the convention approved Burnett's resolutions instead of the majority and minority reports. They preferred Burnett's proposals over the minority report by a vote of 125–30 and over the majority report, 142–13.[40]

The vote, lopsided as it was, failed to settle the resolutions issue. The *Yeoman* said that "Judge Edmonds, of Caldwell"—probably Judge Edwards—offered three resolutions in lieu of Burnett's third and fourth resolutions. The first one said that Garrett Davis, former governor Charles A. Wickliffe, and other Union men "deserve the condemnation, scorn, and contempt of every loyal, patriotic, and true-hearted son of Kentucky" for their efforts "to inaugurate civil war in the State of Kentucky" by furnishing Lincoln guns to Union party members in the northern part of the state. The second resolution declared that Kentucky was a sovereign state and thus "in defense of her reserved rights and the liberty of the people, has the undoubted right by and through the will of a majority of her people, expressed at the ballot-box, to determine the political status of the State and its relations to the General Government, and it is the duty of the minority to submit thereto." His last resolution maintained "that the cause of the South is the cause of civil and religious liberty. It is the cause of Kentucky—and that it is right to give it all the aid in our power, consistent with the present political attitude of the state, and that we use all fair and honorable means to place Kentucky in her true position, side by side with the South." The delegates rejected all three proposals, 132–23.[41]

Finally, the convention got down to renominating Burnett for Congress on the Southern Rights ticket by a vote of 124–31. Burnett had held the seat since 1855. According to the *Yeoman*, the thirty-one anti-Burnett votes were split among four others, apparently Turner, Machen, and Cissell among them. After Burnett won, the convention voted a second time to make his nomination unanimous.[42]

Having backed Burnett for reelection, the convention resolved unanimously "to open a poll at the election . . . headed 'for the South,' 'for the North,' and that citizens be requested to cast their votes on the subject." Apparently, the convention adjourned afterward. The *Yeoman* claimed its story proved "that the glorious patriotism of the First District stands vindicated against all the malign imputations of partisans impeaching the loyalty of its noble-hearted citizens." The capital city paper concluded, "They stand proudly and consistently upon the constitutional platform of States Rights, and immovably loyal to their beloved Kentucky, whose fortunes and fate, to be determined by the lawfully expressed will of her sovereign people, they mean dutifully to accept as their own destiny."[43]

The *Statesman* ran a shorter story about the convention. Nonetheless, it shed more light on the proceedings. The Lexington paper said the convention also had six secretaries: R. W. Walker of Hickman County, Ervin Anderson of Graves County, Robert Burnett of Trigg County, Thomas F. Terrell of McCracken County, J. C. Gilbert of Marshall County, and Ben Harrison of Union. Thirteen counties answered the roll call: Fulton, Hickman, Ballard, McCracken, Graves, Marshall, Calloway, Trigg, Caldwell, Lyon, Livingston, Crittenden, and Union. Hopkins and Webster Counties were unrepresented.[44]

In addition to naming members of the resolutions committee, the Lexington paper also listed members of the Committee on Organization: Alfred Johnson of Marshall County, state senator John L. Irvan of Calloway County, Robert Wooldridge of Trigg County, Dr. J. N. Calvert of Caldwell County, R. Cobb of Lyon County, T. S. Croft of Crittenden County, Dr. J. W. Singleton of Livingston County, G. W. Paschall of Fulton County, E. R. Ray of Hickman County, W. M. Coffee of Ballard County, G. H. Morrow of McCracken County, and A. R. Boone of Graves County. The *Statesman* also listed a "Dr. J. J. Barnett" but did not list a county of residence. Singleton was also on the resolutions committee.[45]

The *Statesman* also reported that while the convention committees deliberated, "several distinguished gentlemen from Tennessee" gave speeches. They "disclaimed any intention of Tennessee invading the soil of Kentucky, unless *invited* to do so." The visitors "felt satisfied that the sympathies and destinies of the two States were now blended and would soon be firmly riveted together in one common line of defense against northern fanaticism and aggression." The paper said Colonel Austin "was particular in defining the true attitude of his State in relation to Kentucky." He assured the western Kentuckians that "the South understood the peculiar position of this State, and when the Abolition hordes of the North landed on Kentucky soil against the wishes of her citizens, all that this people had to do was raise the war-whoop and the brave legions of Tennessee—the sister cohorts of the 'Sunny South' would rush forward to your rescue."[46]

While the *Kentucky Yeoman* story did not mention Austin's call for a military training camp at Columbus, the *Statesman* did. Perhaps Yeoman editor S. I. M. Major figured discretion was the better part of valor. The Unionist-majority General Assembly adjourned before the Mayfield convention. But doubtless Union lawmakers would view such an obviously Confederate facility as a clear violation of neutrality. Did Major not wish to give the opposition ammunition? In any event, the *Statesman*'s account of Austin's remarks was not as detailed as Beadles's version of what he said. Editor Thomas Ben Monroe Jr. would join the Confederate army later in 1861. But his paper did not inform its readers about Gholson's call for the creation of local militia companies in the Purchase or his suggestion that young men desirous of more active service ought to join the Confederate army in Tennessee. Nor did the *Statesman* say anything about Austin's offer to furnish Purchase men weapons with which to shoot Yankees. Nonetheless, the Lexington paper did report that Austin said "a Military Camp to train Southern soldiers is soon to be formed at Columbus, for the purpose of 'home protection.'" He declared, "Our aim and policy is not to *assail*, but to defend." He urged, "let the noble sons of liberty in the South prepare to defend their firesides from the desecrating tread of hostile aggressions, inimical to our institutions, from the grasping blue-nosed Yankees, and illiterate abolition scum of the North." The *Statesman* said Austin's remarks "elicited warm and frequent rounds of applause, and there was a general shaking of hands on his quitting the stand."[47]

The paper also elaborated on Tilghman's remarks. The major was outraged over "certain vile slanders which had been circulated against him." Somebody called Tilghman "an abolitionist, but when he attempted to trace up the author, he had come up 'missing.'" Tilghman vowed, "if there was one ounce of abolition flesh in his frame, he would cut it out. Thank God, he was an honest man—a true and loyal son of the South, and any man who asserted to the contrary was a base liar and a villain, whom he dared confront him." He said those who were defaming him were also "vilifying" Magoffin and Breckinridge. Tilghman thundered: "These slanderers were traitors to the South, and were ready to sell their country for a 'mess of pottage.' They should be marked and hustled from our soil to where they belong—with their brethren north of Mason and Dixon's line."[48]

Tilghman added that he had "five hundred brave soldiers," all "ready to battle wherever needed, no matter how great the odds against us." He said he and his men "have sworn to support the Constitution of Kentucky and the United States, and having done so are ready to 'war to the knife' with any party who trample upon its provisions and seek to oppress us, on our own soil."[49]

After Tilghman finished speaking, the delegates were asked to meet in the courthouse to hear from the committee on organization. At the same time, "the large concourse of spectators" gathered in the market house and listened to speeches from "several distinguished gentlemen."[50]

The committee on organization recommended that the convention accept the named officials, vote county by county "on all contested points," and go by the parliamentary procedures that governed the legislature: "Delegations from each county were allowed one vote in each 100 voters in their county, and a half vote for each fractional fifty." Delegates unanimously approved the recommendations.[51]

The *Statesman* article only included Burnett's resolutions. But the paper said Dr. Barnett moved that the incumbent be "declared unanimously nominated for Congress." The *Statesman* said that in his acceptance speech, Burnett "could not say for certain that he would take the oath at Washington. If he could take his seat with honor to his constituency, and if he could be useful, he would enter the walls of Congress in July next." He said that if he decided to go to Washington, "it was his firm determination to arraign the traitor Lincoln at the bar of his country for treason, and if, in his endeavors to bring the usurper to justice, he should lose his life, he expected that Kentuckians would avenge his death."[52]

After Burnett spoke, Cissell endorsed Burnett's resolutions, praised Magoffin as a "pure patriot and noble statesman," and denounced the Unionists in the legislature for inserting into the measure creating the Military Board a clause that required state guards and home guards to swear an oath to support the US and Kentucky constitutions before they could receive weapons. "This clause was superfluous, and was designed by those who framed it, to disarm the Southern Rights men of the State," he argued. Cissell added that he had been told that many men refused to swear the oath. He had taken the oath often and would do so again. "I tell you to take this oath cheerfully, and in doing so you can as honest men, seize your musket and fire upon that man or party who you find violating that Constitution which you have thus sworn to protect and abide by," he said. "You are not required to swear to support Lincoln's administration." He said the president had "vilely and falsely" violated his oath of office. Lincoln was thus a "despot and usurper" who had "trampled on" the constitution's "most sacred provisions and asks you to help him destroy that noble charter of human liberty." The South, according to the senator, was "battling for the Constitution as framed by our fathers." The *Statesman* story also ended by reporting the convention's resolution to add "for the South" and "for the North" to the ballot for the congressional election.[53]

Because Beadles, the *Courier*, the *Yeoman*, and the *Statesman* failed to name the county-by-county vote on the resolutions, it is impossible to say if the convention's rejection of Turner's minority report was districtwide. While Campbell of Paducah presented the majority report, it seems likely, based on the congressional election returns, that the bulk of the opposition to Turner's "pet" came from the counties east of the Purchase. The Purchase vote sent Burnett back to Washington. He lost every other district county except Trigg, where he barely won. He piled up landslides in every Purchase county.

In any event, one wonders what else the *Uniontown News*, the source of the *Yeoman* story, had to say about the Mayfield convention. Regrettably, no copies of the paper are known to exist. Contemporary accounts of the Mayfield convention to the contrary, Judge Carr declared that the gathering approved the creation of a Confederate state from western Kentucky and western Tennessee. In his speech, Carr declared: "In May 1861, a convention was held in the city of Mayfield, Ky., and attended by delegates from the Jackson Purchase, many settlers of which had always been dissatisfied with being a part of Kentucky and Tennessee, and in this convention a resolution was introduced, voted upon and adopted that the people of the Purchase secede from their respective states and form a new state of their own."[54]

In the last analysis, without official records, the full story of the Mayfield convention will never be known. The *Journal* saw a fiendish plot to split the state. But every pre-convention story the paper ran was based on anonymous and unattributed sources. It is both odd and intriguing that the only surviving eyewitness account of the convention itself is that of a Unionist. Beadles's name is on the *Journal* story and on the *Tribune* reprint. But was he genuinely objective? Civil War newspapers are a mother lode of American media bias. Yankee and Rebel newspapers unashamedly slanted stories. Yet what Beadles recorded is essentially what the pro-Confederate *Courier*, *Yeoman*, and *Statesman* reported.

On the other hand, if the convention did not approve secession, why did

Carr flatly and publicly say it did? Had his memory failed him? If he were stretching the truth, Carr must have known of other locals who could have disputed him. Like Beadles's, Carr's sympathies must be taken into account, especially given the timing of his statement about the Mayfield convention. By the early twentieth century, even erstwhile Unionist sections of Kentucky had embraced the myth of the Lost Cause. Confederate memorials were sprouting on courthouse lawns in Mayfield and Murray. Rebel memorials went up at whites-only cemeteries in Fulton, Hickman, and Mayfield.

Carr's claim that "many settlers" of western Kentucky and western Tennessee "had always been dissatisfied with being a part of Kentucky and Tennessee" is probably overstated. But such assertions were not uncommon. Yet whatever it voted to do, the Mayfield convention appears to have been unique in the Civil War. In addition to western Virginia and eastern Tennessee, there were pockets of defiant Unionism throughout the Confederacy: Winston County, Alabama; Jones County, Mississippi; upland North Carolina and Georgia; and German settlements in Texas. But there is no record of any part of another loyal state seriously contemplating any sort of union with the eleven states in rebellion. Missouri had a rump, minority Rebel government like Kentucky's, which arose from a convention of disgruntled secessionists that met in Russellville, behind Confederate lines, in November 1861. Several luminaries in the Mayfield convention played a major role in the Russellville convention. Burnett would be president.[55]

4

Flag Snatching and Gun Grabbing

The Purchase, squeezed between hostile armies a mere fifty miles apart, looked like the place where neutrality was most likely to be violated. Citizens sweated, and not just from the June heat. Both sides coveted Columbus, where the local secessionist majority feared the Yankees might beat the Rebels to town, especially after they captured the town flag.

Buckner was powerless against the warm weather, but he could at least try to cool passions. To that end, on June 8, he traveled to Cincinnati to meet McClellan. The Yankee general agreed to abide by Kentucky neutrality, and the state guard commander promised to safeguard federal property in the state, enforce federal law, and maintain neutrality against the Confederacy. In turn, McClellan would keep his soldiers off Kentucky soil. However, if the Rebel army invaded Kentucky and state troops could not drive them out, then McClellan would send federal soldiers to expel them and leave after the job was done. If either McClellan or Breckinridge wished to change his mind, then the other party was to be informed.[1]

Technically, at least, the Yankees breached neutrality in Ballard County on June 5, according to state guard captain Charles Wickliffe, commander of the Ballard Grays. On June 6, he wrote to the guard adjutant general, Scott Brown. Wickliffe claimed that troops from Cairo had come to disperse a dozen men from Columbus camped at the Bluff of Mayfield Creek, about nine miles from Cairo. The spot was also known as Elliott's Mills. The Hickman County men had rifles and were part of an independent company, according to Wickliffe. He said that by the time the Yankees reached the campsite, the men were gone. Though the Union soldiers also departed, Wickliffe hastened to Cairo to see Prentiss, who had been promoted to brigadier general on May 17. The post commander said his men had been invited to Kentucky. He read Wickliffe a petition dated June 5 and "signed by some fifteen or twenty" Ballard County citizens living near the Mississippi who wanted his protection "against apprehended violence by that party of men from Columbus." Further, Wickliffe said Prentiss told him that Paducah Unionists had sought his "protection, and that he thought of sending there a force from his command for that purpose." Wickliffe informed Brown that Prentiss warned him "he would send force into Kentucky whenever he thought proper to do so, regardless of the Governor's proclamation [of neutrality]."[2]

In addition to Wickliffe's letter, the *Courier* published a letter from Captain M. H. Wright, commander of the Columbus company, to Magoffin and a subsequent petition from other Ballard County citizens "humbly, but earnestly" asking the governor to enforce neutrality against the "abolition troops" at Cairo. Wright said he and his "Independent Rangers" had gone to Ballard County "with the view of drilling, hunting, and fishing for a few days" and arrived at Elliott's Mills on June 3. Wright claimed the Rangers were surprised to hear about the Yankee foray. Wright claimed that the blue-clad troops woke up three families and placed guards around their houses. He said they asked Thomas Richardson to raise a US flag, swear fealty to the Constitution, and promise not to fight the northern army. Richardson refused, saying he was a veteran. The entreaty, signed by C. H. Blake, V. A. McCutchen, and J. S. Petril on behalf of "the North Ballard Military Company," backed up Wickliffe and Wright. The petitioners claimed the Columbus men were innocently "fishing and hunting" and "committed no crime nor violated any law." Their only offense, according to the petitioners, was "that of being 'Southern Rights' men." The trio added that on the march from the Mississippi to the camp, the "detachment of Abolition troops, numbering some two hundred or over . . . arrested and held as prisoners several of our citizens, thereby depriving them of their liberty." More than "apprehended" violence might have motivated Prentiss. It seems likely that he suspected the Columbus men were spying on his camp, which they might have been.[3]

Buckner was wary of Columbus, too. On June 10, he moved to restrain its citizens from "acts of lawless aggression," meaning threats against Cairo. He dispatched Tilghman and six of his state guard companies to the town. Given the well-known sympathies of Tilghman and his men, Prentiss probably was not reassured.[4]

Indeed, it looked like Columbus might finally be in the path of the long-anticipated Rebel move against Cairo. On June 11, McClellan telegraphed Magoffin that Tennessee troops had been ordered to occupy Island Number One, a half-dozen miles down the Mississippi from Cairo. He called on the governor "in accordance with my understanding with Gen. Buckner" to stop the Confederates. Magoffin replied that Buckner had gone to Paducah and Columbus "and has orders to carry out his understanding with you." Meanwhile, Magoffin said he was investigating "the questions of jurisdiction" over the reputed Rebel objective and would telegraph McClellan the next day. He informed McClellan that Island Number One was indeed Kentucky territory.[5]

Also on June 12, Prentiss sent the *City of Alton* on reconnaissance down the Mississippi. The steamboat carried Colonel Richard Oglesby and two companies from his regiment, the Eighth Illinois Infantry. A six-pounder and a twelve-pounder howitzer on deck provided more potent firepower, according to Private Charles W. Wills, who was aboard the boat.[6]

As the *Alton* chugged past Columbus, the Yankees spotted a fifteen-by-seven-foot Confederate flag "with eight stars and three stripes" fluttering over the town, Wills recalled. The boat continued downriver for about two miles, where Oglesby, a future general and Illinois governor, "expected to find a secesh force." No Rebels were detected, so the *Alton* came about and headed for home. This time, the boat paused at Columbus, where Wills claimed "the flag was still waving," all the stores were closed, and a large crowd had gathered on the levee. The Union soldiers espied just one "gun," presumably meaning an artillery piece. In any event, Oglesby shouted to the townsfolk to take down their flag. When they refused, the colonel "said he would do it himself then." The crowd dared him to try. Wills explained what happened next: "We were drawn up then round the cabin deck guards next [to] the shore in two ranks, with guns at 'ready,' and the captain jumped ashore and hauled down the serpent. We were all sure of a skirmish but missed it. . . . They raised another flag one hour after we left and sent us word to 'Come and take it.'"

The Union troops did not return. But Wills immensely enjoyed the adventure, writing home, offering to send "scraps" of the flag and declaring that "the ride on the river was the best treat I've had for two years."[7]

The *Courier* provided another account of the flag seizure, citing a June 13 letter to the *Cincinnati Enquirer*. The author claimed that the officers aboard the *Alton* told the Columbus citizenry to take the flag down but got no reply. So they called for a Union man to lower the flag, offering him protection. When no one obliged them, the Yankee brass, the *Alton*'s skipper, mate, and cooper, went ashore, cut down the flagpole, and carried the offending banner on board "amid much cheering from" the Yankees. The *Enquirer* correspondent added that Oglesby and a Colonel Morgan wanted "to shoot the flag down, but Capt. Hopkins, in command of the guns, told them he could not do it without damaging property and probably spilling innocent blood." The citizens did not resist, but a woman defiantly told the unwelcome visitors "she had material left to make another flag of the same description, and that it would be flying before sundown." The letter writer added that when the *Alton* arrived at Columbus, a railroad handcar left town for Union City.

"No doubt had the boat and crew remained a few hours there would have been a warm time." When the *Alton* got back to Cairo, the soldiers and civilians went "wild with excitement. All wanted a piece of the captured flag, a small piece of which was several times sold for a dollar, and five dollars was offered for a star of the same." As a sort of postscript, the correspondent said that the *Cheney* had just come in from Columbus bringing "reports that they have another Secession flag afloat on the same spot that the old one was on. Immense excitement prevails there and at Union City." The correspondent also claimed that when the handcar rolled into Union City with the men aboard bearing news of the *Alton*'s advent, the Confederates broke camp and boarded a train "for Columbus, but the invasion order was countermanded."[8]

The flag snatching aside, the *Alton* affair raises interesting questions. What happened to the troops and artillery allegedly spotted in Columbus in April? Were Tilghman and his guards not in town? There are no specific references to guard troops in any accounts of the flag's capture. Had they been present and resisted, then June 12, 1861, might have been the day when the war started on Kentucky soil. Blood might indeed have been spilled had Oglesby tried to blast down the flag with his cannons. What might have happened to Kentucky neutrality then? The Southern Rights Party certainly would have played up a shootout for all it was worth, branding the Yankees as wanton violators of Kentucky neutrality. Had the guard fought back, the secessionists would have portrayed them as brave men defending Kentucky homes and firesides. Doubtless, too, the secessionists would have thundered in even greater outrage had Oglesby fired at the flag and ended up killing or wounding civilians. Would waxing Kentucky Unionism have waned?

Meanwhile, back in Columbus, editor Len G. Faxon of the *Crescent* sharpened his poison pen and cut loose against the Yankee flag stealers and their commander. As noted before, objectivity was hardly a hallmark of Civil War journalism; vitriol and vilification were the stock-in-trade of editors and reporters, Yankee and Rebel. Yet few verbal broadsides were as blistering as Faxon's blast in the *Crescent*. It even astonished the "world's first and greatest" war correspondent, Sir William Howard Russell of the London *Times*. Russell recorded Faxon's fulminations in *My Diary North and South,* his American Civil War journal. If not for Russell, Faxon's fusillade might have been lost. No copies of the 1861 *Crescent* are known to survive. Russell, who reported the Indian Mutiny and the Crimean War for the *Times,* was at the Union camp at Cairo on June 20 when he came by a copy of the *Crescent* with Faxon's version of the *Alton*'s unfriendly visit.[9]

Russell also described his river and rail journey to Cairo, which he reached on June 19, via the *Cheney*. "Columbus is situated on an elevated spur or elbow of land projecting into the river, and has, in commercial faith, one of those futures which have so many rallying points down the centre of the great river." He said the transfer steamer "carried no flag, and on board presented traces of better days, a list of refreshments no longer available, and a bill of fare utterly fanciful."[10]

Russell's account of the train trip suggested that Columbus had become all but a Confederate outpost. He wrote that several Rebel soldiers rode the train to Columbus, including a Mississippian who said he was a veteran of prewar filibustering expeditions mounted by proslavery southern mercenaries to seize Cuba and Nicaragua. Russell added that when the man got off the train in Columbus, "a good number of men in uniform joined him, which led me to conclude that they had some more serious object than a mere pleasure trip to the very uninteresting looking city on the banks of the Mississippi, which is asserted to be neutral territory, as it belongs to the sovereign State of Kentucky."[11]

At Cairo, Russell said he found himself amid what Columbus folk had described as "abolitionists, cut-throats, Lincolnite mercenaries, foreign invaders, assassins, and plundering Dutchmen." His informants did not include Faxon, who was away in the Confederate army and missed the flag grabbing. Russell identified him as "Colonel L. G. Faxon of the Tennessee Tigers." In any event, he soon returned home and opened fire in the June 19 *Crescent.* According to Russell, Faxon apologized "for the non-appearance of the journal for several weeks." Faxon explained that before he left, he had "engaged the services of a competent editor, and left a printer here to issue the paper regularly." Though Faxon's absence had been longer than he expected, the editor maintained that "the aforesaid printer promised faithfully to perform his duties, but left the same day we did, and consequently there was no one to get out the paper." Faxon concluded, "We have the charity to suppose that fear and bad whiskey had nothing to do with his evacuation of Columbus."[12]

Russell quoted Faxon's observation that "the Irish are for us, and they will knock Bologna sausages out of the Dutch, and we will knock wooden nutmegs out of the Yankees." He added his wish that the folds of the captured flag "had contained 1000 asps to sting 1000 Dutchmen to eternity unshriven." The Yankees probably would have been too besotted to feel it, according to the editor: "The mosquitoes of Cairo have been sucking the lager-bier out of the dirty soldiers there so long, they are bloated and swelled up as large as spring 'possums. An assortment of Columbus mosquitoes went up there the other day to suck some, but as they have not returned, the probability is that they went off with *delirium tremens;* in fact, the blood of these Hessians would poison the most degraded tumble bug in creation."[13]

With that, Faxon reloaded and fired again: "When the bow-legged wooden shoed, sour craut stinking, Bologna sausage eating, hen roost robbing Dutch sons of—had accomplished the brilliant feat of taking down the Secession flag on the river bank, they were pointed to another flag of the same sort which their guns did not cover, flying gloriously and defiantly, and dared yea! double big black dog–dared, as we used to say at school, to take that flag down."[14]

The bluecoats declined, Faxon claimed: "The cowardly pups, the thieving sheep dogs, the sneaking skunks, dare not do so, because their twelve pieces of artillery were not bearing on it." After flaying the federal soldiers, Faxon lambasted their leader Prentiss, a tough-as-boot-leather soldier who would become a Union hero at the battle of Shiloh in April 1862. Faxon dismissed him as "a miserable hound, a dirty dog, a sociable fellow, a treacherous villain, a notorious thief, a lying blackguard, who has served his regular five years in the Penitentiary and keeps his hide continually full of Cincinnati whiskey, which he buys by the barrel in order to save his money—in him are embodied the leprous rascalities of the world, and in this living score, the gallows is cheated of its own."[15]

Finally, Faxon hurled down the gauntlet: "Prentiss wants our scalp; we propose a plan by which he may get that valuable article." The colonel could choose 150 of his best fighters "or 250 of his lager-bier Dutchmen." Faxon would recruit 100 Columbus worthies as challengers. "Then let both parties meet where there will be no interruption at the scalping business, and the longest pole will knock the persimmon," Faxon vowed. "If he does not accept this proposal, he is a coward." Prentiss ignored Faxon. But Russell guessed that Prentiss was more wounded by the editor's poison pen than the general cared to admit.[16]

The *Alton*'s stop at Columbus naturally worried Magoffin and Buckner. The day after, the state guard chief, accompanied by Bullock and two other Kentuckians, met with McClellan in Cairo. Buckner wanted McClellan to confirm their Cincinnati agreement. He did and protested that the boat was not supposed to call at Columbus and that volunteer troops like those aboard the steamer were difficult to control. Bullock said McClellan even promised that if Kentucky citizens asked him for military help, "he would refer them to the judicial and military authorities of Kentucky" and not send aid.[17]

Magoffin also sought reassurance from Harris that Tennessee, too, would respect Kentucky's neutrality. To that end, he sent Buckner to Nashville. On June 12, Pillow, in Union City, had asked the governor to dispatch him additional troops, evidently for taking Columbus. After meeting with Buckner, he told his impetuous general that reinforcements would not be forthcoming; the troops would not be sent because he was "satisfied that the Federal Government will not attempt to quarter troops in Kentucky." Harris informed Pillow that Buckner had told him of his agreement with McClellan. Further, he said Magoffin had promised him he would preserve Kentucky neutrality "by repelling from his territory any troops of either of the belligerents that may be quartered within the limits of that State, to enable himself to do which he has sent General Buckner to Columbus to call out and organize a regiment or battalion of Kentucky troops to be quartered at or near Columbus."[18]

Tilghman and most of his men would soon be in Confederate service. Doubtless, they hoped to enlist in a Confederate Kentucky. But the special congressional election strongly indicated that Kentucky was trending the other way. The terms of the state's ten House members had expired on March 4. Union candidates swept to lopsided victories in nine of Kentucky's ten congressional districts. The First District, with the Purchase as its western anchor, reelected Burnett. But outside the Purchase, he only carried his home county, Trigg, and it by a scant twenty votes. Burnett bested Unionist Lawrence Trimble of Paducah, the district's Douglas elector in the presidential election. Districtwide, Burnett triumphed, with 8,988 votes to 6,225 votes for his opponent. The Purchase gave Burnett 5,626 votes to 1,785 for Trimble.[19]

Trimble's hometown *Herald* conceded "the complete triumph of the Union party in the State—every District, we believe, except the glorious and unterrified old First." Editor Noble asked "What next?" and answered, "Though overwhelmed, we are not conquered—though beaten, we are not subdued." The Southern Rights side got drubbed because "our friends in every portion of the State except below the Tennessee river" had blundered and campaigned on "false policies," meaning neutrality, he argued. Naturally, Noble bragged on his paper and his region: "In the 'Purchase,' where the Herald boldly threw out the banner of secession, and where the contest was distinctly made upon that issue, we have triumphed gloriously and by thousands." He claimed that in the First District, east of the Tennessee, "where the voice of Burnett, [Willis B.] Machen, Cissell and others would have been potent with a bold issue, we are defeated, because the dodge game proved to be really an aid to the Unionists instead of a weapon of destruction." Noble argued that neutrality meant only "to *stand still,* and to stand still is the position of the Union party of Kentucky." He claimed that Magoffin, Breckinridge, and other leaders of the Southern Rights Party were secessionists at heart but chose not to make "a bold, manly, honest, open fight for Secession." Noble argued, "They acted upon a mistaken policy, and we have lost the State, and would have lost even the First District had not a few bold men below the Tennessee river forced the true issue and won the district by the innate power and truth of Secession."

The editor looked to the August 5 election for the state legislature, challenging its members to "make the fight in favor of *Secession and the Southern Confederacy.*" He claimed Tennessee secessionists had "first tried the dodge policy and failed." But when they "then took honest ground," they "carried the state by sixty thousand majority. The Kentucky Purchase took honest ground in favor of Secession and won by five or ten to one. The balance of the State took a politic dodge, and lost by thousands." The *Herald* thus urged the Southern Rights Party to campaign "upon the fair issue of Secession or no Secession—to remain with the abolition North or join the South—to remain a slave state or abolish slavery." He concluded with a warning suggesting that the spirit of the Mayfield convention was still alive in Noble's neck of the woods: "Kentucky *must* leave the abolition Union. The Kentucky Purchase, at least, *will* do it."[20]

Noble, of course, was almost surely wrong about why his party had lost. Had the Southern Rights candidates campaigned harder "upon the fair issue of secession," they likely would have attracted even fewer votes. Of course, the *Herald* editor wrote with the certainty of the most doctrinaire of secessionists. No doubt, he reflected the views of most citizens of his town and of his region. But Noble was blind to—or simply unwilling to accept—the political realities in the rest of Kentucky. So were many others of like mind in the Purchase. The August elections proved them dead wrong.

In any event, some secessionists evidently boycotted the election. The total Southern Rights vote was 37,700, compared to 53,143 for Breckinridge. It is also possible that some Breckinridge voters had turned out to be Union men. But the total Union vote of 92,540 was only 513 less than the Bell, Douglas, and Lincoln total.[21]

Indeed, the congressional election was even more evidence that the Purchase was Kentucky's only Rebel region. A majority of voters in the Pennyrile, the Knobs, the Bluegrass, and the eastern mountains cast Unionist ballots. Elsewhere in the state, almost all Bell and Douglas men formed the core of the Union Party. In the Purchase, the congressional election strongly suggested the opposite: most Bell and Douglas supporters had joined the majority Breckinridge Democrats in the Southern Rights Party. Burnett received 1,079 more votes than Breckinridge did.[22]

For example, Fulton County barely went for Breckinridge but gave Burnett 631 votes to 38 for Trimble. In keeping with the Mayfield convention resolution, county officials put "For the North" and "For the South" and "For Neutrality" on the ballot. Voters cast 645 ballots "For the South," none "For the North," and three "For Neutrality." In Clinton, voters could also opt for "Secession" or "Union." "Secession" won 213-0, while Burnett topped Trimble 211 to 3 in the Hickman County seat. In nearby Moscow, the choice was "Secession" and "Against." It was "Secession" 115 and "Against" 0; Burnett bested Trimble by a like margin. In McCracken County, Breckinridge ran third, behind Bell and Douglas. Burnett carried the county 612 to 298. In addition, Bell pocketed Ballard, but the county went for Burnett over Trimble 687-177.[23]

The *Courier,* whose editor was Walter N. Haldeman, had little else to cheer about over the election and happily reported returns from the Purchase, especially from McCracken County, where, according to a Paducah correspondent, the "election passed over very quietly, as the 'boys' were determined that every vote should be polled, and a full, free and fair expression of opinion had." The correspondent added, "There was not a single fight in the town. No drunken men, and no one, either Union or Southern Rights, molested either going to the polls." He added, "The oldest citizens say they never saw so orderly an election. By agreement the coffee-house keepers all refused to open and everyone seemed determined to use every exertion to avoid difficulties of every kind." Perhaps even more remarkable was the drubbing Trimble got in his hometown. Paducah went for Burnett 354–153; Trimble even lost his home precinct, 54–20.[24]

Elsewhere in the Purchase, Burnett outpolled Breckinridge, who claimed 67 percent of the vote in Calloway, Graves, Hickman, and Marshall Counties. Almost 75 percent of their vote was in Burnett's column.[25]

Also in June, several more Purchase men voted with their feet and headed south into the Confederate army. More than a few were state guards, who were honor bound to safeguard Kentucky neutrality against both sides. But they were virtual Confederate soldiers. On June 24, Buckner ordered six guard companies under Tilghman to Columbus to "preserve the neutrality of the state in that neighborhood." Tilghman resigned and was replaced by Colonel Ben Hardin Helm. Both men would become Confederate generals and die in battle in 1863, Tilghman at Champion Hill, Mississippi, and Helm, Lincoln's brother-in-law, at Chickamauga, Georgia.[26]

On June 25, the "Dukedom Rifles" were still part of the state guard. The southern Graves County men were at Camp Sheppard at State Line Station—Fulton—"awaiting orders from Col Austin" to go to Columbus, according to a letter First Lieutenant Samuel Paine Ridgway of Mayfield wrote, but never mailed, to his future wife, Jennie Stanfield of Graves County. The letter is especially interesting for the questions it raises. Ridgway did not supply Austin a first name. But was he the Colonel Austin of Memphis who spoke just before Tilghman at the Mayfield convention? If so, why was he still in the Purchase? In any event, Ridgway's epistle stated the obvious: the militiaman expected to fight the Yankees at Cairo, not to enforce neutrality against both sides. "We have to be governed by the preparation made at Columbus to receive us and we dont want to go until the Cairo forces are ready to fight us," Ridgway explained. He said the guards had a half-dozen thirty-two-pounder cannons. He did not say where the artillery came from but added that "the Boys nurse them night and day." The guns were "to be planted at Columbus whenever we go." He said the "Rifles" "learned this morning that there were three Companies landed there yesterday. Austin said there would be a thousand men at Columbus by tonight." Meanwhile, Ridgway confided that "the boys are all going wild, if they stay here many days we will have to tie them to a stake." He vowed "every boy says his sweetheart is the prettiest & would fight in a minute if any body disputed it—It would be laughable to you to hear them rattling to each other and if you dont come down to Columbus whenever we get there I will never come to your house again to rob the bees—you hear me!"[27]

Meanwhile, Tilghman's home county had contributed all or part of two companies to Tennessee regiments. One group of twenty-one volunteers was included in Company G of the Fifteenth Tennessee Infantry Regiment. The outfit numbered nine Graves countians, plus thirty-four refugees from southern Illinois. Eluding Illinois home guards, these Rebel refugees arrived in Paducah by steamboat on May 27. They "were welcomed as heroes by Paducah's Confederate community." Captain Thorndike Brooks, commander of the Jackson and Williamson County volunteers, led his men to the popular St. Francis Hotel, where the proprietor, Augustine Shields, an Irish-born Catholic southern sympathizer, greeted the mostly, if not all, Protestant band "like long lost brothers." The hotelkeeper happily furnished the weary wayfarers soft beds and hard liquor. Those inclined to partake were provided food and drink "until the wee hours of the morning." One of the "slightly hung-over" guests arose early to find the hotel "thrown wide open to our company." Secessionists came and went bringing food, clothing, and other gifts. Brooks also ordered his men to fan out and seek recruits. They kept at it for the rest of the day and into the morning of May 29, when Clare Shields, the innkeeper's wife, presented Brooks with a Rebel flag, "which was [then] carried through the streets of Paducah at the head of the company." That afternoon, bolstered by the McCracken County volunteers, including Augustine and Claire's son David, they caught a train to Mayfield, where they spent the night in the Old Cargill Hotel. They called for recruits on May 30. In his memoirs, southern Illinoisan Frank Metcalf, who grew up in Mayfield, said there was less fuss made over the recruits in his boyhood home than there had been in Paducah. Perhaps that was because they arrived in the midst of the Mayfield convention. In any event, the company, with the Mayfield additions, continued its southward journey that evening. The troops arrived at the Rebel camp in Union City early the next day. Meanwhile, King received the men he had asked for in the Mayfield convention. Mostly McCracken countians and dubbed the "Pillow Guards Number Two," they became Company K of the Twenty-first Tennessee Infantry Regiment on June 13. Later, King and his men left the Volunteer State infantry outfit and became the nucleus of a Kentucky cavalry battalion popularly known as the "Hell Hounds."[28]

While some Purchase men left for the Rebel army, other southern sympathizers stayed home and started vigilante groups. On July 1, Marshall County Southern Rights supporters met at the courthouse in Benton and established a "Central Vigilance Committee" and local committees that were supposed to protect the citizens against "any movements calculated in the least to injure" their "rights or property." The committees were "to dissolve all meetings of slaves which shall appear in the least dangerous; [and] to find out from all suspicious looking strangers the objects of their visits, and if they shall be proved culpable, to act with them as the public safety shall require." Caleb Lindsey chaired the gathering, and J. W. Dycus was secretary.[29]

Vigilantism seemed to be on the rise in Paducah, too. On July 16, "Sentinel" wrote the *Journal* again, this time claiming that "the Union men are having a hard time still—no quarters are given them by the secessionists. Men have been forced to leave their families at the mercy of the world, and some of their families are in a distressed condition. . . . Our worthy mayor [John W. Sauner] has been called on for protection. He refuses to give any—rather aids and abets the secession party." Even so, "Sentinel" was happy to report that on the night of July 14, somebody cut down a Confederate flag in town. He predicted that just as the Rebel banner fell, so would secessionism, "at a future day, I am in hopes not far distant." The correspondent added that George Washington Lafayette Bickley, who founded the Knights of the Golden Circle before the war, happened to be in town. The fiercely proslavery Knights was a secret society that wanted the United States to seize a "golden circle" of territory in Latin America and the Caribbean and turn it into American slave states. During the war, the Knights spread into the border states and the North, where they were accused of conspiring with pro-Confederate "Copperheads" to subvert the war effort. After the flag was hoisted back up, Bickley gave a half-hour speech that "failed entirely to rouse the patriotism of the people," "Sentinel" said. Next, a traveler from southern Illinois on his way to Tennessee—and evidently taken for a secessionist—was called on to talk. But he delivered a pro-Union speech that "was a damper on the crowd." Next up was Dr. Guilford "Shellbark" Jones, a local Methodist pastor and a secessionist, who "harangued for some time to the great delight of the audience." "Sentinel" suggested that Jones "would make a better politician than he is a preacher, as he affects more zeal in his stump speeches than in his pulpit orations."[30]

The letter also touched on the trouble brewing over the state guard muskets and artillery sent by rail from Paducah to Mayfield in May. So did a missive from the Graves County seat that the *Journal* also printed on July 23. Judge Boone, who was also captain of the "Mayfield Guards" of the state guard, had charge of the firepower. He inherited six brass cannons sent from Frankfort to Tilghman for a state guard company in Paducah. He also received about nine hundred muskets that "had been repaired and rifled at the United States Armory in St. Louis at the expense of this State." The small arms were supposed to have been shipped to Louisville, but they wound up in Paducah under Tilghman's care. On June 14, the military board ordered Tilghman to distribute to home guard companies in the First and Second Districts their allotted shares of the muskets. Any leftovers were to be returned to the state arsenal at Frankfort as quickly as possible. When Tilghman failed to carry out the order, the board, on July 9, sent Commissioner G. T. Wood to get them. The board feared that the arms were so close to the Tennessee line, which is about twenty miles south of Mayfield, that they were in danger of being captured by "lawless persons."[31]

The "Great Graves County Gun Grab" followed. The heist did not make the history books, but Unionists elsewhere in the state viewed it as more proof that the Purchase was Rebel to the core. On July 13, a Saturday, King took it upon himself to seize the Kentucky ordnance for Confederate use. He and his men rode a train to Paducah but returned to Mayfield by evening train. That night, "he was observed in private talk on several occasions with Southern Rights men, some of whom it is said to have advocated the forcible seizure of the arms." A guard was put on the weapons. Trouble seemed to be brewing; twenty or more men reportedly had gathered "in the suburbs of town towards Pryorsburg," a community about six miles south of Mayfield on the railroad to Union City. Also that night, four wagons and teams approached town. Reportedly owned by Jonathan Pryor, William Pryor, Jonathan Richards, and Milton Sexton, the wagons evidently were for hauling away the weapons. But the wagon drivers turned back when spotted; the men at the edge of town apparently went home. The ordnance remained unmolested, at least for the present.[32]

Boone was away and did not return until Sunday afternoon. Perhaps his absence was deliberate; there seems to be no evidence either way. Meanwhile, Captain J. J. Lane, who had raised a local home guard company and was due a portion of the muskets, heard the weapons had been seized: "Thereupon, he gathered up some thirty of his company and came to town with shot guns, and such private arms as he could command." When Boone arrived, Lane and his men offered to help him guard the weapons. If not, they would go home, since their weapons had not been taken. Before Lane showed up, Judge Williams had decided to issue a writ ordering the sheriff to "summons good responsible men of all parties to protect these arms." He also had sent a message to a home guard outfit at Milburn, in Ballard County, which was supposed to get some of the muskets, too. He advised the Unionists "that it was their duty to protect the property of the State equally with the State Guards." Boone, fearing bloodshed, declined Lane's offer and promised Williams and other Unionists that he would protect the muskets with "the remnant of his company of State Guard." If he needed help, "he would call on the citizens of the town indiscriminately." But Boone stressed he did not want help from avowed Union men or secessionists, "as he feared the consequences." Both sides agreed with him. Meanwhile, some Southern Rights men "had gone into the country in different directions to secure the attendance of friends, and had rallied . . . several hundred." However, other secessionists stopped them from coming to Mayfield. Around two a.m., Captain Pugh and about thirty of the Milburn home guards were approaching Mayfield, evidently on horseback, but they stopped at Williams's house, which was on the road to Milburn, about a half-mile from town. After the judge told them that Boone had pledged to protect the arms, they went home.[33]

King returned to Union City, but not before he delivered a speech on the night of July 15 that convinced the *Journal* he was at the center of a secessionist plot to inaugurate "war upon Kentucky soil." The paper predicted "an explosion within the next ten days" and trusted "that the heads of its authors will roll upon the ground like balls." The *Journal*'s alarm was based on the letter it published on July 23. It came from a Mayfield Unionist—"a perfectly reliable source, a source from which nothing but truth ever comes." The correspondent wrote on July 17 that the town was "filled with leading secessionists, representing nearly every county in the Purchase, with sundry officers and privates from the army of the Southern Confederacy." He added that a twenty- to thirty-man company, evidently intent on taking the state guard weapons, had come to the edge of Mayfield on the night of July 16 but withdrew after hearing "that a strong guard" was protecting the ordnance. He said he had it on "I think good authority" that armed men would seize the weapons on the morning of July 18. "It is publicly announced by secessionists that the arms here shall never go into the hands of Union men," he warned. The letter suggested that separationist spirit expressed in the Mayfield convention was still alive. In a speech on the night of July 15, King reportedly predicted that Kentucky would ultimately exit the Union, "but if it did not, the Purchase would, as a majority ought to, and would control it." At that point, "the Union men would . . . have to come in; if not, they would be given three days to leave; after which time, if they did not take up arms for the South, they would have to fall." The Unionist admitted he did not hear King's remarks but learned the gist of them "from several sources." The letter writer added that King "said many much harder things in the private circle than the above" and warned "something desperate is on hands; look out for startling news soon."[34]

Boone was doubtless relieved when King departed on July 19, taking an early morning train for Paducah. Even so, he had not seen the last of the impetuous captain and his command. King and his men, still unarmed, evidently aimed to take 100 to 120 rifles and muskets normally stored at the Paducah arsenal. But Mayor Sauner had removed them the day before for safekeeping with C. Dailey and Company, local merchants. Later in the day, the captain discovered the whereabouts of the ordnance and, the next morning, took forty of the weapons by force. "But upon being remonstrated with, [he] surrendered them up again to the authorities." Even so, King said he intended to seize the muskets and cannons at Mayfield. "But upon the citizens of Mayfield and Paducah objecting to his doing so, he pledged his word that he would not remove the arms." Thus, he and his band rode another Union City–bound train on the evening of July 20.[35]

King got no further than Fulton Station on the state line, where "he was met by a number of citizens from Kentucky and Tennessee" who apparently talked him into taking the ordnance at Mayfield. Most, if not all, of his men went back to Mayfield, loaded their night train with the nine hundred muskets, six cannons, "and baggage wagons &c." and returned. King kept his word, at least technically; he stayed in Fulton while the ordnance was swiped. Back in Fulton, the weapons were divvied up; "citizens of Fulton county" received four hundred muskets. The rest of the ordnance went down the tracks to Union City. Of course, Judge Boone, Senator Johnson, and Albert P. Thompson shared King's southern sentiments. But on the evening of July 21, they hurried to Union City to persuade the Confederates to give the arms back. Cheatham was away, but Colonel William Travis told Boone that neither "he nor the authorities there approved of the act, but most emphatically condemned the whole thing," and promised to return the guns to Fulton Station, if that was what the judge wished. However, Boone said he, Thompson, and Johnson agreed that locals might seize the weapons. So they asked Travis if he would keep the firepower until Kentucky authorities should need the weapons. Travis agreed but suggested that the Kentuckians get Cheatham's approval, which he was sure would be forthcoming.[36]

Four days later, Johnson wrote Magoffin about Travis's disapproval of King's mischief, adding that the colonel "holds the property, subject to your order." In reply, Magoffin said he was sending Wood to Union City and Hickman—where the four hundred muskets were taken—to recover all of the arms. As Wood was already in Mayfield, Magoffin directed Johnson to tell him to get the weapons.[37]

Meanwhile, on July 21, Cheatham had learned of King's action. Immediately, he wrote Colonel W. T. Withers, commander of Kentucky volunteers at newly opened Camp Boone, Tennessee, north of Clarksville and about three and a half miles south of the Kentucky state line. He said that the arms "are subject to your order as Kentuckians" and that he expected that "in retaining them you of course get the consent of Governor Magoffin, of Kentucky." On July 24, Withers wrote Secretary Walker that "I have declined to receive the arms, informing General Cheatham that I would refer the matter to you." Two days before, Frank Stone had given a speech in Murray seeking volunteers for the Kentucky brigade at Camp Boone, but "not to fight in the Southern Confederacy." Stone's aim was to get arms and equipment with which "to go to Louisville and sink that *damnable black Republican city* to *hell,* and open the L. & N.R.R. or tear it up from end to end." Unionist William T. Carr included Stone's threat in a letter the *Journal* published on July 20. Carr added that "Maj. Cargle of Mayfield" and other Camp Boone–bound men confirmed to him that the brigade was being organized to attack Louisville. The *Journal* claimed Carr's information was "the uncolored truth" and confirmed that the Kentucky volunteers from Camp Boone indeed planned to return to their home state to destroy Louisville and the railroad and force Kentucky into the Confederacy: "The design might be inferred from the movement even without this bold and audacious avowal of its leaders, but the avowal puts the matter beyond all question." "Cargle" was apparently Major William M. Cargill, a quartermaster in the Third Kentucky. He evidently was the "W. M. Cargill" who was secretary of the big Union meeting at Mayfield on January 21, 1861. "Stone" was likely R. F. Stone of Benton, an officer in the regiment's Company A. In any event, on July 31, the whole affair of the stolen weapons appeared to be settled when A. T. Bledsoe, representing Walker, wrote Withers that if the arms belonged to Kentucky, then they should be handed back.[38]

Yet the issue was not settled. Colonel Wood was unable to recover the arms for the state, and he returned to Frankfort. On hearing his report, the Military Board resolved to bring Governor Harris and General Cheatham up to date on the stolen weapons. The panel also ordered a special agent to convey the information personally to Harris and Cheatham. He was to see to the shipment of the arms to the state arsenal in Frankfort. However, before the agent could be sent, Representative Lannom went to Frankfort to meet with the board. He told Magoffin and one of the commissioners that Cheatham had complied with his request to send the battery and the muskets he possessed back to Fulton County. The ordnance was "two or three miles within the limits of this State, where they were guarded by our own citizens." He added that at public meetings in Fulton and Hickman County, citizens had voted to dispatch him to Frankfort to suggest to the board that locals "would give bond and security as 'Home Guard' companies" in order to keep them. But Lannom warned that he doubted his constituents "would permit any removal of these arms from their vicinity, if their proposition was rejected." Owing to Lannom's sympathies and the sympathies of the great majority of his constituents, the board stuck to its position that the muskets and the cannons had to be turned over to the state. As a last resort, the Military Board tried to sue the residents of Fulton and Hickman Counties who were responsible for keeping the weapons, but to no avail. An exasperated board ended up reporting to the legislature "that all the muskets which had been returned to Kentucky from Union City, Tennessee, which were said to be guarded by our own citizens, have been taken off, but by whom, what their destination, or whether they will ever be recovered, remains to be seen."[39]

It seems a safe bet that "whom" were Purchase recruits whose "destination" was the Confederate army. The trickle of volunteers that had begun in the spring became a flood in midsummer. In July, Tilghman and most of his state guards went to Camp Boone, where they and other western Kentuckians became the Third Kentucky Infantry Regiment on about July 20. Tilghman was elected colonel and Albert P. Thompson lieutenant colonel. Soon afterward, Tilghman earned brigadier general's stars, and Thompson replaced Tilghman as colonel of the regiment. Apparently, Tilghman's troops were not armed with many of the state guard muskets. In his book *History of 3d, 7th, 8th and 12th Kentucky C.S.A.,* Seventh Kentucky veteran Henry George wrote that the Third Kentucky "had been partially supplied with Belgian rifles, but owing to the scarcity of any kind of arms, numbers of them had to use the old flint-lock musket; they retained these arms up to and including the battle of Shiloh."[40]

The famous Virginia-born artist Conrad Wise Chapman served briefly in the Third Kentucky, abandoning his art studio in Rome, Italy, to sign up at Camp Boone. He recalled: "At that time a great variety was to be seen in the gallant 3d Ky. . . . Every variety from the Backwoodsman blouse to the dandy State guard uniform and the country squire's dress and the city nay-bob, some with old flintlocks[.] I remember mine was such, other[s] their shot guns and others whose time of service in Yankee hands had expired with their owners."[41]

On July 14, Paine Ridgway wrote Jennie from Camp Boone that the volunteers who would become the Third Kentucky would be mustered in the next day, though they were without uniforms or arms. Ridgeway and the "Dukedom Rifles" and the "Mayfield Guards" would merge as Company E. Ridgway said Tilghman promised military duds and weapons "in two or three weeks." The Graves countian added that he had overheard Lieutenant Colonel Thompson explaining "that we would defend Kentucky & that we would be stationed west of the Cumberland River, if so, we will not be so far from our old homes and Friends that some of them can come see us If we go back to Kentucky & her soil." But he found Camp Boone a pleasant enough spot to learn soldiering. "We are situated in a grove of beautiful oak trees with good neighbors around us and every comfort of Life." Ridgway bragged that his outfit would capture "Old Abe Lincoln on the blue waters of the Ohio River take him by the ears, drag him to the Tennessee line and tell Jeff Davis here is his mule." He gave Jennie his love but vowed, "I am a soldier until the South has her rights & are permitted to live in peace free from all Northern fanaticism & aggression."[42]

He wrote Jennie again on July 21, assuring her, "we have everything that would make us happy, except we havent as many privileges as we enjoy at home. Our officers are our masters & have has much control over us as Slaves, rise at their word & never speak, nor make excuses." Ridgway said Colonel Withers told the troops about the Rebel rout of the Union army at the battle of Bull Run, Virginia, on July 21, the war's first major clash of arms. Paine told Jennie that the fight was between "General [P. G. T.] Beauregard & old Abe's robbers" and "black hearted abolitionists." He claimed the Confederate victory proved conclusively to him "that the Southerners are in the right, that God is on their side."[43]

While the Third Kentucky was being readied for war, James W. Moss and his "Columbus Rifles" showed up at Camp Boone. So did Lewis Slayden and the "Boyd Grays," more Graves County guardsmen. Moss and his men, Ballard County and Hickman County recruits, became Company A of the Second Kentucky Infantry Regiment, and Slayden's men formed Company D of the same regiment. Moss and Slayden were elected captains of their companies. Moss's company "was the first to clear a space and pitch a tent at Camp Boone." A native of Greensburg, Kentucky, the thirty-nine-year-old Moss was a veteran of the Mexican-American War, during which, coincidentally, he had been captain of Company A of the Second Kentucky Infantry Regiment. When Moss saw his lieutenant colonel fall mortally wounded from his horse at the Battle of Buena Vista, the captain displayed "the presence of mind, in the sad confusion that momentarily ensued, to perceive that the regular infirmary detail was not available and accordingly ordered some of his men to bear him from the field, and one of them . . . was killed while thus engaged." The lieutenant colonel was Henry Clay Jr.[44]

Meanwhile, Tennessee regiments continued to attract Purchase recruits. Also in July 1861, William Lindsey and a party of Fulton and Hickman countians crossed into Tennessee and enlisted as Company F of the Twenty-second Tennessee Infantry Regiment. Also, King ultimately left the Twenty-first Tennessee. Augmented by three more companies of Purchase men, his outfit became King's Battalion, Kentucky Cavalry. But it was merged into the First, and later the Sixth, Confederate Cavalry. King—or somebody else—dubbed the troopers "King's Hell Hounds." Local Unionists might have considered the nickname appropriate for men they considered hellish.[45]

As summertime heat rose in the Purchase, so did fear of an attack from Cairo. Most of the state guards and many other young men had left for the Confederate army. As a result, the seven counties were practically defenseless, and Frankfort was not apt to arm the Rebel region.

Therefore, the secessionists took matters into their own hands. In Hickman, Thomas McMahon raised a "Home Militia" that was supposed to protect the town against Yankee boats whose crews might be tempted to grab another Rebel flag. A big Confederate banner also flew over Hickman. McMahon's men reputedly were prepared to defend their standard to the death "with rifles, flint-lock muskets, pitchforks, battle axes, spears, spades and other hostile weapons." But Union gunboats from Cairo reportedly chugged past "without so much as even noticing the defiant banner supported by its valiant defenders." Despite their bravado, Hickman's "Home Militia" and similar would-be defenders of the Purchase would have stood no chance against an invasion from Cairo. As summer waned, the region remained essentially wide open to both armies. Most Purchase citizens hoped and prayed for the advent of the Rebels, who were just over the state line in Tennessee. At the same time, many doubtless feared the Yankees at Cairo would arrive first. Doubtless, in church pews and over supper tables throughout the region, many were the supplications to the Almighty for deliverance from the "Hessians," only a river's width away.[46]

5

Politics, Pirates, and More Purchase Perfidy

The Purchase stayed stuck in the status quo as summer wore on. The Yankees were still at Cairo; the Rebels were at Union City and other points in West Tennessee. Kentucky was officially off limits to both sides. But perceived military necessity soon trumped political considerations. Paducah-based pirates helped turn the Union side toward invading Kentucky. Likewise, when the Rebels feared the Yankees were about to grab Columbus, they were determined to get there first. Thus, the Bluegrass State's precarious, if ultimately untenable, neutrality ended in the Purchase.

On July 12, Major General Leonidas Polk took command of Confederate Military District Number Two, which embraced West Tennessee. Polk shared Pillow's enthusiasm for capturing Columbus. A long letter to the *Memphis Appeal* printed on August 6 seemed more proof that westernmost Kentucky would welcome the Rebels. The missive from "J.P." in Hickman also suggested that the idea of regional secession was not dead. The author began by taking exception to a July 20 *Appeal* story that said Unionism was still strong in the Purchase. J.P. said a recent trip through "several counties" in the region had convinced him that the Purchase was "as completely united on the principle of Southern Rights as the Western district of Tennessee." He declared that "in Fulton county, with a voting population of eight hundred, there are not exceeding twenty union men." He said Hickman County was equally pro-Confederate, numbering about nine hundred voters with no more than "thirty union men among them." He claimed the same ratio existed throughout the Purchase, except probably in Graves County, where he said the "voting population of about 2,500 included nearly 600 Unionists." The correspondent vowed he was "certain that in a voting population of about ten thousand west of the Tennessee river, there are not exceeding eight hundred Union voters." He concluded: "We are determined, if the State refuses to go with the South, that we will take this portion of the State out of the Rump Government or take ourselves out." J.P. added that the *Appeal* and the *Louisville Courier* were popular in the Purchase, but that anybody spotted reading the *Louisville Journal* was "thought not to be very 'sound on the goose question.'"[1]

Four days later, the *Courier* reprinted observations of a visitor to the Purchase and West Tennessee that had been published in the *St. Louis Republican.* The wayfarer was unprepared "for the intensity of the bitterness of feeling which appears to prevail everywhere against the North and the people of the North." He said that "towards Cairo there exists a special spite, as the location of the blockade which has deprived the South of so many necessities, conveniences and luxuries." He reported that at Columbus he "did not hear a single Union sentiment expressed. There are, however, a very few Union men at that place." The man wrote that Columbus had furnished four companies to the Confederate army, including a company that was at the Battle of Bull Run on July 21. (He evidently meant Crossland's company of the First Kentucky Infantry, but the regiment did not fight in the battle.) The correspondent said one company, "The Columbus Rifles," was "to be presented a splendid silk banner, from New Orleans, one of the finest company flags I ever saw." He also reported that many men, mostly Missourians, were riding trains from Columbus to the Confederate forces in Memphis. "They go partly on foot through Missouri and Cairo, and many have gone openly on the Cheney."[2]

Meanwhile, Polk, after settling into his headquarters at Memphis, received a series of letters from the Purchase alleging new federal threats toward Columbus. On July 30, D. O. Dixon wrote the general from Columbus that cannons at Cairo were being shifted across the Mississippi to Bird's Point, Missouri, where seven thousand troops were congregated and two thousand more had been expected on the night of July 28. Also on July 28, Major General John C. Fremont, St. Louis-based commander of the Federal Department of the West, was in Cape Girardeau, Missouri, about twenty miles north of Bird's Point, with two thousand men, according to Dixon.[3]

At the same time, the Confederate brass suspected Prentiss was using the *Cheney* to spy on Columbus. Accordingly, on July 28, a colonel, a captain, and a lieutenant departed Mobile, Alabama, for Columbus, evidently by train, to seize the packet boat. When the trio arrived at their destination, they discovered that the *Cheney* was "running under the orders and signals of Gen. Prentiss." Still, before grabbing the boat, the colonel wanted to make sure the packet's owners were from Yankee Cairo, not Rebel Columbus, so he sent the captain, incognito, to find out. He reported back that the *Cheney* "belonged to the enemy" and "that the packet carried United States troops secreted upon her." When the colonel told "a few reliable friends in Columbus" that he intended to capture the vessel, T. W. Doughty, S. W. Rennick, and Washington Gray agreed to help. When the *Cheney* routinely docked at Columbus on August 1, the Rebels and their civilian accomplices arrested the unsuspecting captain and his crew and forced them ashore. The colonel ultimately captained the steamer down the Mississippi and handed it over to Polk at Memphis. The Columbus citizenry gave the *Cheney* a grand sendoff: "As she left . . . a shout arose from a large assemblage on the levee." When the boat paused at Hickman, the Rebel crew "was presented with a Confederate flag, and three hearty cheers for the success of the adventurers were given." As the *Cheney* chugged down the Mississippi, "salutes were fired; and other demonstrations of joy manifested." Valued at approximately $25,000, the *Cheney* reached Memphis on August 3. On the same day, J. P. Gray of Columbus informed Polk that eight transports loaded with troops had landed at Cairo on August 2 and that Union pickets were on the Missouri shore opposite Columbus that night.[4]

On August 5, Kentucky election day, Brigadier General Charles Clark wrote Polk from Union City, declaring that the Union force at Cairo had grown to at least twelve thousand troops. He heard "from two sources, both of which are believed to be reliable (one of them certainly so), that General Prentiss had assured the Union men of Ballard County, Ky., that he will send troops to protect them, and that after Monday (to-day) he would not regard the neutrality of Kentucky, and only delayed until the election was over lest it might have an unfavorable desire on their friends." Clark said his forces were in poor shape and warned, "If the enemy is permitted to occupy the heights above Columbus, which I hear is a very strong natural position, we may have some trouble to dislodge them. It is to be regretted that we are not permitted to occupy them first and fortify them."[5]

The following day, Charles Wickliffe wrote Polk from Blandville. The state guard officer shared Clark's concerns. "We are threatened with invasion by General Prentiss as he said to two of our citizens Saturday afternoon [August 3] that after the August election 'Kentucky neutrality would go up,' and that he intended to send a military escort with Mr. Thomas Owens to Milburn to-day." Wickliffe added that Prentiss warned "that he should send reconnoitering parties into Kentucky to watch the enemy in Tennessee." Additionally, Prentiss said he was "'expecting orders to occupy Kentucky'; also that when his troops came into Kentucky the people should 'change to Union men or keep their mouths shut.'" Wickliffe promised, "we shall try to defend ourselves against aggression upon our political and personal rights" and asked Polk to "communicate the above facts to such persons as ought to know them."[6]

Polk suspected the Yankees might indeed be poised to take Columbus. On August 6, he informed Secretary Walker that he had "reason to believe that the enemy is concentrating troops at Bird's Point and at Cairo, with the aim of making a movement down the river." If Prentiss's words were true, they amounted to no more than wishful thinking or a bluff. The attack from Cairo did not materialize, and Polk sat tight for nearly a month before advancing to Columbus.[7]

On the other hand, Prentiss was right if he really predicted that "Kentucky neutrality would go up" after the August 5 elections for a new state legislature. The Union Party won its greatest victory yet. In the House of Representatives, it took seventy-six seats to twenty-four for the Southern Rights side. In the Senate, including half of the members not up for reelection, it held the majority, twenty-seven to eleven. At the same time, James H. Garrard, a Unionist, was reelected state treasurer, easily defeating a pair of secessionists, James R. Barrick and Gobias Terry. Terry pulled out before the election, leaving Barrick to soldier on to defeat. Garrard collected 83,151 votes to 12,160 for Terry and 3,845 for Barrick, according to the *Louisville Daily Journal*. In the Purchase it was Terry 3,769; Barrick 196; and Garrard 533.[8]

Of course, had the rest of the state voted like the Purchase, Kentucky soon would have left the Union or, more accurately, would have been in the Confederacy long before. Southern Rights candidates won all six House seats; at least five of them were unopposed. None of the three Purchase senators was up for reelection. Yet Union candidates carried every other region by big margins. Even friends of the Union beyond Kentucky crowed over the secessionists' drubbing. On August 10, the *New York Times* mockingly quoted the *Herald*'s clarion call before the vote: "Let us make the fight for the Legislature. Let it be done upon the fair issue of Secession or No Secession—to remain with the Abolition North or join the South—to remain a Slave State or abolish Slavery. Let us be honest. We all mean Secession. Magoffin means it. Breckinridge means it. Powell means it. Burnett means it. We all mean it. Then why not say so, and come out and advocate it openly and honestly?" The *Times* jabbed, "We hope the *Herald* is satisfied with the response of the people."[9]

Again, Noble was deluded by his and his region's fervent secessionism. Magoffin was proslavery, and he believed states had the right to exit the Union. But he was unwilling to lead the state out of the Union, as Governor Claiborne Fox Jackson had attempted to do in Missouri. While Senator Breckinridge and Representative Burnett sided with the Confederacy, Senator Lazarus W. Powell would remain in Washington, albeit as a sharp critic of the Lincoln administration.[10]

A *Times* Louisville correspondent was elated over the vote. "We have won another glorious victory," he crowed. He happily predicted "noble deeds from our new Legislature." He was confident that lawmakers would place Kentucky squarely on the Union side and crack down on Confederate sympathizers, including "the violent Secessionists in the Purchase or elsewhere in the State."[11]

At Camp Boone, Paine Ridgway was pleased with the canvass, but because he was misinformed. "I have some hopes for Kentucky since the last election," he wrote Jennie. "I heard of a good many counties that were strong for the union in the last election for Representatives in congress that have elected secession Representatives to the legislature." Unknown to Ridgway, precious few counties had switched. Nonetheless, he said the election "is some proof that Ky. will some day be right." Meanwhile, he told Jennie he was proud of her for saying she "could kill an Abolitionist," adding, "I believe you have the courage to go into the Battle field if it was necessary. That is encouragement to me, and ought to [be] to every one who calls himself an American human."[12]

Meanwhile, secessionist successes in the Purchase and a few other far western counties were of little consolation to St. Louis attorney and Livingston County, Kentucky, native Given Campbell. He was in Louisville the day before the election. "From what I could learn I felt that it was already decided, and that my native State had already forfeited her birthright of bravery & loyalty, for the loaves and fishes of the administration, and the Election the next day, justified the opinion, for Ky. has elected a large majority of Union men to her legislature," he wrote his wife, Bettie, on August 10 from Paducah. (Livingston County went secessionist by a wide margin, too.) Added Campbell, who was en route to Camp Boone to enlist: "The next step will be to run out the States Right men, when she will be sealed with the Covenant of Abolitionism." Campbell, too, brought up the prospect of regional secession. He predicted that "if the upper part of Ky adheres to the Union the Southern part will go with Tenn or form a new state."[13]

The Purchase vote showed that a majority of Purchase citizens shared Campbell's views. Boone triumphed in Graves and J. Q. A. King in McCracken. It is apparently unknown if a Unionist ran against Boone; returns for the House races in Graves County were evidently not reported in the Louisville, Frankfort, or Lexington papers. But W. R. Coffee was elected unopposed to the House from Ballard County, Daniel Matthewson from Calloway, and George W. Silvertooth from Fulton and Hickman Counties. In McCracken County, King had no opposition. He collected "every vote at each precinct except fifteen—his vote run up to 655," correspondent

"SOUTHERN RIGHTS" wrote to the *Louisville Weekly Courier*. The correspondent added that since "Old Abe" issued his war proclamation in April, "more than 300 Southern Rights men and voters" had departed the county for the Confederate forces. If a Unionist had challenged King, "SOUTHERN RIGHTS" claimed, "his majority would have been between 600 and 700 votes." Jesse C. Gilbert trounced Unionist Wesley Minter in Marshall County, 698 to 110. Absent published election returns, the state treasurer's race might be the best gauge of Union sentiment in Graves County and perhaps the balance of the Purchase. Terry and Barrick polled 747 Graves votes to 300 for Garrard.[14]

Without the Graves County returns, it is difficult to make a precise comparison between the state election and the congressional election in the Purchase. But in Ballard, Calloway, Fulton, Hickman, Marshall, and McCracken Counties, the secessionist candidates polled 370 fewer votes than Burnett collected. The Southern Rights vote increased in Calloway and McCracken Counties. In any event, voter turnout almost always decreases in elections where candidates are unopposed or virtually uncontested. At the same time, several Purchase men who doubtless would have voted the Southern Rights ticket were away in the Confederate army.[15]

Few, if any, of the Rebel recruits came from Milburn, a tiny Ballard County hamlet about fourteen miles east of Columbus that emerged as a pro-Union islet in a Rebel sea for reasons unclear. But some of the townsfolk evidently were fairly recent immigrants from Unionist counties of central Kentucky. They paid dearly for their beliefs, some with their lives. The *Journal* reported several alleged atrocities against Unionists: "Mr. Picket, a Union man, was hung in the woods near his own home, but a few miles from Milburn." The paper did not name the perpetrators but later alleged that the day before the election, a Rebel officer from Union City had given ten families from "the neighborhood of Columbus," probably meaning Milburn, two hours to leave or be hanged. A half-dozen "young men, between the ages of fifteen and twenty," escaped to Louisville. The exiles were from the Busby and Harp families. "Mr. Busby, the father of two of the young men . . . is an aged man, nearly blind, and has a family of six young children," the paper claimed. He was forced to forsake "a large crop, ungathered, and a vast amount of business unsettled." Collecting "hastily whatever he could," Busby and his family fled. "There is no accusation whatever against the individuals thus driven from their homes save that they entertain Union sentiments." The story did not tell the fate of the rest of the Busbys and Harps and the other Union-sympathizing families. But the youths reportedly reached Louisville on August 10 with blistered feet, torn clothes, and lacerated flesh: "They were forced to travel at night and lie by during the day, in order to avoid scouting parties of secessionists, many of whom they encountered along their way." On August 11, the lads departed for Shelby County, where they had kin.[16]

The Unionist *Daily Louisville Democrat* reprinted the *Journal* story, challenging, "Cannot something be done to protect the people of Southern Kentucky? Are they to be powerless and down-trodden by mobs countenanced and sustained by the Tennessee troops?" The paper chided Magoffin, claiming "our Governor is prompt in all movements *against* Union men—cannot he now do something to protect Union men and Southern Rights men from lawless mobs in that section of the state? Cannot that vile vigilance committee be somehow suppressed in time to prevent the citizens in that section of Kentucky from engaging in open warfare?" It is interesting that the *Democrat* included "Southern Rights men" as needing protection. But the paper did "not believe that a tenth of the persons of that portion of the State have any sympathy with these outrages; that while very many are what they call 'Southern Rights,' yet it is only feed plunderers and thieves, who, in concerted bands, rove about that portion of Kentucky, devastating and threatening destruction and driving off good citizens without cause." The *Democrat* was sure most Purchase dwellers wanted peace but advised "that an armed force of a hundred can hold in awe and dictate to a thousand unarmed, peaceful citizens." Even the *Courier* publicized the violence in Milburn, but obviously without the pro-Union commentary. Two days after the election, the state's leading Confederate paper reported "a bloody affray at Milburn" in which Unionists and secessionists, including representative-elect Coffee's brother F. J. Coffee, shot it out; Charles and William Elliott, and officers from the "Dixie Rangers," a local Confederate company, "assailed a crowd of seven or eight Union men, who retaliated in the most fearful manner." When they slew Charles Elliott, Coffee, an ex-deputy sheriff, pulled his pistol and fired all six rounds, gunning down a Unionist named Jackson and wounding three of his compatriots. Before fleeing "precipitately," Coffee "snatched the revolver from the hand of his dead companion" and fired the three bullets Elliott had left. The Unionists got off no fewer "than twenty shots" at the retreating Coffee, who suffered only "a wound of a very trifling nature."[17]

But on August 24, the *Courier* published a letter from a Blandville secessionist who claimed the Union men, not Coffee, had run away and that Jackson survived. The author did not mention the Rangers and claimed bullets flew after Charles Elliott and the Unionists exchanged insults. He said that they killed Charles and shot William in the lung while Coffee stood his ground unscathed, though "several balls passed through his clothes." The secessionist side managed to wound a pair of Unionists, "one of them dangerously." The letter writer added that the Union men, evidently including Jackson, escaped that night to Cairo, where Prentiss purportedly rewarded two of them with a pair of Colt pistols. The writer asserted that "the cowardly conduct of the 'Union party,' as they call themselves, in this unfortunate affair, caused much excitement among our people, but prudent counsels prevailed, and no further violence has been committed."[18]

But an August 4 letter from Milburn, printed in the pro-Union *Lexington Observer and Reporter* and republished in the *Journal,* told of more machinations against Milburn dwellers. The *Journal* headlined the letter, "The Reign of Terror in Southern Kentucky." "The war excitement has got so high here that the Union men are leaving (all that can get away)," George W. Stone wrote his brother in Fayette County. He said secessionists from Columbus and Blandville had ridden into Milburn, taken over the town, and shot it out with Unionists: "We killed two of them and lost one—he is not dead yet, but is not expected to live as the rebels put seven balls in him." He complained that the enemy was "ranging in large companies every day. The Union boys that were in the fight have made their escape. They have got Sam Todd and several others in Blandville. I can't tell what they will do with them." Stone declared that a company of Confederates from Union City was in Milburn: "They catch all the Union men they can, and run them into the South. If we don't get home in a few days, we will all be taken and forced into the South." Stone confided that one of the Rebels had allowed him and "Will," possibly his son, to escape to some woods. Stone also mentioned that the Harps and Busbys were fleeing and leaving "all they have." Stone said he had "no money to get away. I have about 200 bushels of wheat but can't sell it at Columbus. Men are constantly coming to me to get me to leave, but I can't bear the idea of leaving my family. I will try to send them up to your house in wagons. They might get through safe." He concluded that although "the election comes off to-morrow . . . I don't think any Union [men] will be allowed to vote." Stone added a postscript explaining that "the Harp and Busby boys have left on foot," forsaking "all their things and crops" and "badly scared." Stone said unless the Unionists received protection, he would have to leave.[19]

Another Milburn émigré described his plight in a letter to the *Journal* written from Mount Eden in Spencer County on August 16:

> I have been driven from my home in Milburn by the secessionists, simply because I am a Union man and prefer the government of my fathers to the so-called Southern Confederacy.
>
> The secessionists from Blandville came over to Milburn three times in the course of as many weeks to curse and abuse the Union

> men of the latter place, and on their third visit they got up a row, in which several men were shot and killed. In this fracas the Union side got the best of it, as I hope they ever will, and drove their cowardly assailants off. After this, bands of armed men were constantly scouring the country, taking some of our friends to prison, threatening others, and filling the community with alarm.

The author said soldiers, apparently from Union City, threatened him and his family: "Families are leaving that section daily, being unable to bear the annoyance, and powerless to defend themselves against the cowardly brutality of the secessionists." On his trek east three other Unionist families had overtaken him. A young man with them said "parties were going through Hickman county and forcing men to swear allegiance to the Southern Confederacy." The letter writer added that "about the time I left, many families of Shelby, Spencer, and Nelson Counties were preparing to leave, being unable to find protection or safety. We left our stock, crops, furniture, and all, having no time to dispose of or secure them." The correspondent also claimed that other refugees told him "there were some 3,000 or 4,000 Tennessee troops encamped near Columbus, Ky., where they have been for some four or five days before."[20]

If there were troops at Columbus, then they would have been what was left of Tilghman's state guard contingent. In any event, on August 17, the *Journal* published a lament from a Paducah Unionist that referred to the pre-election shootout in Milburn. He claimed such secessionist-provoked "excitement" had depressed the Union vote. The author wrote that after the gunplay, "many exaggerated tales were told and circulated all over the country in reference to the matter to the great injury to the Union party in this region." He said Wickliffe "telegraphed all over the country that Gen. Prentiss . . . intended sending troops into Kentucky and restor[ing] some two or three of the parties engaged to their homes. By these means and other similar ones the excitement was kept up until after the election." He added that "a great many threats were made against families in Milburn and vicinity on account of their Union sentiments, which caused some thirty families to move to Illinois." Thus, Union supporters had "almost come to the conclusion that they have no Government to protect them."[21]

In Paducah, the secessionists ran five hundred citizens out of town, according to the letter. Before Bickley left, he evidently organized or inspired a Paducah branch of the Knights of the Golden Circle, according to the Unionist who wrote the *Journal.* The Paducah group was headed by a "Committee of Thirteen," which had "inaugurated an independent police, numbering one hundred and seventy-five, twenty-five of them on watch every night." Additionally, he mentioned the seizure of the *Cheney* at Columbus by Confederate "rogues" from Mobile. He presumed that they "had nothing to steal down South now." He predicted a battle at Bird's Point, Missouri, opposite Cairo, and protested that "the Union men here are now *completely* overpowered; they are watched with the eyes of hawks and when the 'seceshers' hear anything they think will do to tell, they inform the Committee of Thirteen . . . whose duty it is to attend to his or their case, as it may be." The author concluded with the story of yet another alleged atrocity, this one in Columbus: "Some few days ago three Germans were mobbed . . . one of them has since died. They were from New Orleans on their way North, molesting no one, only getting from the South as easy as possible."[22]

Evidently, the Knights were also active elsewhere in the Purchase. On July 27, about twenty of them left north Graves County for Clarksville, Tennessee, there to join Bickley. Another group of about the same size from "the same neighborhood" was expected to follow, "all on horseback."[23]

On August 20, the *Journal* ran a long article alleging months of multiple misdeeds against the Union and its supporters in western Kentucky, notably in the Purchase. "Rarely has such a catalogue of outrages and crimes been committed in so small a territory and in so short a time as that committed in the First District . . . during the last few months," the paper maintained, then presented its indictment. The *Journal* cited the usual suspects, including Representative Burnett and a trio of Purchase perpetrators—Oscar Turner, Albert P. Thompson, and George W. Silvertooth. After Breckinridge lost the presidential election, they and others, including erstwhile Bell and Douglas men, worked in vain for a Confederate Kentucky. The *Journal* said the legislature's refusal to put Kentucky out of the Union was followed by "a system of terror, aided by the State Guard." The paper recalled the stolen muskets and cannons and the Mayfield convention, whose "avowed purpose" was to forge "a military alliance with Tennessee and of finally seceding from Kentucky and going into the Confederacy, despite the will of Kentucky." The "project met with much favor in the convention, which was said to be by far the largest ever assembled in the district; but it was not finally carried." The *Journal* denounced the district's refusal to fully participate in the border slave state convention election and the intimidation of citizens who wanted to vote the Union ticket. The paper lamented "this full spirit of secessionism" that gripped Paducah, which was under the sway of the KCG group, "a committee of lawless, irresponsible men headed by Maj. Woods, White Fowler and Uliss Milliken." Woods and company "insulted and outraged whomsoever they pleased, even offering violence to and driving from town Union men who were not citizens but were only casually there on business, and ordering off old citizens of the town, &c." The *Journal* claimed wealthy and influential secessionists "would condemn this in private by words, but none *took the necessary steps to prevent it,* therefore the whole party must be held responsible."[24]

One of the out-of-towners was Judge Williams of Mayfield. He "was on one occasion threatened by a serious excitement growing out of a most wanton falsehood published by a secession Doctor of the name of McFarlan." The paper said Williams had boarded the Cairo mail packet merely to post a letter to the Union Democratic Central Committee in Louisville. McFarlan claimed he heard Williams say he was taking the boat to Cairo to bring back Prentiss and his soldiers. As a result, a crowd gathered at the wharf boat to stop him. "His returning from the packet saved him from violence or insult, for he knew nothing of this matter until after his return from the boat and after the excitement had subsided." Had Williams tried to go with the boat, "he would most likely have been detained by force."[25]

Next, the *Journal* maligned the Marshall County vigilante organization as "most scandalous and unlawful." The paper said the group was headed by "a Dr. Irvan, one of the most violent and lawless men in the country. Associated with him, is a Mr. Palmer, a New Englander by birth and education and a lawyer by profession, but quite lawless by practice." The committee judged "who are good citizens and who are not" and threatened and ordered to leave "some of the oldest and best citizens of the county because of their Union sentiments." The *Journal* condemned a similar committee in Calloway County. Headquartered in Murray, its leaders included "a violent, lawless secession Doctor of the name of Boggs. In the work of wickedness, this committee has far outstripped its compeer of Marshall County." The *Journal* charged that the vigilantes ordered a Mr. Jones, a Calloway native, to leave after he refused to join a company of Confederate volunteers heading for Camp Boone. Jones hesitated but did clear out. Nonetheless, Jerry and John Span, Arch Bogard, and Arch Miller tracked him down and took him to the Rebel camp at Union City. When the Confederates refused to relieve the Calloway countians of their captive, the quartet took him back to Kentucky. Near Boydsville, on the state line in Graves County, "he was shot in three places and left to die in the road." Jones managed to drag himself to a nearby creek, "where he got water and was found by a neighbor; he lingered two days and died, leaving a widow and two small children, entirely penniless, to mourn his death." On August 3, the *Journal* published a slightly different version of Jones's murder. That story said that the secessionists ordered two pro-Union brothers named Jones to leave. They were "the sons of a Methodist preacher, obscure, but honest and respectable." The siblings went to a relative in Tennessee, but "several neighbors, among them a Mr. Spear, followed, forcibly seized the elder Jones, and took him to . . . Union City." Brigadier General Benjamin F. Cheatham "would have nothing to do with" the Kentucky Unionist. "But the poor fellow only got a short distance from the encampment before he was shot through the head. He leaves his wife and two small penniless orphan children dependent on him for support."[26]

In addition, the August 20 *Journal* reported the lynching of Picket but added that he was murdered while he was fishing on a Saturday evening. "In Graves County there has been talk of hanging Union men often, as we are informed," the paper said. In Mayfield, a pro-Union merchant was almost mobbed when he ordered some pistols for his friends, according to the *Journal.* "When his pistols arrived, and it became known, a Mr. Cargill, late the census taker for Graves county, but now a Lieutenant in a company at Camp Boon [*sic*], being home on furlough, tried to raise a mob to kill the merchant and take the pistols because they were bought for Union men." The *Journal* charged that many Graves County citizens wanted King to take the state arms at Mayfield: "Prominent secessionists both in Mayfield and in the county not only encouraged this but assisted in the matter." The paper named J. M. Coulter, *Yeoman* editor C. C. Coulter, and R. T. Waller. The trio, together with many others, told Wood they would resist turning over the muskets and cannons to him "even should the Tennessee authorities surrender those [weapons] in their possession." The *Journal* named more purported perpetrators of the gun grab: "Kingman, another of the lawless New England lawyers in that region, Josiah Parker, Samuel Lundrun [likely Landrum] and Dr. Alexander." The paper claimed "companies had been formed without authority of law and put in possession of the weapons. These men keep up a regular guard at the State line depot on the railroad to prevent the arms, taken to Tennessee, from being returned to the arsenal at Frankfort, if surrendered to Col. Wood." In addition, the paper condemned the capture of the *Cheney* at Columbus, characterizing the local men who helped the Rebels—Watson Rennick, Washington Gray, and Mr. Dowdy—as a group of "irresponsible, lawless revolutionists." Further, the *Journal* elaborated on the seizure of the steamer *Pocahontas* in early August. The steamboat had chugged up the Tennessee River to Pine Bluff in Calloway County for a load of tobacco. The crew had loaded "several hogsheads" when the *W. B. Terry,* a cannon-armed steamer, suddenly appeared, pirated the tobacco and other freight aboard the *Pocahantas,* and carried the booty to Tennessee. Most of the *Terry*'s owners were from Paducah.[27]

Meanwhile, according to the *Journal,* Unionists, too, were in peril in the section where Hickman, Ballard, and Graves Counties joined. Here, Ephraim

Sherfield was boss of "a company of lawless desperadoes, organized, officered and armed with guns and large knives, similar to bowies, calling themselves Rangers." Sherfield's lieutenants were "his son, and two sons-in-law, John and Halcom Jackson, all men of bad and lawless characters." The paper said Sherfield was so bad that when he was called to testify as a witness in Hickman circuit court, "a large number of his neighbors and acquaintances on their oath said that his moral character was such that he was not entitled to credit on oath." The paper said the Rangers terrorized Unionists at night. "They visited on two occasions the house of Captain Pugh who, having had notice, had left his dwelling." Sherfield's band and others "have spread such terror in that section that Capt. Pugh and some fifteen families have actually left their crops, stock, and property" and taken "what little they could carry in their wagons, and are now on their way to places of safety." The refugees fled to "those counties in the middle of the state whence they emigrated. Several of the families are returning to Shelby County."[28]

Besides in Milburn, gun battles between Unionists and secessionists erupted in Dublin and Pryorsburg, both in Graves County. In Dublin, one secessionist was killed and a pair wounded; at Milburn, "one secessionist was killed and one badly wounded, and one Union man seriously wounded." In Pryorsburg, middle-aged Jerry Pryor shot to death "an old man of the name of Tucker." A few days later, a young man named Clusterman, a Rebel soldier at Union City, gunned down Pryor. Everybody involved in the Pryorsburg fight was a secessionist, according to the *Journal.*[29]

The paper could not resist adding one more "great outrage," telling its readers that "a Union man and merchant at Mayfield, who has also a branch at Feliciana, had some articles shipped from his establishment at the latter to the former place by railroad." The goods included a small keg of powder and lead bars. "But the secession Conductor, named Linn, would not deliver the powder and lead to Mayfield; he carried it on to Paducah where White Fowler and his confederates seized it." The paper claimed Linn was the conductor "who ran the train down from the State line at the hour of midnight and carried off the stolen guns taken from Mayfield." The *Journal* warned, "It would be well for the road that this Conductor should be immediately discharged, and it would be well for the authorities of Paducah to put an end to this committee of Wood [Woods?], Fowler, and Milliken, for, if there is not enough morality and power about Paducah to do this, it will be sought and found elsewhere."[30]

Despite the Unionists' suffering, the paper begged them not to forsake the Purchase: "Bide your time yet a little longer, you will soon have the omnipotent power of your State for your protection." The *Journal* added that

Union sympathizers need not fear that the First District would secede from the state after all: "Kentucky will maintain at every hazard and under every difficulty the integrity of her territorial limits, and her fair proportions." The paper admitted "it may cost money, it may cost trouble, it may cost blood, but, no matter what it may cost, she will maintain the supremacy of her constitution over her whole territory and protect her loyal citizens though it take one, five, ten, twenty, thirty, yea fifty thousand armed soldiers." The *Journal* labeled the First District "the infected district of Kentucky" and declared "a vast change must be wrought there, and that right speedily."[31]

Meanwhile, before the election, Unionists, including navy lieutenant William O. Nelson of Maysville, had made plans to start a training camp for Union volunteers in Kentucky, but they waited to begin military instruction until after the canvass. The recruit depot was named Camp Dick Robinson, after the owner of the Garrard County farm where it was sited. Magoffin protested to Lincoln that the camp was a violation of Kentucky neutrality, but it remained open, attracting volunteers from Kentucky and Unionist eastern Tennessee.[32]

From western Kentucky Edward I. Bullock of Columbus also denounced Camp Dick Robinson in a long letter to the *Courier* published on August 26. "I speak what I do know when I say that just as sure as God liveth, unless the force now threatening Cumberland Gap and East Tennessee is speedily dispersed, just so certain will there be raised and put into the field an equal force in Southern Kentucky," he warned. "The thing is inevitable. No constraints of law, no consideration of personal consequences can prevent it." Bullock said his intent was not to frighten his friends elsewhere in Kentucky. Rather, he wished "in sober seriousness to arrest now at the threshold, and prevent, if possible, the direst of all calamities, a civil war in Kentucky."[33]

After the state elections, secessionists like Bullock had good reason to fear the state might finally swing behind the Union war effort. Heretofore, the Southern Rights Party had denounced neutrality in no uncertain terms. Now, desperate to forestall Kentucky's outright Unionism, they embraced neutrality. If Kentucky would not side with the South against the North, the state could at least stay out of the war, they reasoned. The legislature was to meet on September 2. Thus, starting in August, the Southern Rights Party sponsored peace or neutrality gatherings across the state. The secessionists-turned-neutralists hoped to sway the Unionist majority in the General Assembly to stay the nonaligned course. Many of the meetings resolved to send delegates to a Southern Rights peace convention called for in Frankfort on September 10. Like the March Southern Rights conclave, the peace convention was supposed to impress lawmakers.[34]

The *Louisville Democrat,* feeling less charitable toward the Purchase, declared that the Southern Rights men were anything but peaceful and neutral. On August 22, the paper said three pro-Union families whom secessionists had run out of Hickman County had arrived in Louisville. The exiles were on their way to Oldham and Shelby Counties. "They left their homes with such articles as they could bring, leaving behind their farms and crops," the paper said. "They report that about fifty families left the county at the same time they did." The *Democrat* editorialized, "This is the freedom and toleration of the white rag peace party of Kentucky, where they obtain a decided majority." The paper added that two sons of one of the émigrés had been sent away the night before the family left so he could avoid being forced into the Confederate army.[35]

On August 24, more than peace and neutrality seemed to be on the minds of citizens who gathered in a mass meeting in Cadiz, Burnett's hometown. They hinted anew at regional secession. The Trigg countians approved a resolution calling on western Kentuckians to meet in Mayfield again in September, "to take into consideration our most effective means of securing our rights as neutrals in the war," according to the *Journal.* The "people of Trigg County" also vowed "that we will, individually and collectively, resist the collection of the direct tax levied by the last Congress, to aid in defraying the expenses of the war now being waged by the North against the South." One must wonder if the Trigg County Southern Rights men had an ulterior motive for another meeting in Mayfield. Did they plan to revisit the idea of regional secession? Burnett was still an avid disunionist. On August 29, he gave a lengthy speech to a crowd in southern Christian County, Trigg's neighbor to the east. Standing on a platform "decorated with two big Confederate flags," Burnett hailed South Carolina "as a bright pattern of heroism, and denounced Union men as Lincoln's dogs." Burnett counseled armed resistance to the war tax "if necessary," declaimed Kentucky's Union leaders as hypocrites and traitors of the worst sort, "abused the United States Government in the most ferocious terms," and wished the Rebels had annihilated the Union army at the battle of Bull Run. At the same time, the congressman said "all the affections of his heart were centered in Jeff Davis' government." Burnett, too, vilified German immigrants, many of whom were conspicuously antislavery. The congressman said he would not live in the Confederacy "unless foreigners were forever excluded from its borders." It was all too much for the state's top Union paper, which cut loose on the Purchase hero. The *Journal* asked, "is it not passing strange that this Congressman who blusters and raves like a bedlamite against the Lincoln Government, as he calls it, should go to the Lincoln Congress and pocket Lincoln gold? Is it not strange that this flaming secessionist has no scruples whatever of making his living off Lincoln's treasury?" The paper said the traitor and rebel Burnett was "a standing monument of the astonishing clemency and tolerance of the American government." The *Journal* said the government should not tolerate his "monstrous conduct" but invited Burnett to decamp "to the Confederacy, which he extols as the most humane and free [government] upon the earth, and which the unanimous voice of the world brands as the most tyrannical in the history of despotism." Among the Rebels, the paper added, "he may console himself with the reflection that no one can retort by calling him a dog, for he is 'A creature / Whom 'twere base flattery to call a dog.'" Likewise, Burnett could "pride himself in the consciousness that although he may not wear a dog's collar, he has brass enough in his impudent forehead to furnish a brace of collars for all the dogs in creation." The *Journal* concluded by branding him a "Kentucky Thersites," who was "admirably qualified for the office of Blackguard Extraordinary and Scullion Plenipotentiary to the Court of Jeff Davis, for his brain is as feeble as his lungs are forcible and his mouth is as dirty as a den of skunks."[36]

In any event, more than a few leaders of the Mayfield convention would show up the Frankfort peace conference. Several, too, would help Burnett and others organize a rump pro-Confederate government at Russellville in October and November. Given all that, it is hard to believe the Trigg countians wanted to meet at Mayfield just to protect their rights as neutrals. It will be recalled that delegates at the May Mayfield convention had rejected regional secession because they were convinced all of Kentucky was bound to join the Confederacy. By August, it was obvious that the Bluegrass State was staying under the Stars and Stripes and edging closer to getting into the war on the Yankee side.

At any rate, the Murray peace meeting, held on August 26, called for an end "to this unjust war," decried the federal war tax, and resolved "never to be shot or bayoneted into a love of the Union in violation of the Constitution." The crowd also resolved to send Senator Irvan and newly elected Representative Matthewson to the Frankfort convention. The meeting, chaired by Thomas M. Jones with Peter S. Hamlin as secretary, also passed resolutions praising Kentucky senators Breckinridge and Lazarus W. Powell, as well as Representative Burnett. Too, the meeting adopted a resolution thanking Representative Clement Vallandigham of Ohio and Senator Jesse D. Bright of Indiana "and other such Northern patriots" for their pro-southern efforts in Congress. Matthewson, Hamlin, Jones, and F. W. Dodd, who helped draft resolutions for the meeting, were part of the county's delegation to the Russellville convention.[37]

The Yankees at Cairo doubtless would have questioned the patriotism of the antiwar and anti-Lincoln Vallandigham and Bright, who were scorned as "Copperheads" in the North. They certainly disbelieved the fealty of the Purchase. Perhaps encouraged by the state elections, if not the results in the Purchase, the Union military brass became bolder toward deep western Kentucky, especially the Paducah-based *Terry* and its crew of pirates who stole the tobacco off the *Pocahantas*. Colonel Oglesby, who had succeeded Brigadier General Prentiss as post commander, decided to send the wooden gunboat *Lexington,* skippered by Commander R. N. Stembel, to Paducah to seize the *Terry,* the little steamer "employed in the rebel trade and carrying their flag." To make sure the Yankee tars got the right boat, Oglesby had Stembel carry a man who could identify the *Terry.* Secrecy was evidently on the colonel's mind; instead of sending Stembel written orders, Oglesby, at midnight on August 21, told Stembel to go get the *Terry.* Stembel arrived at 7:03 a.m. on August 22, "ran alongside of her, cut her out, made her fast to the Lexington, and immediately returned to" Cairo. Stembel said he "was not opposed in the performance of this duty by either the citizens of Paducah or the officers and crew of the Terry, for the latter, evidently suspecting my object, left the boat hastily, with such articles of clothing as were at hand." Stembel was unsuccessful in capturing any of the purported pirates. Thus the *Terry*'s crew was able to even the score quickly by commandeering the *Samuel Orr,* the regular Paducah-to-Evansville, Indiana, mail steamer. Captain W. H. McClurg, three crewmen, and a pair of lawyers claimed "the actors in the seizure were Captain Johnson, late commander of the steamboat W. B. Terry, White Fowler, A. M. Winston, and about 40 or 50 other persons, we believe all citizens of Paducah." They added that "several shots were fired by the assailants, wounding two persons." McClurg and the others protested that "we were all of us hurriedly driven from the boat, without allowing us (except in one or two instances) the privilege of bringing away our clothing or baggage." They conceded "that some of the leading citizens of the town were loud in their condemnations of this act, but no measures were taken, as far as we know, to prevent it." They said the *Orr,* whose principal owners were from Evansville, was new and worth about $15,000 and carried a mixed cargo they valued at approximately $10,000. Oglesby wrote Fremont that he "had indisputable proof, which an examination of papers found on board confirms, that [the *Terry*] . . . was running in the employment of the Confederate states." He valued the vessel and its furniture at $3,000 but added that "to the Confederates three times that sum will not compensate the loss." Oglesby confessed he did not know what else to do with the *Terry* legally. Yet he planned to use the boat "if necessary to do so." He said the *Terry*'s capture had thrown Paducah into "confusion" and suggested Magoffin "may become indignant." Oglesby said the subsequent seizure of the *Samuel Orr* was "more vindictive than sensible, as they thus destroy the last means of illicit trade with the border States north of the Ohio." The *Orr*'s captors evidently ran the vessel up the Tennessee because Oglesby concluded with the wish that he could go ascend the river and "make the reprisal." Fremont did not grant permission. But soon enough, Paducah would be in Yankee hands.[38]

Paducah secessionists feared another unwelcome visit by the Union navy. As a result, a delegation of Confederate sympathizers reportedly made haste to Union City, seeing firepower, including a trio of sixty-four-pounder guns, according to C. D. Millar, Cairo correspondent of the *Cincinnati Commercial.* The *Courier* quoted Millar's stern warning that before "the . . . snake battery is planted, our gunboats will anchor in front of the city, and give the citizens of that place sixty minutes (commonly called one hour) to pay for the steamer Sam'l J. Orr and her cargo." He said "loyal citizens (d—n the secesh!)" would be invited to seek refuge aboard the vessels. "If the demand is not fully complied with to the dead letter, Paducah *must sink to rise no more!*" He claimed the army and navy brass at Cairo "will execute the above programme unless Gov. Magoffin insures the immediate release and return of the stolen steamer, together with her cargo." Not surprisingly, the *Courier* took the Yankees to task and added a challenge to the *Journal:* "The infamous creatures threaten to demolish Paducah, damning the Secessionists, and say the town must sink to rise no more. Can't the editors of the Louisville Journal throw a few expletives at the heads of the Cairo 'ruffians,' ain't they 'excited by infernal passions' to thus, in a spirit of 'anarchy,' threaten to destroy a whole town[?]" The *Courier* also quoted a *Missouri Democrat* story about the *Terry-Orr* affair, which described the group that grabbed the *Orr* as "a party of about fifty Secessionists," who were armed with "rifles, pistols and bowie knives." Nonetheless, "the crew and passengers were kindly treated by many of the citizens . . . who expressed great regret at the occurrence, and said that the boat should be brought back but there is little hope of any such thing taking place." Indeed, the newspaper said the secessionists ran the *Orr* up the Tennessee River. Likewise, crews took the *Eastport,* the *Sam Kirkman,* and the *Dunbar* upriver to forestall their capture. Fowler owned the *Eastport* and was part owner of the *Dunbar.* The *Dunbar*'s other owners were Unionists who were dismayed with its seizure. Likewise, pro-Union Captain J. V. Throop of the *Kirkman,* which was partly owned by Paducah men, "protested against her seizure." In addition, the story reported that the *Diadem* and other boats had stopped at Evansville awaiting a gunboat escort. The correspondent said "the rebels" were bringing a number of sixty-four-pounders from Columbus to Paducah, where they intended to use the big guns to block the Ohio and the mouth of the Tennessee River. The paper said Paducah was "a grand strategic point with the rebels and should be closely watched by the Federal Government." The *Democrat* story raises more interesting questions about Columbus. Were the big guns there, and if so, when were they brought to Columbus? Were there Confederate soldiers at Columbus, or by "rebels" did the correspondent mean state guard troops?[39]

Meanwhile, back in Evansville, McClurg and other *Orr* crewmen told the *Evansville Journal* about their brush with the Paducah pirates, who fired "several pistol shots" and wounded a man. In the story, republished in the *Louisville Journal,* the Orr's clerk said the crowd numbered close to one hundred men, who "yelled and screeched like a pack of ravenous wolves." "A ruffian" pulled a pistol and threatened to shoot him, but "a Mr. McConnell" talked him out of it. The mail agent also had a narrow escape from "several of the pirates" who were "brandishing knives and pistols about his head." He ran, hid in the pantry, and somehow managed to sneak ashore. But the mob caught and kidnapped two African American firemen who were "likely to end their days on a cotton plantation," according to the *Journal.* McClurg confessed that his suspicions were aroused when the *Orr* steamed into Paducah, and he spotted the *Eastport* towing the *Dunbar* up the Tennessee. He continued his appointed mail rounds because the Fowlers, who were subcontractors for the Paducah-to-Evansville mail route, had "pledged their honor that no harm should overtake the Orr while in" Paducah. When he saw an unusually large crowd at the town landing and on the wharf boat, McClurg "watched carefully, expecting, if any evil designs were contemplated against his boat, some friend would have him a warning signal." Seeing no such signal, he decided to land. McClurg quickly discovered there were no friends in the crowd, only enemies intent on stealing his boat. The *Orr* had barely touched land "before several men sprang on her lower deck." White Fowler was among them; he climbed the stairs to the hurricane roof, where he found McClurg, who asked him "what was the excitement." Fowler replied "nothing" and asked the captain what cargo he had for Paducah. McClurg told him and then proceeded to dock the *Orr* at the wharf. When a crowd boarded the vessel, Fowler "drew a pistol, cocked it, and presenting it at McClurg's head, told him he was a prisoner." McClurg replied that he was unarmed and thus "could make no resistance." Fowler ordered the captain to go ashore, "or he would blow his brains out." After McClurg complied, a "pirate" named Johnson spotted a man untying the *Orr* from the wharf boat. Believing the man was fastening the rope, Johnson fired, wounding him. "Fowler rang the bell immediately, and the boat shoved out with the greater part of the Orr's crew still on board." Fowler dropped them off—many of them "in their shirtsleeves"—a mile up the Tennessee while the "highwaymen" helped themselves to the crew's clothes. White Fowler deviated from the customary mail run: he delivered the mail and the *Orr* into "the hands of the authorities of the Southern Confederacy." The *Journal* also scorned Captain Gus Fowler for his complicity in the "highway robbery." He had always been welcomed in Evansville "in the most kind and friendly manner" and had repeatedly assured the *Orr*'s officers that they "would not be interrupted or mistreated" in Paducah. Yet he was seen aboard the *Dunbar* when it passed the *Orr*, and "he failed to give the latter a single hint or warning as to the danger that threatened her." Back in Evansville, McClurg suffered insult added to injury over a rumor that he and his officers were in cahoots with the Fowlers. According to the tale, they had agreed to let the mob have the *Orr* knowing the Rebels would wind up with the vessel. McClurg accused Phy. D. Viets, agent of the steamer *Charley Bowen*, of "circulating reports derogatory to the loyalty of the officers and owners of the *Samuel Orr*," and the captain "beat him most terribly." The Evansville paper said it did not know if the rumors were true but editorialized that "those who witnessed the occurrence assert that the punishment was altogether disproportionate to the alleged offence, and reflects no credit upon Mr. McClurg, who is, physically, altogether superior to Mr. Viets."[40]

The McClurg-Viets fisticuffs probably went unnoticed at Fremont's headquarters in St. Louis. The *Terry-Orr* affair did not. On August 25, Fremont wrote Adjutant General Lorenzo Thomas in Washington that "events have thus transpired clearly indicating the complicity of citizens of Kentucky with the rebel forces, and indicating the impracticability of carrying on operations in that direction without involving the Kentucky shore." Fremont added that Oglesby had telegraphed him that on August 26, he would receive a delegation from Governor Magoffin and had "furnished them a safeguard."[41]

The delegation was coming to protest more than the *Terry*'s capture. Also on August 22, a Yankee force from Cairo, said to comprise "a thousand armed horsemen," had crossed over to Ballard County, arrested two citizens, and taken them to back to their base. This incident, coupled with the capture of the *Terry*, convinced pro-Confederate Paducah residents that a full-scale invasion from Cairo was imminent. Consequently, soon after the *Lexington* left with the *Terry* in tow, the secessionists convened a mass meeting. The citizens approved resolutions protesting the arrest of the Ballard countians and the seizure of the *Terry* and demanding Kentucky's "protection and redress for such outrages." If the state "could not, or would not, afford it," then the people "would feel compelled, in self defense, to call on the Tennessee troops at Union City for aid."[42]

It seems likely that the mass meeting included members of the newly organized Paducah branch of the Memphis steamboat association. Paducah captains, clerks, and engineers had joined in protest of the Cairo blockade against suspected Confederate cargoes and resolved "to a man to fully stand up to Southern Rights." In addition, the gathering resolved to advance "Southern interests" and "neither employ nor run with men known to be hostile to the South." They agreed to exclude from their organization "all except men known to be devoted to the South." The meeting was more proof that the Purchase was continuing to look to Tennessee for help, the same idea reflected in the Mayfield convention.[43]

Though the steamboat men complained about the Yankees interdicting river shipments at Cairo, the McCracken County sheriff reputedly "attacked and emptied" the *Pocahontas* of most of its cargo, according to the *Louisville Daily Journal.* En route to St. Louis, the boat called at Paducah. "The Pocahontas then went on to Cairo with only fifty barrels of lime. The cargo consisted of bacon, &c, in which large quantities of contraband goods were packed." At about the same time, Union authorities in Evansville confiscated Paducah-bound cargo aboard the *Emma Duncan.* The goods included "fifty bags of coffee, twenty casks of bacon, twenty barrels of whisky, with a large lot of soda, candles, soap, salt, pork, &c." The freight was to be kept "until some arrangements are made about the return of the steamer *Samuel Orr* and her cargo." Rumors continued to fly about Confederate military aid for Paducah. When the *John Gault* called at Paducah, its officers said they heard the citizens had asked for a cannon from Union City. A Yankee gunboat had escorted the *Belle Creole* past Paducah on August 23, the *Journal* reported. "We presume the gunboats will cruise in the vicinity of Paducah and protect passing boats. . . . The blockade of Paducah and the Tennessee river is complete."[44]

Meanwhile, Senator Johnson, representing Magoffin, reached Oglesby's headquarters on August 25. Doubtless Oglesby knew Johnson was a secessionist. In any event, the men had been released, but the senator failed to secure the return of the *Terry.* Likewise, the *Orr* remained in Confederate waters, apparently at Fort Henry on the Tennessee River. Oglesby told the Kentuckian that he had dispatched the troops to Ballard County because he saw an unusually large number of men on the Ballard shore across from Cairo. He took them for Confederate troops or engineers "sketching a profile of the grounds, with a view to its occupation for military purposes." Oglesby put his force at a mere "company, or squad, of men." As it turned out, the crowd had gathered in anticipation of watching a battle; they had heard the booming of cannon, apparently practice firing. All fled but the two men who were arrested and taken to Cairo. Both captives admitted they were secessionists but were turned loose after Ballard County judge Charles S. Marshall, a Unionist, came to Cairo and vouched for them as "good, law-abiding citizens."[45]

Three days after Johnson's visit to Cairo, Fremont appointed an obscure, cigar-smoking, most unmilitary-appearing brigadier general of Illinois volunteers named Ulysses S. Grant to the command of the federal forces at Cape Girardeau, Missouri. Fremont made it plain what he ultimately wanted Grant to do: "occupy Columbus, Ky., as soon as possible." On September 2, a Union force led by Colonel G. Waagner was at Belmont, Missouri, opposite Columbus. "The rebels fly the secession flag from a lofty pole in the center of the village in defiance of our gunboats," the colonel reported to Fremont. Waagner also wanted to know what he was to do with Columbus, Hickman, and New Madrid, Missouri. That night, Oglesby sent a steamboat to Belmont to communicate with Waagner. From his headquarters in Cairo, Oglesby spotted in the sky above Kentucky "rockets and balloons, small, announcing to some other post the coming and return of the steamer." Presumably, the signalers were Rebel soldiers or secessionist citizens.[46]

Downriver at Memphis, a September 2 meeting of Kentuckians living in Bluff City, probably including Purchase expatriates, urged the creation of a military force—"a Kentucky legion"—comprised of Bluegrass State natives residing in the Confederacy. They also organized a committee to compose an address entreating all former Kentuckians in the seceded states to unite with them "in the redemption of Kentucky from the toils of Federal power and northern abolitionism."[47]

At the very moment the Kentucky expatriates were issuing their call to arms, the Confederate army was poised to invade Kentucky. On September 1, Polk wrote Magoffin, "I think it of the greatest consequence to the Southern cause in Kentucky or elsewhere that I should be ahead of the enemy in occupying Columbus and Paducah." Consequently, Polk ordered Pillow, at New Madrid, Missouri, to take Columbus. On the night of September 3, he moved upriver to Hickman. Pillow stopped in deference to the Union force at Belmont, which Grant ordered withdrawn on September 4. Pillow arrived in Columbus the same day.[48]

Also on September 4, the gunboats *Tyler* and *Lexington* went looking for the Confederates. At Hickman, the Union vessels dueled with a Confederate gunboat. "The boat fired a shot at us, which we replied; a number of tents extending for half a mile were upon the shore fronting the river," Commander John Rodgers, the *Tyler*'s skipper, reported to Fremont. "When three or four shots had been exchanged a battery on shore fired several guns, then another battery opened upon us." After swapping about twenty shots with the Rebel gunboat, the Union vessels retired.[49]

On September 4, too, Grant moved his headquarters from Cape Girardeau to Cairo. Predictably, the *Appeal* was unimpressed: "Gen. Prentiss, who has been commanding the Cairo suckers, it seems, has become tired of fighting these ferocious gallinippers that sport in that delicious region, and has accordingly thrown up the sponge and quit the trade. He is succeeded by some unknown Hessian, responding to the name of Grant." In a few months, that "Hessian" would have his headquarters in Memphis.[50]

Grant's arrival in Paducah sealed Paducah's fate. A man who said he was a scout for Fremont reported to Grant with the latest news from Rebel-occupied Columbus. The scout said Confederate troops were on the way to Paducah or were preparing to march on the city. Losing no time, Grant decided to beat the enemy to "the Charleston of Kentucky." He telegraphed Fremont that he was ready to move on Paducah unless he received orders to the contrary.[51] Grant said he did not want to arrive before daybreak, so he did not start until 10:30 p.m. on September 5. His flotilla consisted of a pair of gunboats and a trio of transports carrying the Ninth and Twelfth Illinois Infantry Regiments and a four-gun field artillery battery. Commodore Andrew H. Foote of the US Navy accompanied Grant, thus beginning an interservice partnership that won laurels for both commanders. Grant's soldiers and Foote's sailors would team up to capture Forts Henry and Donelson in Tennessee in February 1862, twin blows that would compel the Confederates to give up Kentucky and open the way for a Yankee invasion of the Rebel interior.[52]

That invasion started in Paducah, most of whose citizens had hoped that their city might become a springboard for military operations in the opposite direction. From the start of the secession crisis, or at least until after Fort Sumter, the city had shown deep Confederate colors. Paducah and McCracken County had voted secessionist in the August state election; the *Terry-Orr* affair was more evidence that the McCracken County seat really was "the Charleston of Kentucky." But the Bluegrass State's "Charleston" was about to become a Yankee-ruled city for the rest of the Civil War. History would be kind to Grant, though he was never popular in Paducah. He was the Civil War's most successful combat commander and ended up in the White House. On the other hand, almost all local historians have been decidedly unkind to an officer who came with Grant. They have made him out to be the meanest man who ever trod Purchase soil. He was Brigadier General Eleazer A. Paine, commander of the Ninth Illinois.

6

"Abolition Invaders" and Rebel Deliverers

"It was the best of times, it was the worst of times"; these are the oft-quoted opening words of *A Tale of Two Cities,* Charles Dickens's famous novel set in London and Paris during the French Revolution. The prose might also apply to the Jackson Purchase in September 1861. It was the best of times for most citizens of Hickman and Columbus and other Rebel-run territory in the region. They were overjoyed with the advent of soldiers they saw as their salvation from the "abolitionist" army at Cairo. On the other hand, the secessionist majority in Paducah and its environs endured their worst of times, the arrival of Grant and his troops.

Grant reached Paducah at 8:30 a.m. on September 6 with the Ninth and Twelfth Illinois Infantry Regiments and a four-gun battery of light artillery, "a magnificent show of offensive initiative." The general, an eyewitness later recalled, stepped ashore puffing on "a big cigar and . . . dressed in regulation military uniform with epaulets as the only distinguishing mark." Grant's advent finished off what was left of Kentucky's always fragile neutrality. Of course, neutrality was never popular in Paducah. For weeks, most residents of the city had pined for a Confederate Kentucky, and they fervently hoped the Rebel army would get to town ahead of the "abolition invaders." Officially, Paducah was part of a loyal state, but Grant knew he was in enemy territory.[1]

"Found numerous secession flags flying over the city, and the citizens in anticipation of the approach of the rebel army, which was reliably reported 3,800 strong 16 miles distant," the general wrote in his official report of Paducah's capture. His intelligence was faulty; the Rebels had not left Columbus. But Grant almost bagged a Confederate bigwig, Brigadier General Tilghman. Yankee gunboat sailors under Grant's command would snare him soon enough; Tilghman would surrender Fort Henry to Commodore Andrew H. Foote, chief of the bluejackets, on February 6, 1862. Grant said Tilghman, his staff, and a recruiting major, with a company of volunteers from Paducah, escaped on a train, "taking with them all the rolling stock." But Grant must have been relieved that he did not have to contend with Pillow's army. "I landed the troops and took possession of the city without firing a gun," he wrote. When Grant's troops fanned out from their transport boats, some women jeered, taunting them as "abolition invaders" while "repeatedly cheering for Jeff. Davis and the Confederate States." Other citizens fled "panic-stricken to sections south and west of the city."[2]

Indeed, most Paducah residents, the general recalled, were badly frightened: "When the National troops entered the town the citizens were taken by surprise. I never after saw such consternation depicted on the faces of the people. Men, women and children came out of their doors looking pale and frightened at the presence of the invader. They were expecting rebel troops that day." Grant aimed to reassure the citizens that if they behaved he would do them no harm. So he proceeded to the southeast corner of First Street and Broadway and read an official occupation proclamation. Because few townsfolk heard him, Grant summoned Mayor Sauner, handed His Honor the proclamation, and told him to publish it. Sauner obeyed, but the document—a slip of white paper, seven by ten inches—was so hastily produced that the printer used three different typefaces:[3]

> To the Citizens of Paducah:
> I have come among you not as an enemy, but as your fellow citizen; not to maltreat or annoy you, but to respect and enforce the rights of all loyal citizens. An enemy, in rebellion against our common government, has taken possession of and planted his guns on the soil of Kentucky, and fired upon you. Columbus and Hickman are in his hands. He is moving upon your city. I am here to defend you against the enemy, to assist the authority and sovereignty of your government. I have nothing to do with opinions, and shall deal only with armed rebellion and its aiders and abettors. You can pursue your usual avocations without fear. The strong arm of the government is here to protect its friends and punish its enemies. Whenever it is manifest that you are able to defend yourself and maintain the authority of the government, and protect the rights of citizens, I shall withdraw my command.

Evidently, Grant's offer of protection was less than reassuring. "The citizens did not appear to appreciate the favor," wrote the Cairo correspondent for the *Cincinnati Enquirer*.[4]

In any event, the train Grant mentioned may have been the one William George Pirtle heard chugging down the rails "from Paducah, whistleing danger signals continualy and running at a rapid speed." He "was at home three miles distance," heard the commotion, and galloped off on horseback to Water Valley station to investigate. "Quite a noumber of persons had gathered before I did, all highly excited. Some one had threw off a message saying that the yanks were landing in the city. We all went home that evening with sad hearts." The following Saturday was regular drill day for his state guard company, the "Feliciana Invincibles," which was commanded by Captain J. G. Pirtle, his brother. "Quite a crowd of people collected in town, but little driling though lots of talk as to what to do. We learned that the C.S.A. army was moving from Union City to Columbus."[5]

Meanwhile, back in Paducah, secessionists evidently figured discretion was the better part of valor. They removed the Rebel flags before Grant's troops landed. He ordered the Stars and Stripes hoisted up the poles from which the secessionists hauled down their Confederate banners. One of the Rebel flags had fluttered above the St. Francis Hotel. Paine and other officers wanted to replace it with a US flag, but innkeeper Shields protested, "saying that it would bring him trouble, and he did not want its protection." Paine ordered him "to keep quiet" and advised him that the Stars and Stripes would supplant his "secession flag." The general warned Shields "that if he or other rebels interfered with the flag, or pulled it down, they would be led out and shot." Such "assurance" from Paine "quieted his nerves, and the flag floated, defying the rebels, despite many remarks by them that 'the damned rag must come down.'"[6]

Grant also sent his troops scurrying to take over every enterprise that might be militarily useful. Baker George M. Oehlschlaeger, in business at 825 South Third Street, was soon providing bread for hungry Yankees. Soldiers whose firearms needed repair began calling at Ferd Hummel Sr.'s gun shop on Broadway near Second Street.[7]

Elsewhere in town, Union troops seized the railroad station and telegraph office. At the former, Grant's men found "a large number of complete rations" and two tons or so of leather, all bound for the Confederate forces. The general confiscated the leather goods and distributed the food to his troops. Meanwhile, he heard the Rebels were descending the Tennessee "in large force" but correctly doubted the truth of the rumor. Grant completed the occupation of Paducah by positioning his troops so they would "best command the city and least annoy peaceable citizens." Too, Grant lost no time in sending part of his force upriver to capture Smithland, at the mouth of the Cumberland River. While the Civil War would turn out to be America's bloodiest war, the occupation of Hickman, Columbus, Paducah, and Smithland was accomplished without bloodshed. In any event, having secured

Paducah, Grant turned the city over to Paine and left for Cairo. He cautioned Paine to go easy on the locals and to "exercise the strictest discipline against any soldier insulting citizens or engaging in plundering private property." Grant saw no point in ruffling the feathers of Rebel civilians who did not cause trouble.[8]

Doubtless, most Paducah citizens wished Grant had taken his whole army with him. On the other hand, Columbus was ecstatic at the arrival of the Confederates. Polk showed up in time to enjoy the adulation. On September 5, a group of townsfolk handed the general a lengthy letter asking him to "permit a few of the citizens of this city and its vicinity, so recently oppressed and suffering from the tyrannical rules of the Northern Government, to express to you our profound gratification at the advent of the army under your command." The letter also included "a brief history" of alleged Yankee evil-doings in and around Columbus and statewide. The epistle claimed that the Confederacy had always respected the state's neutrality while the Union side repeatedly had violated it and even "scoffed at those who trusted to it for protection." Columbus had feared attack from Cairo "from the first hour" the city "became a military encampment." The Union troops also allegedly menaced Confederate sympathizers across the river in Missouri, arresting and jailing homeowners or chasing them into canebrakes while offering "insult and indignity . . . to unprotected and defenseless females." The Missourians had "dared to think and express the thought that a sectional President, elected by a sectional party and administering the Government upon purely sectional ideas, was a bane and a curse to the nation." Columbus citizens had "offended in like manner" and thus knew they "stood within the danger of similar treatment." The communiqué claimed the "Columbus Rangers," the outfit Prentiss sent troops to disperse in May, were innocent youths recruited by the "honorable" Captain M. H. Wright "for the mere purpose of drill, to learn camp life, and to amuse themselves in hunting." Yet on their way "to capture or slay" the Rangers, the neutrality-disrespecting Yankees rousted peaceful citizens from their beds, put them under guard, and forced them to swear allegiance to the Union. The letter denounced the whole affair as "a wanton, unprovoked invasion of Kentucky soil to hunt down and murder Kentucky citizens." The letter also recalled the capture of the Columbus flag in June as yet another example of the Yankees' "utter disregard of the rights of the people of Kentucky." The authors claimed local Unionists also had a flag. (No accounts of the flag-napping mention a Union flag.) The letter also denounced McClellan, claiming he had gone back on his agreement with Buckner. Additionally, the letter condemned Union restrictions on Kentucky trade, the war tax passed by Congress, and the massing of Union troops in Louisville and Lexington. Further, Union gunboats were "menacing our citizens," and the Yankees had sunk the Columbus ferry. Gunboats had fired into

Hickman; according to the letter, the Yankee sailors had also shot at Columbus: "We . . . witnessed the inhuman and fiendish act of a bomb hurled into our own town, bursting near a private residence, and in the very midst almost of shrinking, affrighted women." The letter concluded, "It is from hearts filled with such emotions as these that this entire community extends to you and to your gallant army a cordial welcome." The letter was signed "GEORGE C. TAYLOR ET. AL."[9]

Apparently, the Confederates were as happy with Columbus as its citizens were with them. Private John Milton Hubbard of the Seventh Tennessee Cavalry wrote that "the Kentuckians seemed to be pleased with our coming and recruiting went forward accordingly." He also declared that the Jackson Purchase was "'hog and hominy' country and the soldiering was of the holiday kind." Another Tennessean wrote the *Memphis Appeal:*

> I have concluded to give you an inkling of our doings in this part of Old Abe's vineyard. I use the term in no offensive sense to the good people of this part of Kentucky; for a more generous, kind and hospitable set of people that occupy this and Fulton county, below here, it has never been our good fortune to meet. They are a unit in favor of Kentucky taking her natural position with her sister Southern States, thoroughly imbued with true southern sentiments and ready, at any moment, to take up arms in defense of the position they have no hesitancy in declaring. Lincoln's bulls and Fremont's proclamations have no terror for them. Prompted by a patriotism which knows no sacrifice—too great for the cause in which they are wholly enlisted—they are ready to meet the issue, be what it may. They bend no knee to the Baal of Lincolnism—know no altar save their country's honor, to which they are ready to bring their most costly offerings. In a word, a more generous, brave and noble people do not live than the Southern Kentuckians. Their many acts of kind hospitality will long be remembered by our whole army, and when the bloody strife shall come, if come it must, to save these people from the fanatical rule of an abolition despot, there is no man here that will not lay down his life in their defense. And the time is not far distant, in my humble opinion, when Kentucky will shine as brilliantly in our constellation of southern stars as any that now grace our beautiful banner.[10]

Unlike the Columbus populace, the Kentucky General Assembly flatly opposed the Confederate invasion. On September 9, Unionist senator Walter Whittaker introduced a resolution in the upper house demanding that the Confederates withdraw from Columbus, and Hickman and Senator Johnson, as chairman of the Committee on Federal Relations, dutifully wrote Polk to that effect.[11]

On September 8, Polk wrote Magoffin defending his action. He said he had reliable information that Union troops were poised to seize Columbus, thereby endangering western Tennessee. Polk added that as his troops neared the town, "Federal troops were found in formidable numbers in position upon the opposite bank, with their cannons turned upon Columbus." The general claimed that the inhabitants "had fled with terror, and not a word of assurance of safety or protection had been addressed to them." Polk offered to leave the state if the federals did likewise. Yet Polk wanted a guarantee, which he promised to provide "reciprocally for the Confederate Government," that Union troops would not be permitted "to enter or to occupy any part of Kentucky in the future." The next day, Polk replied to the pro-Confederate Johnson's letter that told him to withdraw. He said the Union party forced his hand: "The Union speakers and papers, with few exceptions, claimed up to the last election that the Union vote was strict neutrality and peace." Polk added that "these facts and events gave assurance of the integrity of the avowed purpose of your State, and we were content with the position she assumed." The general maintained that he invaded Kentucky because after the election, the state "allowed the seizure in her ports (Paducah) of property of citizens of the Confederate States," because some Kentucky members of Congress had voted money and supplies to carry on the war against the South, because Kentucky had permitted the federal government to cut timber for Union warships in the state, and because of Camp Dick Robinson. He concluded with the same offer he made to the governor: both armies should leave Kentucky and promise not to return.[12]

Polk stayed in Columbus, and Union forces did not budge from Paducah: "Thus Polk, at great cost in public opinion, preempted Grant and won the strategic prize of Columbus, effectively blocking the Mississippi, and Grant in turn preempted Polk with the capture of Paducah, gaining the Union still another splendid base of operations and assuring access to the Tennessee River that crisscrossed the heart of the South." Time would tell that Grant had made the better move.[13]

Despite Whittaker's resolution, the Southern Rights Party's "Peace Convention" met in Frankfort as scheduled. Delegates registered from more than seventy counties, most of which had voted the Union ticket in August. Senators Irvan and Johnson and Representatives Boone, King, Matthewson, and Silvertooth comprised the Purchase delegation. Desperate to keep the legislature from embracing all-out Unionism, the gathering resolved that Kentucky was being driven into an unnatural war and urged the people to remain neutral. The delegates also called for the removal of federal troops from the state and, for extra measure, added that if the Confederates did not follow, Kentucky troops should expel them. In addition, the convention claimed the North had started the war and denounced Fremont for his order freeing the slaves of Confederate sympathizers in Missouri.[14]

Not unexpectedly, the legislature spurned Polk's proposition of a mutual withdrawal. On September 11, the senate approved Whittaker's resolution by a vote of twenty-five to eight. Irvan and Jenkins voted nay; Johnson did not vote, perhaps convinced it did not matter. The next day, Senator Cissell countered with a proposal demanding that both sides leave the state. The senate killed the bill on September 13, with Irvan and Jenkins voting aye. Again, Johnson did not vote.[15]

Also on September 11, the house, by a vote of seventy-one to twenty-six, passed a resolution ordering only the Confederates to exit Kentucky. At the same time, lawmakers voted sixty-eight to twenty-nine against Representative King's proposal calling for both armies to depart so "that the peace and neutrality of the State may be maintained inviolate." Boone, Coffee, Gilbert, King, Matthewson, and Silvertooth voted in the minority on both bills.[16]

On September 13, Magoffin vetoed the General Assembly's resolutions, but both houses overrode him. On the senate side, Irvan and Jenkins voted to sustain the veto; the five Purchase representatives backed the governor.[17]

Five days later, the senate and house called for the organization of a military force to aid the Union and named Brigadier General Robert Anderson, the Union hero of Fort Sumter and a Kentuckian, as its commander. Once more, Irvan and Jenkins voted with the senate minority, with Johnson not voting. Boone, Gilbert, Matthewson, and Silvertooth were in the house minority. Coffee and King did not vote, possibly figuring it was meaningless. At any rate, the last vestige of Kentucky neutrality was gone—the state was firmly in the Union camp.[18]

Meanwhile, some Confederate leaders opposed Polk's occupation of Hickman and Columbus on political grounds. Like the Kentucky Southern Rights Party—what was left of it—they believed a neutral Kentucky was eminently preferable to a Unionist Kentucky. A nonaligned Kentucky could provide a buffer between the Confederacy and the North, especially shielding Tennessee. Hence, on September 4, Governor Harris telegraphed Polk that his move into the Bluegrass State was "unfortunate, as the President and myself are pledged to respect the neutrality of Kentucky." Harris hoped the Confederate troops "will be withdrawn instantly, unless their presence there is an absolute necessity." Polk sent Harris his regrets "that a movement so entirely acceptable to the people of Kentucky, or at least this portion of Kentucky, and so essential to the security of Western Tennessee, does not permit me . . . to concur with your views." He added that he "had never received official information that the President and yourself had determined upon any particular course in reference to the State of Kentucky."[19]

On the same day, Secretary Walker telegraphed Polk, ordering him out of Kentucky. The determined Polk went over Walker's head, appealing to President Davis to let him stay. Polk said he had taken Columbus because Union troops were undoubtedly set to seize the town from Missouri. Thus, he had afforded "its citizens that protection they unite to a man in accepting, and also to prevent in time the occupation by the enemy of a point so necessary to the security of Western Tennessee." Davis backed Polk, replying, "the necessity justifies the action." That settled the issue. Polk held his ground, and Columbus and Hickman secessionists were glad he did.[20]

A Columbus contingent penned a "Letter to the Citizens of the Commonwealth of Kentucky," explaining why they were happy to have the Confederates. The letter, essentially a rewrite of the letter Taylor and others had presented to Polk, concluded:

> You may ask fellow-citizens, why we citizens of Kentucky desire that no censure should attach to the Confederate army. We promptly answer, that if we must have an armed soldiery quartered in our midst, our experience and observation, as well as our sympathy and judgment, induce us to prefer the southern to the northern soldier. You may differ with us about this matter. But we beg you to remember that it is our wives and daughters, our property, our slaves, and our homes, whose honor, safety and indemnity is involved, and not yours, and that this is a matter in which of all others you should grant as license to judge for ourselves. When the administration forces, being collected in other parts of the State, were sought to be dispersed, Mr. Lincoln put his refusal to do so upon the ground that their presence in that locality was agreeable to the people of that community. Apply the same doctrine to this army, and if, upon their removal, a northern army is to be substituted to enact such scenes as we have witnessed on the opposite side of the river, it will be a great while before the change is made by our consent.[21]

Meanwhile, down at Camp Boone, Ridgway was itching to get at the Yankees. "From the news we learned this morning I expect there is fighting now in Paducah—Hope to God it is so," he wrote Jennie on September 7. He guessed the Third Kentucky would be ordered to Paducah straight away but confessed, "don't know anything more than all the straws are drifting that way." If his outfit did go to Paducah, he invited Jennie to "come up and we will make you a Captain." The Graves County Confederate also boasted, "If there ever is a fight between these Kentuckians & the Lincolnites they are as sure to be Whipped as the sun shines."[22]

Up the Ohio at Louisville, few locals shared Ridgway's opinion of Grant and his troops, according to the *New York Times* of September 12. "Gen. Grant's Paducah proclamation is the theme of general praise on our streets," a Falls City correspondent wrote the paper. "They say: 'That's right and proper,' 'That's the point,' 'That's just what the Purchase has needed a long while' and 'That's the best and the only move the Government can take to sustain itself and protect its loyal citizens there, and the great mass of Kentuckians should and will back the Government in it, and in all similar moves, under similar circumstances.'"[23]

The Union army's advent in Paducah stood in stark contrast to Polk and Pillow's triumphal entrance into Columbus. The *Enquirer* scribe added that local merchants had closed their stores and most of the men had gone away, at least for the present. The coming of the "Abolition Invaders" disrupted civilian steamboat traffic; only "Government boats" were allowed to run. The *Tom Scott,* the Paducah-to-Cairo packet, was traveling only as far as Metropolis, Illinois, ten miles down the Ohio, but regular service was expected to be restored. At the telegraph office, Grant's soldiers found most the wires had been cut down and most were missing, presumably taken south: "The line from Smithland . . . has all been carried away." Union troops were sent south down the railroad to guard bridges and trestles against an anticipated Rebel attack.[24]

Paine evidently would have welcomed a chance to battle the Rebels at Paducah, though he remained in charge of the town only briefly. Even so, it was long enough to rile the "secesh." They hated him, and he hated them back. On September 7, Fremont named Brigadier General Charles F. Smith commander at Paducah. "This change met with approval among the people, who were dissatisfied with Paine's ruthless manner."[25]

Paine returned to command in Paducah for two more days in February 1862 and for fifty-one days in 1864. His last appearance went down in local history as Paine's "reign of terror."

After dark on the same day Fremont tapped Smith as Paducah commander, Private Aaron Loder Mastin arrived in Paducah with the Forty-first Illinois Infantry. "When we got there the town was almost deserted, and there was an apprehension of an attack on the place by the Rebels from Columbus," he penned in his diary. "The Secesh flag had been waving there and the Secesh elements greatly predominated." Nonetheless, he added, "We was greeted by the waving of hats and ladies waving their handkerchiefs." For the next two days, Mastin and his mates fished and set up camp. "Our camping ground was exceedingly beautiful, being on the river bank in the west part of town familiarly known as Jersey." On the night of September 13, Mastin pulled guard duty at the wharf boat, where he said "there was an immense lot of provisions stored away which had been taken from the Secesh, they having it ready to ship to Columbus for the Rebel troops." Mastin said he and his buddies "found a box of candy in there and we soon emptied all the contents." He figured his baptism of fire had come on September 16, when he heard a big force of Rebels was within fifteen miles of the city. "What few citizens was left behind began to get away as fast as their legs would carry them. I saw several females crying and going on as if they were about to go into fits over the fear of having a fight here. Some of them having husbands, some fathers, some brothers, and some of them children in the rebel army." The Confederates did not show, and Mastin found himself back in the daily routine of camp life. He stood guard on September 22, while his fellow soldiers were "running all over town (such of them as can get out) and buying themselves rich in pies, cakes, melons, and soda and ginger pop."[26]

Smith, a mustachioed fifty-four-year-old career soldier, apparently had little use for such volunteer soldier tomfoolery. But he tried to pacify the secesh. No matter, the *Appeal* and *Courier* devoted many column inches to news from occupied Paducah. The *Appeal* quoted a *Nashville Union* story that alleged "that Lincoln's vandals commenced, immediately on their arrival at Paducah, Kentucky, pillaging the private dwellings of the citizens, taking whatever their cupidity of fancy might covet." The *Appeal* said the wharf boat, which belonged to the Fowlers and company, "has been despoiled of its office furniture, and is now in possession of the soldiers." The Memphis paper declared that the Yankees were not satisfied with mere "plunder of ordinary property." They were "endeavoring to entice the negroes of the citizens away." According to the Nashville paper:

> A number of soldiers stopped at the house of Mr. Flournoy [evidently Judge Flournoy] and entered into conversation with one of his negro women, when the gentleman called his servant into the house, with a threat that if she did not come in he would whip her, when the insolent soldiers informed him of their presence, and that the day for whipping negroes was past, and that he had better leave himself.[27]

Another issue of the *Appeal* quoted a description of Paducah that the Cairo correspondent for the *St. Louis Republican* had penned for his paper:

> Considerable terror has arisen among the inhabitants, and thousands would leave if they could. Household furniture is being removed in skiffs, and what other conveyances can be got, to safer points. If affairs in Kentucky continue in their present state three weeks longer, the town will be almost depopulated. Although numberless elegant residences are deserted and stand monuments of blighting secession, society seems to have already fled, and gloom and horror taken possession. Not a carriage is seen upon the streets, or lady upon the beautiful walks.
>
> The stores are many of them closing, and wagons with the boxed up goods standing instead of customers before the doors. In no place yet have I seen so bitterly hostile a feeling existing against the Union as here. Scowling, angry glances watch with what seems an intense hatred, every movement of a passing soldier. Some of the wells have been poisoned where the camps get their water, and many similar acts perpetrated. Secession is the rule, and Union the rare exception. Whether Uncle Sam has any medicine as strong as the complaint, is still an open question. On the streets people wear secession caps, and boast that before the week closes every Federal will be driven out. The telegraph wires have been cut through the town and lie across the sidewalks, or are twined around trees.

The *Appeal* editorialized that Paducah's purported plight was "the condition that the venal press and tory representatives in the Legislature have brought Kentucky to by 'loyal neutrality.' An outraged people will remember the authors of the evil."[28]

Also according to an *Appeal* correspondent in Columbus, the Confederate army there was "anxious to avenge the outrages that have been committed by the Federal soldiers in and around Paducah." The Yankees promised they came to protect the citizens and their property. Instead, "they take what provisions, etc., they want, without paying for it." Union troops were being quartered in private houses, and if a homeowner objected, "his life is threatened, his cattle and horses carried away, and it is often the case that his barn is burned." Smith, the paper said, had promised "that no one would be harmed on account of his political opinions," yet Union troops were "arresting every man in and around Paducah, who entertains the opinion that a State has the right to secede; and if the men escape and come to the Confederate camps for protection, they arrest the women." The Union dragnet extended for twenty miles around Paducah, the *Appeal* asserted. "Old men, whose locks are white with the frosts of many winters, have been captured and sent into the Northern States as prisoners." When the spouse of Phil Wallace, a Rebel soldier from Paducah, learned she was to be arrested, "she daringly made her way through the guard lines and picket guards, and started to this post." The Union troops went after her "and like bloodhounds on the track, pursued her until their cowardly hearts prompted them to return." She reached Columbus and her husband, but back in Paducah, the Yankees took over the Wallace house, "and one of their generals therein makes his headquarters," the *Appeal* claimed.[29]

Smith's troops got busy fortifying Paducah. The city's main strongpoint would be a cannon-bristling earth-walled bastion built around the Marine Hospital along the Ohio River. The Yankees turned the facility into a military medical center, and though it later burned, the fort stood until the end of the war. Mastin said that while the "ten or twelve hundred on fatigue duty" dug the breastworks, he and a fellow soldier went foraging and "got some persimmons of which the woods is full of them here at Paducah."[30]

The Yankees named the works Fort Anderson in honor of their hero of Fort Sumter. Also, they spanned the river with a pontoon bridge to the Illinois shore, thus providing the army an escape route should the Confederates attack and overpower them. It was said to be the longest floating bridge on record. Mastin said the bridge was "composed of flat boats run up side by side and sleepers or ties thrown across them and then planked over that again so I think when high water comes it will all wash away." He would be proved prescient; on October 8, the Ohio suddenly rose as much as fifteen feet and broke apart the mighty span.[31]

A *New York Times* correspondent observed the bridge building. "A dozen steamboats, pouring from their chimneys immense volumes of dense black smoke, and laboriously puffing forth their white, hard-drawn breath, are busily engaged in towing barges to and fro, to form a bridge across the Ohio at this point," he wrote on September 22. "When completed, it will be an immense affair, capable of sustaining a whole Army at a single burden." He added that it was apparent from the bridge building that the Union brass appreciated "the vital importance of Paducah, and that it will figure, largely in the history of the expedition of the Mississippi." The scribe also claimed Paducah "may be considered safe" from enemy attack: "The rebels look upon it with a longing eye, and would like very much to have it. It would be worth an army of fifty thousand men to them. They have made two or three advances upon it, but never could screw their courage up tight enough to come within striking distance." He said the Confederates "seem to have finally concluded that Paducah grape was sour grape, not wholesome for rebels," and after advancing to Mayfield, the enemy thus retreated to Milburn, citing a shortage of water. "But there is plenty here in the Ohio; why did not they come and get it?" The correspondent could not resist mocking Polk, a former Episcopal bishop, describing him as "the epauletted man of God" and "the mitred Thug."[32]

The pontoon bridge, which spanned the river near the present site of the Irvin Cobb Bridge, was repaired, because it was featured in an October 26, 1861, *Harper's Weekly* story about Union-occupied Paducah. Drawings of the bridge, steamboats, the Marine Hospital, small earthworks and cannons, and the courthouse illustrated the article. J. C. Beard and Bill D. Travis, the latter a soldier in the Twenty-second Illinois Infantry Regiment, provided the artwork. "The bridge at Paducah surpasses any thing of the kind ever before attempted in the United States," Beard wrote. "The river at the bridge is 3600 feet across." He added that the plank span rested on "a hundred coal barges, strongly braced together, twelve feet apart, connected by trestle-work." The planked bridge deck was "twenty feet wide" and could accommodate "the heaviest ordnance." The bridge also supported telegraph poles and wires and featured a moveable midsection to permit the passage of river craft.[33]

Beard said Paducah was "a beautiful little city, full of respectable and often elegant residences. It now wears, however, a deserted and melancholy appearance." He added that "whole streets of tenantless buildings stretch from the landing to the intrenchments; and the few inhabitants who remain, although entirely unmolested and secure, look guilty and sullen." Beard said he and some of the troops had tried to reassure skeptical locals by staging an impromptu concert in a deserted "secesh church." With one of the Yankees playing away on the organ "and most of us having assisted before on such occasions, we did our best to convince those within hearing that although we belonged to the 'Northern rabble' we were not altogether heathen and benighted." Travis wrote that the federal government had spent fifty thousand dollars building the Marine Hospital in 1850–51 but that because Paducah was "considered the most healthy place in the West," the facility had "not had much business yet."[34]

The *Appeal*'s Columbus correspondent told a different story, claiming that a third of the six-thousand-man Union garrison was hospitalized. The rest were "strongly intrenched behind works which our delay [in attacking Paducah] has given them ample time to construct." The reporter also mentioned the pontoon bridge. In addition, he said that the Yankees' artillery and cavalry were deployed "in a most novel and effective method" to help protect from attack the "most exposed points" in the Union lines, which consisted of "formidable earthworks." The soldiers had also blocked all roads into town but one with abatis, or trees felled outward with their limbs interlaced. The troops had carefully trimmed and sharpened the branches so they would "impail anything belonging to the animal kingdom larger than a weasel," the *Appeal* said. Then, shifting away from more or less straight news reporting, the writer denounced "the despotic and mercenary character of the policy of the Federalists," adding that southern sympathizers in Paducah and its environs "are loud in their applications for release from their worse than Egyptian bondage." The *Appeal* also reported that the Yankees had apparently taken Mayfield. The Graves County seat, like Paducah, was "surrounded by men in sympathy with the South, and the brief period of our occupation of the place encouraged them to take a stand which is interpreted as treason by the Praetorian bands of the Washington despotism." Union troops were making "numerous arrests" to keep Confederate sympathizers from escaping to Columbus. Another story, reprinted from the *Daily Confederate News* at Columbus, provided additional details about the Yankee visit to Mayfield. An infantry regiment and a "troop of Lincoln's cavalry" advanced to Viola, in north Graves County, where the foot soldiers halted and the horsemen galloped on to the county seat. As soon as the troopers hit town "they commenced the work of arresting private citizens," including former state senator John Eaker and his son. The *News* could not resist a swipe at Judge Williams. The *News* claimed that the senior Eaker was Williams's friend, yet the judge abandoned him "to the peril of his own fortunes and the beggary of his family."[35]

In any event, the *Times* considered the Paducah fortifications newsworthy, too. "The lines occupy over a mile in extent, and every road or other approach to the place is guarded by strong batteries, built by the soldiers of the different regiments, under the direction of the excellent engineers from Gen. Fremont's staff," the paper noted, quoting from a story a *Detroit Advertiser* correspondent filed from Paducah on October 18. "The batteries are well supplied with some of the best siege guns that have yet been sent to the West, and manned by experienced artillerists." The Yankees were handy with axes, too. "When we came here the town was skirted by a dense forest of mostly young trees, but now for several hundred yards outside the batteries this timber is cut down, the branches chopped off about eighteen inches or two feet from the trunks of the trees, in such a manner as to leave the ends sharp, with the buts [*sic*] of the trees turned inward, and the limbs that will make stakes are sharpened and driven into the ground, thus making an obstruction that cannot be passed by either infantry or artillery," the correspondent wrote. "This has made a vast amount of work for the soldiers; in fact, the cutting of the timber has been nearly as much labor as the building of the batteries that now command all the principal points around here."[36]

The Detroit reporter said the Union force numbered about eight thousand, and he praised the troops as "among the most efficient of any in the West. They are entirely armed with either the Enfield or Minie rifles, and are under the most perfect discipline, and it would be hard to find eight thousand better officered, better drilled or equipped troops in the grand army or the Union." He described Smith as "an officer of the regular army, who possesses the unbounded confidence of the men. He is about fifty years of age, and is next to Gen. [William S.] Harney, the most soldierly-looking officer I have seen during the war, and, so far, his actions have not belied his looks."[37]

Although he and his comrades-in-arms were frequent objects of disaffection from the locals and Rebel newspapers, Wills was impressed with Paducah. "I fell in love with Paducah while I was there, and I think I will settle there when the war is over," he wrote home. "I never saw so many pretty women in my life. All fat, smooth skinned small boned, highbred looking women. They hollered 'Hurrah for Jeff' at us, some of them, but that's all right. I could write until to-morrow morning about Paducah, but I must go and confiscate some corn for dinner."[38]

With neutrality gone, both sides quickly moved into Kentucky. Following Grant's occupation of Paducah and Smithland, Union forces seized Louisville and Muldraugh's Hills, southwest of the city. The Confederates took Bowling Green, Cumberland Gap, and Cumberland Ford, while improving their defenses at Hickman and Columbus. Major General Albert Sidney Johnston, a Kentucky-born Texan, was in command at Bowling Green. One of his lieutenants was the newly commissioned brigadier general Simon Bolivar Buckner.

But Columbus was the destination for the "Invincibles." On the morning of September 10, they gathered in Feliciana and prepared to march off to the Confederate army. Pirtle said they left amid "a multiplicity of people all feeling great interest in the company and desireous of seeing them off. As no one seemed to know much about moving an army we were late getting into line on the road." The state guards were ready by eleven. They "moved out and on for three or four miles, halted for dinner and then on again." He said the men "were a great amasement to the people along the road, especially in Clinton." The company reached the Obion Creek bridge about sundown and made camp for the night. Pirtle pulled guard duty for the first time: "About dark I was conducted up the creek some two or three hundred yards and instructed to keep a sharp lookout and report if anything took place that I did not understand. This was a very lonesome place and if it had not been for the hoot owls I do not know if I could have stayed awake. After a long time, it seemed most a day, a relief came, went back to camp and slept the balance of the night. The boys having hooped and yelled all day were exhausted so they slept sound all night."

The next morning, "after a wonderful chauco of nois and hurraw, we got into line and on the move for Columbus, five miles off, and reached [there] in due time." Pillow assigned the "Invincibles" a campsite on the Mississippi near the railroad station.[39]

Elsewhere in the Jackson Purchase, the northern and southern armies strengthened their positions. The Yankees built Fort Holt on high ground next to the Mississippi just downriver from Cairo. Named for important Kentucky Unionist Joseph Holt, the earthwork was near the site of the old wooden-walled Fort Jefferson. By the end of 1861, seventeen hundred soldiers were camped at Fort Holt, which consisted of a lower and upper redoubt connected by a small trench for infantry. Besides soldiers, the earthworks shielded five long-range guns and five field guns.[40]

The Confederates employed more than ten thousand slaves to help them turn Columbus and its bluffs into the most strongly fortified spot in North America. Some of the bondsmen were officers' personal servants; others were "hired" from their owners. Slaves and soldiers cut trees, creating broad fields of fire. On the Iron Banks, the Confederates planted triple-tier artillery batteries. Fifteen feet above the shore, a water battery bristled with several ten-inch Columbiad guns and eleven-inch howitzers. They emplaced more guns about halfway up the bluffs. On top, the Confederates constructed "bull pen forts" that shielded more cannons. Fifty to one hundred yards square, the bastions featured thick walls made from corn sacks stuffed with sand. One fort protected what was reputedly the Confederacy's largest gun—a monster cannon capable of hurling 128-pound shells dubbed "lampposts" three miles. The soldiers christened the gun "Lady Polk" in honor of the general's wife. As extra protection for Lady Polk and the rest of their firepower, the Rebels dug a ditch ten feet wide and eight feet deep that ran in a great semicircle around the forts. Beyond the ditch, they cleared underbrush and chopped down trees, sharpening and interlacing the limbs into an abatis. A mile or so north of town, where the bluff jutted out flush with the Mississippi, work crews cleared off a shelf of land to accommodate yet another battery. All told, Polk massed 140 guns at Columbus and commanded a garrison of more than seventeen thousand men.[41]

Polk's heavy ordnance was impressive, but the most talked-about feature of his defenses was a mile-long chain and anchor that blocked the river. The iron barrier may have been "Pillow's Trot Line," the chain the general had stretched across the Mississippi at Fort Pillow, just north of Memphis. General Pillow had shipped forty guns from the fort to Columbus, and he may have dispatched the chain upriver as well. At any rate, the Rebels evidently buried the anchor inside Fort De Russey atop the Iron Banks; twelve-foot oak logs helped hold it in place. The anchor was massive, nine and a half feet long and weighing between two and six tons, depending on the source. Each link weighed about twenty pounds. The Rebels ran the chain down the bluff side and across the river to Camp Johnston, their “camp of observation.” Log pontoons supported the chain, whose end was wrapped around two sycamore trees on the Missouri side. The Rebels worked a capstan between the trees and the river to adjust the chain’s tension. “This enormous, costly, imaginative, clumsy obstruction failed, snaring only a riverboat that drifted too close.” Nonetheless, it symbolized Polk’s unshakable will to hold the Mississippi.[42] Yankee gunboats and troop ships would have a hard time even getting close to the chain. The Rebels anchored mines—called “torpedoes” in the Civil War—to the riverbed in front of the barrier. Floating just below the surface, their purpose was to destroy attackers that managed to evade Polk’s long-range rifled guns. If the mines failed to sink the vessels, then the Mississippi’s powerful current would pin them against the chain, making them easy targets for short-range smoothbore guns. The Confederates sowed contact and electrically fired mines at Columbus. The former type exploded when a boat struck a lever or pulled a wire attached to the mine. Wires connected electrically detonated mines to telegraph batteries on shore. They would be set off when a Yankee vessel was seen passing over them.[43]

Naturally, the military goings-on at Columbus attracted visitors from throughout the Purchase. Many were friends and families of the soldiers; all were well-wishers. Eighteen-year-old Alice Henderson Phipps, whose brother, uncle, and cousin were in the Confederate army, traveled to the “Gibraltar” from her family’s two-thousand-acre plantation on the river between Columbus and Hickman. “It was a perfect picnic for us young folks,” she recalled. “The officers would have their wives with them in camp.” She said the officers brought along their slaves to cook for them and that every regiment had a band. “We got up parties every few days to go out there on the M and O train and had a wonderful time,” Phipps added. “They had a pavilion made so we danced and met such nice people from Memphis and other states.” She did not welcome bluejackets from the North. Union gunboats, she said, would hide behind a forested point on the Missouri side of the river and bombard Columbus. “The point was covered with dense timbers and we would not see the gun boats but the shells were bursting in the streets and we had to be guided by the noise they made to enable us to get out of the way.” She said Grant “ordered the shelling although he knew the town was full of women and children.” Phipps compared the shelling to German atrocities in Belgium in World War I.[44]

Also in the fall of 1861, the Confederates established three other positions in the Purchase. In September, they laid out Camp Henry C. Burnett two miles west of Clinton on the road to Columbus as a rendezvous for Confederate recruits. The "Invincibles" were evidently the first men in camp. In any event, on September 12, an officer from Columbus lined up the Graves countians, about sixty in number, and swore them in "for one year if not sooner discharged," wrote Pirtle. They elected J. G. Pirtle captain, and brothers J. A. "Fon" Collins first lieutenant and A. D. "Lon" Collins second lieutenant. William G. Pirtle was made a sergeant.[45]

Soon, other Purchase volunteers joined the "Invincibles." "In about a week, we had eight companys present, ours from Feliciana next to one from Clinton, then two more from Graves County, one from Fulton County, and one from Marshall County," Pirtle wrote. "Those companys were all camped near each other but in no regular order." He remembered that few of the companies "knew any thing about how to drill except ours, it had been drilling all summer, and was pretty well up on that line, and many were the je[e]rs we hurled at the awquard squad, but they soon became our equals." Ultimately, the western Kentuckians became the Seventh Kentucky Infantry. Wickliffe was elected colonel and Lannom lieutenant colonel. Editor Warren of the *Hickman Courier* was made assistant quartermaster. One of the "Invincibles," Private Henry George of Feliciana provided a detailed description of camp life:

> The men were armed with any kind of arms they could get, some with the old flint-lock musket, but they were soon furnished with a musket which had been changed from a flint-lock to a percussion, and a very destructive gun. . . . As soon as the companies were organized into a regiment they were put to drilling almost constantly every day; they soon became quite proficient in both the movements and manual of arms. The men were furnished with tents, cooking utensils, and such other things as were necessary to make the camp comfortable. Here the men were put through the seasoning process of camp life. The most of the men were not far from the homes of their people, who constantly sent them great quantities of good things to eat, and hundreds of articles of wearing apparel for which they had no sort of use. Nearly every man had a big knife from eight inches to two feet long, made from big files, buggy or wagon springs or tires; these were the instruments of warfare with which they intended to prosecute the war against the Federal armies in the event they could not get arms. They were all left behind, however, on the first march.[46]

Before that march, the *Crescent,* renamed the *Daily Confederate News* with Bullock as editor, cheered them on: "Let the brave Purchase boys rush to the standard and fill up these ranks, remembering, as says Erin's sweet bard: Far dearer the grave or a prison, / Illumed by the patriot's name / Than thy trophies of all who have risen / On Liberty's ruin to fame!"[47]

Bullock told his readers he wanted to make his paper "equal to any daily published in the South." To that end, the editor said he had made arrangements by which the *News* would be privy to "the earliest intelligence of every important result that may transpire in other sections, and also one by which we will be enabled to give our readers all the information touching the army in Kentucky and at this place which can be communicated, compatible with the safety of our troops and the success of our arms." In the November 1, 1861, issue he predicted that "this most unnatural war, forced upon the South by a bigoted and insolent party at the North, like all earthly things, must end sooner or later." Bullock confessed he did not know "when and how" the conflict would stop. But the editor was sure the war's termination would leave the South "a united people, under a constitutional government, in which individual and State rights will be fully recognized and protected." He was also confident the border slave states would ultimately join the Confederacy. Elsewhere in the paper, Bullock claimed "duplicity has marked Mr. Lincoln's administration from the time of the delivery of his inaugural to the present time." The editor added, "The ultra school of Abolitionists are clamorous and fierce in their denunciations of him because he will not openly endorse their Red Republican ideas of liberty, and by proclamation emancipate all the slaves in the Southern States." Bullock was certain the president, "in his heart of hearts, desires every slave freed, not so much from philanthropic considerations, as deep-seated hatred of Southerners; but then there are Missouri, Kentucky, Maryland, and little Delaware to be looked to, and such an ultra course he fears would effectually crush Unionism in these States." Further, Bullock opened fire on Kentucky's "Abolition Legislature," claiming Unionist lawmakers were "as much under the pay of Lincoln as the soldiers who have crossed the Ohio to invade the state." He denounced Kentucky neutrality as dishonorable. What followed was worse, according to Bullock: submission to the North: "The people see and know this, though their legislators will not.—They have been sold like cattle on the hoof." No matter, Bullock was sure Kentucky "will come forth from her shroud with a shining countenance. She will pluck her star from the cold and cheerless banner of the frozen North, and set it where the impulses of the people are as warm and as generous as the Southern sun which shines on their escutcheon."[48]

Meanwhile, in late September, the Rebel brass decided to establish an outpost between Columbus and Fort Henry, which was on the Tennessee River, just south of the Kentucky state line. The idea was to protect Polk's right flank and hold the center of the Columbus-to–Fort Henry line. On September 30, Polk ordered Lieutenant Joseph Dixon to scout the country on a line between Columbus and Mayfield and find "a suitable place in an advanced position for an intrenched camp" that would protect the railroads and form part of the Columbus–Fort Henry defense line. Polk wanted a camp convenient for water and wood and close to the New Orleans and Ohio Railroad. Dixon, an army engineer, chose a high hill a mile and a quarter north of Feliciana and a mile and a half northwest of Morse Station (Water Valley today). The site was on a wooded ridge known locally as "Mobley's old campground." The spot was near the natural springs of the Bayou du Chien creek, and the high ground seemed perfect for repelling an attack. The Rebels could see the Yankees coming long before they got close.[49]

The Confederates named the camp for General P. G. T. Beauregard, the Rebel hero of Fort Sumter. Feliciana provided many comforts for the troops. Most locals were Confederate sympathizers. While their community was not on the railroad, it had a quartet of stores, a pair of hotels, a Masonic lodge, a school, a druggist, four doctors, a lawyer, a magistrate, two blacksmiths, a boot and shoe maker, a tanner, a painter, and two tailors. There was also whiskey aplenty, which earned more than a few soldiers brief stays in the guard house. One veteran confessed he "was very wicked at Camp Beauregard," explaining he "was only 20 years of age, and wanted to fight the Yankees." He said he atoned and was baptized a Christian in 1864. The soldiers from Camp Beauregard were from Alabama, Arkansas, Florida, Kentucky, Louisiana, Mississippi, Missouri, and Tennessee. The Kentuckians were the "Hell Hounds"; King and his men were evidently the only soldiers in camp who knew the territory. L. B. Wardlow, a veteran of the Twenty-second Mississippi Infantry Regiment, recalled the time a colonel of one of the out-of-state regiments ordered a lieutenant and a detail of soldiers "to go out in the front and reconnoiter." Puzzled, the lieutenant asked his superior, "Colonel, how far is it to reconnoiter?" The colonel snapped, "You d—n fool, go ask your Captain."[50]

The third Rebel outpost was Fort Heiman, in southeastern Calloway County, almost directly across the Tennessee from Fort Henry, Tennessee, which was built on low ground next to the river. In early September, Captain Jesse Taylor, a veteran artillerist, visited Fort Henry and learned from local farmers that winter rains would flood the fort. He warned Polk, but to no avail. When Tilghman took command of Fort Henry, he, too, knew the earthen bastion was in the wrong place. He calculated that if Union gunboats did not overpower Fort Henry—which they did—the river would and almost did. Tilghman looked across the river and saw high ground better suited for a fort. Thus, construction began on a fort named for Colonel Adolphus Heiman. Tilghman and his officers believed that if Fort Heiman could be finished in time, the Confederates could catch attacking gunboats in a fatal crossfire. Also, if floodwaters necessitated the abandonment of Fort Henry, then the garrison could at least put up a fight at Fort Heiman.[51]

If Calloway County southern sympathizers had gotten their way, the Confederates would have established themselves at Wadesboro or Murray, too. Colonel John S. Bowen, the Camp Beauregard commander, wrote Polk's headquarters in Columbus on behalf of secessionists who wanted him "to establish a command" at either location. The pro-southern county residents proffered plentiful provisions for soldiers, offering to "sell cheap to the Confederacy—corn, 25 cents per bushel; wheat, 60 cents, &c." Bowen added that there was "a strong position immediately east of Murray (a mile, say), with plenty of running water." The colonel also called attention to Eggner's Ferry on the Tennessee River, sixteen miles northeast of Murray. "No force coming up the Cumberland can cross the Tennessee and fall in rear of Eggner's without building their roads through a country of 'ravines,' 'backbones,' and 'lime-sinks,' unless they go up as high as Dover, on the Cumberland." Bowen reported that a good road connected Murray to the ferry. He suggested that by stationing troops in or around Murray, the Confederates would be able to cover considerable unprotected ground, while establishing "a strong line of defense from the Mississippi to the Tennessee," thereby safeguarding the left flank of the Rebel army in Bowling Green. Bowen added, "Whether it would be advisable to have General Tilghman's command move up to Eggner's Ferry and a brigade stationed at Murray must of course depend on the disposable force." The general explained that he could not abandon Camp Beauregard without leaving the northern border of Weakley County, Tennessee, open to Yankee raiders, "even if it does not weaken Columbus by having the right and rear opened."[52]

Throughout the fall of 1861, Calloway and the other Purchase counties continued to furnish volunteers for the Confederate army. R. H. Fristoe and another band of Graves County volunteers went to Hopkinsville, where they became Company C of the Eighth Kentucky Infantry Regiment. Calloway County furnished two independent cavalry companies, Captain James M. Bolins's and Captain James M. Melton's, and Company B of the Thirty-third Tennessee Infantry.[53]

With the Rebels at Columbus, Hickman, Camp Beauregard, and Fort Heiman, much of the Purchase became Confederate territory, at least militarily. Yet officially, Kentucky was now in the war on the Yankee side. Hence, many secessionist legislators saw Frankfort as an "enemy" capital. Like southern lawmakers who left Washington after their states seceded, the most outspoken Southern Rights senators and representatives turned their backs on Frankfort. They included all six Purchase representatives and Senator Johnson. Irvan and Jenkins remained in the senate until their terms expired in 1863.[54]

On September 20, the senate granted Johnson indefinite sick leave to go home to Paducah. But he headed to Confederate-occupied Bowling Green, according to the *Journal.* His detour suggested that "he thought the company of Gen. Grant would not be as congenial as that of Gen. Buckner." To further prove the senator's treachery, the paper reprinted a September 26 New Orleans newspaper story supposedly based on a telegram from Johnson, in which he said "the Federals have been committing all manner of depredations" around Frankfort. Johnson claimed "a boy sixteen years of age was shot dead in the streets of Frankfort for cheering for Jeff Davis, and his murderer was not arrested." The *Journal* jabbed, "The Doctor is growing like Falstaff in more ways than one, and in obesity and falsehood particularly. If he gave the information telegraphed from Bowling Green to New Orleans, he reported what was false and reported it knowing it to be false." The *Journal* added, "He feigned sickness to escape from his legislative duties at Frankfort, went to the rebel camp, concocted most injurious lies about the feeling of public opinion, and then impudently wrote back to the State Capital asking for travelling expenses in the service of the Senate." The paper was convinced that no "one man in Kentucky . . . has done more towards placing the State in her present unhappy attitude than Dr. Johnson." The *Journal* charged that Johnson had counseled the Confederate army to occupy Paducah and kept the Rebels informed while he was investigating the *Terry-Orr* affair as the governor's representative. Too, he "was a spy upon the movements of the Union men at home." Thus, "steeped . . . to the very lips in treason, he went to Frankfort, took his seat in the Senate, and used every energy, by vote and speech, to embarrass the Union cause and aid that of the Confederates." The *Journal* was certain there was "no bigger scoundrel of a rebel in all Kentucky, except [Confederate Brigadier General] Humphrey Marshall, who has the advantage by avoirdupois, though not perhaps in heart."[55]

Ultimately, Silvertooth, Boone, Coffee, Gilbert, King, and Matthewson also made their way to south-central Kentucky. But their ultimate destination was Russellville, the Logan County seat, about twenty-nine miles southwest of Bowling Green. They joined Johnson and other secessionists from the Purchase and statewide in creating a Confederate "provisional government" for

Kentucky. Many supporters of the idea had been at the Frankfort peace convention in September. No one worked harder for the movement than George W. Johnson of Scott County, who took great pains to convince Jefferson Davis of its merit. As a first step toward a "Confederate" Kentucky, secessionists representing thirty-two counties—most of them majority Unionist—met on October 29. The secessionists asserted that the General Assembly had acted illegally in abandoning neutrality and siding with the Union. Of course, the legislators had been freely elected. The secessionists declared their action was lawful under the state constitution, which gave Kentuckians "at all times an inalienable and indefeasible right to alter, reform, or abolish their government, in such a manner as they may think proper" and which said, remarkably, "that absolute and arbitrary power over the lives, liberty, and property of freemen exists nowhere in a republic—not even in the largest majority." Further, the secessionists urged Magoffin to convene the legislature beyond "the lines of the Federal bayonets." The secessionists were building a straw man. They knew the Unionist majority legislature would stay put in Frankfort and that Magoffin could not or would not make lawmakers leave the capital. So the delegates called a sovereignty convention for Russellville on November 18. Before adjourning, the meeting appointed Breckinridge, who had left the senate, and others as a committee to carry out the program.[56]

On November 18–20, the Russellville convention met as planned. Burnett, having resigned his house seat, presided over a gathering of about two hundred men from sixty-five counties—again, most of the counties pro-Union. The Purchase was the only region of Kentucky that could claim legitimate representation. Johnson and all the House members elected in August attended, along with a large group of others from the region. Apparently, only one other lawmaker elected in August, Representative George R. Merritt of Livingston and Lyon Counties, which adjoin the Purchase, was at the Russellville convention.[57]

The body drafted a secession ordinance that declared Kentucky "a free and independent State, clothed with all power to fix her own destiny and to secure her own rights and liberties." The framers claimed that President Lincoln and the Republican Congress had contemptuously violated the constitution "and usurped to themselves the power to interfere with the rights and liberties of the States and the people." Too, the president and his party had thrown over "the highest forms of national liberty and constitutional government" for "a central despotism, founded upon the ignorant prejudices of the masses of Northern Society, and instead of giving protection with the Constitution to the people of fifteen States of this Union, have turned loose upon them the unrestrained and raging passions of mobs and fanatics." The secessionists protested that "because we now seek to hold our liberties, our property, our homes, and our families, under the protection of the reserved powers of the States," the northern-dominated federal government had "blockaded our ports, invaded our soil, and waged war upon our people for the purpose of subjugating us to their will." Further, they declared that "our honor and our duty to posterity demand that we shall not relinquish our own liberty and shall not abandon the right of our descendants and the world to the inestimable blessings of Constitutional Government." In addition, the document blasted the legislature's "factious majority" for abandoning neutrality in support of the North's "war against the people and institutions of fifteen independent States of the old Federal Union," despite Magoffin's vetoes "and the solemn remonstrances of the minority in the Senate and House of Representatives."[58]

The written record of the Kentucky convention does not appear to be as overtly racist as the printed proceedings of conventions in Confederate states. For example, in justifying disunion, Texas secessionists said Lincoln's election meant the country had been taken over by "a great sectional party . . . proclaiming the debasing doctrine of the equality of all men, irrespective of race and color—a doctrine at war with nature, in opposition to the experience of mankind, and in violation of the plainest revelations of Divine Law." Mississippi secessionists said Republican ascendancy left them "no choice . . . but submission to the mandates of abolition, or a dissolution of the union, whose principles had been subverted to work our ruin." They declared, "We must either submit to degradation and the loss of property worth four billions of money, or we must secede from the Union." But the Kentuckians were motivated by what Charles B. Dew characterizes as an overarching, concern among all secessionists: "the fate of the South's slave system in a United States ruled by a Republican majority." By claiming the power to determine Kentucky's future and safeguard the state's "rights and liberties," the delegates clearly meant they aimed to preserve the freedom of white Kentuckians to enslave African Americans. The "fifteen States" they cited were Kentucky and the other fourteen slave states. "The people" were whites, and "mobs and fanatics" were abolitionists like John Brown, who seized the federal arsenal at Harpers Ferry, Virginia—now West Virginia—in hopes of arming a slave rebellion or sparking a war against slavery.[59]

The delegates created a provisional government consisting of a governor, a council of ten, and lesser offices. The council comprised representatives from each of the state's ten congressional districts. Delegates named Bowling Green as the state's Confederate "capital" and named Johnson "governor." Because the secessionists considered their provisional government the true state government, they retained the old constitution and the old laws not inconsistent with what they had wrought. Finally, the convention called for the creation of a permanent Confederate government "so soon as an election can be held, free from the influence of the armies of the United States."[60]

Kentucky's lawfully elected governor, though a Southern Rights man, strongly condemned the Russellville convention as rebellion against Kentucky. But he protested he could not suppress it because he was "without arms, without money, without men." Before adjourning, the commissioner designated Burnett, William Preston of Louisville, and William E. Simms of Paris as commissioners to the Confederate government. Davis, convinced that the heart of his native state was with the South, recommended Kentucky's admission to the Confederacy. On December 10, Kentucky was brought into the fold as the thirteenth Confederate "state" and permitted ten congressmen. Missouri became the twelfth Confederate state by action of an equally dubious rump Rebel government. Burnett represented Kentucky's First District and could at least claim some legitimacy based on his election on the secessionist ticket in June, albeit to the rival congress.[61]

Kentucky Unionists denounced the Russellville convention, rightly pointing out that the gathering did not represent majority opinion in the Bluegrass State. Historical accounts of the meeting gloss over, or do not address, how the delegates were chosen, leaving one to conclude that they simply appointed themselves. But a letter Dr. Caleb Jones of Farmington, in Graves County, wrote to his children in Paris, Tennessee, on November 1, 1861, suggests that Boone was elected to represent Graves County. "Between this & the 18th we go to the poles [*sic*] and vote for our choice Governments, not by order or authority of the Legislature, but by our own independent acclimation," he penned. Apparently, no record of such a vote, if one took place, survives. But one wonders if there were more such "poles" in other Purchase counties or anyplace else in Kentucky.[62]

In any event, the physician also fulminated against Yankee soldiers. He claimed "300 dragoons" had ridden into Mayfield, "pillaged it for six hours," and perpetrated "every kind of insult & plunder." But he added that local secessionists had "disarmed" Union sympathizers, "demons," to Jones, who added that "many of them have joined Judge Williams at Paducah." Jones also advised that he, Thomas Cochran, and E. Hendrix were "the special objects of Paducah vengeance" in the Farmington neighborhood.[63]

Williams was not just enjoying the company of the Union troops. He was trying to boost their numbers with local volunteers. According to the *Appeal,* he had help. P. D. Yeiser, a lawyer from Eddyville, the Lyon County seat, was raising a company at Smithland and had seventy-five men signed up, most of them from Crittenden County.[64]

Not surprisingly, the *Confederate News* flayed Williams. "This gentleman, holding a commission as Circuit Judge of this judicial district, under the Constitution and laws of this State, in direct violation of that Constitution which he was sworn to protect, accepted of a Colonel's commission under Lincoln's government, and is endeavoring to raise a regiment," Bullock blasted. He claimed that some years before, the judge "was utterly bankrupt in fortune and seriously damaged in character" and that "a trusting and confiding people, comprising this judicial district, made him all he is and more than he ever deserved to be." Then Bullock lowered the boom: "With a full knowledge that nine-tenths of the people who elevated him to office, are heart and soul with the Confederate States, holding on to his office as Judge, he is endeavoring to prostitute that high place, to aid him in recruiting Lincoln forces. Whatever may be the issue of our unhappy difficulties, he is doomed. Nothing but curses and execrations will ever greet his ear from his old friends and constituents."[65]

Naturally, the *Journal* put a different spin on Williams's activities. "Judge Williams, who has doffed the judicial toga for the soldier's uniform, and is now Colonel Williams, is recruiting his regiment with great success in the First District, and will soon succeed in raising the full complement," the paper predicted. "At Smithland and other points on the Ohio river, our men are coming in daily as fast as they can escape from the interior and slip through the Confederate pickets." The *Journal* claimed the volunteers "are all animated by the purest patriotism and moved to action by the persecutions and indignities they have suffered at the hands of the rebels." The paper explained that when Williams's regiment was organized, many of the men would be able "to revisit their families, from whom they are now exiled, and also open the way for others to join the Union ranks, who are now placed under such strict surveillance that they find it impossible to leave their homes."[66]

Williams was unable to raise a full regiment. The volunteers he collected became part of the Twentieth Kentucky Infantry, a regiment organized for three years' service. Most of its men joined up in Lexington and at Camp Dick Robinson. Williams either served briefly or not at all; in 1862, he was elected to the Kentucky Court of Appeals, then the state's highest court. He served for eight years and was chief justice for his last two years.[67]

About the only Purchase men to sign up for the Twentieth Kentucky were in a group of approximately one hundred Marshall County volunteers, who formed Company G, with Thomas B. Waller as captain. His brother, Benjamin Rush Waller, was first lieutenant. Their father, Wiley Waller, was one of the few outspoken Unionists in Marshall County: "So great was the prejudice against him, that on different occasions, he was subjected to cruel treatment in both person and property, and lived in almost constant danger of assassination."[68]

Meanwhile, Grant had no fewer than 20,000 men who he said were spoiling for a fight with the Rebels at Columbus. They had to settle for a foray against the Rebels' outpost at Belmont, against which he moved on November 6 with a little more than 3,000 men he collected from Cairo and Fort Holt. Grant's troops headed downriver aboard transport steamers and escorted by the wooden gunboats *Tyler* and *Lexington.* The next morning, he led his men ashore above Belmont, just out of range of the big guns at Columbus; the general planned to capture Belmont, break up the enemy camp, and go back to Cairo. Grant's troops easily seized Camp Johnston, but the Rebels rushed reinforcements over from Columbus, and suddenly the general found himself surrounded. The Yankees expected their commander to surrender, but Grant coolly announced "that we had cut our way in and could cut our way out just as well." The Union troops rallied, pushed past the Confederates, and got safely back to their transports. Grant put his losses at 485, killed, wounded, and missing. The Confederates captured about 125 of his wounded troops, but Grant's force returned to Cairo with 175 Rebel prisoners and two of their cannons. The Yankees spiked and disabled four other enemy guns. Grant said Confederate losses totaled 642 men killed, wounded, and missing. All told, Grant went into battle with 2,500 men; 500 were left to guard the transports. The Confederates threw about 7,000 men into the battle.[69]

Twice, Grant nearly became a casualty himself. When he returned to his transport boat, Grant entered the captain's cabin adjacent to the pilothouse and lay down on a sofa. "I did not keep that position a moment, but rose to go out on the deck to observe what was going on," Grant wrote. "I had scarcely left when a musket ball entered the room, struck the head of the sofa, passed through it and lodged in the foot." The day after the battle, he met with some of Polk's officers aboard a truce boat to make arrangements for burying the Union dead at Belmont and to negotiate a prisoner exchange. He mentioned to one of the Confederates, a man he had known from West Point and the Mexican-American War, that he had been on horseback in a cornfield close to the Rebel army. Grant said he was wearing a soldier's overcoat. The officer said he and his general had seen Grant but did not recognize him. Polk had suggested to some of his nearby troops, "There is a Yankee; you may try your marksmanship if you wish." Grant said no one had fired at him.[70]

The Purchase Confederates were not in the Battle of Belmont. The Seventh Kentucky's baptism of fire came on the first day of the Battle of Shiloh, April 6, 1862. On November 7, 1861, the men were still at Camp Burnett, where they experienced "a real alarm sounded by the booming of cannons and the rattle of musketry in the direction of Columbus," George wrote, adding that it sounded like the Yankees were attacking the strongpoint. "For hours the deadly rattle of the battle continued; it was the first the men of the Seventh ever heard."[71]

Pirtle said that "about sunup," the troops heard firing to the west, toward Columbus. "It became heavier . . . knew that a fight was on . . . but how or where we could not determin." Wickliffe ordered the regiment's equipment piled onto wagons and sent the conveyances in the direction of Columbus. He "called the men in line on the parade ground," while sending couriers to Polk "asking what to do, but all the word he could get was to stand fast and keep a good watch for the enimy." The distant din "was wonderful to us, the roar of musketry, and belching of big guns, O how wonderful, perhaps not a man in the whole regment had ever heard any thing of the kind before." Pirtle recalled that the Seventh Kentucky "stood in line all day, listened to the fireing as long as it lasted until one or two Oclock in the afternoon." Not until after nightfall did the regiment move out to Columbus: "Off we went in light marching order as we had sent everything off not reserving any thing, not even a blanket, had no dinner or anything for supper." He said it was close to midnight when they arrived on the bluffs above the town close and "found some bresh and logs that answered to build fires, did the best we could the balance of the night, and by morning was conclueding that a soldiers fare was hard, nothing to eat since the morning before and no prospect that we could see for any thing soon." But there was news: "the fight was on the other side of the river."[72]

Four days after the Belmont fight, the *Journal* published what it claimed was more evidence of Purchase perfidy. The paper had Oscar Turner living in Mayfield, claiming that when Union soldiers searched his Graves County seat dwelling—he was evidently absent—they purportedly found a February 17, 1861, letter from Merritt, who was from Eddyville. The letter advised, "We are endeavoring to organize a party which shall sweep the First District. . . . The whole country will flock around our standard, save a few emancipationists, since Col. W. B. Machen has arrived at home and declared that he has no hope of any adjustment being made, and that Kentucky must go with the Southern Confederacy." Merritt, a Bell elector, according to the *Journal,* said "a large proportion of the Bell party are straight-out secessionists, and all of the prominent men of the Democratic party." He conceded "there is a large element of both parties in the country opposed to us, but that is because they have not been enlightened upon the subject." Merritt concluded by advising, "would be pleased to receive any suggestion from you as to present ourselves in the best attitude."[73] Machen and Merritt attended the Russellville convention.[74]

A letter from a Paducah Unionist that the *Journal* published on November 20 called the convention "treasonable" and claimed "this heretofore rampant secessionist city, now under the benign influence of about 10,000 well-behaved and orderly federal soldiers, is gradually assuming a decent respect for law and order." The Unionist claimed "a large majority of the citizens now here are loyal to the United States and the seceshers begin to recognize the fact that we have a government." He said "many of the most rabid are returning to their houses after a search of about two months in the Southern Confederacy for their rights." He added that "the little brush at Belmont" had "thrown a gloom" over the leading secessionists in the First Congressional District, "and many of them heartily regret voting for that arch-traitor Burnett against that able and tried friend of the Government, L. S. Trimble, who the Union men of the district now intend to place in the councils of the nation, and, if possible, by his wise and prudent councils heal some of the ghastly wounds inflicted upon it by Burnett and his deranged followers."[75]

Five days later, the *Journal* reported the "deserved fate" of a Burnett supporter, John Milliken, the ex–Paducah postmaster who died in a shootout with Mayfield Unionists. Milliken, the paper said, had fled to Mayfield when Union troops occupied Paducah and "has since been unscrupulous and unsparing in his persecution of every one who was loyal to his country." On November 19, he entered a home, found two Union men, and began cursing and threatening them. "Having lashed himself into fury, he finally struck one of them," the *Journal* said. "As quick as the thunder follows the lightning flash, the report of a musket was heard and the ruffian received its entire contents, killing him instantly." The *Journal* hoped "this terrible retribution will . . . have the effect to deter others from the commission of similar outrages." The paper said Unionists were anxious to go to Paducah and enlist in Williams's regiment, "but the rebels will not permit them to leave their homes, and they subject them to all kinds of indignities." The judge's "four or five complete companies" were "a terror to the secessionists, because they will be able to identify them and bear witness against them for their ruthless deeds." The *Journal* hoped that the Military Board would give Williams extra time to raise a full regiment and not consolidate his recruits into another regiment. His men "know every foot of ground in the infected district south of the Tennessee river, and in a short time they will be able to clear it of every sneaking rebel who is committing depredations."[76]

It seems doubtful that "a large majority" of Paducah citizens had undergone a Road to Damascus experience and gone over to the Union side. By October 10, Smith had concluded that his pacification effort was not very effective. "Perhaps it may have done some good," he mused in a "To all whom it may concern" message. "But the course taken by some of the inhabitants of this city, and by many in the neighborhood, satisfies him that the conciliatory policy ceases to be a virtue." Smith warned that he would, "accordingly, take such measures as the circumstances call for and justify." Coyly, he offered no specifics as to "what those may be," explaining that time would tell. But he did announce that only citizens judged to be loyal could get passes to travel from Paducah or to ship "goods or stores of any description" out of the city.[77]

Doubtless, Robert Owen Woolfolk would have been ineligible for a pass. He persisted in flying a Confederate flag over his large, two-story brick house at 631 Kentucky Avenue. The Tilghmans had lived in the dwelling before the general and his family departed for the Confederacy. Smith ignored the enemy standard, which led to a Yankee-versus-Yankee dustup that the *New York Times* could not resist reporting.[78]

Quoting a letter from Cairo, published in the *St. Louis Democrat,* the *Times* said Woolfolk "hurrahed for Jeff. Davis" and hung the flag from his window when some Union troops passed by. He had shouted for the Confederate president and displayed his flag "before on several occasions." Smith was told about it, but he let the flag fly. Smith's refusal to haul down the flag "caused great indignation among the troops, and doubts of his loyalty were freely expressed in Paducah." No Yankee was more outraged over the flag than Brigadier General Lew Wallace. He dispatched his aide-de-camp and a squad of men to make Woolfolk remove "the traitorous flag." If he would not do so, they were to take it down and run up the US flag over his home. Woolfolk, knowing Smith outranked Wallace, would not yield. So Wallace's aide "forcibly took down the rebel flag, and hoisted the Stars and Stripes in its stead." Woolfolk protested to Smith, who sent his aide to order Wallace to take down the US flag from Woolfolk's home. "Wallace refused to obey the order, and sent word to Smith that the flag should not be taken down while there was a live man in his brigade." Wallace's subordinate declared that "Woolfolk should sleep under a loyal flag one night, anyhow." When General Smith's staffer "replied that he did not consider that any great honor," Wallace's man knocked him down. "As Gen. Smith had nobody but his discomfited Lieutenant to enforce his order, 'the old flag still waves.'"[79]

On November 20, Smith issued a general order protesting the "breach of military discipline, remonstrating against like occurrences in the future, and reminding the troops that they were sent into Kentucky as protectors of a loyal State, and that moderation and forbearance should be exercised toward unarmed enemies, and that they should ever show themselves the champions of law and order." The *Times* reported that another account of the fracas "says that Gen. Wallace went with his whole regiment [the Eleventh Indiana Infantry] to tear down the obnoxious flag, and that he made a congratulatory speech to his soldiers after the affair was over." In addition, a Missouri regiment reportedly "started with a fire-engine to wash out Gen. Smith's headquarters, which they were dissuaded from doing by Gen. Wallace. There was much feeling against Gen. Smith."[80]

As 1861 drew to a close, Paducah became crowded with refugees, Purchase Unionists like Williams, escaped slaves, and Union sympathizers from the Volunteer State. "Within the past week about one hundred men have come in from the bordering counties of Tennessee," an anonymous correspondent wrote the *Journal* from Paducah on December 9. "They represent matters as in a terrible condition in their sections of country." The author thus concluded that in West Tennessee "the unity of the people for separation and the military despotism of the South seems to be a myth, a fancy, a falsehood." Between one thousand and fifteen hundred refugees were expected to reach Paducah "in a few days." The letter writer added, "It is thought that about that number will come from Weakley county," where reportedly "the Union men are in open revolt in that county against the authorities, and a collision is anticipated." Weakley County had voted against secession in June.[81]

But just as the Paducah letter the *Journal* published on November 20 almost certainly overstated Union sentiment in Paducah, the December 9 letter likely exaggerated the extent of Unionism in West Tennessee. Nonetheless, heretofore hard-pressed Purchase Unionists had something genuine to cheer in December. On December 3, the House had formally expelled the "Kentucky Thersites" Burnett for being "in open rebellion against the Government of the United States." According to the *New York Times,* Representative Charles A. Wickliffe of Bardstown blistered Burnett, declaring that he intended to deliver Burnett's "obituary notice" but changed his mind because his "late colleague" had "showed himself in extraordinary colors. He is now in armed rebellion, at the head of a Provisional Government in Kentucky, and the leader of a revolutionary Convention." Wickliffe also blasted Burnett's military commander, Buckner, claiming he was "much more wicked, than Simon Gerty [*sic*], who headed the Indian tribes in an attempt to conquer Kentucky in the days of her first settlement." Burnett, according to Wickliffe, "got up this Convention, composed of the young, and reckless, and desperate men who were already in arms under this man Buckner." Burnett preferred Richmond, the Confederate capital, to Washington anyway. From February 19, 1862, to February 18, 1865, he served as a senator from Kentucky's rump

Confederate government, which exited the state with the retreating Rebels in early 1862.[82]

In addition, the Unionists also got a special Christmas gift four days before Yuletide. The state house and senate expelled Boone, Gilbert, King, Matthewson, and Silvertooth. Coffee resigned in October. The house accused Boone, Gilbert, King, Matthewson, and Silvertooth of being "directly or indirectly connected with, and giving 'aid and comfort' to, the Confederate army, repudiating and acting against the Government of the United States and the Commonwealth of Kentucky." The house further faulted Boone, Gilbert, Matthewson, and Silvertooth for being "members of the Russellville Convention, which organized and established a Provisional Government in Kentucky, in violation of the Constitution, laws, and will of the people of the State, and which was revolutionary and rebellious." Coffee and King also were at the convention.[83]

Back in deposed Representative King's hometown, the Union military buildup continued unabated. When army doctors found themselves shorthanded, they asked nuns who were teaching at St. Mary's Academy to help them. Sister Mary Lucy Dosh, a twenty-two-year-old Pennsylvania-born music teacher, was among the volunteers. Some of her patients were Confederate prisoners of war; she provided the same care to Yankees and Rebels. Her act of Christian charity cost the nun her life. She caught typhoid fever, evidently from one of her patients, and died on December 29: "She was held in such grateful esteem and affection that her body, escorted by an officer and a detail of soldiers, was taken to the U.S. gunboat *Peacock* on a caisson, put aboard and transported to Uniontown, Kentucky, where it was carried to St. Vincent's Academy in Union County." Twelve of her patients made up her honor guard: six Union and six captured Confederate officers. The nuns served in all of Paducah's army "hospitals which were soon filled with cases of typhoid and other infectious diseases, and later with sick and wounded from the battlefields." It was said that Sister Lucy sometimes sang softly as she worked and ate less food so her patients could have more. Thus weakened, it was claimed, she came down with the deadly fever.[84]

Would the Confederates succumb to deadly fire from attacking Yankees? Could the Yankees hold Paducah against an equally determined assault from the Rebels? After all, southern newspapers and public opinion in general considered the Battle of Belmont a "glorious victory" and a "glorious repulse" of Grant and his "insolent invaders." Grant would soon resume the offensive, but not from Cairo against the Confederate "Gibraltar." He would depart from Paducah to strike deep into the Confederacy.[85]

7

Gibraltar Crumbles

January 1, 1862, marked less than a happy New Year for most of Paducah's citizenry. The Yankees had been in their midst for almost four months. It seemed less and less likely that the Rebels would rescue them from the "abolition invaders." Yet it soon went from bad to worse for the secessionist majority in the Purchase—and minority in the rest of the Kentucky. Confederate sympathizers were branded as disloyal by their own state government and denied the vote, jailed, or otherwise punished. Even so, most Purchase secessionists remained resolutely Rebel, eagerly smuggling supplies to the Confederates, spying for the southern side, and still hoping some army in gray, any army in gray, would come back.

Burnett's ouster necessitated a special election to replace him. The vote was set for January 20, and two candidates—both Unionists—vied for the open seat. Trimble decided to try again. His opponent, Samuel L. Casey of Caseyville in Union County, had been US treasurer in President Franklin Pierce's administration. The turnout was tiny, but Casey won, 541–442. In the Purchase, polls opened only in Calloway, Graves, Marshall, and McCracken Counties, which gave Trimble 326 votes to Casey's 251. Trimble carried his home county 297–70.[1]

The *Louisville Journal* printed the *Evansville Journal*'s claim that few ballots were cast because "the secessionists did not recognize the election and the Union men were afraid to vote." The Louisville paper also printed a letter published in the Evansville paper that claimed the vote was light because "the whole country where the rebels have possession is full of guerrilla bands playing the devil generally." Most of McCracken County was firmly under Union military control. Indeed, the paucity of the vote suggests that few citizens had come to rue casting a Burnett ballot.[2]

Two days after First District Unionists sent Casey to Congress, secessionists elected Burnett to the Rebel senate, though no record of the vote apparently exists. Machen became First District representative.[3]

On the other hand, the Purchase remained voiceless in the Kentucky house. In February, the more deliberative senate looked to clean itself of absent secessionists and voted unanimously to expel John M. Johnson of Paducah and William T. Anthony of strongly Unionist Allen County. Both were elected in 1859 and attended the Russellville convention. Neither Irvan nor Jenkins voted on the two expulsion resolutions. The senate investigated Irvan but chose not to remove him. Unionist Thomas A. Duke of Paducah won a special election to succeed Johnson.[4]

Meanwhile, from its "capital" in Confederate-occupied Bowling Green, the Rebel government tried to exercise some authority over the part of Kentucky it—or rather the Confederate army—controlled. Reportedly, commissioners went into the First Congressional District to remove all civil officials "who have refused to take the oath to support the Russellville nuisance." Rebel officials reputedly were "making arrangements to collect the taxes by force, rebel sheriffs are levying on the property of Union men, and advertise it to be sold, while those men are driven from their homes."[5]

Senator-elect Burnett was away from his Cadiz home, but he was not yet in Richmond. He had gone to Rebel-held Hopkinsville, the Christian County seat, to raise the Eighth Kentucky Infantry. On November 11, Burnett was elected colonel of the regiment but never took command. Not surprisingly, the *Journal* was singularly unimpressed and heaped more scorn upon "the expelled member of Congress." The paper claimed to have seen a letter from Hopkinsville cataloging "his excesses of passion and his cruelty towards the Union men." The Louisville paper added that when Burnett heard about a skirmish between Brigadier General Nathan Bedford Forrest's cavalry and Union troops at Sacramento, in McLean County, on December 28, "he raved and swore like a maniac." Never mind that the small battle was the soon-to-be-famous Rebel cavalry commander's first Civil War victory. Burnett, according to the *Journal,* "went about the streets, ordering all loyal men to leave their homes, threatening to hang them or cut their throats."[6]

The *Journal* said Burnett's tirade prompted "his commanding and subordinate officers" to insist that he apologize "to those whom he insulted, which he did the next day." The *Journal* editorialized that "a traitor to his country must always prove a tyrant and a traitor toward the defenceless." The paper predicted that in the Confederate senate he "will most fittingly represent the atrocity, violence, plunder, and pillage of this accursed rebellion, but, as an exponent of the honor and loyalty of the proud old State, the seal of righteous condemnation has been set upon him by the vote which expelled him from the House of Representatives at Washington."[7]

From Hopkinsville, Burnett traveled with the Eighth Kentucky to Fort Donelson, the Rebel bastion on the Cumberland River near Dover, Tennessee, which Buckner surrendered to Grant's attacking army-navy force on February 16, 1862. Grant assaulted the southern strongpoint on February 12, six days after his force captured Fort Henry on the Tennessee River. After Henry, Johnston feared Donelson was doomed, so he ordered his army, including the Third Kentucky, to forsake Bowling Green for Nashville. Burnett eluded capture at Fort Donelson by fleeing for the Tennessee capital on a steamboat with Major General John B. Floyd and his Virginia troops. Afterward, Burnett doffed the uniform of a Rebel soldier to return to Rebel politics.[8]

The Yankees commanded the lower Tennessee and Cumberland Rivers after the fall of Henry and Donelson. But both sides still vied for control of the Mississippi River between Cairo and Columbus. Cairo-based Yankee captain William D. "Dirty Bill" Porter challenged Columbus-based Rebel skipper Marsh J. Miller to "come out here, you cowardly rebels, and show your gunboats," according to the *New York Times.* On January 13, 1862, Miller picked up the gauntlet: "Sir: The iron clad steamer Grampus will meet the Essex, at any point and any time your Honor might appoint, and show you that the power is in our hands. An early reply will be agreeable to." One was forthcoming "to the traitor Marsh Miller, commanding a Rebel Gun-boat called the Grampus: 'Commander Porter has already thrashed your Gunboat Fleet; shelled and silenced your Rebel Batteries at the Iron Banks; chased your miserable and cowardly self down behind Columbus.'" Porter added, "But if you desire to meet the Essex, show yourself any morning in Prenty's [probably Puntney's] bend, and you shall meet with a traitor's fate." The affair of honor never came off. Porter was skipper of the USS *Essex,* "the most powerful ironclad gunboat on the Mississippi River at the time," according to Clinton historian and writer John Kelly Ross. The *Grampus* was a small sternwheeler steamboat. The *Essex* was based near Cairo; the *Grampus* was from Columbus. "The *Grampus* was Porter's nemesis. The Union gunboats would test the defenses of Columbus," Ross says. "The *Grampus* would wait for them a few miles above Columbus and, blowing her steam whistle, the little scout boat would race ahead of the Yankee fleet to warn the Confederates." Not surprisingly, the *Times* correspondent also maligned Miller. "The *Grampus* is well known to be a species of spouting-fish, and this particular one frequently runs up the Mississippi to blow, and then runs down again," he wrote. "We are going down the river to-morrow to see if his courage is up to the standing point; but we are afraid he will draw a bee line to Columbus, as he has heretofore always done." Porter, on the other hand, "is not one of those rose-water heroes, and he will not be expected to waste compliments on men whose treasonable and cowardly conduct he holds in supreme contempt." Miller's vessel was unarmored and apparently had only one cannon, compared to multiple guns on the *Essex.* Hence, the captain prudently preferred flight to fight. Even so, the plodding *Essex* almost caught the speedy *Grampus* one time. Ross says the accommodating Captain Miller stopped his boat upstream from Columbus so his crew could go ashore and pick paw-paws: "When they saw the Union fleet, the men rushed back to the boat and got away to Columbus." The *Essex* would have made kindling out of the *Grampus,* Ross maintains: "The *Grampus* was . . . just a little wooden boat. But Porter was able to get a little cheap publicity out of the affair." Miller kept the *Grampus* out of range of the *Essex.* The boat escaped with the Confederates when they abandoned Columbus.[9]

Doubtless Burnett was remorseful about the fate of the twelve to fifteen thousand Rebels who gave up to Grant on February 16. These defenders of Henry and Donelson had expected to whip the Yankees; now they were on their way to prison camps up north. The captives included the Second and Eighth Kentucky and Buckner, who was a friend of Burnett and Grant. Like Confederate prisoners, Union casualties went by boat down the Cumberland. But military hospitals in Paducah and elsewhere were the destination for the wounded Union soldiers. Mastin wound up as a nurse and helped treat some of them.[10]

At Columbus, where the Rebel army's days were numbered, the soldiers of the Seventh Kentucky were detailed as military police. Polk named Wickliffe military governor of Columbus; in turn, he made his infantrymen provost marshals. The bishop-general prohibited booze, and Pillow the teetotaler added his "amen." Dutifully, Wickliffe's men patrolled against purveyors and purchasers of illicit alcohol. Liquor flowed freely, though the "strictest martial law" was the rule. Two civilians caught peddling whiskey were flogged in the middle of town as a warning to citizens and the soldiery.[11]

Polk's alcohol ban encompassed "liquor of all hues and colors in Columbus and environs of ten miles," "A.M," a Louisiana soldier, complained in a letter to the *New Orleans Picayune.* He claimed the bars of steamboats calling at Columbus "must be kept hermetically sealed, under penalty of being entirely excluded from visiting here." Wickliffe's troops had to inspect all parcels, except those addressed to officers, for liquor. "The Contraband stuff" was to be seized "for the benefit of the sick and wounded soldiers." Provost marshals had to "know the bowels of a box or package at first sight, and" understood "that boxes marked 'sweet oil,' and bottles labeled 'medicines' need the closest investigation." The Seventh Kentucky wintered comfortably enough in log huts on the edge of town. Nonetheless, an outbreak of measles killed a number of soldiers, George wrote. "Nothing of very especial importance occurred during the winter, the men performed their routine duty, patrolling the town."[12]

The loss of Forts Henry and Donelson and Bowling Green left Columbus "the only stronghold which [the Confederates] . . . retain north of Nashville, and the only fortified position of formidable strength from Cairo to the Belize [Louisiana]," the *Times* reported on February 23. The paper predicted "a grand assault might carry Columbus, but it would be at an expense of loyal blood and treasure." The paper suggested only two ways Columbus could be conquered: "One is to attack it by regular approaches, the other to surround it, and starve out the swaggering rebel chivalry." Interestingly, the *Times* said the Confederates had been fortifying Columbus "for eight months past." Yet the Confederate army had arrived a little over five months before. Did the paper consider Columbus to be under Confederate control when the state guards came to town and reportedly planted long-range cannons?[13]

The longest-range cannon, "Lady Polk," accidentally exploded after the battle of Belmont, killing five men and wounding several others. Polk, standing nearby, was unscathed, though the blast shredded his uniform and somewhat burned his face. But the Rebels still had at least five more big guns with nicknames: "Soul Searcher," "Snorter," "Yankee Smolluxer," "Rib Smasher," and "Cunning Cuss." If the cannons were "no safer institutions than their 'big rebel' that exploded . . . the Rebels will be a pack of fools if they don't apply slow matches, and run like quarter horses themselves," the *Cairo City Weekly Gazette* mocked. "The reputation of some of the Columbus cannon is such that a person would likely consider himself to be as safe at one end or the other."[14]

Not a drop of Yankee or Rebel blood was spilled at Columbus. The Rebels moved out, and the Yankees moved in. Editor Bullock, apparently deciding that discretion was indeed the better part of valor, went with the departed southern troops. His editorials in the *Daily Confederate News* had grown even more bloodthirsty. On January 3, he thundered:

> The time has come—the hour arrived—the period pregnant—we are determined to rush to the rescue of our country. Therefore we make known to all that should the Yankees attack Columbus we are ready and willing, and will be in the fight, although we are no volunteer. We want to kill a Yankee—must kill a Yankee—never can sleep sound again until we do kill a Yankee, get his overcoat and scalp. Indian-like, we want a scalp, and must have it. We'd think no more of scalping a dead Yank than cutting the throat of a midnight assassin—not a shade's difference between the murderer and the deceptious Yank.[15]

The *Times* touted Columbus's uncontested capture by the "deceptious Yanks," quoting a *Cincinnati Daily Gazette* correspondent who accompanied the Union forces to "the Gibraltar of America, as our Southern brethren have been prone to style what will be better known as Columbus, Ky." Before the Union armada set out for Columbus ahead of sunup on March 4, rumors flew in Cairo that Columbus had been evacuated, reinforced, or burned or had been "neither reinforced, evacuated or burned." The scribe suggested that Commodore Foote believed the enemy were still in Columbus since his flotilla consisted of a half-dozen gunboats, four mortar boats, and three transports carrying forty-five hundred troops. Foote, aboard his flagship, the ironclad *Cincinnati,* led the way. One of the army generals aboard would also achieve military greatness. He was a red-bearded Ohioan named William Tecumseh Sherman. The day dawned "clear, bright and cold," before the Union fleet reached its objective. When the soldiers and sailors sighted Columbus, they could not determine if the Confederates were still in town, so the gunboat crews prepared for battle, manning and loading the guns. The mortar boats were towed into position on the Missouri side of the river, and the transports stood ready to land troops. But no gun was to be fired nor a single soldier put ashore until the brass determined if "there was anything to attack." The fleet was three miles upriver from Columbus, too far away to tell for sure. Peering through spyglasses, two men said the Rebels and their big guns were still there. A third man viewed "table bluffs," which he suggested "might once have been in use for fortifications of some kind." But another spotter with a spyglass saw "in the dim distance large clouds of smoke, and felt quite sure that a great conflagration was in progress—that military stores and army quarters were in flames, and that the rumored evacuation had certainly taken place." Foote had a healthy respect for well-emplaced shore batteries. The long-range guns of Fort Donelson had beaten up his gunboats, some of which still needed repair. Thus, "he did not wish to get within rage of the rebel guns until he had satisfied himself, and seen that there was or was not somebody there to fire them." Just then, the commodore caught a break. The Yankees espied a Missouri farmer running through a cornfield behind what was evidently the man's house. The *Gazette* man suspected the gunboats had scared him and that the poor fellow "was beating a hasty retreat from what he feared would be the scene of bloodshed." Foote sent his tug scuttling "to the river bank, to hail him, and get from him what information he had about the rebel stronghold." The commodore listened as the man swore that the Rebels had abandoned Columbus, taking "their arms and munitions with them." They also "had burned the greater part of the town." The Yankees believed their informant. The reporter said he seemed to be "an honest, hard-working man, one of a class largely represented in Kentucky, Missouri and Tennessee—who love the Union and abhor secession, but cannot easily reconcile themselves to the horrors of war, and pray for peace and the Union, though they know the two cannot be maintained at the present time." The farmer's testimony clinched it for Foote; he was confident the Rebels were indeed gone. Even so, doubt returned, if briefly, when the Yankees, through their telescopes, spotted a big flag flapping on a hilltop. "It was too large for a rebel flag, we thought, and had too many stripes on it. We therefore concluded that the rebels had all vacated the town, leaving behind them, as they generally do, a leaven of Unionism, which had already begun to work," the *Gazette* reporter wrote. They were wrong. Columbus citizens had not hoisted the banner; Yankee soldiers had.[16]

Unbeknownst to the men afloat, troopers of the Second Illinois Cavalry had galloped into town on the evening of March 3, found the enemy gone, "and were in joyful possession" of Columbus when the fleet arrived. Their flag of welcome was hardly regulation, according to the *Times.* The paper said the innovative horsemen had fashioned it from "colored calico—the object being to present to the gaze of Commodore Foote a banner of almost any description, provided it intimated that treason did not rule supreme." In any event, Foote took the flag as a symbol to debark his troops. Less than five minutes after the first soldier was ashore, the Yankees "unfurled a beautiful silk flag," which "proudly floated where blatant Southrons have boasted of treason's impregnability." The banner "had a magical effect upon every one in our fleet, and cheer after cheer resounded through the surrounding woods and hills."[17]

The *Gazette* man thought that the fortifications at Columbus were not as fearsome as the Yankee brass believed. He held that the bastion had been poorly scouted, leaving the generals "ignorant, from the first, of the real strength of the rebels at this point." The reporter said the works crowned a 150-foot bluff immediately north of town, admitting that "the position is admirably adapted to defence." He said by felling many trees at Belmont, the Confederates were able "to command a perfect view of the river for a distance of four miles." He said the bluff faced north and projected slightly into the river beyond a ridge that extended a mile north of it. "There are, or rather there were, three rows of batteries upon it, the first about fifteen feet above the river, the second about — feet above this, and the third on the top of the hill." The reporter said it was "difficult to say how many guns either of these mounted, as the rebels threw most of their heavy pieces into the river, or attempted to do so, though many of them failed to reach their destination, and stopped on the bank, where they are now visible." He guessed that the Rebels' three main batteries had fifty cannons, "and we have the evidence of citizens, who frequently visited the camp, to this effect." Nonetheless, Union attackers would have had one big edge: "There was no shelter erected for the artillerymen; and those who worked the guns in the lower batteries would be exposed during the entire action to the fire of the gunboats."[18]

He said the water battery, which was "on a sort of table about fifty feet long and twenty feet deep," would have been an easy target for a good gun crew. "If the gunboats could have held out against it for any length of time, it would have been silenced." The upper batteries were not as exposed, but none of them provided gunners adequate shelter from exploding shells, grapeshot, or canister fire. The whole works on the bluff sprawled for approximately four miles: "The fortifications are equally strong on all sides, and calculated to repulse an army attacking from the south as well as from the north. The fort can be reached from the town of Columbus by four different roads, cut through the high hills at an immense outlay of labor." The correspondent saw a number of small huts or cabins, adding that there "are enough of these apartments to accomodate thirty thousand men." He said regimental and company officers had similar lodgings, "but a little more tastily finished." The main magazine was close to the Mississippi, below the water battery. The correspondent described the ammunition storehouse as "a subterranean work, about twenty feet square, easy of access from all parts of the fortifications. About half way up the bluff—75 feet above this—is another magazine, equal in size and similar in construction to the first." He added that the troops got their water from the river "by means of a force-pump worked by an engine."[19]

In addition, the reporter cited "Pillow's great chain" as "among the objects which excited curiosity" among the Yankees. "It is a very strong and heavy looking affair, stretching down the hill and into the river, where, I believe, it is broken."[20]

The *Gazette* man was unimpressed with Columbus, describing the town as "a small, unimportant place, with a population, in its palmiest days, of about 1,000 inhabitants." He said the railroad brought the town "a business significance that would not otherwise belong to it," adding that the "mud and dirt" of Columbus streets "resembles Cairo." The reporter said Columbus contained "four large brick buildings in the town—one of them a hotel, whose principal patronage was that of railroad passengers." He found vacant houses, closed and empty stores, and a shortage of food. He said the Rebels had driven the citizens away when they "took possession of the hills," "cleaned out the stores," and "depleted every farmer of his produce without giving him even Confederate scrip therefor." He declared Columbus "one of the poorest and gloomiest towns I have come across, even in the benighted regions of Secessia."[21]

Junius Henry Browne, the famously acerbic *New York Tribune* correspondent, was also with the flotilla, riding on a transport boat. He said the flag the soldiers and sailors spotted was indeed "the glorious old Stars and Stripes" shining "out bright and clear." The men doffed their hats, "and three cheers for the Union rang out across the silent bosom of the Mississippi. The cry was caught up from the gunboats, and the distant bluffs echoed the joyous shout." But Browne did not like the music army bands struck up—"Dixie," which he panned as "that detestable air which I am sorry Secessia has not been allowed to monopolize." Yet, "with waving hats and banners, we were soon passing the Rebel fortifications, whose guns had been dismounted—and steaming into the landing of the famed and fearful town." Browne explored the defense works, speculating that the Confederates "must have been extremely jocose. I found a number of Valentines the troops had sent each other, with droll letters, showing their fondness for, and appreciation of humor." He explained, "We found a number of stuffed figures of President Lincoln, General McClellan, [*Tribune* editor] Horace Greeley, and others, represented in the most grotesque form, and always associated in some way with the gallows and negroes." The effigies "were 'gotten up' with bottles in their hands in every instance, and some ultra-Abolitionist sentiment invariably ascribed to them." He also said the Union troops found in the camps "various letters and documents, all breathing the most fervent spirit of orthodoxy, the loftiest appeal to Providence, the largest faith in its determination to overthrow the wicked Yankees, who would not let the saintly Rebels alone in the enjoyment of their rights. . . . The idea of the Almighty arraying Himself on the side of Treason, Oppression, Cruelty, and Slavery, would be monstrous, if it were not ridiculous." Browne suggested, "Murderers might as well pray to Him to shield them from harm during the progress of their assassinations, or profligates ask His assistance in the betrayal of an innocent maid as *they* invoke the protection of Heaven, or claim its sympathy with their unholy cause." He added that the Union troops grabbed as trophies pikes and large knives the Rebels had left behind: "In ancient days, the valor of a nation was determined by the shortness of their weapons; but I opine the nation did something more than throw them away at the approach of real danger." The pikes, he reported, "proved serviceable to our men in climbing the steep bluffs of Columbus, though they did not deem them adapted to the sanguinary pursuits of war."[22]

The general accuracy of the *Times* story and Browne's account was borne out in the official reports of Foote, Union brigadier general G. W. Cullum, and Polk. Sherman, also a brigadier, and Cullum commanded the troops. A jubilant Foote wrote navy secretary Gideon Welles on March 4: "Columbus is in our possession. My armed reconnaissance on the 2d instant caused a hasty evacuation, the rebels leaving quite a number of guns and carriages, ammunition, and a large quantity of shot and shell, a considerable number of anchors, and the remnant of chain lately stretched across the river, with a large number of torpedoes. Most of the huts, tents, and quarters destroyed. The works are of very great strength, consisting of formidable tiers of batteries on the water side and on the land side, surrounded by a ditch and abatis." Sherman had sent part of Second Illinois from Paducah to scout toward Columbus. But unaware the horsemen were in town, he and Lieutenant Commander S. L. Phelps boarded a tug, apparently Foote's, with thirty soldiers and "made a bold dash to the shore under the water batteries." After discovering that the cavalry were in Columbus, they hoisted "the American flag on the summit of the bluff, greeted by the hearty cheers of our brave tars and soldiers." Foote said Cullum and Sherman had prevented a blazing powder magazine from exploding, thus saving the lives of many Union soldiers. Foote also praised other army and navy officers. Cullum, chief of staff and engineer for Major General Henry W. Halleck, who succeeded Fremont in command in St. Louis, also wrote his boss on March 4: "Columbus, the Gibraltar of the west, is ours, and Kentucky is free; thanks to the brilliant strategy of the campaign, by which the enemy's center was pierced at Forts Henry and Donelson, his wings isolated from each other and turned, compelling thus the evacuation of his strongholds of Bowling Green first and now Columbus." Cullum, though he was ailing and abed, "could not resist landing to examine the works, which are of immense strength." He suspected Columbus had been "evacuated hastily," considering all the ordnance the Rebels left behind: "Desolation was visible everywhere; huts, tents, barracks presented nothing but their blackened remains." Cullum said he had prevented the magazine from blowing up and urged Foote to press on and attack the Confederate strongpoints downriver at Island Number 10 and New Madrid, Missouri. Foote declined: "that gallant commodore, after consulting with his brave officers, was of the opinion that two or three days of repairs to the gunboats was indispensable."[23]

Polk's March 2 preliminary report to Confederate secretary of war Judah P. Benjamin was more succinct: "The work is done. Columbus gone. Self and staff move in half an hour. Everything secured." He also telegraphed Beauregard that he was leaving Columbus.[24]

After they settled in, some "deceptious Yanks" of the Second Illinois took over the newspaper office and started publishing the *Federal Scout*. The first issue—March 11—listed the names of the approximately two hundred troopers who had beaten Foote's force to town. The paper also told how they had gotten to Columbus, explaining that on March 2, Sherman ordered the Second Illinois to ride out and see if the Rebels really were leaving Columbus. When Milburn citizens told the troopers the Confederates were indeed forsaking their "Manassas of the West," Lieutenant Colonel Harvey Hogg ordered them "Forward to Columbus." Any Rebels encountered on the way were to be given "*the cold steel!*" of their sabers. They reached Columbus just before sundown on March 3: "Seeing no enemy, neither stopping to consider whether there was any danger, we drew our sabers and dashed into town." The paper said they ran a regulation Stars and Stripes—not "colored calico" cloth—up a pole "amid deafening cheers for the Union, and our gallant Colonel and Major, who had so successfully lead [*sic*] us into the strongest hold or rebellion in the West." They planned to present the flag to Illinois governor Richard Yates. Most of the horse soldiers moved into empty houses and a hotel, stabled their horses, and helped themselves to sugar, molasses, "and many little items of special need" from abandoned stores. The paper satirized the Rebels in poetry, prose, and artwork, the latter a cartoon based on advertisements for runaway slaves. The drawing, captioned "Secesh Leaving Columbus," depicted a runaway Rebel, a stick resting on his shoulder and his belongings tied in a tiny bundle at the other end. A pig was fleeing in front of him.[25]

Meanwhile, Polk did not get around to writing a detailed report of the loss of Columbus until March 18. He was in Humboldt, Tennessee, about seventy-five miles south of the fallen "Gibraltar." He said he had carried out the evacuation of Columbus "with as much celerity as the safety of my command and the security of the public property at risk would allow." The evacuation began on February 25, with most of his troops heading thirty miles downriver to Island Number Ten and New Madrid. The fortified island was at the upper base of a big loop in the river that separates Madrid Bend, Kentucky, from the rest of the Bluegrass State; the Kentucky-Tennessee line was nearby. The Confederates burned and otherwise destroyed much of what they could not carry. The evacuation of troops, guns, ammunition, and supplies lasted until March 2, when Polk and his staff left town at 3:00 p.m.[26]

Reporters and sketch artists naturally followed the Union troops to Columbus, feeding a steady stream of stories to news-hungry northerners. Writer-artist Alexander Simplot thrilled readers of *Harper's Weekly* with three large sketches and a story about the water and land mines. The "fiendish" gadgets were designed to blow unsuspecting boat crews and soldiers to kingdom come. One of Simplot's drawings showed some of the "torpedoes"—river mines—plus their weights and anchors, forsaken on the levee. The other two illustrations were panoramas of the water batteries and the town from the bluffs. The newspaper included a *New York Herald* account of Columbus after the Rebels were gone:

> The river batteries have been almost entirely demolished—three tiers of them—their guns dismounted and thrown into the river, the gun-carriages mutilated and magazines demolished, leaving nothing to mark their former presences save ruined breast-works and huge piles of cannon-balls and shells. Just below the upper river battery, a huge chain, which has been christened "Pillow's Folly," emerges from the water, extends up the almost perpendicular band a hundred feet or more, and disappears under the soil, where it extends to—the Lord only knows where. This is the Kentucky end of the chain which the valiant inside-ditchdigger had stretched across the river to obstruct the passage of our gun-boats.[27]

Meanwhile, the Confederate exodus from the Bluegrass State included the Third Kentucky, which had joined Johnston at Bowling Green in September. On February 24, a weary Paine Ridgway of the Third Kentucky wrote Jennie from Murfreesboro, Tennessee. He described a march from his native state that had taxed body and soul: "We were in all that snow and rain last week, from twelve to sixteen miles per day. And one day we marched twenty six miles double quick two miles. Oh, miserable! How we suffered from sore feet and fatigue no one but a poor soldier can imagine." He promised Jennie he would never forget her though he might end up confined "in a Yankie prison where hundreds of my friends are suffering tonight." He vowed he would have stayed in Kentucky "& fought as long as . . . we would have been allowed to do so. I would have thought it a greater honor to have been killed in Ky than won a victory down here. These are things that we could not control you know."[28]

The Seventh Kentucky was equally powerless to stop the evacuation of Columbus. The regiment had been relieved of provost duty about the first of February and returned to perhaps equally dreary infantry drill. Pirtle recalled the day when the regiment received orders "to cook rations" and move out to Fort Donelson: "We made all preperations that we could expecting to start next morning, thus we continued from day to day for several days." He added, "All the word we got was to keep ready to move at a moments notice. During this delay some of the boys threatened to run away and go without orders." Orders finally came, but not to battle the Yankees. "While waiting in suspence, one night was awakened by a heavy lumbering nois and when day light came, could see that every thing in fort was being run down the bluff near the river and all loaded on steamboats." Pirtle and his mates "were troubled, could not understand the movement, but by noon learned that fort donalson had surrendered, and evacuation of Columbus had began. Every thing was in great commotion, soldiers moving in every direction. This hubbub continued several days."

About noon on March 1, according to Pirtle, Cheatham formed up his division, including the Seventh Kentucky, on the Clinton Road. The Graves County soldier could "see smoke in every direction, every thing was being burned that we could not carry with us." The soldiers tramped to familiar territory, Camp Burnett, where they spent the night. They continued their withdrawal through Clinton, turned south to Moscow, and made camp at Cayce, on the railroad. After dark, a locomotive pulling flat cars backed in from Union City. The footsore western Kentuckians clambered aboard and rode to Humboldt, Tennessee. They and their comrades in the Third Kentucky did not know it, of course, but they were a little over a month shy of their baptism by fire along the banks of the Tennessee River deep in Tennessee. The battle was named Shiloh for a little log Methodist meetinghouse around which much of the fighting swirled. Pirtle would survive unscathed. But Colonel Wickliffe would be among the Rebel dead.[29]

At the same time they retreated from Columbus and Hickman, the Rebels abandoned disease-ravaged Camp Beauregard, which seldom rates more than a few lines in history books. A state historical marker on US Highway 45 in Water Valley tells motorists about Camp Beauregard, now a local cemetery. A gray stone monolith commemorates the campsite. Rowed up, soldierlike, are sixteen military tombstones that mark individual graves of Mississippi and Missouri troops. But most of the Confederates who succumbed to disease were buried in mass graves and are thus unidentified. "In memory of the loyal men who died here September 1861 to March 1862 for the Confederate States of America, and were thus denied the glory of heroic service in battle," the inscription on the monument reads. Yet the first troops did not arrive at Camp Beauregard until October 6, 1861; the camp was finally abandoned and burned on February 21, 1862. In any event, the late Graves County historian Lon Carter Barton likens the local Rebel outpost to Valley Forge. Between twelve and fifteen hundred southern soldiers perished, not from Yankee bullets but from typhoid fever, measles, and cerebrospinal meningitis.[30]

The troops were ultimately housed in small log cabins on the hilltop. At first it might not have mattered if the shelters were less than cozy; the autumn weather was unusually warm. But in late November, it turned unseasonably cold. Sunny skies clouded; freezing rain lashed the soldiers. A three-inch snowfall blanketed the ill-fated camp on November 30. Worse, a full-scale epidemic struck. Colonel John S. Bowen, commander of the First Missouri Infantry and Camp Beauregard, reported that just 3,361 of his 4,260 officers and men were fit for duty. The epidemic was so bad that even Smith and the Yankees in Paducah heard about it. Among the camp's hard-pressed doctors was G. C. Phillips, surgeon of the Twenty-second Mississippi Infantry. He recalled that measles ran through the soldiers of his regiment, "in many cases leaving some broncial [*sic*] or intestional [*sic*] trouble, rendering them easy marks for pneumonia and typhoid fever." He remembered the cold rain, followed by sleet and snow, harsh weather that made drilling and picket duty doubly difficult. Phillips added that the men were not used to the camp diet, "mostly fresh beef and flour, no vegetables, with plenty of coffee, tea and whiskey." Typhoid fever and pneumonia followed the measles. "There were 75 cases of typhoid fever and typhoid pneumonia in my hospital tent during one month," Phillips remembered. "It was as bad or worse than other regiments. Then the most terrible disease, cerebro-spinal meningitis broke out, killing nearly every case attacked, and frequently in a few hours." He remembered one time "the men in a certain mess had just come in from drilling, and whilst waiting for their dinner to cook, one of them commenced to talk queer, then jerk his head back and fell over into convulsions." Another soldier dashed to Phillips's tent and yelled, "Come, Dr., quick, one of our men has that thing." By the time Phillips arrived, another soldier had been similarly stricken, and both of them died within three hours. "The drs. were all at sea. None of us had ever seen a case of this disease. We knew the brain and spinal cord were affected, but why so many similar cases?" He said meningitis was deadlier than yellow fever, a disease common in the South. "We knew that a disease very similar in symptoms to this attacked the new recruits in the French Army during Napoleon's campaign in Egypt, but this did not help us, as no remedy was known for it." Phillips said the commander of the regiment, Colonel D. W. C. Bonham, summoned him and asked frantically if anything could be done to stop the unseen killer. "It was worse than a battle," Phillips remembered. "The men became depressed and gloomy, each one feared that he would be the next one taken, and if so it meant death. Men in apparent perfect health, on going to bed, would be taken in the night, and by the next night might be dead." Desperate to stop the disease, Phillips suggested to Bonham that he shift the campsite, if merely a half mile, and order his men fed "corn meal, bacon, dry salty meat, turnips, potatoes, onions and cow peas." Phillips confessed "this was an experiment, but I could advise nothing else." The change of diet seemed to work, or more likely, the epidemic simply ran its course: "For the two weeks afterwards that we remained there (being then ordered to Bowling Green, Ky.) we had no more of this terrible disease and typhoid fever and pneumonia fell very markedly." But the troops who remained at Camp Beauregard "continued to suffer," Phillips wrote.[31]

The commander of the small Confederate force that burned Beauregard on February 21 confessed his sadness over the destruction of the hard-luck camp: "As the flames consumed the labors of the brave boys who had built and occupied those cabins, I could not but think of them as roofless wanderers, exposed to every inclemency of weather, yet contented with a hasty bivouac, and finding their reward in the service of their country." Phillips said the Confederates "who suffered and died at Camp Beauregard, were just as brave and patriotic as their comrades and friends, who fell upon the great battlefields of the War Between the States, and in whose honor and memory beautiful and noble monuments have been erected. They should be honored in the same way." He added, "It was no fault of theirs that they did not live to be killed at Shiloh, Vicksburg or Franklin, where so many of the regiment were killed, and whose resting places are marked by headstones and beautiful monuments—erected by loving descendants and friends in memory of their heroism, courage and glorious death." The Camp Beauregard dead got their memorial through the efforts of Lizzie Lowe Fuller of Mayfield, the Kentucky Division of the United Daughters of the Confederacy, and the Beauregard Monument Association of Louisiana. Lowe spearheaded a fund drive that raised almost thirteen hundred dollars for the stone, and she presided over the dedication of the monument in 1920.[32]

The winter of 1862 was indeed the winter of discontent for the Purchase's secessionist majority. The Union army dug in deeper in Paducah; the Confederates abandoned the Purchase and joined a wholesale Rebel retreat from Kentucky. The southern conquest of Hickman and Columbus had been bloodless, as was the Union occupation of both towns. Columbus proved less than Gibraltar-like. Yankee soldiers moved behind the battlements and held them unchallenged, except for occasional small guerrilla forays, for the rest of the war.

8

Yankee Occupation

After driving the Confederates out of Kentucky, Union forces seemed unstoppable in the Western Theater of the war. As the Yankees pushed the enemy ever southward, Purchase hopes for a Confederate reconquest of the region dimmed further. With Union troops to protect them, the Unionist minority asserted themselves. But this was a conservative Unionist group. Almost all of them favored the preservation of the Union with slavery. Though they detested the region's pro-Confederate majority, almost every Purchase Unionist shared the secessionists' disdain for abolitionism, Lincoln, and his Emancipation Proclamation.

The Yankees permitted no rest for the weary Rebels at New Madrid and Island Number Ten. Union forces captured the former on March 13 and the latter on April 8.[1]

The surrender of Island Number Ten ended significant military operations in the Jackson Purchase, except for Forrest's raid on Paducah in March 1864. Even so, the Yankee occupiers, however far from the big battles, did not have it easy. Guerrillas plagued them for the rest of the Civil War, a conflict most people think of in terms of mighty armies clashing, not guerrillas, writes historian Daniel Sutherland in *A Savage Conflict: The Decisive Role of Guerrillas in the Civil War.* The title reflects the thesis of his book: "It is impossible to understand the Civil War without appreciating the scope and impact of the guerrilla conflict, although that is no easy thing to do." Sutherland says that "the guerrilla side of the war was intense and sprawling, born in controversy, and defined by all variety of contradictions, contours, and shadings." Union military commanders applied a broad-brush and derogatory definition of "guerrilla." They commonly used the term to describe bands of horsemen who insisted they were regular Rebel cavalry or claimed to be "rangers" or "partisan rangers," designations the Confederates applied to their government-sanctioned guerrillas starting in the spring of 1862. But as the war dragged out, "guerrillas grew increasingly independent and ungovernable, very nearly waging their own war." Recognizing the threat posed to Union military operations, federal commanders cracked down hard: "They treated rebel guerrillas as brigands, not soldiers, and they punished rebel civilians who supported or encouraged guerrilla warfare." When Union forces encountered the countryside united against them—guerrillas and civilians who supported them—Union political and military leaders understood that winning conventional battles would not bring the war to an end, Sutherland writes. They had to "crush rebellion on the southern home front." Such comprehension wrought profound changes in how the Union side waged war: "Those changes, in turn, produced a more brutal and destructive war that led to Confederate defeat." So it would go in the Purchase—and the balance of Kentucky—from the withdrawal of Confederate forces from the state in early 1862 to the end of the war. In 1863, the Union army officially drew a distinction between partisans and guerrillas in General Orders No. 100. Signed by President Lincoln, the document was an attempt to establish rules of warfare. It was also known as the Lieber Code for its author, Francis Lieber, a Prussian-born legal scholar, historian, and philosopher. General Orders No. 100 defined partisans as armed and uniformed soldiers who were detached from the main bodies of their armies and who operated in enemy-controlled territory. If captured, they were "entitled to all the privileges of the prisoner of war." On the other hand, guerrillas were men who committed "hostilities, whether by fighting, or inroads for destruction or plunder, or by raids of any kind, without commission, without being part and portion of the organized hostile army, and without sharing continuously in the war." Guerrillas intermittently returned to their homes and work or occasionally assumed "the semblance of peaceful pursuits." Because such men divested themselves from "the character and appearance of soldiers," they were not to be considered prisoners of war if caught. They were to "be treated summarily as highway robbers and pirates."[2]

In any event, the heretofore hard-pressed Unionist minority in the Purchase was just glad to see the Rebels go. They started having mass meetings of the sort the secessionists were always getting up before the Rebels came and during their occupation of the Purchase. Ballard County Unionists gathered triumphantly in Blandville on March 24. Chaired by M. C. Thompson with J. C. Depoyster as secretary, the meeting endorsed Judge Williams for election to the Fourth Appellate District seat on the Kentucky Court of Appeals, then the state's highest court. After helping raise the Twentieth Kentucky Infantry Regiment, Williams had opted to return to the bench. The election was scheduled for August 4; a First District nominating convention was set for May 1 in Henderson. The meeting also chose Ballard's delegates but resolved that if they could not attend, then Graves County's delegates would be their proxies.[3]

Five days later, Marshall County Unionists met at Flat Rock and endorsed Williams. Dr. W. T. Chiles and A. Johnson led the meeting as chairman and secretary, respectively. The Union men appointed county delegates to the Henderson convention and resolved if none of them could go, then Mayfield attorney Lucian Anderson should "cast the vote of Marshall county as an alternate."[4]

Williams had competition when the convention met. Some counties in the eastern part of the district favored state representative George H. Yeaman of Owensboro. But he bowed out, and the convention unanimously nominated Williams. Anderson, who put forward Williams's name, "addressed the convention in a short but stirring speech." The grateful candidate "returned thanks to the Convention, and pledged himself to a vigorous canvass." The convention included delegates or alternates from all of the Purchase counties. Each county got one vote for every one hundred Union votes cast in the August 1861 state elections. But special dispensation had to be made for those counties where Unionists had not run. Convention rules were written to permit them to substitute their Union vote in the June 1861 congressional election. Even so, that eliminated Fulton and Hickman Counties, neither of which gave Trimble one hundred votes. Graves County delegate Richard Neel, a Mayfield lawyer, offered a resolution urging "every loyal man of this State to vote for no candidate for official station whose loyalty to the Federal Government and the State of Kentucky is not above suspicion." The proposal passed without a dissenting vote.[5]

Colonel Silas R. Noble, Union commander at Paducah, suspected several court officials in the Purchase and its environs were disloyal. On May 13, circuit judge Wiley P. Fowler of Smithland was holding court in Marion, the Crittenden County seat, when cavalry troopers from Paducah interrupted him. The horsemen stood guard at the door while their captain handed Fowler a letter from Noble. The colonel had heard several officers of Fowler's court in different counties were secessionists and had not sworn the oath of allegiance. They were "constantly oppressing Union men, and talking treason in the very presence of the court." Noble said his job was to "punish treason wherever it may be found, whether in high or low places." Allegiance must be sworn, he warned, and he demanded "*a record of such oath sent to these headquarters.*" Fowler refused Noble's order and ordered the court adjourned. The captain announced that nobody could leave the courthouse until the oath was sworn and that Fowler was under arrest.

The Yankees did not clap the judge in irons and frog march him away. They released him upon his promise that he would appear before Noble in Paducah on May 21. Likewise, four lawyers who spurned the oath were arrested and placed under bond to report to Paducah. Fowler appealed to Magoffin in a letter. In his reply of May 20, the governor urged the judge to ignore Noble and "go on, and hold your courts, under the laws and constitution." The judge replied to Magoffin on May 23, explaining that he went to Paducah "in obedience to his parole" and to help secure the release of John T. Bunch of Henderson and Senator Cissell of Union County—two of the lawyers arrested with him in Marion. Bunch was the Southern Rights candidate for Congress from the Second District in the June 1861 election. Bunch and Cissell said they refused to swear the oath because it required them to "surrender their rights, if proceeded against for its violation, from the civil to a military tribunal." Officers of such a tribunal had the power to convict and even execute persons they judged guilty of oath-breaking. Bunch and Cissell said they would swear a loyalty oath without the provision for a military trial, though "as attorneys, they had repeatedly taken the oaths prescribed in the constitution and laws of Ky." In addition, Noble, evidently no relation to Editor Noble, tried to force Judge Flournoy and McCracken County clerk Thomas D. Grundy to swear the oath. They protested to the colonel that they "had taken all the oaths required by the laws of Ky., and could not and would not take any other, nor would they resign their offices." Noble immediately stopped the duo "from exercising any of the functions of either office, and the clerk's office was closed to business." Magoffin, on May 25, wrote Crittenden in defense of the beleaguered western Kentuckians. On June 2, Crittenden wrote Secretary of War Edwin M. Stanton on their behalf. Five days later, Stanton wrote Crittenden that he had contacted Major General Henry W. Halleck, commander of the Department of the Mississippi. Evidently, nothing came of the senator's protest. On July 8, Magoffin received yet another entreaty from one of Noble's suspected secessionists in Paducah. Joseph M. Bigger wrote the governor that military authorities in Paducah had warned him not to run for circuit judge. If he did, he would be arrested and sent to Louisville. Bigger had been Albert P. Thompson's law partner. But he insisted he had "the constitutional qualifications" to seek the office.[6]

On June 10, Brigadier General Jeremiah T. Boyle, the new Union commander in Kentucky, had cracked down hard on the enemy. Confederate soldiers, along with citizens who aided them in any way or spent time behind Rebel lines, had to report to provost marshals and swear allegiance to the Union. They also had to promise their future loyalty. Anyone refusing to obey the order was subject to arrest and transportation out of the state. As a result, many "notorious and dangerous rebels" wound up behind bars or free on $5,000 to $20,000 bail. On July 21, Boyle ordered that "no person hostile in opinion to the government and desiring its overthrow, will be allowed to stand for office in the district of Ky." Boyle's order warned, "The attempt of such a person to stand for office will be regarded as in itself sufficient evidence of his treasonable intent to warrant his arrest."[7]

Federal authorities also defined disloyalty as trading with the Rebels. Kentucky presented a dilemma: How could Uncle Sam permit the state to carry on its lawful trade and simultaneously halt all commerce with the Confederate states? Not surprisingly, the first rigorous trade restrictions applied to the Purchase and the adjacent territory west of the Cumberland River. Treasury Secretary Salmon P. Chase forbade all trade with the region, "drawing no distinction between it and Tennessee." After Grant promised Paducah citizens he had come to protect them against a common enemy, he disallowed trade between far western Kentucky and Illinois. Soon afterward, all steamers plying west of Louisville had to have permits, and they could stop only at approved places. Permits were mandatory for all freight consignments; passengers had to show passes to continue their trips. Ultimately, boats were not allowed to stop between Evansville and Paducah, which included Smithland, where the Cumberland joins the Ohio, and all ferry operations were suspended on the Ohio.[8]

Even so, commerce between Kentucky and the South continued, especially after the fall of Forts Henry and Donelson, which portended the reopening of the lucrative prewar trade routes up the Tennessee and Cumberland. Cargo and passenger steamers began to churn the muddy waters of the two rivers as soon as Grant gave his blessing. But circumstances necessitated regulation. By March, a permit system was created to control the trade and stop smuggling. Officials kept a close watch on who got the permits and their frequently required renewals. Occasionally, officials granted a certain amount of leeway, notably toward traders who gained the favor of army officers or treasury agents. But the leniency was sometimes used as a trick to trap suspected smugglers and grab their boats for military purposes.[9]

Also by the summer of 1862, federal authorities made the Ohio River the boundary of the restricted commercial area. Thus, in terms of trade, Uncle Sam considered the Bluegrass State part of the Confederacy. Louisville was the only port on the south bank of the Ohio in Kentucky where cargo could be shipped without a permit. However, government agents monitored all commerce and sometimes traveled on steamboats. The system was extended to wagons and trains; if the carrier and the shipper lacked permits, then federal officers were authorized to seize the freight. Anyone seeking a permit had to describe and put a dollar value on the goods and name the consignee. The destination and transportation route had to be stated. By awarding permits only to faithful Unionists, the government hoped to put out of business southern sympathizers and lukewarm Unionists alike. Permits went only to those who swore allegiance to the Union and promised they had never aided the rebellion. If the loyalty of an applicant was questionable, the endorsement of six Union men was required. In 1864, federal authorities outlawed trade in arms and munitions of war statewide.[10]

Meanwhile, endorsements for trade permits might not have been easy to get in the Purchase, where the Union men—like Unionists across the state—were focusing on the August election. Purchase Unionists particularly wanted to clean courthouses of the numerous secessionists who ran county governments. They aimed to replace the ousted secessionist lawmakers with true Union men, too. Doubtless, they figured the presence of Union troops would be helpful. In any event, on May 26, Ballard County Unionists again met in Blandville and made Henry Boswell chair of the gathering and Henry Quigley secretary. The assemblage unanimously endorsed Unionists for several local offices, including M. O. Hawthorne to succeed Coffee in the state house of representatives. In turn, the Unionists unanimously backed Marshall to replace Williams as circuit judge. The meeting also passed a series of pro-Union resolutions, including two that mirrored the views of almost every loyal Kentuckian, namely fealty for the Union and simultaneous support for slavery. Subsequent Union meetings in Mayfield, Murray, and again in Blandville approved similar resolutions. On March 26, the Ballard County Unionists insisted slavery "is a creature of the States and as such unknown to the Federal Constitution." They recognized "no power on the part of the Federal Congress to interfere with the institution in [any] . . . way, save to protect it." Second, they resolved "that the present war is not waged with any view to interfere with the institution in any way, nor is it waged to reconstruct the Constitution, for we hold that is unbroken; but that the war be waged to preserve the Union and uphold the laws—State and Federal—with all the rights, dignity, and equality of the several States unimpaired; and when that object is accomplished the war ought to cease—*and not until then.*" They organized a Union Party for the county that was to mirror the resolutions. The party would nominate candidates "who shall pledge themselves to that well-known platform—The Union, the Constitution, and the Enforcement of the Laws." That was Bell's presidential platform in 1860, suggesting that the Union men, or at least most of them, voted the Constitutional ticket in 1860. Statewide, as has been noted, Bell and Douglas supporters made up the core of the Union Party.[11]

On June 16, Lucian Anderson opened the Mayfield meeting with a nearly two-hour speech "in his usual happy and impassioned style, and to an attentive and appreciative audience." Afterward, the Unionists called Mayfield attorney Thomas H. Mayes to be chairman and Richard Neel secretary. The delegates endorsed Marshall for circuit judge and Major P. D. Yeiser, who had moved to Paducah, for commonwealth's attorney from the district. Like the Ballard Unionists, the Graves men endorsed "the Union, the Constitution, and the Enforcement of the Laws," and "the Constitution as it is and the Union as it was." They also resolved "that abolitionism, like secessionism, is unauthorized by the Constitution, and we regard them both as inimical to the free institutions of our country and destructive to the interests of the American people; a foul blot that should be eradicated from American politics." In addition, the Unionists addressed the growing guerrilla danger in their midst: "The system of guerrilla warfare which has been partially, and is likely to be generally, inaugurated by those in rebellion, is in violation of civilized warfare, and those engaged in it or aid and abet in it in any way are outlaws, and should be treated as banditti by the Government."[12]

Two days later, Calloway County Unionists met in Murray and endorsed candidates for several local offices. R. B. Rose was chairman of the caucus; J. B. England was secretary. The Unionists resolved "that the Constitution and the laws of the United States are the supreme law of the land, any State Constitution by law to the contrary notwithstanding, and all good citizens should submit to them peaceably; if not, they should be forced to do so; and every citizen owes paramount allegiance to the Constitution of the United States, and to the state in which he lives." Further, the Union supporters resolved that "the time has come when the line of distinction should be drawn between loyal men and those who are disloyal, and no man should be trusted with an office of honor or profit under the Constitution and laws of the State of Kentucky, who at heart are opposed to them, or whose sympathies are with those in rebellion." They also resolved that "abolitionism, like secession, is unwarranted by the Constitution, destructive to the interests of the people, and both these political heresies should be put down—peaceably if it can be, but by force if necessary." Another resolution condemned guerrilla warfare, blaming it on the Confederates and characterizing such strife as "in conflict with the rules of civilized warfare." The resolution also said that "all who engage in it, or give aid and comfort to it, are the enemies of mankind, and should be sternly dealt with." They further pledged support for "the Constitution as it is, and the Union as it was" and endorsed Marshall for circuit judge and Yeiser for commonwealth's attorney.[13]

On June 26, the new Ballard Union Party met in Blandville. They were "not the quasi concern, the half and half gentry, who do things with a 'but,' and an 'if,' but the genuine Union party, men always true and loyal, even under the guns of the rebel stronghold at Columbus," claimed the author of a letter from Milburn that the *Journal* published on July 9. "Two hundred, not less in number" attended, he added. Again, conservative proslavery Unionism showed through as the Union passed "resolutions giving to the South, under the Constitution and in the Union, all the rights to which she is entitled." They said the issue was simply "Union and disunion" and sought support at the polls from "all good citizens, no difference what their previous opinions may have been." They endorsed Marshall to succeed Williams as circuit judge; Thomas F. Hayes was their nominee to replace Coffee. The Unionists also claimed that after the convention adjourned, "the disunion party" announced its own candidates, including Bigger—who must have sworn the oath after all—and father and son Jacob and Thomas Corbett. The former wanted to keep his job as county and circuit clerk; the latter was standing for commonwealth attorney. Jacob Corbett, who had held both offices for twenty years, was "without exception the most bitter and unrelenting rebel in the country" and had sent "his negroes to Dixie, fearing their confiscation, where they still remain, as I am informed," the letter writer said. He added that Corbett had taken the oath of allegiance, and "says he is as loyal as any man," yet he "denounces the *Journal* with bitter anathemas, and avows that [the paper's] . . . columns never uttered a single truth in all their existence." The Unionist admitted his side was "in a great minority. Two hundred and fifty against 800 or 1,000 is fearful odds." He challenged, "Shall the loyal men of Ballard submit to be governed and represented by men who, though now comparatively quiet through fear, await but the favorable moment to rivet the chains of that infernal despotism, the Southern Confederacy upon us[?]"[14]

Tilghman, the Purchase's highest-ranking "riveter," was a prisoner of war. No doubt, he was chagrined if he learned the fate of the place where he worshipped in Paducah; the Yankees converted Grace Episcopal Church into a hospital. It was one of the most unusual buildings in Paducah. The tiny wood-frame building—thirty by sixty feet—had been nailed together in Louisville, floated down the Ohio on a boat, and erected on the west side of South Second Street between Washington and Clark Streets. Tilghman himself had "beautifully colored" the church's "diamond shaped" windows. Now, to make room for cots, the medical staff put the pews—"plain little wooden benches"—outside in the yard, where they became casualties of war: "Army mules 'sharpened their teeth' upon their crude backs." In addition, the staff turned the Reverend Thomas J. Pickett's rectory, next door to the church, into quarters for nurses and doctors.[15]

Paducah Union men probably approved of secesh churches becoming military Union hospitals. But they, like all Unionists, could not have been surprised when their party swept to victory in the state elections in the Purchase and across Kentucky, though the turnout was light. Marshall beat Bigger, 2,014 to 839. Yeiser turned back Thomas Corbett, 1,455 to 804. In Graves County, Lucian Anderson was elected county attorney "by 466 votes though not a candidate." Reportedly Unionists went with Anderson "because of some dissatisfaction about Mr. Mayes, the regular nominee, who received 280." The Graves returns suggest that the Union cause had not advanced very far in the county; in the congressional election, Trimble won 610 votes, to 1,270 for Burnett. At the same time, it is remarkable that Bigger and Corbett managed more than 800 votes apiece, despite the state and military authorities' best effort to keep all but demonstrably loyal men from voting. Bigger carried Fulton, Hickman, McCracken, and Marshall Counties. Corbett won Fulton, Marshall, and McCracken Counties.[16]

At any rate, the election wrought a sea change in the Purchase delegation in the state house of representatives. The new lawmakers were all Union men: William Mercer of Ballard County, Leroy Brinkley of Calloway County, Elisha Beasley of Fulton and Hickman Counties, Richard Neel of Graves County, Wiley Waller of Marshall County, and J. W. Boone of McCracken County. The McCracken County senate seat would remain Duke's until 1863, when Unionist W. T. Chiles replaced him.[17]

Some Ballard County Unionists opted to do more to show their loyalty than just vote Mercer to Frankfort. A group of men—likely from in and around Milburn—volunteered for the Eighth Kentucky Cavalry, recruiting for which began in August. The Ballard countians formed Company L under Captain Elisha Owens. During the fall and winter, the regiment, whose men agreed to serve a year, patrolled against guerrillas in western Kentucky. But in 1863, the Eighth Kentucky joined Yankee forces pursuing Kentuckian John Hunt Morgan and his Rebel cavalry raiders across the Bluegrass State, Indiana, and Ohio. The regiment was present at Morgan's capture at Salineville, Ohio, on July 26, 1863. Afterward, the regiment returned to Kentucky and mustered out on September 23, but several of the troopers enlisted in other commands.[18]

The day before, Lincoln had shaken the faith of many Kentucky Unionists with his preliminary Emancipation Proclamation. The president decreed that after January 1, all slaves in Confederate-held territory would be free. Thus, the president turned the Civil War from a war to preserve the Union into a war to save the Union *and* destroy slavery. Of course, almost every white Kentuckian who supported the Union favored a Union with slavery. Thus, Lincoln's action was "a stunning blow"; even the staunchest Bluegrass State Unionists were outraged, though their "full vigor of opposition would be reserved" for when the proclamation took effect. Nonetheless, "occasion was taken at this time to condemn abolitionism again and all who stood for it. . . . Abolition was considered to be just as much treason as secession was." Though preliminary, the proclamation linked Lincoln "with the abolitionists, in Kentucky." The Reverend Robert J. Breckinridge of Danville, the Union's strongest supporter in Kentucky, "held that Lincoln's policy concerning slavery was dangerous and unwise."[19]

Lincoln was doubtless disappointed with his home state's response to the proclamation, but he could not have been surprised. On July 12, he had summoned representatives and senators from Kentucky and the other border slave states to the White House, tried to sell them on gradual, compensated emancipation, and essentially failed. "I regard the whole thing, as far as the slave states are concerned, as full of arsenic, sugar coated," groused Senator Lazarus Whitehead Powell of Kentucky. Ironically, Samuel L. Casey, the Unionist congressman who represented the Purchase, Kentucky's only pro-Confederate region, favored Lincoln's plan.[20]

Powerful Confederate armies under General Braxton Bragg and Major General Edmund Kirby Smith were in central and eastern Kentucky when Lincoln issued his proclamation. On September 3, the Confederates under Kirby Smith captured Frankfort—the only capital of a loyal state to fall to the Rebels during the war—and, on October 4, tried to inaugurate Richard Hawes of Paris as the state's Confederate governor, but fled at the approach of Union forces. Yet relatively few Kentuckians rallied to the Rebels, who ultimately retreated from the state after Major General Don Carlos Buell defeated Bragg at the Battle of Perryville, in Boyle County, on October 8. The bloodiest battle ever fought on Kentucky soil, Perryville was a tactical draw. Strategically, it was a Union victory because never again would the Confederates be able to invade Kentucky in force.

Paducah is about 230 miles west of Perryville. Doubtless to the disappointment of most Purchase citizens, the Confederate forces did not come anywhere close to where they lived. "Things here continue *in status quo,*" "Sigma" wrote the *Journal* from Paducah on October 24. "The rebels here outnumber the Union men at least twenty or more to one, and it is really amusing to hear them talk about the Confederates and the Federals." He added that every battle that the newspapers reported was "a great Southern victory" to the Confederate sympathizers, who dismissed reports of Union victories as "Northern lies." "Sigma" also wrote that the Emancipation Proclamation "is emphatically and universally condemned by almost every man of every class—Union men being as loud in its condemnation as many others." He added, "It is the general opinion that if it is *enforced,* it will destroy almost every vestige of Union sentiment, not only in the South but in the border slave States." Meanwhile, "Sigma" said "the secesh here and hereabouts manifest great anxiety to see Paducah and the country in possession of rebel soldiers." But he claimed, "as great rebels as they are, and anxious as they may be to have the 'Yankee devils,' as some of them term the soldiers of the Union, driven out of the country, and as bad as they hate the Federal Government," the secessionists preferred Yankee greenback dollars to Confederate currency. They "are as anxious to get hold of them as if they were gold and silver." In any event, "Sigma" was sure Confederate troops would rue the day they attacked Paducah: "I will not say what is the amount of our force, at Paducah, but they are sufficient and prepared to give any Rebel force that may be so presumptuous to attack them a good fight, and give a good account of themselves."[21]

Rebel troops would not show up in Paducah until March 25, 1864, when Forrest hit town. Many of them would be western Kentuckians. The Yankees would shoot dead one of the Confederate commanders, Colonel Albert P. Thompson. He would die directing a failed attack on Fort Anderson, reportedly in sight of his home. Among the troops who gave "a good account of themselves" in keeping the Stars and Stripes flying over the fort were western Kentuckians, white and African American.

Meanwhile, another group of Purchase men enlisted for the Yankee army in the fall. They mustered into the Fifteenth Kentucky Cavalry, a Paducah-based one-year regiment that mustered out on October 29, 1863. Representative Waller was major of the regiment. Company A, commanded by Captain Samuel Duncan of Benton, was from Marshall County. Captain Samuel M. Purcell was a Graves countian; his Company B was mostly comprised of Graves and McCracken men. Captain L. A. Hanson, also of Graves, led Company E, largely Graves volunteers.[22]

By mid-December, Grant was far from Paducah, his first Civil War conquest. He was in Mississippi, hoping that he would soon take Vicksburg, the Rebel fortress city on the Mississippi River. Grant was commander of the vast Department of the Tennessee, territory that stretched southward from Cairo to northern Mississippi and was sandwiched by the Mississippi and Tennessee. He had plenty to distract him from a Vicksburg campaign. Marauding guerrilla bands—supported or at least tolerated by civilians—bedeviled his soldiers. Too, more than a few civilians continued to ply a lively, illicit trade with the enemy. Jews were a tiny minority in his vast district. Yet Grant was convinced they were the most notorious smugglers. The result was the infamous General Orders No. 11, "subsequently described as 'the most sweeping anti-Jewish regulation in all American history.'"[23]

Grant spent the rest of his life apologizing—and atoning—for the order that nonetheless haunted him until his death in 1885. Issued from Grant's headquarters at Holly Springs, Mississippi, on December 17, it declared: "The Jews, as a class violating every regulation of trade established by the Treasury Department and also department orders, are hereby expelled from the department within twenty-four hours from the receipt of this order."[24]

However, "in the end, only a few Jews were seriously affected" because "a fortunate communications breakdown and Abraham Lincoln's prompt decision to revoke the order greatly limited its impact." Prussian-born Cesar Kaskel of Paducah almost single-handedly got the order revoked. One of the Jews banished, he fought exile all the way to the White House on "his Paul Revere-like ride" to Washington. Wherever he went, he spread the news of Grant's order. Kaskel won the support of the press, politicians, and Lincoln. Kaskel's Unionist credentials seemed impeccable. He was vice president of the city Union League Club, and his younger brother, Julius, was helping recruit soldiers for the Union army. Kaskel's battle began on December 28, when the Paducah provost marshal told him he had twenty-four hours to leave. Other Jews received the same ultimatum.[25]

All along, Kaskel was buoyed by the confidence of an innocent man. Ironically, the enemy helped his cause. On December 20, Rebel cavalry raiders captured and burned the Union supply base at Holly Springs. At the same time, Forrest and his cavalry raided to the north and destroyed fifty miles of railroad and telegraph lines, thereby cutting communications between Grant and his commanders in the department for weeks. As a result, implementation of his order was delayed. Kaskel arrived in Washington on January 3 and soon gained an audience with the president, who knew nothing of the order. "And so the children of Israel were driven from the happy land of Canaan?" he reportedly asked Kaskel. "Yes, and that is why we have come unto Father Abraham's bosom, asking protection," his visitor replied. "And this protection they shall have at once," Lincoln assured him. The conversation probably did not take place, but the president ordered Halleck to revoke General Orders No. 11. On January 6, Grant complied. By then, Kaskel was home. When the Paducah military brass demanded by whose authority Kaskel had returned, he declared, "By order of the President of the United States." Lincoln had restored Kaskel's faith in his adopted homeland. But the majority of Purchase citizens still put their faith in the Confederacy.[26]

Fort Anderson and the Marine Hospital (Courtesy of the Kentucky Historical Society)

Congressman Lucian Anderson (Courtesy of Pogue Library, Murray State University)

The Hell Hounds (Courtesy of Pogue Library, Murray State University)

Paine's fort at Mayfield (Courtesy of Pogue Library, Murray State University)

Union "timberclad" gunboat on the Ohio River at Paducah (Courtesy of the Kentucky Historical Society)

Governor Beriah Magoffin (Courtesy of the Kentucky Historical Society)

Richard D. Gholson (Courtesy of the Washington State Historical Society)

Paducah war scenes (Courtesy of the Kentucky Historical Society)

John C. Breckinridge
(Courtesy of the Library of Congress)

Congressman Henry C. Burnett
(Courtesy of the Library of Congress)

General Grant's soldiers crossing Mayfield Creek Bridge (Courtesy of the Kentucky Historical Society)

State Representative Lawrence D. Husbands (Courtesy of Pogue Library, Murray State University)

The *Dacotah* and other steamboats on the Cumberland River (Courtesy of the Kentucky Historical Society)

Q. Q. Quigley
(Courtesy of Pogue Library, Murray State University)

Gideon J. Pillow (Courtesy of the Library of Congress)

General Lloyd Tilghman (from *A History of Kentucky,* published in 1916 by Elizabeth Shelby Kincaid)

The bluffs at Columbus (Courtesy of the Kentucky Historical Society)

Oscar Turner (Courtesy of Pogue Library, Murray State University)

Nathan Bedford Forrest (Courtesy of the Library of Congress)

Leonidas Polk (Courtesy of the Library of Congress)

Pontoon bridge at Paducah (Courtesy of the Kentucky Historical Society)

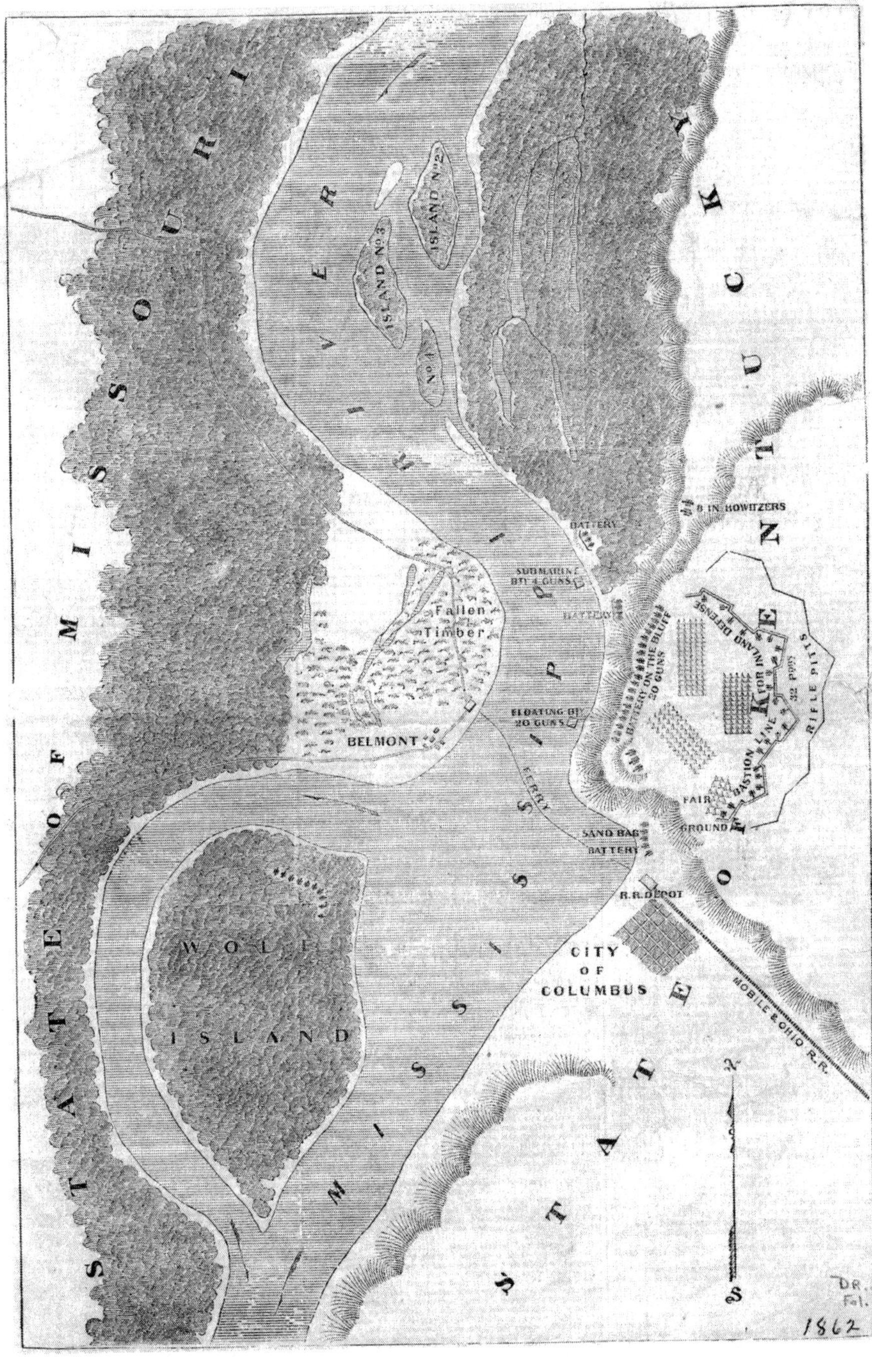

Confederate fortifications at Columbus (Courtesy of the Kentucky Historical Society)

Oscar Turner (Courtesy of the Library of Congress)

Soldiers of the 134th Illinois Infantry at Columbus (Courtesy of the Library of Congress)

Simon Bolivar Buckner (Courtesy of the Library of Congress)

Officers of the 134th Illinois Infantry at Columbus (Courtesy of the Library of Congress)

Stephen G. Burbridge (Courtesy of the Library of Congress)

USS *Peosta* (Courtesy of the Library of Congress)

Lew Wallace (Courtesy of the Library of Congress)

USS *Essex* (Courtesy of the Library of Congress)

Charles F. Smith (Courtesy of the Library of Congress)

9

Traitors Beware

The Emancipation Proclamation, though it did not apply to Kentucky, added more strain to the fraying relationship between Lincoln and his native state. All along, almost all Kentucky Unionists favored a Union with slavery. Nearly every Kentucky soldier in blue was fighting for the preservation of the Union, not for the abolition of slavery. Across the state, thousands of Kentuckians who were prowar turned to the "Peace" Democrats. The Purchase stayed stubbornly secessionist.

When the Emancipation Proclamation took effect on January 1, 1863, it brewed in Kentucky a "storm of disapproval . . . which had never been equalled up to that time. Virtually no one could be found to support Lincoln." Governor James F. Robinson, successor to Magoffin, who had resigned under Unionist pressure in August 1862, said the proclamation was a great injustice to the state and showed Lincoln's ingratitude for Kentucky's refusal to secede. He also argued that emancipation would only make the Confederates fight harder. The legislature, with only three dissenting votes, denounced the proclamation as "unwise, unconstitutional and void." Too, Kentucky whites feared that freed slaves now would pour into the state from Confederate-held territory. As a result, the legislature enacted laws that "contemptuously thrust aside the emancipation proclamation." African Americans "claiming or pretending to be free" as a result of the proclamation were forbidden to enter Kentucky. Those who did were subject to arrest and jail. As a result, newspapers were filled with advertisements inviting out-of-state slave owners "to come forward, prove property, and pay charges," or their chattels would be resold after a month. As fast as slaves freed by the proclamation set foot in Kentucky, "they were seized and enslaved again." Amid such defiance of Washington, Union military authorities feared the Unionist legislature was about to vote Kentucky out of the Union and prepared to arrest lawmakers and judges. Additionally, several Kentucky officers in the Union army resigned their commissions when they learned the proclamation was in effect.[1]

Samuel L. Casey's support for the Emancipation Proclamation doubtless turned almost all First District Unionists against him. A Union man in Crittenden County, just east of the Purchase, wrote the *Journal,* advising, "I live in Sam Casey's District, and voted for him, and I think he cannot find half a dozen men in his district who will endorse the President's Emancipation Proclamation. I never saw *one* myself." The *Journal* accused Casey of cutting "as clean from his constituency as he has from the principles he once avowed." The paper thundered, "except in bare constitutional form, he is no more the representative of the First District in Kentucky, and no more a representative of Kentucky at large than Owen Lovejoy or George W. Julian or John A. Bingham is."[2]

Despite the uproar over emancipation, few Kentuckians joined the Confederate army. People still drew a sharp distinction between disdain for Lincoln and emancipation on the one hand and devotion to the Union on the other: "Opposition to the latter did not constitute hostility to the former." Even so, secessionists in the Purchase and elsewhere in Kentucky doubtless cried, "We told you so." On January 7, Quigley judged Lincoln guilty of "the blackest act in my judgment ever done by Christian man."[3]

Almost every white man and woman in the Purchase shared Quigley's views. The Union cause had made little headway in Graves County, according to a long lament from a Mayfield Unionist the *Journal* published on January 14. The letter, signed "FAIR-PLAY," also provided a glance backward to when the Rebel army was at Columbus, Hickman, and Camp Beauregard. But "FAIR-PLAY" was particularly vexed over the recently concluded November circuit court term. Though Judge Marshall was a devout Union man, "sixteen straight-out secessionists and disunionists" comprised the grand jury, thanks to the perfidy of the southern-sympathizing sheriff, said "FAIR-PLAY," who nonetheless did not name the lawman. He explained that the May 1862 court term lasted approximately a week, "owing to the then unsettled state of affairs in this part of the State." Judge Williams, who was still on the bench, forgot to name jury commissioners, whose job was to fill the grand and petit jury pools. As a result, the sheriff got to choose the jurymen. He lost his job in the August election, but "smarting under his defeat" and seeing an "opportunity to gratify his petty spleen and malice on Union men," the lame-duck lawman packed the grand jury, whose foreman was none other than known secessionist John Eaker. "FAIR-PLAY" might have been doubly angry with Eaker because he was at least a conditional Unionist in early 1861. He had chaired a Union meeting in Mayfield in January and written Senator Crittenden about it. The meeting's secretary was W. M. Cargill, who joined the Confederate army. In any event, despite their known Confederate sympathies, the grand jurymen swore the required Union loyalty oath, according to the letter's author. He alleged that Eaker had headed a "Safety Committee" organized to "*save Union men*" and keep them from leaving without buying a ten-cent pass from him. When the Rebels arrived in Mayfield, Eaker "got on the railing around the public square in the midst of hundreds of persons, men, women, and children, and saluted them with hat off with cheer after cheer for Jeff Davis and the Southern Confederacy." Also, Eaker had been part of "a secret conclave" to invite the Rebels into the state "and signed a petition to that effect." Worse, according to "FAIR-PLAY," Eaker was, in effect, an accessory to murder in the death of J. F. Conner, a Unionist jailed in Mayfield for shooting John Milliken, the pro-Confederate ex–Paducah postmaster, on November 19, 1861. Eaker had reputedly helped pass the news of Milliken's demise to the Confederates at Camp Beauregard, knowing soldiers would come to town to murder Conner, which they reputedly did. The soldiers may have been from L. B. Wardlow's regiment, the Twenty-second Mississippi Infantry. He remembered that "our boys" went into Mayfield and killed a saloonkeeper: "It was an act that I did not in any way approve of and did not participate in." He could not recall the victim's name.[4]

Further, "FAIR-PLAY" claimed the Graves grand jurymen knew their county was home to "at least five hundred men who had committed treason against the State." No fewer than fifty of these Confederate sympathizers, including Mayfield residents, had helped steal the state guard arms, worth $35,000, in 1861, he charged, adding that local men had also helped burn bridges to halt the advance of Yankee troops. Nonetheless, the grand jury reputedly refused to indict for any crime any of the guilty parties, though Eaker and the grand jurymen knew who they were. Instead, they gratified "their damnable prejudices on Union men . . . by indicting them for breaches of the peace, and for . . . interfering in elections." "FAIR-PLAY" wrote that two-thirds of the indictments were "for alleged minor offenses." Those bound over for trial included "an old gray-headed Union man by the name of Cooper seven times charged with stealing guns, horses &c, and not a man on the Grand Jury who knew him believed him to be guilty." At the same time, the grand jury indicted a trio of Unionists over alleged irregularities in the January 20 special congressional election to replace "the traitor Burnett." The Union men had allegedly failed to have "the election at the proper place of voting in the district." Yet "FAIR-PLAY" complained that the grand jury chose not to indict the secessionists, who opened a poll at the courthouse for the Confederate congressional election, which Burnett won.[5]

He predicted the sixteen secessionists would get their comeuppance when another grand jury met. He expected that some of them and other local southern sympathizers would be imprisoned "to expiate for the treason and corruption they have been guilty of." He singled out Eaker, challenging: "Now the question is asked, was diligent inquiry made by these men (and especially by said John Eaker, foreman as aforesaid) of all treasons and felonies committed in this county? Let this old traitor answer this question in his own time and wait for the wagon, which will pass along in due time; then we will all ride, not to the so-called Southern Confederacy, but to the Temple of Justice, erected by Kentucky, to try all traitors to her Constitution and laws."[6]

An irate Eaker responded to "FAIR-PLAY" in a January 23 letter the *Journal* published eight days later. He signed his name to his missive, which included his vow to vindicate himself and the rest of the grand jury from the "foul imputations" of "FAIR-PLAY." He challenged "FAIR-PLAY" "to unmask himself" and "acknowledge the paternity of his literary offspring." If he refused, Eaker would "only leave him to the scorn and contempt of an honest community as a slanderer who uses publicly and vilely the names of others while ignominiously concealing his own to avoid exposure and personal responsibility."[7]

Statewide, though not in the Purchase, a majority of Kentuckians did not share the views of men like Eaker and his fellow grand jurymen. The Southern Rights Party had lapsed into dormancy after Kentucky declared for the Union, but the Emancipation Proclamation gave the party's adherents a new lease on life: "In addition to Southern sympathizers, who were its chief support, it was an ever ready refuge for those Unionists who could no longer endure the Lincoln administration and the military regime." The arrests, the Emancipation Proclamation, and "various military rigors so troubled the political waters that the State Rights Party leaders might fish in them with some hope of success."[8]

The Southern Rights men figured a name change was in order if they were to win over erstwhile Unionists, so they started calling themselves the Democratic Party. Hoping to make considerable political hay off the Emancipation Proclamation, they announced plans to hold a state nominating convention for candidates to run in the August 3 state elections, in which Kentuckians would elect a governor, members of Congress, state legislators, and local officials. The gathering was set for Frankfort on February 18. Unionists feared the conclave was part of a scheme to pry Kentucky yet out of the Union, perhaps in cahoots with Rebel troops, including John Hunt Morgan and his famous cavalry raiders, who were wreaking havoc in parts of the state. The Democrats wanted to meet at the capitol in the house chamber, but lawmakers voted no. So they assembled elsewhere in town on the appointed date, but not for long. Colonel E. A. Gilbert of the Forty-fourth Ohio Infantry mustered troops who broke up the convention. Gilbert warned that the military would not permit the convention's candidates to run or to serve, if elected. Nonetheless, the party persisted and became known as the "Peace Democrats." It became "the logical party for those to support who favored secession, if any there should be, for those who were looking for peace, and for those who wished to register their protest against the military regime and the various unpopular acts of the National administration." The Peace Democrats worried the pro-Union and prowar—through not pro-Lincoln—"Union Democracy." Some leading Union Democrats, including Lawrence Trimble, had defected. The Union Democrats blasted everybody on the other side as "secessionists, rebels and traitors, and even abolitionists—the Union Democrats using this last term to ward off as far as possible the use of the same term against themselves."[9]

Meanwhile, the Union Democrats girded for political battle, holding mass meetings across the state, including in the Purchase, in preparation for their convention, which was set for March 18 and 19 in Louisville. On February 28, "a large and enthusiastic meeting" of Graves County's "Union Democracy" convened at the courthouse in Mayfield. Led by Lucian Anderson, his uncle Crawford Anderson, W. A. Terrell, and others, the Unionists also passed resolutions declaiming disunion and abolitionism "as the twin causes and coworkers in the destruction of the Government and the people." They resolved that "armed treason is to be put down by bullets, moral treason by ballots." Other resolutions praised Gilbert and panned the greatest despotism and iniquity of earth, known as the 'Confederate States of America,' with 'King Jefferson the First' at its head." The Unionists also denounced the Emancipation Proclamation "as wholly unconstitutional and an outrage on all the loyal men of the slave States." However, they added that they "can find no remedy for these evils in secession, but regard it as the immediate cause of all our curses." Further, they castigated Eaker's "traitorous grand jury" and pledged their "unshaken faith in the conservatism and patriotism of the Northern people" as allies in preserving "the Constitution as it is and the Union as it was." The Unionists also sympathized "with the masses of the seceded States," promising them a warm, brotherly welcome when they abandoned "their traitor leaders" and returned "to the old union under the ample folds of its Constitution." The Graves Union men did not overlook the elections and the possibility of the Peace Democrats winning. Consequently, they resolved that only "straight-out" Union men who supported "putting down this infamous rebellion" should be allowed to run for and hold office. They also said delegates to the state convention should favor "no man for office . . . whose loyalty to the Government is not firm and unfaltering."[10]

McCracken County Unionists adopted similar resolutions at their "large and respectable meeting" on March 7 in Paducah. Dr. R. H. Hall chaired the gathering, and Thomas M. Redd was secretary. The Unionists approved several resolutions, the first one declaring that it was the duty of loyal Kentuckians "to unite (without distinction of party names or titles) in order to suppress the present rebellion against the best government ever established by man." The Union men conceded that their party did "not endorse all the acts of the present Administration" but favored continuing "the war until peace shall be restored to our once happy and prosperous country." The Unionists also linked disunion with abolitionism, declaring the secessionists to be "the practical abolition party of our State" because "they have brought about just such a state of affairs as the abolition party of the North desired, namely, the virtual abolition of slavery in our State." They rejected "both the abolition and secession party" as "twin sisters" who were "equally subversive of our civil and political rights." Further, they endorsed the military draft, supported Joshua F. Bell of Danville for governor, and lauded Gilbert for breaking up the Democratic convention, recommending that "all loyal commanders in the state, in such cases . . . pursue a similar course."[11]

Four days later, Marshall County Union Democrats met and chose P. Washam and William M. Bondurant as their convention delegates. If they failed to attend, Graves County's delegates would represent Marshall County, the gathering resolved. The Marshall Union men also jabbed at the Emancipation Proclamation, resolving, "we cannot endorse all the acts of the present Administration." But the Union men pledged, "we will vote for no man who is opposed to voting men and money for a vigorous prosecution of the present uncalled for rebellion." Further, the delegates added their "most hearty approval" of Gilbert's "action . . . in breaking up and dispersing the traitors and rebels who met at Frankfort for the purpose of concocting ways and means for the destruction of our Government." They were sure that if Kentucky had more soldiers like Gilbert, then "treason would soon be crushed and driven from the soil of our glorious old Commonwealth."[12]

The Marshall men made it to the Louisville convention, along with delegates from every Purchase county except Fulton and Hickman. Lucian Anderson represented the Purchase on the credentials committee and Redd on the resolutions committee. The delegates nominated Bell for governor—all of the Purchase Union men were for him—but he declined. So the Union Democrats chose Colonel Thomas E. Bramlette of Columbia, commander of the Third Kentucky Infantry.[13]

In April, several Purchase men signed up for the Twelfth Kentucky Cavalry of the other side. The commander was W. W. Faulkner, a guerrilla chieftain whom the Yankees had captured and released. Organized at Tupelo,

Mississippi, the regiment "was recruited in Southern Kentucky, and from West Tennessee and Northern Mississippi." The Kentuckians came principally from the Purchase—"the Counties of McCracken, Ballard, Carlisle, Graves, Hickman, Fulton and adjacent counties." Faulkner had been first lieutenant of the Woodville Cavalry, a McCracken County state guard company. The Twelfth Kentucky's second in command was Lieutenant Colonel Lannom, the ex–state lawmaker, gun grabber, and Seventh Kentucky Infantry light colonel.[14]

Meanwhile, back in Kentucky, slave owners had warned their chattels that the Emancipation Proclamation did not apply to them. Nonetheless, many slaves understood Lincoln had put the peculiar institution on the road to extinction. Consequently, a number of African Americans took what they believed was the road to freedom—they ran away to "Mr. Lincoln's Army." On the other hand, other chattels, given the fiercely proslavery stance of almost all Unionists in Kentucky, "may have imagined that both sides in the Civil War were equally opposed to the freedom of the slave." To be sure, "public pronouncements on both sides made abundantly clear the hatred both Unionists and Confederates felt for abolitionists." However, "slaves understood early on that the preponderance of large slaveholders and their most zealous advocates tended to side with the South, not the Union. And slaves understood that conservative rhetoric to the contrary, a Union victory over the slaveholder's rebellion was the best chance for emancipation."[15]

In Kentucky, the first slaves began trickling to the Union forces as soon as the blue-clad troops entered the state in September 1861. Paducah was their first destination in the Purchase. Several, too, went to Smithland; one, Andrew Jackson Smith, would ultimately be permitted to enlist in the Union army and would earn the Medal of Honor.[16]

Other slaves slipped away to Columbus after it fell to Union forces. At first, the advancing Union armies had no settled, uniform policy for dealing with escaped slaves; initially, they sent some slaves back to bondage. Yet some officers resisted the reenslavement of African Americans. At Columbus in July 1862, a captain who refused to follow orders to return slaves seeking freedom—known as "contrabands"—was arrested on orders from Brigadier General Grenville M. Dodge, the post commander. Nonetheless, the slaves kept coming. In December, Grant ordered Brigadier General Thomas A. Davies, Dodge's replacement, to quarter escaped slaves in tents and vacant houses, feed them, and put them to work while he found out from the secretary of war "what final disposition shall be made of them." In the meantime, a Christian missionary reported that the two thousand fugitives at Columbus were poorly housed and clothed and suffering greatly from exposure and lack of nourishment; twenty-two died in one night. Too, they had not been paid for their work. Even so, the lure of freedom was strong; slaves kept escaping to the Union forces at Columbus, Paducah, Smithland, and elsewhere. Consequently, Grant, in January 1863, wrote Halleck, asking, "What am I to do with the surplus negroes?" He said he had recently agreed to let an Ohio philanthropist "take all that were at Columbus to his State at government expense." Grant said he "would like to dispose of more in the same way."[17]

At first, slaves could not join the Union forces, but many toiled for the army at Columbus and elsewhere. Statewide, Union officers impressed many slaves, regardless of their owners, for military-related labor, a policy that angered some Unionists. The government paid loyal slave owners for using their bondsmen. Pro-Confederate masters were not compensated; instead, the government paid the slaves and provided them food. Some of them never went back to their owners.[18]

At Columbus, which became an important Union supply depot and transportation center, African Americans loaded and unloaded steamboats and trains and helped keep the fortifications in repair. Some were sent as far as St. Louis and Cincinnati when Union commanders asked for laborers. However, records are unclear as to whether or not the African Americans were compensated for their labor. But at Cairo, the Union navy signed up "contrabands" as gunboat crewmen and paid them eighty dollars a month, ten dollars less than white sailors.[19]

Most of the blue-clad troops who came into Kentucky were from the Midwest. Few were abolitionists, but in general they did not like what they saw of slavery. Many came to sympathize with the runaway slaves, especially after hearing their stories of severe abuse under their "Rebel owners." Too, "masters often alienated soldiers when they appeared at camps and threatened to whip or shoot fugitives who resisted returning to slavery." As a result, many junior officers and their soldiers became reluctant to send fugitives back to bondage. Often, male slaves fled with their families, swelling the number of refugees inside the Union lines. In August 1862, slave women were forbidden to come to Columbus. Still, the number of African American men and women seeking refuge at Columbus overwhelmed the army's ability to care for them and provide them living space. Therefore, after the Rebels gave up Island Number Ten, about one thousand former slaves were settled there in a farming colony protected by Union soldiers.[20]

The Emancipation Proclamation opened the door for African Americans to become soldiers. After January 1, 1863, a freed slave could do as he wished, even fight for his freedom. Nearly every white Kentuckian despised the idea of putting ex-slaves in military uniforms and arming them. It was beyond their comprehension "that anyone could advocate the elevation of an inferior being, a slave, into a soldier, a rank of distinction held particularly high in the traditions of the state. . . . No Kentuckian in authority could ever be found to tolerate the idea." Indeed, lawmakers in Frankfort roundly condemned Lincoln as "a usurper and a tyrant" for permitting slaves to be turned into soldiers. At the same time, whites saw African Americans with guns as "dramatic affirmation of a manhood systematically denied for more than two centuries. Here was a powerful affront to notions of white supremacy, to white social control over blacks." Whites, from army officers to Union party leaders—"men of hitherto unquestioned loyalty"—now openly denounced Lincoln and the Republican Congress.[21]

Many whites in Kentucky, "who had traded their loyalty to the Union in return for protection of slave property," viewed the enlistment of African American soldiers as "the ultimate blow, the final realization that the Union cause had evolved and was no longer their own." Black soldiers "offended Kentucky whites on several fronts. In addition to the fact that the draft hastened the loss of their slave property, many felt that the very dignity of the Union war effort was compromised by having black troops join the fight 'side by side and shoulder to shoulder' with whites. . . . The change in racial order stung all the more because in Kentucky the Federal army often employed black troops locally, rather than sending them to fight on some distant battlefield." The result was "contentious confrontations between masters, mistresses and former slaves."[22]

Despite white outrage in the state of his birth, Lincoln saw African Americans as a new and much-needed source of soldiers for what was becoming America's bloodiest war. In May 1863, the War Department created the Bureau of Colored Troops. Ironically, the Union army signed up some of the first Kentucky blacks in the state's only Rebel region—the overwhelmingly proslavery and pro-Confederate Purchase. Many enlisted at Columbus, which would become the second-largest recruit center and refugee camp for African Americans in Kentucky, trailing only Camp Nelson in Jessamine County.[23]

In July 1863, the Second Regiment Tennessee Heavy Artillery (African Descent) was organized at Columbus, with many of its men coming from the area and from Confederate-held territory, where the Emancipation Proclamation was in effect. Like other African American units in the Civil War, the regiment's officers were white. The army designated the regiment the Second Tennessee because Kentucky political leaders did not want "Kentucky" to be part of any black outfit's name. The Second Tennessee was renamed the Third Mississippi, the Third Heavy Artillery, and, finally, the Fourth US Heavy Artillery (Colored). The regiment's companies were scattered throughout western Kentucky and Tennessee. The men mostly guarded railroad bridges, important roads, and river ports, and they patrolled. The troops at Columbus escorted trains out of town. On October 11, eighty-five men from the regiment defeated a Confederate cavalry force "composed of parts of three regiments" near Fort Donelson. The soldiers were in Tennessee helping recruit an African American infantry regiment, whose white lieutenant colonel praised the bravery of the black artillerymen fighting as infantry. By October 31, the Second Tennessee numbered 594 men; by Christmas Eve, the regiment's ranks had swelled to 878.[24]

Meanwhile, the number of white volunteers from the Purchase increased a bit in the spring of 1863, when the army organized the Sixteenth Kentucky Cavalry. Records of the regiment are sketchy; it merged with the Twelfth Kentucky Cavalry on March 25, 1864, the day of the battle of Paducah. At least part of the Sixteenth evidently was at Lebanon, Kentucky, in May, June, and July 1863. But Major George F. Barnes raised the regiment's first battalion in the fall of 1863. Captain Charles Bachmann's Company A was from McCracken County. Captain John E. Williamson of Paducah commanded Company B. Company C, led by Captain J. H. Starks, and Captain Thomas Carter's Company D were composed of men from Marshall, Calloway, and McCracken Counties, though Carter's outfit included a sprinkling of Tennessee Unionists.[25]

On June 18, a group of "radical Union" Democrats met in the McCracken County seat, shunted Casey aside, and named Lucian Anderson their man for Congress. Quigley was unimpressed. "I have not seen nor heard what character of resolutions they passed but from the character of [the] man they nominated, they endorsed the administration of Lincoln and a total destruction of States' rights," he harrumphed. Quigley named Trimble and L. A. Duke, also of Paducah, as "independent candidates upon the platform of the Northern or Vanlandigham [*sic*] democracy." He added that as near as he could tell neither one was "in favor of the war as now conducted."[26]

The Peace Democrats were still rising in opposition to the war. They nominated Charles A. Wickliffe of Bardstown for governor. Trimble was their man against Anderson for Congress in the First District. Trimble and Wickliffe were typical of conservative Unionists of 1861, who gradually turned against the war and Lincoln, especially after the Emancipation Proclamation and the enlisting of African American troops. Before he officially declared his candidacy, Trimble allegedly tested the political waters at Mayfield, where he addressed "a large crowd of traitors" for two hours, according to a long letter the *Journal* published on June 4. The author, "CONSTITUTIONAL UNION," said Trimble claimed that when Lincoln had asked him to run against Burnett, the president had promised him "slavery was not to be interfered with." Thus assured, Trimble said, he came home and ran against Burnett. He told the crowd that Lincoln had thus "deceived him . . . in the object for which the war was being prosecuted." He admitted "that men who turned secessionists upon the idea that the war was being waged to destroy slavery were correct" and that "the war was now being prosecuted in violation of the Constitution, and for the destruction of slavery." He characterized the conflict as an "abolition war," adding that the Confederates were justified in rebelling because "they were right in their belief that it was to be a war on slavery." The writer added that Trimble "had nothing to say against Jeff Davis and those engaged in this wicked rebellion" and that "he was repeatedly cheered by traitors who have taken the oath to support and defend this government against all enemies." "CONSTITUTIONAL UNION" claimed "all parties have regarded him as a secesh for eighteen months." When asked if he would vote "men and money to prosecute the war," Trimble replied evasively but "was understood by all present that he would not." His response brought loud cheers from "the secesh" and hisses from the Union men. Trimble claimed he was not a candidate for office, but "CONSTITUTIONAL UNION" said "everybody believed he would be, and that his speech was only thrown out as a feeler to see how it would take with traitors, as he well knows he cannot get a Union vote in the district." Detractors aside, Trimble found his reception in the Graves County seat so "very satisfactory, that within a week" he announced his candidacy for Congress, the correspondent claimed.[27]

Meanwhile, local Unionists wanted Anderson to expose Trimble and put him where he belonged: "with the enemies of his country and untrue to the Union." The two met on a county court day in Mayfield. Both men spoke; Anderson challenged candidate Trimble to come clean with the voters on "his sentiments in regard to furnishing means for carrying on the war." Trimble hedged, especially angering fathers of sons in the Union army; they demanded a straight answer. Trimble put his hand in his pocket, as if preparing to produce a pistol, turned to Anderson, and warned "that if he wanted a difficulty with him then he could have it." Anderson coolly replied that he was not looking for trouble; he merely wanted his question answered. He queried his opponent yet again. Trimble "writhed and twisted," hesitated, then admitted he "would vote neither men nor money." Trimble exited the speaker's platform, "declaring as he went that he was as good a Union man as anybody." Anderson got off a parting shot, challenging Trimble to endorse the actions of the March Union convention in Louisville and support its nominees. Trimble refused, whereupon Anderson promised the crowd "that he was for voting the last man and dollar for putting down the rebellion." His retort prompted "several traitors" to interrupt Anderson. The naysayers included Anderson's southern-sympathizing brother, Ervin, who had been voted out as circuit court clerk. With that, Marshall banged his gavel, and calm ensued. The correspondent also wrote that "traitors" were spreading the word that Trimble had told them he had the blessing of the Union military to run for Congress. "CONSTITUTIONAL UNION" was skeptical, considering that Trimble's speech represented the "last, meanest, and most cowardly phase of secession, and one that takes from the brave soldier in the field everything that sustains him."[28]

All the while, in the Purchase and elsewhere in Kentucky, guerrilla combat continued apace with political combat. The Hungarian-born brigadier general Alexander Asboth, the new commander at Columbus, was determined to stamp out the guerrilla menace, especially to railroads. In February, he had issued an order threatening even execution of civilians who provided money, food, ammunition, shelter, or intelligence to guerrillas. "These citizens will be held responsible, with their persons and property, for the acts of guerrillas whom they cherish and support," he further warned. Asboth said that for every guerrilla raid on the railroad, steamboats, or government transports, families living nearest "the scene of the outrage will be arrested and held as hostages for the delivery of the real perpetrators." Asboth vowed, "the civil law re-established in Kentucky for the benefit of the loyal shall never shield the traitor from his doom."[29]

Asboth may have heard of Columbus's big "traitor" flag the Yankees from Cairo tore down and took away in June 1861. In any event, an even larger Stars and Stripes fluttered atop a 160-foot pole in Columbus in the summer of 1863. One awestruck Yankee wrote that the banner was 50 feet long. That was probably a stretch; it was likely a standard garrison flag, which was massive enough at 36 by 20 feet. The flagpole cost $150 and was erected in two sections. With a base diameter of thirty inches, the pole gradually slimmed to eight inches square at the top. It is unclear where the flag flew, on the riverbank or inside Fort Halleck—the renamed Rebel Fort De Russey—atop the bluffs. If it was on the high ground, then it would have towered more than 350 feet above the Mississippi.[30]

In late May, possibly before the flag went up, Canadian-born social reformer, abolitionist, and Underground Railroad member Laura S. Haviland of Michigan arrived in Columbus by steamboat after a stop at Island Number Ten. Reared in New York State, widowed young, and a devout Methodist, she traveled widely, bringing money and supplies to Union hospitals and other facilities and to camps for refugee slaves. Obviously, the Island Number Ten settlement had grown; she found about three thousand former slaves. As soon as she arrived at Columbus, Haviland saw a funeral procession "of colored people, and a number of officers and soldiers." The cortege, which Haviland joined, was for a runaway Missouri slave fatally wounded by his young master two days before. The slave had wanted to join the Union army at Columbus; he was rowing his mother and two small sisters across the river in a skiff when the master appeared on the bank with a gun and ordered them to return, or he would fire. When they refused to turn back, the master shot the son in the arm, but the mother grabbed the oars and rowed "with all her might." The master fired again, hitting the son in the lung. His mother completed their freedom flight. Soldiers rushed the wounded man to the post hospital, where "he received the best surgical attendance, but to no avail," Haviland wrote. "Much sympathy was expressed in behalf of the bereaved mother, who was left with two little girls." She added that grief "was no new trial for . . . [the mother]." Her husband had been sold away from her a few years earlier. She also told Haviland that her "two big boys" had been sold just before the war and that she did not know where they were. The mother sobbed to Haviland, "An' now my poor boy is shot dead by that young massa I nussed with my own boy. They was both babies together." The murder angered the troops at Columbus. A soldier told Haviland that he and "a large company" of men were awaiting permission to go to Missouri and "strip" the plantation from which the family had escaped. The soldier said the mother "seemed to be such a nice woman; they all felt so indignant they hardly knew how to wait for orders."[31]

Haviland left the tragic scene and headed for the Soldiers' Home, which was operated by the Western Sanitary Commission, a private charity similar to the USO. The facility, where transient soldiers could find food and lodging, had been the Buchanan Hotel, which the Confederates had used as a hospital when they were in Columbus. On the way, she spotted a white man, evidently a civilian, pushing a wheelbarrow loaded with bricks; a heavy iron ball was attached to his ankle, and an African American soldier was guarding him. A white officer told her the captive "was a strong secessionist, and was a hard master over a large plantation with more than one hundred slaves, and he was taken prisoner, and all his slaves came into our camp." The younger slaves joined the army. When the slave owner tried to flee, soldiers shackled him with ball-and-chain. His guard had been one of his bondsmen. "What a turning of tables!" Haviland exclaimed. "Yes, you will find the same turning of tables within our lines all over the South," the officer replied.[32]

As Haviland passed an open tent, she noticed "a large, square block of iron, weighing sixty to eighty pounds, to which was attached a ring." She asked a black man about the block, and he said it was from the plantation where he had been enslaved: "When master had a mind to punish us he ordered us locked to that block, and from one to a dozen of us sometimes were locked to it with a long chain; and when we hoed corn, we'd hoe the chain's length, then the one next the block had it to tote the length of the chain, and so on till we did our day's work." The man said that since he and other former slaves had arrived in Columbus, they had "seen nine of our masters chained to that same block and made to shovel sand on that fortification yonder. There were forty of us that belonged to our plantation standing in this yard looking on." The man said when he watched, he "cried like a baby." Haviland asked him why he wept. Came the reply: "O, to think what great things God is doing. Man could never, never do it." He said some other freedmen "laughed, and one man said, 'Ah ha, you see now how sweet 'tis to tote that old block, don't you?" Haviland asked if the ex-slave owner had heard the man. "O no, we's five rods off."[33]

Haviland also wrote that she heard troops were burning several houses three miles beyond the Union lines. A man, evidently an ex-slave, agreed to show Haviland and another woman helping at the Soldiers' Home the Moss mansion. They boarded an army ambulance and soon reached the smoldering remains. The owner was "raking over the debris for gold and silver or other imperishable treasure." In the ashes she spotted "hand-cuffs, chains, shackles, and other slaveirons." Moss had moved to a slave cabin, "as the long row was vacated by seventy of his former slaves." Haviland wrote that Moss was supposedly one of the richest planters in the state. She added that a year before the war started, he reportedly lost "seven valuable slaves." Haviland said that while a Cairo carpenter was doing work for Moss and some other plantation owners, he allegedly helped ten slaves escape, Moss's seven plus three more belonging to other masters. While he was still in Kentucky, some local men captured the carpenter, who protested that "he knew nothing whatever of their slaves." The men refused to believe him and proceeded to tar and feather him "and treated him to a ride on a rail-horse." Afterward, they gave him soap and lard to clean himself off, then strongly implied they would kill him if he came back. The carpenter reputedly wrote Moss, promising that if he got a chance, he would get even with "those who had heaped upon him these abuses." Moss claimed he had seen the carpenter and three other men in Union uniforms a few days before his house burned, but he did not believe the carpenter was really in the army. Moss said he "did not think a Union soldier would do so mean a thing." A Union officer said Moss "was a hard master, and a warm secessionist, but was now very tame."[34]

Back in Columbus, Haviland interviewed other former slaves, some from far down the Mississippi. They told of cruel masters who sold off children from their parents and forced female slaves to have sex with them. She said her attention was drawn by another scene, "different . . . but truly revolting—a young mother of only fourteen years, with a very sick infant; the grandmother of a very light complexion, and the great-grandmother a mulatto." Haviland wrote that they "were the children of their old master, whose hair was white with age. He was the father of the great-grandmother, and of each generation to the fourth, and master, all in one." As repelled by it all as Haviland said she was, she "was compelled to believe it, as his former slaves told me of his licentious character from his early youth to eighty years. He was never married, and was the owner of a large plantation, and his many slaves sought the first opportunity to escape." Before she left Columbus for home on May 30, Haviland also toured the post hospitals. She found them "tolerably well cared for except one regimental hospital, where were a number of sick and emaciated soldiers, who had no pillows but their haversacks, and no covering but their overcoats, and they piteously begged for milk." A surgeon told Haviland she was welcome to bring them milk, but that the patients, who were suffering "camp diarrhea," would likely trade the milk for whiskey. She fetched boiled milk, pillows, and quilts anyway, and the sick soldiers received her gifts with gratitude.[35]

Though Asboth doubtless meant business when he laid down the law to the local secesh, his "many good social qualities . . . won him a number of warm personal friends even among his bitterest enemies in war," the *Columbus Dispatch* recalled in 1871. He greatly admired flowers and native birds, taking "great delight" in cultivating the former and taming the latter. He had a cage full of wild fowl, prompting a visitor to offer to bring the general a feathered friend he did not have. This "Mr. S—" allegedly "loved a practical joke better than it was possible for him to like any Federal officer." Anyway, Asboth's command of English evidently was limited, for when "S" offered to fetch him an "owl," Asboth did not understand. "S" said an owl was a rare bird, one that "sings in the night when all other birds were asleep." He added, "Its notes are loud and clear, and so sweet, you would think a woman was singing to you." Asboth was purportedly "a great admirer of the ladies." In any event, Asboth had to have such a bird. When "S" produced an owl, the grateful general put the newcomer in the cage with the other birds and happily went to bed. That night, the owl ate all of his mates, leaving only "a few quill feathers and well picked bones." The distraught Asboth slew the owl. "S" steered clear of the post commander "for some days, until fully assured that General Asboth had recovered equanimity." When they finally met, Asboth told "S" what had happened. "S" offered a mock apology and suggested to the general that he should have cut off the owl's talons and fed him before caging him. "But the general was inconsolable."[36]

At the same time, Asboth and the Union brass were worried about the election. Never mind that the state's civilian and military authorities did all they could to ensure Union success at the polls. On July 10, Governor Robinson issued a proclamation reminding Kentuckians that under special war measures the legislature had passed, their expatriated fellow citizens could not vote and should be barred from taking part in the election: "In this campaign and election the army became the dominating factor, issuing orders and prohibitions on all sides to such an extent that the freedom of the election was almost destroyed." The army decided Wickliffe would not be governor "even if every Kentuckian in the state should want to vote for him." On July 25, General Boyle issued an order permitting authorities to seize the property of any Kentuckian who voted for Wickliffe. He said such a vote was proof of Confederate sympathy. On July 31 came the crowning blow: Major General Ambrose E. Burnside, commander of the Department of the Ohio, issued General Orders No. 120 declaring martial law in Kentucky "for the purpose only of protecting, if necessary, the rights of loyal citizens and the freedom of election." He said Kentucky had been invaded "by a rebel force"—meaning Morgan's raiders—whose "avowed intention" was "overawing the judges of elections . . . intimidating the loyal voters, keeping them from the polls, and forcing election of disloyal candidates." Only the army could prevent such machinations, according to Burnside. Thus, the only question over the election was how big the Unionist landslide would be. In many counties, officials crossed Wickliffe's name off the poll books. Likewise, they removed Trimble's name in several First District counties. Soldiers arrested him and kept him locked up until after the election.[37]

Perhaps nowhere were Union soldiers more diligent in keeping down the Peace Democratic vote than in the Purchase, the northernmost part of Major General Stephen A. Hurlbut's Sixteenth Corps command area. On July 14, the general issued Special Orders No. 159, commanding his troops in the Columbus District to stop anyone from voting or running for office "who is not avowedly and unconditionally for the Union and the suppression of the rebellion." His decree required all civilian election officials to demand a loyalty oath of suspected southern sympathizers; anyone refusing to swear it could not cast a ballot. On July 15, an approving Asboth notified Hurlbut that he had communicated the orders to local civilian and military authorities, explaining to them that troops would arrest violators.[38]

On June 29, Hurlbut had issued Special Orders No. 144, which subjected the Purchase to martial law. On July 6, outgoing state senator Thomas A. Duke of Paducah, a Unionist and a candidate for Congress, wrote Lincoln, expressing his disapproval of the general's action. The missive revealed the growing gap between conservative and unconditional Unionists. Duke, who included a newspaper clipping of the order, obviously figured Anderson was the "avowedly and unconditionally" Unionist candidate Union authorities had in mind. Duke said he feared Hurlbut's order might "be abused and missunderstood [*sic*] and in several Counties may be used against me by preventing my friends from giving me their support." Duke promised the president he had always been "a union man" but said that he, Representative Casey, and other "union men & candidates" spurned the Paducah convention that had nominated Anderson. "These gentlemen & myself are independent Candidates for Congress," he explained. Duke felt duty-bound to call Lincoln's "attention to an order so pregnant with danger to the elective franchise." He hoped the president might modify the order to "prevent its abuse by designing parties," evidently meaning Anderson and his supporters. He claimed the Purchase had grown quieter than any other part of the state; "the people are at home sowing that they may reap—& they will continue to do so to the end of this rebellion." He said "designing & bad men," an apparent swipe at Anderson and the other unconditional Unionists who nominated him, had "poisoned the minds of the administration" against the Purchase "from motives of interest—Selfishness alone prompted them." Duke said Union commanders in the region, past and present, would back him up and "testify . . . that there has not been a rebel Soldier (except those who have voluntarily returned home) in any of the Counties west of the river for Sixteen months or more."[39]

Duke seemed to be splitting hairs. True, the Confederate army was long gone. But guerrilla bands, harbored, or at least tolerated, by the citizenry, continued to bedevil Union troops. Thus, it is hard to imagine the Union brass would have called the Purchase quiet. In any event, on July 29, Asboth issued his own General Orders No. 47 to insure there were no doubts "as to the intent and meaning of Special Orders, No. 159." His edict warned that "no person shall be permitted to be voted for or be a candidate for office who has been or is now under arrest or bonds, by proper authority, for uttering disloyal language or sentiments." Asboth told county judges to appoint only "avowedly and unconditionally" Union men as election judges and clerks. They were to fire judges and clerks "who are not such loyal persons." Also, election officials were "not to place the name of any person upon the pollbooks to be voted for . . . who is not avowedly and unconditionally for the Union and the suppression of the rebellion, or who may be opposed to furnishing men and money for the suppression of the rebellion." The latter proscription was, of course, aimed squarely at Trimble. So was part of the oath that Asboth mandated for voters and candidates: "I am unconditionally for the Union and the suppression of the rebellion, and am willing to furnish men and money for the vigorous prosecution of the war against the rebellious league known as the Confederate States." Asboth's order also warned that any voter or election officer who failed to obey it "will be arrested and sent before a military commission as soon as the facts are substantiated."[40]

Asboth touched on the election in a July 30 dispatch he had sent to Hurlbut informing corps headquarters about his antiguerrilla operations in the Purchase and West Tennessee. He told Hurlbut that Anderson was campaigning in Columbus the day before. In addition, Asboth included a copy of his General Orders No. 47, explaining that he had issued it because "the rebel sympathizers will struggle to elect disloyal men." Also on July 30, election instructions were part of a message Asboth sent to Colonel George E. Waring Jr., commander of the Fourth Missouri Cavalry, who was out hunting guerrillas with his regiment and thought to be at Feliciana. Asboth included his and Hurlbut's general orders and told the colonel to "see that the ensuing election in your neighborhood is conducted and controlled in accordance to their provisions."[41]

Taking no chances, Hurlbut forwarded copies of both orders to Brigadier General Napoleon Bonaparte Buford, commander at Cairo, and called on him to "send one discreet, well-posted, and firm commissioned officer, with ten men," to each of three evidently suspicious voting precincts in Ballard County: McChristian's, Thorp's, and Fort Jefferson. The soldiers were to carry Hurlbut's and Asboth's election orders. Hurlbut advised Buford that his men had to be at the polls by 6:00 a.m. and that "each officer should have the assistance of a well-posted citizen of known loyalty." Hurlbut also referred Buford to an "unofficial but authentic newspaper report" of Burnside's declaration that was evidently included in the dispatch.[42]

Three days before the election, the *Columbus War Eagle,* the town's soldier paper, issued its own warning to "traitors" who would "vote for Trimble, or any other man who has not publicly avowed himself as an unconditional Union man." They would henceforth "be treated as enemies, and as men deserving on their guilty heads all the punishment which the Government has in reserve for traitors." The paper added, "Other persons of lesser magnitude have announced themselves candidates for the State Senate, and for Representatives in the State Legislature, who are occupying the same position that Wickliffe and Trimble occupy." The *War Eagle* reminded citizens "not to vote for such men" whose candidacies violated Hurlbut's and Asboth's orders. "We tell the people of the District that their only safety and protection depends on voting the straight-out Union ticket. The issue is in your hand, and on your conduct . . . depends your future peace and protection. When you vote for traitors, you can of course expect no protection from the Federal Government."[43]

Not surprisingly, "the straight-out Union ticket" triumphed statewide. Bramlette piled up 67,586 votes to 17,344 for Wickliffe. Unionists claimed every seat in the state senate and all but three seats in the state house. All of the Unionist congressional candidates cruised to easy wins. Anderson trounced Trimble, 4,323 to 711.[44]

In the Purchase, Bramlette beat Wickliffe 1,729 to 554. Anderson topped Trimble 1,650 to 523, handing the Unionist-turned–Peace Democrat his third straight loss in a congressional contest. Even so, Wickliffe and Trimble carried Fulton, Hickman, and Marshall Counties. By way of comparison, in June 1861, Burnett had pocketed every Purchase county and outpolled Trimble 5,626 to 1,785. Duke's protest letter to the president notwithstanding, he polled just 15 votes, all in Marshall County.[45]

In January 1862, 1,001 First District voters—579 of them in the Purchase—went to the polls to replace Burnett with Casey. Unionists claimed the vote was small because "the secessionists did not recognize the election and the Union Men were afraid to vote." Rebel soldiers were still in the neighborhood, too—at Columbus, Hickman, and Camp Beauregard in the Purchase and at Forts Henry and Donelson not far over the border in Tennessee. Guerrillas, at least nominally Confederate, were around in August 1863, but regular Rebel soldiers were long gone. At the same time, Union troops tried to guarantee the safety of most Union voters. Yet in victory, neither Bramlette nor Anderson mustered as many Purchase votes as Trimble garnered in defeat in 1861. Thus, it would seem that few hearts and minds had been won over to the Union cause. Unionists remained a minority in Kentucky's South Carolina.[46]

Kentuckians also elected a new state house and half of the senate in August 1863. Interestingly, none of the Purchase Unionists who replaced the expelled secessionists returned to Frankfort. Perhaps their Unionism had waned, like Trimble's. In any event, the region's new house delegation consisted of Thomas P. Hays of Ballard County, John Whitnell of Calloway County, F. M. Ray of Fulton and Hickman Counties, E. W. Smith of Graves County, Wiley Waller of Marshall County, and Thomas Barchett of McCracken County. In the senate, W. T. Chiles of McCracken County, J. D. Landrum of Graves County, and T. W. Hammond of Trigg County would represent the Purchase. Chiles's district included McCracken and Marshall Counties, and Landrum's included Graves, Ballard, Fulton, and Hickman Counties. Hammond sat for Trigg and Calloway Counties.[47]

Hurlbut and Asboth might have received the election news with mixed feelings. Bramlette and Anderson easily triumphed in the Purchase, but Wickliffe and Trimble managed to carry Fulton, Hickman, and Marshall Counties. Livingston County, just east of the Purchase, also went for the Peace Democratic duo. In the Purchase, Anderson's best showing was in his home county, where he received 682 votes. Trimble got none, apparently because his name was not on the candidate list. By comparison, Trimble had managed 610 Graves County votes against Burnett in the June 1861 race, where Burnett's total was 1,270. In every Purchase county, Trimble had gotten more votes in 1861 than Anderson did in 1863. Neither Wickliffe nor Trimble received votes in Calloway and McCracken Counties, suggesting both their names were crossed out there, too. Bramlette fared best in Graves County, where he piled up 720 votes. The 1863 elections, the last state elections before the war ended, are more proof that Confederate sentiment still prevailed in the Purchase. Based on 1861 and 1863 vote totals, Unionism had increased only in Graves County, and there but marginally. Possibly, too, some southern-sympathizing Graves County men voted for Anderson simply because they knew him and figured he might be able to help them in some way.[48]

10

The Battle of Paducah

As 1863 waned, so did Rebel fortunes of war. Grant's capture of Vicksburg and Lee's defeat at Gettysburg, occurring simultaneously in July, turned the tide in favor of the Union. Afterward, even the most ardent Confederates—including those in Kentucky's "South Carolina"—must have known, or at least feared, all would be lost sooner or later. Yet the Purchase stayed Confederate, its secessionist majority perhaps hoping for a miracle. Forrest's cavalry raided Paducah in March 1864, boosting Rebel spirits. But like Polk's army in 1861, these latter-day "deliverers" also departed, again leaving the rebellious citizenry to the ever-present "Abolition Invaders."

An August 3 story in the *Journal* showed Union ardor was still in short supply in the "the South Carolina of Kentucky" and in much of the First Congressional District. The paper published a table showing the number of white volunteers that each of the state's nine congressional districts had furnished to the Union army up to July 28, 1863. Like the vote, the totals strongly suggested that western Kentucky was still Rebel. Anderson's fourteen-county constituency lagged far behind the rest of the state, providing a mere 1,154 men to the national forces, 560 from the Purchase. Marshall County led the district, but with only 216 volunteers. Fulton and Hickman Counties were at the bottom of the list; Fulton had sent no men to the Union army, and Hickman had sent a mere 9. Statewide, 41,937 Kentuckians had volunteered for federal service.[1]

Most of the white volunteers from the Purchase rode in the Fifteenth and Sixteenth Kentucky Cavalry Regiments; most of the region's African American volunteers were in the Second Tennessee Colored Heavy Artillery but often were used as infantry. Afoot or on horseback, the Purchase men in blue helped pursue the numerous guerrilla bands in the region. The marauders dared not challenge strongly fortified Columbus and Paducah. Even so, Colonel Stephen G. Hicks, Paducah's commander, prepared the people for guerrilla attack. In November, he issued a special order, instructing civilians that if the enemy came, all women and children were to take refuge under the riverbank, and all Union men were to go to Fort Anderson, bringing "whatever arms they may have, to assist in defending the city." Hicks's decree "had the effect of cooling down the ecstasy of the rebel sympathizers, who were impatient for the arrival of their 'deliverers.'" But Paducah's "deliverers" were many miles away and were not heading in the city's direction. Bragg's Army of Tennessee was the main Rebel force in the Western Theater. Grant's Army of the Tennessee, the principal Union force in the theater, was on the verge of pushing Bragg away from strategic Chattanooga into north Georgia.[2]

Grant and Bragg—indeed, almost every other general on either side—considered kidnapping and looting beyond the rules of war. So were shooting up, wrecking, and robbing a passenger train and cold-blooded murder. But, according to the *New York Times,* raiders, apparently Colonel W. W. Faulkner's Twelfth Kentucky Cavalry, were guilty of all such crimes when they galloped into the Purchase in early November. The newspaper estimated their numbers "from 500 to 5,000." Five hundred was probably closer to the force's actual size. In any event, on the night of November 1, they burned a Mobile and Ohio railroad bridge between Columbus and Union City and started their crime spree in Mayfield before dawn on November 2. A hundred raiders surrounded Lucian Anderson's home. A like number encircled the dwelling of a "Mr. Ballinger"—likely J. T. Bollinger, Anderson's friend and fellow Unionist. They seized the congressman-elect, but Bollinger disguised himself and got away. After plundering the town of $18,000 worth of goods, the raiders destroyed a construction train at the depot and cut the telegraph wires. Next, they hid in the woods along the railroad, aiming to ambush a passenger train expected from Paducah. At 11:00 a.m., the train stopped at Hickory Grove Station, about six miles north of Mayfield. The conductor, D. W. H. Boyd, heard the enemy was in front of and behind the train. "Escape was impossible"; nonetheless, he sent the train forward to Mayfield but stopped it "several hundred yards from the depot." When the raiders surrounded the train, the conductor reportedly opted for surrender, but "Mr. Dobson," who had climbed onto the locomotive, pulled a pistol on the engineer and threatened to shoot him if he did not back up. The engineer complied, throwing the locomotive in reverse, and poured on "every pound of steam." The train began rolling "with fearful rapidity down a steep grade, amid a perfect shower of musket-balls." Meanwhile, the Confederates had piled crossties on the rails two miles farther up the line. When the hindmost car smashed into the barricade, the entire train derailed and was "crushed into a wreck." Raiders waiting at the barrier opened "a continuous fire" on the wreckage. Edward Twyman, a local Union official, "received a buckshot in one leg," while "a large splinter was thrust through the other, and several pieces of timber fell across his body." Though he was seriously injured, "the guerrillas rendered him no aid, and refused to permit the citizens to assist him," the *Times* said. He "remained several hours in this situation, suffering greatly from his wounds." Also wounded were Boyd, a passenger named Williams, and the brakeman, "a negro boy." In addition, the raiders stole $500 from Dr. Humble and $600 from the Mayfield station agent. They also "robbed every one who came in their way, taking watches, money, breast-pins and finger-rings." A pair of Union men, William Colly—probably "Colley"—and West Brinkley, fled the scene, but the raiders tracked them down with bloodhounds. Colly, who had been in the state guard, was "fearfully torn and mangled by the dogs." The paper did not say if he died, but Brinkley evidently did. While the ex–home guard captain was holding off the dogs, the raiders showed up and shot him, apparently fatally. Besides Anderson, the raiders kidnapped two other men, a "Dr. Ladruner" and "Irain Anderson," more likely Ervin Anderson, Lucian's southern-sympathizing brother. After suffering no casualties in the one-sided gunfight, "the miscreants" remained around Mayfield until 8:00 p.m., when they rode away, camping about eight miles from town before "finally disappearing altogether." The *Times* said their leaders were "Capt. Faulkner," who "formerly resided in Ballard County," and a "Major Newsome," a former railroad man. "Some of the men were former residents of McCracken and Ballard Counties, and some were sons of residents of Paducah," the *Times* said.[3]

Doubtless Hurlbut heard what had happened in Mayfield and its environs. In any event, he was bound and determined to stop aiders and abettors of guerrillas and Confederate raiders. To that end, he forbade trade beyond Hicks's picket lines around Paducah. His decree led to great suffering, even among loyal citizens—and even death in one case, the *Journal* reported on December 30. The paper said city Unionists had gone to see the governor in Frankfort, hoping he might deliver them from Hurlbut's trade restrictions. "'Jackson's Purchase' is not the most loyal section of the State, it is true, still it contains many inhabitants who have never been seduced into the support of the Confederacy, but, from the first breaking out of the rebellion, have been staunchly loyal to the Union cause," the paper said. "Their lot is peculiarly hard: beset on one side by thieving and merciless guerrillas, and on the other by the unrelaxing rigor of Federal military rule." The "long suffering patriots of" the Purchase "are without the means, arms, and ammunition to expel the guerrillas, and are too honorable to attempt any evasion of the military orders." The paper suggested "the root of all this evil" in the Purchase was the Union military's decision to make Kentucky's westernmost region part of Hurlbut's command. "The whole of our State should be embraced in one department," the *Journal* editorialized. The paper said Hicks was a kind-hearted officer but, of course, he had to obey orders. As a result, about all that was permitted to pass beyond his picket line, "which did not even extend as far as the city limits," was "one dollar's worth of sugar and of coffee, twenty-five pounds of salt, and the smallest bag of flour." Otherwise outside the line, "barefooted women and children cannot get shoes nor a yard of material to make a garment." The paper cited the story of little Eddy, a seven-year-old "loyal seedling from the patriot Richard A. Bacon." Eddy had a tiny Union flag that "he has thrust in the face of every secessionist who had crossed his path since the outbreak of the rebellion." Yet the brave lad had to furl his flag and take to his bed, the unhappy result of "a dangerous attack of croup brought on by the exposure of his little feet—naked but loyal—to the biting frosts of winter, his old father having been denied the privilege of purchasing a pair of shoes for the noble little standard-bearer." The *Journal* trumpeted in outrage: "In the name of God, do the children of Dick Bacon deserve to be treated thus by the government which he would lay down his life to preserve?" The paper alleged that Hurlbut's restrictions also contributed to the untimely end of Mr. Brassfield, "a thoroughly loyal and most estimable citizen of Dresden, Tenn." The weather had turned colder while he was visiting Paducah. Brassfield "complained of serious indisposition" and tried to buy a shawl, blanket, or "some such covering" for the trip home, yet "orders were imperative—no merchants could sell any clothing to a person residing without the picket lines." Brassfield headed for home anyway but came down with pneumonia and died en route. Interestingly, the *Journal* gave the devil his due, claiming that while "the murderous guerrillas who infest the 'Purchase'" regularly stole "heavy goods, ammunition . . . horses," and robbed men of their purses, they at least "frequently abstain from disturbing the small supplies of needy families." At the same time, the paper charged that "men who served in the rebel ranks, and have been known as active smugglers to the enemy, are now living in Paducah, enjoying plenty under the protection of the government, while the ever true and loyal are subjected to the most rigid military restrictions."[4]

Nonetheless, the loyalty of almost all Kentucky Unionists was to their country, not its president. They remained simultaneously pro-Union and anti-Lincoln, and prowar and antiabolition, and could fathom no contradictions in their views. The *Journal* sided with them and against the state's "Unconditional Unionists," who would ultimately go over to the Republicans. On November 9, the paper published the plea of a conservative Paducah Unionist, who wanted to know, "Why is the Kentuckian who was contemptuously called an abolitionist upon the issues of '61 and '62 as vehemently branded *traitor, copperhead, or secesh sympathizer* upon the issues of '63?" He recalled that "two years ago the advocates of secession cursed us for defending the sacred laws and institutions and unity of our country, and now we receive the scorn and jibes of men calling themselves *loyal* for doing the same thing."[5]

Anderson stood among the scorners, according to the *Journal,* which scorned him on January 14. The raiders released him in a prisoner exchange and evidently freed his brother and the other captive, too. While they presumably went home, Anderson headed to Washington, where he fell in with the Republicans. "Mr. Anderson's first act as a Representative was to go into the abolition caucus at Washington; and his second act was to vote for the abolition candidate for the Speakership," the *Journal* reported disapprovingly. According to the paper, the congressman "has been acting with the abolitionists ever since." The *Journal* charged that Anderson "is now confessedly a regular abolitionist in particularly good standing."[6]

The *Journal* story kept pouring it on Anderson, mocking a New Year's Day meeting at his house in Mayfield in which "The Six Radicals of Graves" resolved their "abiding confidence" in Anderson's "patriotism" and promised to "sustain him in the best and most practicable mode of subduing the rebellion and sustaining the Government." The paper reminded its readers of the resolutions approved by the state Union Democratic convention in March 1863, including the one that declared "our institutions are assailed by an armed rebellion one side" and on the other side "by unconstitutional acts of Congress and startling usurpations of power by the Executive," the Emancipation Proclamation conspicuous among them. The *Journal* also recalled that the First District Union Democratic convention that nominated Anderson was called by the Graves County Union Democrats, who wanted a candidate "neither contaminated with secessionism or abolitionism." The *Journal* claimed that Anderson was thus "elected under the most unequivocal and solemn engagements that he as a Representative would act with conservative men and vote for conservative measures." After he made common cause with the Republicans, Anderson and "his associates in apostasy" tried to organize a meeting in Mayfield "to endorse his conduct." After "privately beating up for attendants some ten or fifteen days in all parts of the county, this brace of enterprising radicals succeeded finally" in arranging the January 1 gathering. "Twenty or twenty-five persons, we are assured, were present at the meeting, but only *six* persons took part in the proceedings, and, of these six, one refused to vote for the resolution in question." The *Journal* said just before the pro-Anderson resolutions were to be voted on, a gentleman asked if they were meant "to represent the sentiment of the Union men of Graves." Anderson, "the master-spirit," replied, "No, they are intended to represent only this meeting." At that point, "the meeting of six" adopted the resolutions. "And yet this sexangular concern has had the effrontery to put forth its proceedings in the name of the Union men of Graves." The *Journal* concluded: "When the Three Tailors of Tooley Street met and resolved in the name of the people of England, the thing was very generally looked upon as rather brazen; and so it was no doubt for that age and clime. 'But,' as Gregory says to Sir Jasper in the farce of The Mock Doctor, 'we have changed all that.' The Three Tailors of Tooley Street would be accounted very unassuming craftsmen in our time and country. Compared with the Six Radicals of Graves, the Three Tailors of Tooley Street were not only modest but shy and shamefaced."[7]

Ironically, the First District's Union Democrats dumped the Republican-leaning Casey for the "conservative" Anderson, who had turned "abolitionist." Another Republican-sympathizing, antislavery man was representing the Purchase, the western anchor of the "infected district," in Washington.

Perhaps the *Journal* was doubly disdainful of Anderson because he was an erstwhile favorite of the paper. He had been one of the few brave Union men in "the South Carolina of Kentucky." But Anderson the fearless had become Anderson the feckless, said the January 14 *Journal*. Back on November 2, the paper had stoutly defended Anderson when a rumor spread that the congressman would back abolitionist Republican Schuyler Colfax of Indiana for speaker, thereby spurning his fellow Kentuckian, Representative Robert Mallory of New Castle, who wanted the job. The paper discounted the rumor, pointing out that Anderson "was expressly nominated on the platform of the Union party of Kentucky." He had "expressly accepted the nomination on that platform; and he expressly made his canvass on it, issuing a circular to the voters . . . in which he expressly approved the platform and expressly condemned the policy of the Administration," meaning the Emancipation Proclamation. "We indeed have never seen any declaration of political opinion from Mr. Anderson wherein he did not equally denounce the abolitionists and the secessionists," the paper said. "He was thus nominated and elected not only as the adversary of both abolitionism and secessionism but as the representative of the selfsame position that Mr. Mallory represents." The *Journal* added that the claim that Anderson would support Colfax over Mallory was "a gross insult not merely to Mr. Anderson but to every Kentuckian." Yet Anderson voted for Colfax, turning the *Journal* into his sworn enemy.[8]

While the *Journal* assailed Anderson's vote for Colfax, the army paper at Columbus defended him. "Again we say, Bully for Anderson!" the *War Eagle* cried on December 12. Yet the big news in town was the blaze that had destroyed the military prison. The *War Eagle* lamented the lack of a fire engine. It is hard to believe that many First District residents supported their congressman in making common cause with Republicans, but on December 24, the *New York Times,* quoting the Frankfort correspondent of the *Cincin-*

nati Commercial, reported that "a majority of the members from Hon. Lucien [*sic*] Anderson's district have signed a statement that his cooperation with the Republicans, and his vote for Colfax is not inconsistent with his principles and professions at home, and will meet the approval of his constituents." The *Times* and the *Commercial* were staunchly Republican. Civil War newspapers north and south were wont to bend the truth to suit their side.[9]

At any rate, Anderson objected when Union authorities lifted all trade restrictions on Kentucky. On January 8, the Treasury Department announced "that all products and goods might be 'freely taken into and transplanted within the state as in time of peace.'" After all, by early 1864, the big battles were being fought miles from Kentucky. Thus, Uncle Sam evidently reasoned that it was safe to restore free trade to the Bluegrass State. Anderson disagreed and said so in a January 29 letter he wrote to Secretary Chase. The congressman warned that the policy change would dash "the hopes of the Union men, especially in my district." He said free trade was "what the rebels want." He said absent trade restrictions, "the rebels will be supplied with every thing they desire."[10]

Before January was out, Anderson was rebuked again in newsprint, this time in the *Congressional Globe.* A face-to-face confrontation with the foe followed. Anderson never would have admitted it publicly, of course, but he surely knew he could not have won Union troops, with the blessing of the state's Unionist government, or kept many southern sympathizers, real and suspected, from voting. Representative William J. Allen, a Tennessee-born, antiwar southern Illinois Democrat from Marion, unabashedly challenged the legitimacy of Anderson's election, calling him "one of the President's military appointees from Kentucky." Allen's district, dubbed "Egypt" for reasons not clear, adjoined Anderson's. But they were not friendly neighbors; Allen slurred the western Kentuckian as "one of the President's military appointees" in a speech the *Globe* published on January 27. Anderson said he was ailing, abed, and did not hear Allen's remarks. But on February 2, the Kentuckian was well enough to call Allen to task on the House floor. He said he was "totally unacquainted with" Allen but denounced his remark "as false and slanderous, without any foundation in fact." Anderson claimed that he had been elected by "as true, unflinching, sturdy Union men as breathe upon the continent of America . . . Union men who have been robbed and plundered, who have been imprisoned, Union men who have been hunted with hell-hound ferocity by the rebels in arms against this Government, and who seem to have an apologist" in Allen. Anderson gave "the gentleman from Illinois" a brief history lesson on his part of Kentucky since January 1862, when First District Confederate sympathizers "voted and sent a member to represent" them "in the so-called southern confederacy at Richmond." He said "the Union men took no part in that election, which they regarded as treasonable." Anderson added that "in 1863 . . . those men who had gone to the ballot-box in 1862 went to vote and send a rebel and a traitor to the Congress of the United States, but were prevented from voting, and therefore the Union men there have secured the indignation of the gentleman from Illinois." Anderson added that the Kentucky court of appeals had upheld his election. A heated exchange between Anderson and Allen followed.

Anderson said Allen knew that Rebel raiders "not more than one month before the assembling of this Congress" had invaded that portion of Kentucky adjoining his district. He knew that they "robbed and plundered by wholesale almost every union man in that district," that they wrecked the railroad between Paducah and Mayfield and shot up a train "filled with innocent women and children." Even so, "no denunciation falls from his patriotic lips," Anderson declared. Allen challenged Anderson to deny that Trimble was under military arrest until after the election solely because "he was a candidate in opposition to" Anderson. When Anderson tried to explain, Allen said he could do so after he was finished. Anderson demurred and waited for his chance, which never came. "He says that the Union people of southern Kentucky elected him," Allen scoffed. "The Union people! The bayonets were the Union people that elected him." Allen recalled Hurlbut's election order, declaring that "those who were allowed to vote had to do so in accordance with that order, and not otherwise." Allen confessed he had not seen the election returns but added that he "would be somewhat curious to see how many votes the member received, although his chief competitor was held in bonds, surrounded by a guard." Allen, referring to Anderson's capture and release by the raiders, said the congressman "has had some experience of the kind, and that it is to the good offices of a system of exchange that he owes the opportunity of being able to circulate freely in this Hall to-day and maintain his base subserviency to his masters and his contempt for the popular will of his district." Allen argued that throughout his district, "it is well known that the election in Kentucky was a mere farce; everybody so speaks of it, especially to that *Union* portion of Kentucky the member hails from." The House finally got enough of the feud and agreed it should end. But Anderson did manage a parting shot at Allen: "I had not intended to carry the war to Africa, but only into Egypt, from which the gentleman from Illinois comes."[11]

Though a Republican ally, Anderson had tried to represent the interests of Unionist slaveholders in the First District, though he advocated compensated emancipation. Anderson also initially objected to slaves becoming Union soldiers. Yet he subsequently voted for legislation that included limited compensation to slave owners for the loss of their chattels to the military. In any event, his embrace of abolition and the "Black Republicans" all but assured his defeat in any election where the secesh could vote.[12]

At the same time Anderson was having to endure Allen's war of words in Washington, Union troops at Paducah were getting help in their shooting war against guerrillas. But the new soldiers came from the source almost all Kentucky whites disdained: African Americans. At first, Lincoln, ever sensitive to border state Unionist opinion, authorized the enrollment only of free blacks, whom almost all white Kentuckians hated. The president believed whites in his native state would not care because slaves would not be affected. He erred in judgment; Kentucky whites vehemently protested, believing that enrollment of slaves was sure to follow. Strenuous white objections, from Governor Bramlette and the legislature down, led to suspension of the enrollment plan until February 1864, when all African Americans of military age in the state were made eligible for military service. Meanwhile, Kentucky was permitted to use whites to meet its quota of the three hundred thousand men the military called for in October 1863.[13]

In January 1863, the army had established a recruiting station for black volunteers in "the Charleston of Kentucky." Lieutenant Richard D. Cunningham, a Paducah-based Illinois cannoneer, began seeking soldiers for a heavy artillery regiment, promising a three-hundred-dollar bounty plus freedom for the enlistee and members of his family. Cunningham's efforts proved no more popular in Frankfort than they had in Paducah. The legislature, on Lincoln's birthday, approved a resolution calling African American enlistments "impolitic." Bramlette, who had denounced African American enlistments in his inaugural address, subsequently dispatched a strongly worded nine-page protest letter to Lincoln. Bowing to pressure, the president and Major General Stephen G. Burbridge, commander of the District of Kentucky, agreed that African American troops signed up in Kentucky would be trained out of state. Burbridge made the promise official in his General Orders No. 34. He also offered to pay the owner of each slave who enlisted three hundred dollars as compensation for his loss. Yet such conciliatory efforts did not last long; in March 1865, Congress approved a law granting freedom to the wives and children of slaves, including Kentuckians, who joined the army. By March 1864, recruiting of black soldiers was in full swing across Kentucky under the direction of Adjutant General Lorenzo Thomas. Chetlain, Hurlbut's subordinate in Memphis, renewed his efforts to enlist African Americans in western Kentucky. Reception centers were opened across the state; Paducah was the First District "camp of reception."[14]

Almost all white Kentuckians were horrified at the flood of black enlistments, which "at the very least . . . threatened a calamitous breakdown" of long-established white supremacy. Even more ominous in white imaginations was "the suddenness of the black enlistment stampede," which "heralded the sort of disorderly racial catastrophe befitting the onset of a slave uprising." Further, "African Americans in their midst had become a powerful political force, and unbeknownst to the master class, the newly militarized black population drew energy and organization from decades of kin and social networks built during slavery." Thomas, though born in Delaware, a slave state, did not understand the situation in Kentucky. He suggested that "the unconditional Union men will . . . cheerfully bring forward their slaves to assist in crushing the rebellion." Yet unconditional Unionists were few statewide and fewest of all in the Purchase and adjacent counties. Nonetheless, J. L. Seaton of Smithland was one. In February, he approvingly wrote Anderson that Cunningham had "mustered in about 200 colored men in his regiment." Like Anderson, Seaton was a straight-out Union man on deeply Rebel turf; he called his hometown a "Rank *Secesh Hole.*" Seaton told Anderson that Cunningham was authorized to enlist soldiers only in "Paducah and Vicinity" but that the captain wanted to be able to recruit in a wider area. Seaton argued that blacks should be signed up throughout the First District, though he conceded such a move would cause proslavery Unionists to "cry out and say it is a great violation of the CONSTITUTION of K*ai*ntucky," though "in their hearts they sigh for Jeff. Davis and his hellish crew, to win, so as to save their" slaves. Seaton promised "the true unconditional me[n], who had the honer, to work for your Election, will now, Stand up for you, and we wish you to assist us in having the order Extended, through the 1st District." Seaton also warned "that the Kentucky Conservative Copperheads had made up a purse, and hired some weak kneeded, Union man to go to Washington & endeavor to have the order of Sect. Stantons, *revoked,* so that no more Negroes, should be mustered or conscripted in Kentucky." He concluded, "Now as your friend and the friend of the Government I ask is it not right that Rebel sympathizers negroes, should be taken to put Down this infernal rebellion and restore the Government to its former Dignity & power. Therefore I would respectfully ask you to assist the true Union men of your district in having the order of Sect. Stanton to Extend over this whole Congressional District, as I am informed there are many men anxious to recruit Colored Regiments, if they can get the Authority to do so." At first, the men Cunningham recruited were designated the First Kentucky Heavy Artillery (Colored). But because state political leaders so strenuously objected to the use of "Kentucky" in naming African American units, the regiment became the Seventh United States Colored Artillery (Heavy) and finally the Eighth

United States Colored Artillery (Heavy). Their commander was Colonel Henry W. Barry.[15]

Doubtless, Seaton approved of Cunningham's success in raising and training African American troops. But his opinions were rare as July blizzards in Kentucky. Smoldering white opposition to African American enlistments in Paducah turned violent on March 21, 1864, when some of Cunningham's soldiers tried to draft African American crewmen off the steamboat *Carrie Jacobs.* The white officers and crew resisted and called on white soldiers for help. A "bloody fight" resulted between the white and black troops, "and several are badly wounded on each side." Nonetheless, recruiting continued, and four days later, the soldiers stood as comrades-in-arms, holding Fort Anderson against an attack by Forrest's cavalry.[16]

On the way to Paducah, Forrest would ride through Graves County, where, in early 1864, almost all of the citizenry apparently was still "strongly secesh, the Union men . . . numbering but about four hundred." At the same time, the pro-Confederate majority remained "in the habit of secreting bushwhackers and guerrillas, and doing many things which loyal parties call lending aid and comfort to the enemy." Those "things" included keeping quiet while guerrillas held in Mayfield nine soldiers from the Fifty-eighth Illinois Infantry whom they captured in a January 13 ambush seventeen miles from town. On muleback, the Yankees and their civilian guide—sixteen in all—were hunting guerrillas when the quarry bested them. The guerrillas opened fire from the underbrush, killing the guide, a Mayfield Unionist named Hood, and wounding the sergeant who was leading the patrol. After the Union troops shot one guerrilla dead, the rest of them swarmed the soldiers and captured them all. The guerrilla chieftain rode up, ordered his prisoners to stack their arms, and threatened "to hang at least two of them on the spot." The young soldier who had slain the guerrilla raised his rifle and shot the leader dead; another one fired and killed another guerrilla. Before the guerrillas could shoot them, the duo, joined by three more of their comrades-in-arms, got away. In the days that followed, the Yankees, to no avail, scoured the countryside for their missing men, enduring rain, sleet, and cold. Finally, they decided on one last sweep; if they failed to turn up the missing men, they would go back through Mayfield, then to Paducah, and on to Cairo. The Yankees obviously suspected their men were in Mayfield, because they sent ahead messengers with a dire warning to the townsfolk: if they gave up the guerillas' captives "within a limited time, well and good." If not, the soldiers "gave due notice that they should devote the village to fire and destruction." The threat worked; "the citizens made diligent search" and "produced in double-quick time" the prisoners, including the wounded sergeant, plus Hood's remains. With that, the detachment triumphantly headed for Paducah and Cairo. Mayfield's minority Unionists were "loud in their praise of the Fifty-eighth. They say they have done more to clear out guerrillas and treason-mongers than all the troops ever stationed in the vicinity."[17]

Hicks must have been glad to hear that. But he got bad news from Mayfield on February 22: guerrillas were poised to strike the Graves County seat again. They were evidently not the raiders who had hit town in November, but their visit also resulted in robbery and murder. Determined to stop the guerrillas, Hicks dispatched Cunningham and two hundred of his African American recruits to the Graves County seat. They arrived too late. The guerrillas were gone, but before departing they "killed J. B. Happy, a good Union man, took Parson Dugger prisoner, put him in heavy bonds, robbed three stores (all belonging to Union men), took all the goods they wanted, and destroyed the rest." Hicks ordered his men to stay put and wait for further orders.[18]

On February 29, the *Journal* published a more detailed account of the raid, based on a letter the paper received. The correspondent said Happy was "one of the most prominent and respectable citizens and business men of the town." He added that the guerrillas had opened fire "without cause or provocation—they meeting with no resistance whatever." The armed men robbed several stores and houses "of their most valuable contents, and then . . . departed with their ill-gotten gains, and the life blood of one of the most gentlemanly and magnanimous citizens of the town upon their hands." Mayfield was "an unlucky place," the *Journal* suggested. "It has had so many raids from guerrillas that it must be pretty well used up by this time." The paper surmised that the town's "location must be bad, and we would advise what is left of the Mayfieldites to gather into their haversacks what they have left of the place, and go to some more congenial clime." The paper suggested they might seek shelter with the army at Cairo.[19]

On February 27, Union troops dogging guerrillas chased "a squad of rebels" from little Dukedom, a community that straddles the state line between Graves County and Weakley County, Tennessee. The Yankees captured one of the enemy, plus four horses, a like number of loaded revolvers, and a carbine, plus "the hats of perhaps the entire party." On the night of March 6, an especially bold band of about thirty guerrillas tried to sneak into the earthworks at Columbus. Pickets from the Second Tennessee Heavy Artillery spotted them. The black soldiers opened fire, drove the intruders away, and earned high praise from their captain. Apparently, the same guerrilla group put "an obstruction" across the railroad about two miles from Columbus, but the Yankees removed it "before any mischief was done." Soon afterward, guerrilla mischief-makers hit Clinton and Mayfield. On the night of March 10, about forty guerrillas stole thirty-five to forty government horses at Clinton, where they also "broke open two stores, taking what they wanted." The same night, guerrillas targeted Mayfield anew, galloping into town and "robbing the stores of Union men, &c." Several citizens fled to Paducah. After this latest raid, Hicks sent troops of the 122nd Illinois Infantry to garrison the hard-luck community.[20]

It is not known how many Rebel soldiers, far from their homes in Mayfield and elsewhere in the Purchase, voted in the February election for the Confederate congress. But the March 1 *Journal* reported that Machen was reelected to represent the First District, collecting 908 ballots to 15 for John C. Noble of Paducah. "The precincts were 'lying about loose' wherever a squad of the traitor sons of this State could be found in Dixie," the paper explained, listing the dozen winners and their opponents. The election featured a general ticket, which meant that "about one thousand voters elected the twelve members or about 83 1/3 between each favored Representative and his antagonist," according to the *Journal*, which was predictably unimpressed with the canvass. "The result of this noble exhibition of the elective franchise will fill up a proud page in history and we therefore append it for preservation," the paper mocked.[21]

Four days later, Anderson mocked Democrats in a House speech defending his vote for Colfax for speaker. The congressman began with "a short retrospect of the history of this Democratic party of Kentucky," which would show that fealty to the Union was "never found in its actions, and only occasionally its professions." His whole address equated Democrats with disloyalty, drawing no distinction between Union Democrats like Prentice and "the Southern rights alias Democratic party" that had dominated Purchase politics in 1861. His history lesson included the elections for the border slave state convention, Congress, and the state legislature. Anderson said the "pseudo Democracy of Kentucky," facing almost certain defeat, had pulled out of the border slave state convention contest. But on the May morning of the vote, Graves County Democrats had dispatched runners to polling places "with the lying information that both tickets were withdrawn, and no election will be held." Anderson added, "In a majority of the precincts of my county no polls were opened; in some of the Democratic counties of my district, no election was held." Despite such perfidy in the Purchase, Anderson said, "over two thirds of the votes of the state were still for the Union." In the June congressional elections, he bragged that that "nine Union men were elected and one Democrat, that notorious traitor, Henry C. Burnett." He also bragged on the Union victory in the August election for the state legislature: "Thus

Kentucky had, from May to August, pronounced by overwhelming majorities that her people would abide in the Union." Though their party had been "thrice defeated" statewide, the Democrats resorted to "violent lawlessness and disregard of decency unparalleled," according to Anderson: "In most of my district all law and order was broken down; no man who professed Union principles was permitted to exercise the functions of his office." He said the circuit judge of his judicial district—meaning Williams—had been prevented from holding court: "Had he attempted to do so, an excited populace would have taken his life by the most brutal means."[22]

At the same time, "committees were regularly organized, and constant communication kept up with the rebel military authorities in Memphis and elsewhere in Tennessee; these were constantly urging the rebels to possess Kentucky, especially that part of it where I reside." He said the local "State's attorney" had gone to Montgomery, Alabama, then the Confederate capital, seeking "guns to put in the hands of . . . disloyal" citizens, who "openly boasted that that if they could obtain twenty-five thousand stand of arms, they would take Kentucky out of the Union in twenty-five days." The prosecutor evidently was Albert P. Thompson of Paducah; he was commonwealth attorney when he joined the Confederate army. Anderson also recalled the state guard muskets and artillery stolen from Mayfield: "A disloyal Governor, through a disloyal inspector general, had the State arms distributed among disloyal State guards, most of whom went into the Rebel service and took with them the State arms." He said "an extra twelve hundred muskets and a battery of six cannon and caissons were sent to a disloyal colonel of State guards at Paducah, who shipped them out to my town, placed them under the care of a disloyal captain of State guards; and this within thirty miles of the rebel encampment at Union City, in Tennessee." Anderson claimed that, "as was intended when shipped from Frankfort," the firepower "fell into the hands of the rebels; they made a raid one night and got the guns without resistance." Again, Anderson did not name names, but he meant, of course, Governor Magoffin, Inspector General Buckner, Colonel Tilghman, and Captain Andrew R. Boone.[23]

Additionally, he charged that Tilghman's hometown "was governed by a mob. Though the criminal judge of the district [Wiley P. Fowler] lived there, and a county and city judged lived there, and other inferior magistrates, yet there was no law and order, no guarantee to Union men; these were mobbed and driven off, and sometimes murdered." He said the railroad was used to ship contraband to the Confederates, "while the packages of citizens who were Union men were violently opened and searched." Worse, Anderson declared, "the lives of Union men were daily and openly threatened because of their sentiments, and more than twenty murders occurred within a circle of twenty miles of my town, of citizens, before either side had taken military possession." He added, "large meetings were held at which the most treasonable sentiments were uttered, recruiting for the rebel service openly and defiantly made, with the avowed purpose of possessing Kentucky and subjugating her free people." Meanwhile, Anderson recalled, "a disloyal Governor had twice called the legislature together to get it to call a 'sovereignty convention,' but it persistently refused."[24]

After failing "to accomplish their wicked designs, through the firmness and patriotism of the people and Legislature, they resorted to means which, although more wicked, was more promising." The secessionists tried a statewide petition drive for a convention and gained thousands of signatures. The *Louisville Courier* and the *Paducah Herald* supported "this great abomination," yet "the loyal men in various ways made it known to the Governor in that his life would be the forfeit of any such wickedness." He also brought up the May 1861 Mayfield convention, which he said fathered the November 1861 Russellville convention, which created the state's rump Rebel government:

> All their nefarious projects having miscarried, these *par excellent,* patriotic, and much oppressed Democrats of the first congressional district—a part of the people of which I have the honor to represent, the others being represented by one Willis B. Machen in the rebel congress, placed there by their votes openly and notoriously given at a public election—called a convention, to meet at my town, Mayfield, for the purpose of making a military alliance with the then seceded State of Tennessee, and separating the entire first congressional district from the State of Kentucky. The address that called forth that immense convention—the largest ever held in my district—was one of the most treasonable documents ever put forth by the most unblushing traitor. It was signed by three now prominent Democrats of my section. The bold and treasonable utterances of that convention were not excelled by South Carolina. Who were chief actors in that traitorous conclave? Without stopping to rehearse their names, I will say they embrace almost every prominent Democrat in my district at this time. In this nest of rebels and conspirators was hatched that most infamous of pretended governments, the provisional government of Kentucky.

The trio of "traitors" evidently was Oscar Turner, William R. Bradley, and Anderson's brother, Ervin.[25] The congressman gloried in Bragg's defeat and retreat from Kentucky in 1862, and in the Confederate army's failure to hold Frankfort and establish a Rebel government. He praised Colonel Gilbert for breaking up the Peace Democratic convention in early 1863 and lauded the subsequent defeat of the antiwar party at the polls. In any event, Anderson protested that "the vote I gave for speaker was in strict conformity with the Union party of Kentucky; and so far as the charge of abolitionism is concerned, it is an old, worn-out charge, always made use of by certain men when they have no other argument." The congressman admitted, "To be a Union man in a slave state is no easy task; he suffers the taunts and jeers of those who are ignorant, led on by designing demagogues, who too cowardly to fight remain at home with an oath on their conscience, protected by the Government, but on all occasions talking about the Constitution and its violation by the President and those aiding him in crushing the rebellion. These are the men in my State who call themselves Democrats." He blamed them and their supporters, "the so-called Democrats of the North," for "prolonging the war." Most Kentucky Unionists were, of course, for prosecuting the war only to preserve the Union, not to abolish slavery.[26]

Meanwhile, back in the Democratic Purchase, guerrillas continued to rob and murder citizens, usually Unionists, with seeming impunity. On March 22, some of them terrorized the little Catholic hamlet of Fancy Farm in Graves County, while others waylaid a train as it rolled into Mayfield. As many as fifty guerrillas rode into Fancy Farm and shot Julian Sanderson, who carried the mail between Mayfield and Columbus. They also destroyed the chapel and cleaned out the Willis & Boswell store. The marauders left with "some 4 or 5 citizens as prisoners." At Mayfield, ten miles east, about thirty-five armed men "killed one negro man and shot several times at a Union man, who escaped," Hicks reported from Paducah. "No Union man can go out of this place with safety in that direction," he complained. "The interior is full of guerrillas. I have no cavalry to send after them." Soon, Hicks would have more than guerrillas on his hands. Unbeknownst to the colonel, Forrest's cavalry was riding hard for Paducah. The foray would be a longed-for homecoming for many of his men. Many Paducah citizens would welcome the Confederates as their deliverers.[27]

On March 1, the Third, Seventh, and Eighth Kentucky Infantry, the latter exchanged after Fort Donelson, were sent to Forrest at Columbus, Mississippi, as mounted infantry. The Twelfth Kentucky Cavalry was to be part of Forrest's force, too. The western Kentuckians were glad on two counts, Henry George remembered. They heard Forrest was bound for deep western Kentucky, and they were proud to get to serve under a commander "admired by every Confederate and feared by the Federals." When the men learned that Forrest indeed was heading for Paducah, "those who could not be furnished with horses indicated that they were willing to start on foot." The journey toward "home and loved ones" began on March 15, "the Kentuckians who could not get horses trudging along afoot, happy in the thought that they were going where they could get horses to ride and comfortable clothes to wear once more."[28]

Pirtle fondly remembered that the men were joyous "over the prospect of seeing home and homefolks again, now more than two years since the most of us had seen any of our people." He missed his spouse and four children, "oldest ten years and down, one a year and a half old that I had never seen, only short two months of being two years since I had seen my wife." But he rode no more than three miles before his horse "began to limp badly from sore feet." He had to detour to a blacksmith shop in Starkville, Mississippi, while the Seventh rode north. Pirtle spent the night waiting for his horse to be reshod and departed the next morning. He rode alone for more than a hundred miles, finally catching up with the regiment at Corinth, Mississippi, four days later.[29]

On March 20, Forrest's advance elements reached Jackson, Tennessee. Four days later, part of his army forced the surrender of federal troops at Union City while he and the rest of his men, including the western Kentuckians and other regiments of Brigadier General Abraham Buford's division, pressed toward Paducah, sixty-five miles away. The Third, Seventh, and Eighth Infantry had been redesignated mounted infantry; the Twelfth was officially a cavalry command. After camping near Mayfield on March 24, the Rebels "were in their saddles early" on March 25, Good Friday, riding toward Paducah, George wrote. At the edge of town, the Confederates drove in the Union pickets and advanced into Paducah.[30]

Before the Rebels arrived, "rumor had a busy day playing on her 'harp of a thousand strings' . . . till about two o'clock . . . when all of a sudden the presence of large rebel force in the suburbs of our city was no longer a doubtful question," according to a Paducah Unionist's account in Frank Moore's *Rebellion Record*. When he saw the raiders heading up Broadway with what he "supposed to be a flag of truce," he hurried home "to provide for the safety of my family." He figured he had at least thirty minutes before battle was joined. Before he reached his doorstep, the rattle of muskets surprised him. "Its sudden commencement can be accounted for only upon the presumption that the enemy's flag of truce was not a flag of truce, or at least was not respected by those who sent it, for Federal pickets were fired on and prisoners taken before the flag could have reached its destination." One of Hicks's officers evidently mistook the flag, too. He advanced toward the Rebels, waving his white handkerchief. The Confederates opened fire, and the officer beat a hasty retreat. "Thus the battle opened," the Union man remembered, "leaving non-combatants, women, and children to make their escape through the rain of shot and shell, which had been provoked by this strange and untimely attack."[31]

While the Union man headed for what he hoped was home and safety, the Kentucky troopers headed for cannon-bristling Fort Anderson. They dismounted and moved in a battle line until they reached "the more densely built up portion of the city," George wrote. They continued forward, filing in columns along "streets, the buildings on either side of which preventing an advance in any sort of line until an open space was reached near the fort." Moving through the streets, the Rebels were "under a constant and withering fire from the fort by both small arms and artillery." When they reached open ground near the fort, "the lines were somewhat adjusted before the final charge was made," he added. The charging Confederates quickly discovered a nasty surprise: surrounding the fort was "a deep ditch with such perpendicular banks as to render crossing impossible." The ditch and the deadly fire from the fort were too much for Forrest's horsemen. "A retreat was ordered back to the buildings," George said. The Rebels went inside, stationed themselves at the windows, and kept up "a terrific fire . . . until near night," when "the whole command was withdrawn a short distance from the city and went into camp for the night."[32]

George recalled that "casualties in the engagement were not large in numbers but in material it was a very serious loss." He mainly meant the death of Colonel Albert P. Thompson of Paducah, commander of the brigade that included the Third, Seventh, Eighth, and Twelfth Kentucky. His gruesome death looms large in local history, but there are multiple versions of how his life ended. George wrote that the colonel "was instantly killed by a cannon-shot while leading his troops in a charge" and that "he fell on the threshold of his home, flushed with the prospect of crushing the enemy." George said Thompson was "one of the most intelligent and valuable officers in Forrest's command. His death was a sad loss to the Kentuckians." Reputedly, the cannonball that killed Thompson also fatally injured his horse, which ran half a block before dropping dead. Supposedly, the steed was buried where it fell; the gravesite is possibly under the city's busy Downtown Loop today. Thompson was buried in Paducah but reinterred near Murray, where he was apparently born.[33]

The Union man's story in the *Rebellion Record* says a cannon shot and a musket ball ended Thompson's life "as suddenly and furiously as the proud oak receives the thunder-bolt." The shell passed clear through him, "tearing to atoms the lower part of the breast and down to the limbs, throwing portions of his body fifteen feet distant." He added, "it is said that just before, and almost simultaneously with the shell, a musket was fired at the Colonel by an ardent young African, which took effect in the forehead." According to another story in the *Rebellion Record*, an exploding shell killed "Bert" Thompson "within forty feet from the fort," and the blast "so badly mangled [his body] that it could not be carried off by the rebels, one arm not being found at all." Union troops took from the dead colonel "several trophies . . . among them his pistols, the stars on his collars, etc.," according to an *Indianapolis Journal* story quoted in Moore's book.

Battle, Perrin, and Kniffen's *History of Kentucky* claims the fatal shot came from a thirty-two-pounder gun "carefully aimed by" Kentucky cavalry sergeant Tom Hayes. The shell "tore the brave commander's body to pieces within 100 yards of the coveted prize." Yet an April 1 *New York Times* story, quoting a *Chicago Times* article, said Hayes was killed in the battle. The New York paper also quoted a *Chicago Tribune* story that said "Col. Thompson was literally torn in pieces by a shot from a siege gun handled by colored men." Writing in *The Story of Paducah,* local historian Fred G. Neuman also maintains that a cannon shot killed Thompson but that the deadly missile came from a gunboat helping defend the fort. J. V. Grief of the Third Kentucky, who, like George, survived the battle, said the colonel was holding "his cap in his right hand above his head when he was struck by a shell, which exploded as it struck him, literally tearing him to pieces, and" ripping the saddle from his horse. In an 1897 *Confederate Veteran* magazine article, Grief also recalled that that the colonel's "flesh and blood fell on the men near him." Grief was within ten feet of Thompson, "and my old gray Confederate hat was covered with his blood; a large piece of flesh fell on the shoulder of my file leader, John Stockdale." Grief remembered "that although Col. Thompson was surrounded by his staff and couriers, only he was hit."[34]

Controversy, too, surrounds Thompson's attack. Some sources say Forrest ordered it, while others claim the colonel did, on his own. Thompson indeed freelanced the assault, according to Forrest biographer Brian Steel Wills, who writes that the attack "was ill-advised, apparently prompted by Thompson's desire to achieve success in his hometown." Wills quotes Captain Henry A. Tyler of the Twelfth Kentucky, who said Thompson told him "I am going to take that fort" and rode alongside him in "the wild rush" against the strongpoint. Grief's *Confederate Veteran* article tells a different story: "In accounts published in Northern papers it was said: 'The Confederates charged the fort, and were repulsed with heavy loss.' The facts are that we did not approach nearer than one square (about one hundred yards), and there never was an order or an intimation of an intention to charge the fort."[35]

George acknowledged claims that Thompson attacked the fort without orders from his superiors but admitted he did not know if that was the case. Yet George also wrote that it was "a well-known fact that Forrest demanded the surrender of the fort, and neither Forrest nor Buford, in their reports, attach any blame to Thompson for moving on to it." According to George, Captain F. G. Terry, Thompson's acting ordnance officer, said the colonel sent "Captain [A. M.] McGoodwin" to Buford to report where he and brigade were "and ask for instructions." Terry added that when McGoodwin returned, he told Thompson, "General Buford says dismount your men and move against that fort, and keep your flanks well protected." George added that "the movement was commenced at once and continued until the death of Colonel Thompson." Pirtle said Thompson "did as instructed and drove the yanks behind their works without the loss of a man." But Pirtle added that Thompson's "egotism got the better of his judgment"; the colonel concluded he would capture Fort Anderson "and ordered a charge." As a result, "he was killed by a cannon shot and many of his men were killed and wounded." When Thompson fell, Colonel Edward Crossland took command. But "within minutes," he was "severely wounded" and carried off the field with McGoodwin, "who was badly wounded by the same shell that caused the death of Colonel Thompson." George said only the Third and Seventh Kentucky charged the fort: "The Eighth Kentucky had been, previously to the charge, deployed as skirmishers and covered practically the whole front of the brigade; and the Twelfth Kentucky was in another part of the field, as was also [Colonel Tyree H.] Bell's Tennessee brigade."[36]

Meanwhile, Hicks had suspected Forrest was on the way. "I have scouts out 8 or 10 miles," he telegraphed Brigadier General Mason Brayman, the Cairo commander, at 11:20 in the morning on March 25. "Have concentrated my force at the fort the three past nights; stand ready at all times." Hicks also said he "had a spy arrested this morning." The man had arrived in Paducah the night before and "wanted to go out on the train this morning." Hicks told Brayman he ordered the train halted "until further orders."[37]

Around noon, Hicks's scouts returned and brought "no news of the enemy's whereabouts," the colonel said in his official battle report. He immediately sent out other scouts, directing them to try the Mayfield road. About three miles out, they collided with Forrest's van. When the Rebels opened fire, the outnumbered Yankees prudently fell back and spread the alarm. "In less than ten minutes after they reported the enemy were driving in my pickets, who opened a skirmish fire and fell back to Fort Anderson, according to previous instructions." Losing no time, Hicks "ordered the little force under my command to double-quick to the fort, which order was promptly obeyed; yet, before they could reach there, such was the impetuosity of the attack that their rear was fired into by the enemy." At 2:00 p.m., the Confederates "took position surrounding the fort and a sharp fight commenced, which in a few minutes became furious and continued for about one hour, when it was announced that a flag of truce was approaching," Hicks said. When the colonel saw the truce party—a half-dozen Paducah Confederates—he ordered a cease-fire. The soldier with the truce flag handed over a piece of paper addressed to Hicks. Written on it was Forrest's demand that the Yankees give up or else: "Colonel: Having a force amply sufficient to carry your works and reduce the place, and in order to avoid the unnecessary effusion of blood, I demand the surrender of the fort and troops, with all public property. If you surrender, you shall be treated as prisoners of war; but if I have to storm your works, you may expect no quarter." Hicks quickly wrote out a reply, also couched in the military formalities of the era: "Sir: I have this moment received yours of this instant, in which you demand the unconditional surrender of the forces under my command. I can answer that I have been placed here by my Government to defend this post, and in this, as well as all other orders from my superiors, I feel it to be my duty as an honorable officer to obey. I must, therefore, respectfully decline surrendering as you may require."[38]

Forrest allegedly took advantage of the cease-fire to improve his position. The *Chicago Times* article charged that while the truce flag flew, "Forrest advanced his sharpshooters and placed them in houses where they could pick off men in the fort and on the gunboats [the *Paw Paw* and the *Peosta,* which backed up the fort]."[39]

Hicks declared that "while the flag of truce was near the fort, and during its pendency, the enemy were engaged in taking position and planting a battery." After the truce party departed with Hicks's refusal in hand, the Confederates "moved forward, and our forces opened on them, and the fight became general." The Union troops turned back a first foot charge, then a second. "They made a third effort, but were forced to abandon their design," Hicks said. "It was in this last struggle that Brig. Gen. [*sic*] A. P. Thompson (Confederate) was killed."[40]

When the Rebels retreated a third time, Hicks took stock of his small-arms ammunition supply. Had the Rebels known what he found out, they might have charged again: "I now discovered, on examination, that my ammunition was growing short, and out of 30,000 rounds (the amount we commenced the fight with) 27,000 had already been expended." Though running perilously low on bullets, Hicks was still disinclined to capitulate; he said he was "feeling fully determined never to surrender while I had a man alive." He told his men to fix bayonets and make every shot count. If they ran out of ammunition, they were "to receive the enemy on the point of the bayonet." Hicks said his no-surrender order "was received with loud shouts and cheers" by his troops. But victory was not quite theirs. Hicks reported that Rebel sharpshooters, concealed in houses near the fort, began to pick off "some of my gunners, shooting nearly all of them in the head." As darkness approached, the Confederates "took shelter behind houses, in rooms, and hollows, and kept up a scattering fire until 11.30 o'clock, when it entirely ceased, and the rebel general withdrew his command out of the range of my guns and went into camp for the night." Forrest was back the next morning, "again making a demonstration by surrounding the fort in the distance." Hicks ordered Major Sidney Barnes of the Sixteenth Kentucky Cavalry to send out men "to burn all the houses within musket-range of the fort, from which the sharpshooters had annoyed us the day previous." While the houses went up in flames, Forrest sent forward another white flag. The bearer carried a note from the Rebel chief proposing a prisoner-of-war exchange: "Sir: I understand you hold in your possession in the guard-house at Paducah a number of Confederate soldiers as prisoners of war. I have in my possession about 35 or 40 Federal soldiers who were captured here yesterday, and about 500 who were captured at Union City. I propose to exchange man for man, according to rank, so far as you may hold Confederate soldiers." Hicks's reply was friendlier: "Sir: I have no power to make the exchange. If I had, I would most cheerfully do it." Hicks said Forrest's proposal listed the names of the prisoners he held, but "all of whom, with one exception, were convalescents in the general hospital, and too feeble to get to the fort."[41]

In his report, Hicks also named the units under his command, their commanders, and their strength: Companies C, H, and K, 126th Illinois Infantry, Major J. F. Chapman, 120 men; Sixteenth Kentucky Cavalry, Major Sidney Barnes, 271 men; First Kentucky Heavy Artillery (Colored), Lieutenant Richard D. Cunningham of the Second Illinois Artillery, 274 men. Hicks said Forrest had 6,500 men against his 665, adding that he had lost 14 men killed and 46 wounded. He put Forrest's losses at 300 killed and from 1,000 to 1,200 wounded. Hicks said that "General Forrest admitted, in conversation with some of his friends in this city, that in no engagement during the war had he been so badly cut up, and crippled as at this place." Hicks said his losses in government property were "inconsiderable," explaining that "the quartermaster's depot, a temporary wooden building, was burned, and in consequence thereof a small lot of quartermaster's property was lost." But he said his commissary stores and most of his horses, mules, wagons, and other property had escaped theft or destruction. Hicks praised all of his officers and men, especially his African American troops. "Permit me to remark that I have been one of those men who never had much confidence in colored troops fighting, but those doubts are now all removed, for they fought as bravely as any troops in the fort," he said. The *Chicago Daily Tribune* also lauded the black soldiers. "It was the negro regulars that fought so well," the *Times* quoted the Chicago paper. "They handled the artillery with great skill and their bravery is on the tongues of all the loyal men." The Chicago paper also credited Representative Anderson for "getting permission to raise a regiment of blacks, which was done against the opposition of the State authorities." At the same time, Hicks commended the gunboats *Peosta* and *Paw Paw,* and their skippers, Smith and O'Neil, respectively, for their "valuable aid in shelling the city and operating on the flanks of the enemy as they surrounded the fort." The *New York Times,* again quoting the *Chicago Times,* said the two gunboats fired about five hundred rounds at the enemy, pouring broadsides into the city, with "scarcely a building" escaping their "terrific fire." Many buildings "were completely riddled by shrapnel and solid shot." The navy men gave considerably more than they got. While Rebel fire perforated the cabins of the two boats, just two tars were wounded, and only slightly. O'Neill "received a slight scratch on his cheek" but escaped injury when "a minie ball passed through his pantaloons."[42]

Nurse Jennie Fyfe of Lansing, Michigan, worried that Hospital No. 2, where she tended sick and wounded soldiers, might become a target for the gunboats if the Rebels sought shelter in and around the building, which they captured. She said Forrest's men ransacked the hospital, stealing medicines, clothing, other supplies, and the horse-drawn ambulance. One soldier tried to rob the patients and nurses at gunpoint but came away empty-handed; they had hidden their money and valuables, according to Fyfe. Like Hicks, she praised the African American defenders of Fort Anderson. "Our colored troops did *nobly* they fought with perfect desperation & nearly all the killed & wounded was among them." When she visited the wounded black soldiers, she "found them quite as intelligent as *most* of the Kentuckians." Fyfe confessed that her "ideas of Kentucky & Kentuckians have been taken down a peg since I came to this place." She found the locals "low & ignorant in the extreme," adding, "so many of them . . . can neither read or write." Four days after the battle, Fyfe heard a rumor that Morgan had joined Forrest and that their combined forces were riding toward Paducah. She feared for the African American wounded should the Confederates capture them: "By dint of effort in many ways we succeeded in getting our colored wounded,—who were in the building opposite us removed to a boat. We knew should the Rascals come, they would show them no mercy but kill every man of them. We were relieved when they were away, yet still one felt much for our sick men, for we knew we need expect but little from the cruel mercies of the Guerrillas." She recalled that during the battle, "Old Forrest" had stood behind the hospital "& gave his orders." She conceded he was "a fine looking man, but how deceiving his looks."[43]

Doubtless "Old Forrest" would have disputed Fyfe's characterization of him and his men. In any event, his battle report to Polk was much briefer than Hicks's account to Brayman, perhaps because the former lost and the latter won. Effusiveness often accompanies victory in all things. Forrest said he left Jackson on March 23 and the next day captured Union City, bagging about two hundred horses, five hundred small arms, and 450 men. Forrest said he moved through Hickman, then attacked Paducah, where "he drove the enemy to their gunboats and forts; held the two for ten hours, and could have held it longer, but found the small-pox was raging, and evacuated the place." Forrest said he "captured many stores and horses, burned up sixty bales of cotton, one steamer and the dry-dock, bringing out about 50 prisoners." He put his losses at Union City and Paducah as "twenty-five killed and wounded, among them Thompson. Forrest reported that Lannom was "mortally wounded" and Crossland and "Lieutenant-Colonel Morton, of the Second Tennessee, slightly wounded." He said Union losses at Paducah were "50 killed, wounded, and prisoners; in all 500." Mum was the word from the general about Thompson's attack on Fort Anderson. Lannom survived, only to be murdered in Paris, Tennessee, in 1872. Crossland's wound almost got him killed by Union home guards near Mayfield, where he stopped for the night after the battle of Paducah.[44]

Buford, a cousin of Napoleon Bonaparte Buford, the former Cairo commander, congratulated his troops "upon the success that has thus far attended the campaign into Kentucky." He cited the hardships they had endured by riding from Mississippi to Paducah in only a week: "The devotion you have exhibited in the cause of freedom, and the valor our skirmishers displayed in their attack upon the fort at Paducah, call for the highest admiration and praise." Buford added that "at the very doors of their homes some of your comrades laid down their lives to rescue Kentucky from the iron heel of abolition despotism, and the rule of the negro." He named Thompson, who "fell as a soldier desires to fall, at the head of his command, a hero regretted by all." Doubtless, Forrest also was sorry over Thompson's demise. But a Paducah Unionist suggested that Buford's boss, a Tennessee slave trader before the war, rued something else, too: the fact that ex-slaves fought so bravely and so well against his troops: "One of the most mortifying things to Forrest, connected with his terrible defeat here, must be the reflection that his men were whipped in part by 'n—r' soldiers, whom he had come to take and shoot, with their officers."[45]

Robertson, who has chronicled Paducah history more extensively than anyone else, says the battle did little to enhance Forrest's reputation as "one of the most effective leaders on either side in the war." He wonders if Forrest perhaps "counted too much on the lack of training of the Federals." Possibly "he acceded too quickly to the demands of the Paducah personnel who wanted to impress the homefolks, or perhaps he felt that sheer audacity would carry the day." Robertson faults Forrest for failing to properly reconnoiter the area around the fort: "The ditch should not have been a surprise." Robertson also suggests that the African American soldiers in the fort might have spurred the Confederates to attack with massacre on their minds. "Forrest let the Kentuckians in his command attack Fort Anderson, as their former slaves were among those in the garrison," he writes. The *New York Times,* quoting the *Chicago Tribune,* reported that before the assault, the Rebels freely made threats "in the streets that they would capture the fort and kill every damned n—r in it." Robertson writes that after the unsuccessful assault on Fort Anderson—"with its African-American defenders as one possible target"—Forrest found another "opportunity . . . to impress on the black population the danger of taking up arms against the Confederacy." He meant Fort Pillow, Tennessee, where on April 12 the Union garrison, including black soldiers, surrendered to Forrest, "only to have the African-American troopers shot, driven into the Mississippi, or buried alive in one of two instances." Robertson said had Hicks given up Fort Anderson, a Paducah massacre might have preceded the Fort Pillow massacre.[46]

Likewise, Ronald K. Huch, a professor of history at Eastern Kentucky University, writes that "it seems reasonable to argue that the frustration the Confederate forces experienced in [Paducah] . . . led them to seek revenge at the first opportunity." According to Huch, the fact that "black artillerymen had been primarily responsible for the setback in Paducah was probably sufficient cause to turn Forrest and his men from angry, battle-weary warriors into mass murderers at Fort Pillow." Huch also doubts that Thompson attacked Fort Anderson without approval: "Forrest, even his biographers admit, was a most arrogant general. At the time of Paducah, his natural confidence had been heightened by the easy victory at Union City, and probably still more by the knowledge that black soldiers were primarily responsible for the defense of Fort Anderson." Union commanders seldom trusted black troops "and they were held in the utmost scorn by Southern officers." Huch added that "Forrest was perhaps the most vehement of all Confederate generals in his hatred of black Union troops." The historian also cites the *Times* article and its quote about the Confederates threatening to kill "every damn n—r in" Fort Anderson. "Based on what is known about General Forrest, it is difficult to believe that he was unaware of these threats," Huch argues. He concludes that if Hicks had surrendered Fort Anderson, there probably would not have been a massacre at Fort Pillow: "An easy victory at Fort Anderson would have confirmed the belief of Confederate soldiers that black troops were inherently inferior and that most blacks preferred to return to their 'masters.'" Hicks's African American solders "seriously challenged" such beliefs. Thus, "Forrest's men needed desperately to reassert what they thought to be their natural superiority. That is why, from the Southern viewpoint, the killings at Fort Pillow were a tragic necessity." Huch quoted Forrest: "the river was dyed with the blood of the slaughtered for 200 yards. It is hoped that this fact will demonstrate to the Northern people that negro soldiers cannot cope with Southerners."[47]

The *Journal* was gratified to learn that Forrest had failed to seize Fort Anderson but concerned that he and his cavalry were able to reach Paducah. "The capture and brief occupancy of Paducah by the rebels must of course be considered a Federal calamity," the paper editorialized. "But it would seem from the statements now before us that the rebels suffered far more injury than they inflicted." Even so, the *Journal* argued, "it does not bode well for the safety and welfare of Kentucky that Forrest and Faulkner, at the head of thousands of Rebels, have been able to invade the State from the Southern Confederacy, penetrate to Paducah, and occupy the city without letting their movements be known to any considerable extent to the Federal military authorities." The paper said that at least in theory Union troops were "watching to detect and thwart every movement of the enemy across the border." In addition, the *Journal* suggested that "if Forrest and Faulkner, after doing what they have done, can now escape or extend their ravages, Heaven only knows what they and others may be expected to do in the future."[48]

Two days later, the Louisville paper ran a news story about the battle, using engineer Oliver of the *Dacotah,* the steamer Forrest's troops burned; adjutant W. H. Walker of the *Cairo Army Times;* and the *Evansville Journal* as sources. Oliver "fully confirmed the heavy loss of the rebels" to the Hoosier paper and spoke "in the most enthusiastic terms of the desperate valor of the colored troops in the fort as well as of all others engaged on the Federal side." The river man accused the Rebels of wholesale plunder in Paducah. Thirteen Confederates had torched the *Dacotah,* which was high and dry at the Marine Ways, a boat repair facility. Before setting the boat alight, they broke into the bar and, after stealing whiskey, robbed the crew of money and their best clothes. The Union man who beheld the "truce flag" moving up Broadway said that women and children had sought refuge in the *Dacotah.* "Dastardly" Rebel sharpshooters also climbed aboard and, "thus protected by" the "sacred presence" of the innocent civilians, "poured their deadly missiles upon the gunboats with impunity." When the Confederates torched the boat "and skedaddled," they left "the women and children to find other quarters," he recalled.[49]

Oliver added that "not over twenty buildings were burned" in the city, most of them by Union troops determined to deny further cover to Forrest's sharpshooters. Oliver said, "Forrest resorted to the usual perfidy of the rebels" by moving his guns into position against Fort Anderson under cover of the truce flag. "But even this trick did not avail him as the rebels were handsomely repulsed at every point," he declared, adding that "intelligent citizens" estimated enemy losses at between three hundred and four hundred. On the Union side, eleven soldiers were killed—seven blacks and four whites—and fifteen to twenty were wounded, Oliver said. Further, the Rebels stole "some 20 government horses and all the [civilian?] horses and mules they could find." In addition, he claimed the cannonball that had killed Thompson "literally knocked [him] inside out" and that after the battle "a large number of rebels were seen hopping back through the streets wounded." Further, a shell fragment killed "a daughter of Capt. Smith, of the Commercial Hotel." Oliver disputed reports that the commissary stores were destroyed as the officer in charge fooled the Confederates, though Oliver did not say how. He also said that a number of gunboats had gone up the Tennessee to look for the Rebels and that troops were arriving and preparing to chase after the Rebels. He said Brigadier General Benjamin Grierson, the famous cavalry commander, was expected to intercept the enemy at any hour.[50]

All during the fight, the *Peosta* and the *Paw Paw* "plied up and down the river, opposite the city, and shelled the streets wherever the rebels appeared," Walker said. He said, "Mrs. Block is the name of the woman who was killed by a shell from the gunboats," adding that the blast also killed her child. Other civilian casualties included John Salter, son of the superintendent of the gasworks, who was killed helping defend Fort Anderson. Walker said a letter received in Cairo from Paducah claimed "the reports in regard to the slaughter of citizens are greatly exaggerated." But he defended the gunboat crewmen, maintaining that the motion of the vessels naturally rendered "the aim of the gunners incorrect, and some balls and shells consequently hit some of the houses in the vicinity."[51]

Meanwhile, in the fort, the cavalrymen had no sabers to help fend off any

Rebels who might climb the fort's walls, Oliver said. All they had were pistols. How many Rebels the troopers hit with their handguns is unknown, but Oliver claimed fifty-seven enemy soldiers remained unburied on the battlefield on March 26. "They took off their dead and wounded in the night of [March 25] as fast as they could," Walker said. "Their loss in killed and wounded was supposed to be from 150 to 400." Thompson "was struck by a shell in the breast and literally torn to pieces," he added. "What was left of his body was taken off under a flag of truce."[52]

He, too, recounted the death of an unnamed Confederate lieutenant who lost his life trying to take horses from "Morgan," evidently a civilian. The officer "was not shot by a Federal soldier, but by one of the strongest Southern sympathizers in Paducah who, passing along the street, heard the conversation and drew his revolver and shot the Lieutenant through the head." The subaltern instantly fell dead; his assailant escaped.[53]

Walker also said that Forrest's troops hoped to get away with "the quartermaster's stores and plunder they had collected" by piling it on a southbound train. But somebody sabotaged the locomotive, prompting the Rebels to burn their booty. In addition, he said around fifteen hundred civilians, whites and African Americans, fled to the Illinois side of the Ohio and had nothing to eat for eighteen hours. At noon on March 26, Hicks's quartermaster, Captain J. A. Finley, sent the people all the food he had: "They were hatless, bootless, and many of them with scarcely any clothing at all." While the small group of Rebels managed to relieve the *Dacotah*'s crew of its cash, "the money in the bank was saved. They entered the Commercial Bank but it was not robbed."[54]

The Rebels missed $2,628 in silver that Oehlschaeger left on a table in his bakery at 825 South Third Street, Neuman wrote. The money was payment from the Yankees, whom he supplied with bread. When the baker heard the Confederates were in town, he spread a newspaper over the pile of cash and fled without his coat. "The next morning a rumor was afloat that the bakery had been burned, but upon returning he found not only the store but the money as well," Neuman explained. "The store was ransacked, but none of the plunderers thought to look under the carelessly tossed newspaper which covered the mound of silver." Other civilians hastily left the city, most of them crossing the river to the Illinois side. They included Louis C. Kolb, who recalled that "the smoke of battle was visible from Brookport [Illinois] four miles below."[55]

Some Paducah women and children fled to Metropolis, Illinois, just below Brookport. The *Chicago Times* correspondent quoted in the *New York Times* saw them huddled around a fire "and apparently making the best of their condition." The steamboat continued on and arrived in Paducah after dark on March 26. He also observed refugee campfires on the riverbank opposite the city. Some of those huddled around the little blazes were men who had volunteered to help defend Fort Anderson but were turned away by Hicks because he had insufficient weapons to arm them. The colonel said anyone wishing to seek safety on the Illinois shore was free to cross. The Paducah man who sighted the "flag of truce" said he was able to get away thanks to "the coolness, tact, self-possession and untiring exertion" of Finley, Paducah's "most excellent quartermaster," whose family was in the flight. Though in "feeble health," he shepherded many of the scared civilians onto the wharf boat, which ended up "freighted with probably a thousand frightened souls, and valuables of a public and private kind." Finley found himself in charge of a "confused mass of human beings," on the boat and ashore, "crying for safety." So were civilians aboard a nearby coal barge, where the flag spotter and his family had sought refuge. The officer quickly "comprehended the magnitude and responsibility of the task" and took "control of the vast crowd, with limited means of escape." Finley, who "seemed to be an instrument in the hands of Providence," ordered the crew of the ferryboat *Blue Bird* to tow the wharf boat and the barge across the river. The ferryboat was small, and hence "insufficiency of motive power was a fearful question," he remembered. All the while, the *Peosta* was firing its big guns "over and around us, causing an awful tremor to seize our vitals," he said. Finley ordered the *Blue Bird* to cast off with its heavy load: "Like a huge leviathan, the trio of boats swung round, the graceful *Peosta* withdrawing a little to give us swing, and we were off to the opposite shore just in the nick of time." The refugee added that "ten minutes later and we would have been in the hands of the rebels, as they had ordered the destruction of every boat in their reach." Obviously a Union man, he jabbed, "Why didn't they take the *Peosta*? She didn't run."[56]

The *Chicago Times* man said food was in short supply among the refugees opposite Paducah until Hicks ordered up more provisions from Cairo. They were to be given to poor people but sold to people who could afford to pay. The reporter disembarked in the darkness and "walked up toward the fort through the smouldering ruins of the once beautiful city." He beheld battle-scarred warehouses and homes. "In many places, nothing but bare walls and chimneys were standing. Scarcely a building escaped the terrific fire of the gunboats, and many of them were completely riddled by shrapnel and solid shot."[57]

The gunners had aimed to hit only the Rebels, who, 1,800 strong, had hit town "on a melancholy Good Friday," according to Neuman's fanciful, and not entirely accurate, account of the battle. Neuman writes that a marker—now long gone—in a sidewalk at the intersection of Old Mayfield Road at

Guthrie Avenue marked Forrest's entry point. The Confederates rode crosswise through town and dismounted at Fifteenth and Broadway to await further orders, Neuman adds: "From there a number of them could see the homes they left to join the Confederate ranks." Grief, shot in the jaw but not seriously hurt, managed a quick visit with his father, mother, children, and some neighbors who had holed up in the cellar of the Grief house, "where they were amply protected from shot and shell." Neuman writes that the Union troops filed into Fort Anderson "like Noah's host into the ark." He says the Third and Seventh Kentucky—180 in number—waited at Ninth and Broadway, "eager for an attack" against the fort. At the same time, "the Eighth regiment was in the heart of the city ransacking commissary stores and raiding Government stables for horses, mules and wagons." Neuman says the Third and Seventh attacked at 4:30. Forrest issued "his unique command, 'Forward men, and mix with 'em!'" The author describes Fort Anderson as 400 feet long and running 160 feet toward the river. The works "were surrounded on the west, north and south by 50-foot ditches filled with water." He says the Rebels, led by Thompson, "ran toward the citadel in the face of bitter fire from within and a barrage of grapeshot and canister from the newly-converted gunboats, the sidewheel tinclad *Peosta* and *Paw-Paw*, the latter piloted by Captain William L. Ballowe (1831–1885) of Paducah." According to Neuman, the Confederates pulled back because they were "unable to ford the watery trenches." He adds that "equally determined resistance" from the Union side broke a second Confederates surge. Half of the attackers charged a third time, "many of them entering residences nearby and firing down into the fort from second-story windows, effecting good aim," Neuman writes. "The fusillade increased until General Forrest rode up. Seeing the futility of capturing the breastworks without heavy artillery, he ordered a cessation of the firing." At that moment, according to Neuman, the cannonball felled Thompson at 516 Park Avenue, where a tablet in the sidewalk denoted "the spot where the brave officer met his death." Neuman piles high the purple prose: "Steadfast till his tragic death, he upheld the waning fortunes of the Confederacy as did Hector those of Troy." Thompson, thirty-five years old, "was a tall, stalwart man, with dark hair and mild countenance." His fellow Rebels lingered near the fort until eight p.m., when they "slowly siphoned from the city, clearing before midnight by the same route they came."[58]

Forrest and his battle-weary troopers bedded down for the night on George Smith's farm, six and a half miles from town. The general tethered his horse to a black oak tree in front of the Schmidt home, a story-and-a-half, three-room log cabin, Neuman writes in *Paducahans in History.* The author again waxes eloquent: "The 'death wagon' was parked under a small tree to the right of the front entrance, and the groans coming from the wounded and dying in it could be heard through the night—faint calls for help like those of the dauntless defenders and fearless assailants who after the Battle of Waterloo and while yet alive found a common grave in the well at the Chateau of Hougoumont." On the morning of March 26, Forrest led his men back to Mayfield, where he gave the soldiers from the Purchase a few days' leave "to visit their homes, from which they had been separated since 1861," George writes. "To their everlasting credit they all returned to their command at the appointed time." George adds that most of them had secured good horses "and comfortable clothing; and in the meantime they had succeeded in gathering up numbers of recruits, which brought the regiments up to something like their proper size again."[59]

The day after the battle, some Union soldiers found one Confederate who did not leave Paducah. He was seated motionless on the ground with his back to a maple tree at Ninth and Madison Streets. The man was dead, and "his eyes were riveted on some object tightly clasped in his hands." The soldier was clutching an ambro-type image of his two children, according to Neuman. "Hardened soldiers though they were, the sight of that man who looked on his children's photograph for the last time in this world, brought tears to their eyes which they could not restrain," the author writes. "Great lumps gathered in their throats," and they stood gazing at the unknown enemy soldier for several minutes. Then they buried the Rebel "with his children's picture clasped over his heart" and, according to Neuman, carved a simple epitaph on the tree: "Somebody's Father. March 25, 1864."[60]

While Grant's occupation of Paducah bore significantly on the outcome of the Civil War in the Western Theater, the battle of Paducah did not. Yet small as it was, the battle of Paducah was large enough to bring the horror of war to the very doorsteps of the city's people. The fate of the Confederacy, which most Paducah citizens still supported, hung in the balance in big battles elsewhere. Lincoln had brought Grant east to whip Lee. Sherman, who had taken over Grant's Army of the Tennessee, was preparing to move on Atlanta. Sherman's horsemen would include Purchase soldiers. On the day of the battle of Paducah, the Sixteenth Kentucky Cavalry was consolidated into the Twelfth Kentucky Cavalry. The regimental surgeon recalled that "not a day passed in the Atlanta campaign that the 12th was not engaged with the enemy."[61]

11

Still Disloyal

As much as it disappointed Purchase secessionists to see Forrest leave, their discomfiture increased with the return of their "General Pain." E. A. Paine came back in July. He was sure that sparing the rod spoiled the secesh. He ended up being portrayed—even today—as the worst villain in Purchase history, the region's Robespierre, whose "reign of terror" allegedly included wholesale murder, though by firing squad, not guillotine. The Purchase's secessionist majority saw Paine as the vilest sort of Yankee: an abolitionist, a Republican, a friend of Lincoln, and an egalitarian given to treating African Americans and whites equally.

Crossland's painful leg wound forced him to stop and spend the night of March 26 at the house of a Graves County secessionist, William Pryor, who lived near Mayfield. It was almost the colonel's last night among the living; he narrowly escaped death at the hands of Captain Thomas Jones Gregory's home guards. George said Gregory's outfit was typical of "gangs of robbers and murderers" who called themselves "Home Guards." He said most of them had some kind of affiliation with the Union armies, adding that if the home guards "did not act under orders from the Federal commanders they certainly made no effort to restrain them." Of course, Unionists said the same about the more numerous Confederate guerrillas. Unionists insisted that home guards were brave men fighting to defend their families and firesides against Rebel guerrillas, who were the real robbers and murderers. George, the ex-Rebel, claimed Gregory and his men "were guilty of as brutal conduct as any gang of cut-throats who roamed" parts of Kentucky and Tennessee from the middle to the end of the war.[1]

Purchase secessionists seem to have ranked Gregory—usually called "Jim Gregory" or "Jones Gregory"—second only to Paine in perfidy, if only because Paine's position was more powerful than Gregory's. The general was evidently fond of the captain and vice versa. While they seemed to form a sort of a mutual admiration society, the Purchase's southern-sympathizing majority despised them both. They might have expected Paine's alleged cruelty. He was, after all, a Yankee-born "abolition invader." On the other hand, Gregory was of the Purchase, a son of Graves County. During the postwar Reconstruction period, southern white supremacists detested Northern men like Paine, denouncing them as "carpetbaggers." Yet their hatred burned more intensely for men like Gregory and, for that matter, Lucian Anderson. White supremacist "redeemers" branded them "scalawags," meaning fellow white southerners who became Republicans or who supported the biracial Republican governments in the old Confederate states. The unregenerate Rebels would see the "scalawags" as the rankest of traitors: betrayers of their race and region.

Such was Gregory's fate. Indeed, he looms large in local Confederate lore as a Civil War version of Simon Girty, the much-feared and loathed "great renegade" of frontier Kentucky during the Revolutionary War. Girty went down in history as the Bluegrass State's worst-ever miscreant, though his purported misdeeds were almost certainly exaggerated. Likewise, it seems Gregory was far from the out-and-out fiend Rebel sympathizers made him out to be.

Girty was pro-British and preferred the company of Native Americans to whites. As a result, Kentucky whites scorned him as a turncoat to his "kind." Southern sympathizers passed the same sort of judgment on Gregory, loathing him as a turncoat to his own people. Yet his disdain for all things Confederate might have been as personal as it was political. When the war began, Gregory and his younger brother were outspoken Unionists, though apparently almost everybody else who lived near their Dublin home was a secessionist: "Being high-spirited men, they could not hear treason uttered without rebuking it, and this obtained for them the ill will of their neighbors, who threatened their lives." The threats were not idle. In the autumn of 1861, when the Confederates were close by at Columbus, "it was determined to 'root out' the brothers, and to make examples of them." Almost a hundred armed men went to the Gregory home planning to hang the brothers. Anticipating the attack, the siblings barricaded themselves inside the house and "calmly awaited the coming of their chivalric neighbors." The bloodthirsty band opened fire, bullets falling "like hail around the house." The brothers shot back, killing three of their assailants and wounding others. "Finding the game somewhat hazardous," the attackers withdrew, "leaving the Gregorys master of the situation." Even so, the brothers knew they were far outnumbered. Thus, still fearing for their lives, they forsook their dwelling, which the secessionists burned down.[2]

Gregory ended up in Smithland, where on January 6, 1862, he joined the Union army as first lieutenant of Company G, Twentieth Kentucky Infantry. He enlisted for three years but resigned on February 5. Military records do not say why, but it may have been to recruit a home guard company in Graves County. On September 12, 1862, "Capt. Jones Gregory" and fourteen of his men foiled "a robbing guerrilla band" that was ransacking Unionist J. T. Bolinger's store in Mayfield, according to a local *Journal* correspondent. Gregory's group surprised the marauders, who were led by "Dr. Hart, of Boydsville." They slew one guerrilla, mortally wounded his brother, broke up the band, and captured most of their horses. None of Gregory's group was hurt. While George and most other Graves countians loathed Gregory, the *Journal* man lauded the captain for "this nice little job." He added, "already the loyal portion of the community feels more protection from this company than has heretofore been assured to them by the Federal army. Indeed these are the only kind of forces that are any protection against the guerrillas." The correspondent was confident that in just a few months, Graves County would be home to "several hundred of these Home Guards, and guerrillas will find this a hot place for them." He praised Gregory as "one of the bravest of the brave, thoroughly acquainted with the country, at all times, cool, collected, and skillful, indeed, he is already a terror to the rebels, for he always gets the better, whether in a fight as a private citizen or a soldier." The correspondent vowed that "the loyal portion of our community are fully determined to protect themselves against the guerrillas, without longer being tied by red tape." He said there were several guerrilla groups in southern Graves County.[3]

Shooting local guerrillas was one thing, but Gregory and his men must have longed to kill or capture a real Rebel officer like Crossland, especially in their neighborhood. They almost dispatched "old Eddie" right after the battle of Paducah. The colonel's son, Samuel H. Crossland, told George his father's version of what happened, and George featured the story in his book. It began with the colonel's arrival in Mayfield, accompanied by his staff and other soldiers, all from the Seventh and Twelfth Kentucky. Crossland saw his old friend and law pupil Stokley W. Slayden, who invited the colonel and his party to spend the night with his father. But adjutant C. H. Roulhac told Crossland that the senior Slayden was afraid the Yankees—perhaps he meant Gregory—would burn him out if he harbored the colonel and his entourage. So they decided to push on to the home of the Crossland's stepmother in Hickman County, about twenty miles away. Yet on the road about four miles south of Mayfield, the Rebels met Pryor, who told Crossland "that the weather was so cold that he would freeze to death before he got to his destination." He insisted they stay with him. Crossland warned Pryor the Yankees might torch his house. "Let them burn," he said. At about 11:00 p.m., Crossland woke up when he heard somebody cursing outside his window. He figured the disturber of the peace was a drunk and ordered him to go away. The man shot at Crossland through the window. The gunfire woke Roulhac and Major James K. Polk Welborne—Crossland spelled his name "Wilborn."

Both men had been sleeping on pallets in the room with the colonel. Crossland told them he thought a crazy man had fired the shot. It was Gregory or one of his home guard, according to Crossland, who added that "by this time the door was burst open and Gregory gave the command to kill the last damn one of them."[4]

The home guards ordered Roulhac to identify himself; when he said he was a Rebel, "he was shot in the breast, and fell dead." Welborne, unseen in the dark room, crawled under the bed. "You damn son-of-a-bitch in that bed, surrender," somebody barked at Crossland. He replied, "I am wounded and helpless, and of course I surrender." A shot rang out, the bullet slicing through Crossland's armpit and lodging in his pillow. "I am killed," the colonel said, then fell back in the bed and played dead. Gregory's men left, entered an adjoining shed room, pounded on the door, and stormed inside. They "cursed, kicked and beat, shot and cut with their sabers a detail of Faulkner's regiment, composed of Lieutenant Oliver, Privates Burns, Front and Hatler." Crossland confessed, "If there were others their names are not remembered."[5]

After Oliver and Hatler surrendered, the home guards took them outside and commanded them to kneel. After Oliver said "he only knelt to his God," his captors shot him dead. Hatler broke and ran. "He was fired upon by a fusillade from Gregory's gang, about twenty-five or thirty in number, and as he ran by the guard he fired upon him, but he was not struck in the legs, and kept running and escaped." The next morning, Hatler was brought to Mayfield, where "surgeons cut twenty-eight bullets out of his body." After slaying Oliver, Gregory's men searched the stable. Seeing his chance to escape but unable to walk because of his leg wound, Crossland crawled to the shed room and tried to exit through the back door, but a guard stopped him. Forced back into the room, the colonel said he encountered a bloody scene: "Burns . . . had been pierced and chopped with sabers; also Front, who had been shot in the melee by Gregory's men." But the two men were still alive, if barely, and had found pistols. They handed one to Crossland, and the trio "determined to sell their lives if again attacked."[6]

When he discovered "things had become quiet," Crossland crawled out of the house to a chicken coop and covered himself with a wagon sheet to keep from freezing to death. Fearing Gregory's men would return and burn the house, thus exposing him in the firelight, Crossland, still dressed in nightclothes, crawled to "a stake-and-ridered fence." But his wound prevented him from climbing over or tearing down the fence. Welborne, having escaped, saw Crossland's predicament and carried him piggyback to safety in the woods. He left Crossland and returned to the house for warm bed clothing to cover the colonel. Inside the house, Welborne discovered that Gregory's men had tried to burn Crossland's bed, which did not catch fire because it "was wet from bathing Crossland's wound." Meanwhile, after Crossland and Welborne escaped, Gregory's men returned to the colonel's room, where Roulhac's corpse lay on the floor. "Ah, yes, old Eddie, we've got you this time," one of the men said, grabbing Roulhac's beard. But Gregory recognized that the dead man was not the colonel.[7]

Crossland and Welborne hid in the woods until morning, when a contingent of Forrest's cavalry came out from Mayfield and took them back to town. "The soldiers who were at Pryor's with Crossland, believing there were no enemies in the country nearer than Paducah, had carelessly left the most of their arms with their saddles and horses at the stables, and, being surprised, were unable to make any defense," Crossland said. He added that "it was learned afterwards" that Mose Saxon, an elderly African American, had told Gregory and his men where they could find Crossland and his party. "The Yankees took Roulhac's uniform coat (rebel gray) and Gregory wore it in the streets of Paducah, riding Crossland's fine roan horse with great parade and gusto," concluded Crossland, who said that "this is a statement of the details of the affair, as I have frequently heard my father relate them."[8]

While Crossland barely eluded death, many of his men enjoyed happy homecomings. Among them were now Second Lieutenant William G. Pirtle and his brother First Corporal J. W. Pirtle. At Mayfield, Buford furloughed the Third and Seventh Regiments and ordered them to report back at Feliciana in ten days with "all the recruits posable, and all, both old and new men to be as well mounted as the country would afford." George wrote, "To their everlasting credit they all returned to their command at the appointed time." The Pirtles may have owed their lives to Thompson. On the way to Paducah, the colonel permitted the brothers and other men from the Feliciana neighborhood to go home for a few hours. As a result, they arrived in Paducah too late for the attack on Fort Anderson.[9]

Thompson told Pirtle to collect his men early on March 25 and meet him in Mayfield at 9:00 a.m. Pirtle said he reached town about an hour after sunup. But stragglers delayed their departure; the Graves County men reached Paducah "perhaps forty minutes" after the attack on Fort Anderson. Pirtle nonetheless enjoyed his visit with the homefolks: "As my wife and children were living with my father, so I found all to gether inclueding one babe now a year and a half old that I had never seen." Pirtle remembered that after Buford furloughed the Third and Seventh Kentucky, the men found themselves on their own. "Brother Wess and Jim had been more careful of their horses" and thus beat W. G. home. "Jim" may have been someone other than his brother, the captain. J. G. Pirtle was seriously wounded at Shiloh and permanently disabled, according to military records. In any event, Pirtle remembered "a wonderful scatering took place, every man going off the best rout home." Pirtle made a beeline for Feliciana and found that his soldier siblings had beaten him home. "Of course had lots to talk about again," Pirtle remembered. "And now for ten days all enjoyed ourselves finely. Had a chance to ride all over the country, go when we pleased, and where we pleased, and stay as long as we please. A great privilidge for old soldiers." He said that on the day of "rendevoze at Feliciana, men began coming in early, in squads from every direction, so that by noon nearly if not all were present with many recruits." Pirtle compared the day to September 10, 1861, when his company marched off to war:

> Now perhaps nine hundred or a thousand men all mounted and nearly all armed, then only fifty muskets and none mounted, except on wagons and buggies. Now every man the custodian of his rations, which consisted of a piece of bread and meat in a sack hung on his shoulder, then rations were packed in large boxes and consisted of bread meats and all the dainties the women of the community had the art to fix up, and I would say, they were not slouches in the culinary art.[10]

George wrote that by April 5, the Third, Seventh, Eighth, and Twelfth Kentucky had come together at Trenton, Tennessee, where they learned that Forrest was sending Buford back to Paducah. Forrest wanted to create a diversion for his attack on Fort Pillow. At the same time, he was after supplies and 140 horses that northern newspapers boasted Forrest had missed on his raid. On April 12, Buford and the Kentucky troops drew near Columbus, where he split them up. Buford sent Tyler and about 150 men to make a demonstration against Columbus while he led the rest of the column to Paducah. Tyler carried out his mission "so successfully as to create the impression on the Federals at that point that they were going to be attacked by a large force of Confederates." As part of the ruse, Tyler pretended to be the general, signing an unconditional surrender demand "A. Buford, Brigadier General." The note was delivered at 6:00 a.m. on April 13 under a flag of truce. Addressed to Colonel William Hudson Lawrence, the post commander, the message claimed the Confederates were "fully capable of taking Columbus and its garrison by force" but that "Buford" wished "to avoid the shedding of blood." Therefore, Lawrence must capitulate. The note said that if he gave up, "the negroes now in arms will be returned to their masters." "Buford" warned, "should I, however, be compelled to take the place, no quarter will be shown to the negro troops whatever; the white troops will be treated as prisoners of war." Lawrence sent a note back, calling the brazen captain's bluff: "General: Your communication of this date is in hand. In reply I would state that, being placed by my Government with adequate force to hold and repel all enemies from my post, surrender is out of the question."[11]

Women and children were given five hours to leave Columbus, and many, especially children, took the steamer *Crawford* to Cairo, which arrived at 1:00 p.m. Just as the *Crawford* left Columbus, a pair of steamboats arrived from downriver with three thousand Yankee veterans heading home on furlough. The troops and an artillery battery were put ashore, which doubtless would have materially altered "the calculations of the rebels."[12]

Buford reached Paducah at noon on April 14 with the western Kentucky troops, about two thousand strong, and "as usual coming in under white flags," Hicks reported. They exchanged fire with Union pickets, and the colonel again moved his garrison inside Fort Anderson. When the Rebels "made their appearance in the skirts of the timber about 1 mile distant," Hicks ordered the big guns in the fort to open fire. Soon afterward, Buford sent forward a note to Hicks under a white flag: "Sir: Reluctant to endanger the lives of women and children and non-combatants, I respectfully request that you order all such out of the town. They will be allowed to pass through my lines, and will be allowed one hour to get out." Hicks again proved he was made of sterner stuff. In his reply, he mixed graciousness and grit: "Sir: I have this moment received yours of this date. Your notice of one hour to let the women and children out exhibits an act of humanity on your part, but do not allow your men to sack the city during that time, nor attempt to take position, or I will fire on you. After that, come ahead; I am ready for you."[13]

Buford did not attack the fort. He made off with about two hundred mules and horses, all "fine animals," George said. Afterward, Buford and his force "moved leisurely back toward Trenton giving some of the men another opportunity of visiting their homes."[14]

Meanwhile, Hicks said that while he was giving women and children notice to leave and holding his fire, "parties of the enemy were going through the upper part of the city, under protection of white flags, breaking into houses and robbing and plundering." When Hicks saw what was happening, he sent Lieutenant Colonel Eaton with two hundred men of the Seventy-second Ohio "to pass up the river under cover of the gunboats and guns of the fort and drive them from the city." Hicks added that when the marauders saw Eaton and his men approaching, they fell back to their main force and immediately beat a retreat toward the Mayfield road. Hicks opened up on the fleeing Confederates with the fort's big guns; for extra measure, the gunboats blasted away. The colonel confessed that he was not sure what effect his shelling had on the Rebels but claimed he "sustained no loss from this raid except in Government horses, about 40 of which were taken during the pending of the flag of truce." Pirtle backed up George, writing that Buford bagged "two hundred horses without the loss of a man."[15]

Paducah women "were the principal encouragers" of Buford's raid, according to the *Journal.* The paper hoped "that means will be taken to establish unmistakenly the guilt of every one of the offenders." The *Journal* had never favored "the infliction of severe punishment upon women or men for light words or other light offences." But the paper warned, "whenever the fact can be established that any of them have invited rebels to a raid or given them information or aided them in any way in the accomplishment of thefts, robberies, murders, and deeds of arson, they should be punished as actual traitors." In such eventualities, "mercy and forbearance are out of place. Even woman forfeits all claims to clemency and respect." Still, the *Journal* repeated its hope that since federal military and civil authority probably had been restored, the case of anyone, "male or female, charged with inciting or conniving at the raid or aiding the rebels or showing signs of exultation over the progress of the work that was done, will be searchingly investigated, and justice administered."[16]

In response, a Paducah woman dashed off a letter to the *Journal* in hopes that Hicks might read it and become "convinced that there is *at least one* among the ladies of Paducah who is *truly* loyal." She had witnessed a flag raising and listened to a nearly ninety-minute speech from Hicks in which he praised his troops for fighting bravely against the Rebel raiders and "made many plain and truthful statements in regard to the war and the situation of our torn and bleeding country." She hoped the colonel would pardon her for saying that "some of his remarks were rather more severe than my *woman's* heart will allow me to fully respond to, yet I know 'the end will justify the means.'" She claimed "it is also true that the colonel *occasionally* mingled the sublime and inelegant, which, although a violation of the strict principles of rhetoric, mattered not, for through all were seen brilliant scintellations of true patriotism and bravery, and all present must have been convinced that Colonel Hicks is a true patriot and brave." The correspondent swore her love for "our Union and its glorious cause, and my heart is ever warm toward those who nobly defend it, whether with the sword or the pen, on the field or in the sanctum, and you Messrs. Editors, are very conspicuous among the number."[17]

Though Forrest only stayed briefly in the Purchase, his advent again brought the region "under insurrectionary control, and so it still remains," warned Brigadier General Mason Brayman, the outgoing Cairo commander. He added with disgust, "The disloyal citizens are open and avowed in their determination to kill, plunder, and expel from their homes all loyal men, and freely declare that none but such as sympathize with themselves shall take any part in the approaching elections." He compared the fealty of the region's hard-pressed Unionist minority's "fidelity to their country and their flag" to "the faith of the early Church"; their loyalty had "withstood the fires of relentless persecution." Brayman rewarded their fealty by permitting Union men at Columbus and Paducah to form home guard companies to fight guerrillas. He said they were "doing good and gallant service" in helping "drive out the armed marauders, silence their sympathizers, and hold Western Kentucky to its allegiance." Brayman said that when he took command on March 19, parts of the Purchase and West Tennessee not under Union military occupation "were under insurrectionary control." He complained that "between those rebels who had taken the oath and remained within our lines and their brothers who were in arms without, full fraternity and correspondence existed." Brayman said armed guerrillas infested the countryside, "engaged in murder and pillage." The guerrillas had "friends at our posts," who kept them well supplied. He condemned "the laxity of trade regulations" and "disloyal persons who, having taken the oath," still "carried on illicit traffic under our protection and favor." Brayman added that "too often" Union officers were complicit in the smuggling, sharing in the crimes and profits. Such were "the efficient means by which disloyalty was fed and the enemy encouraged to remain; honest, loyal men of course being the deepest sufferers." On the other hand, Brayman praised the bravery of Hicks and the black troops at the battle of Paducah. The colonel, "though suffering and partially disabled by wounds received at Pittsburg Landing [the battle of Shiloh], met every responsibility, braved every danger, and performed every duty with the vigor of youth, the judgment of the experienced soldier, and the pluck of a hero who knows not how to fail." He said the African American soldiers proved their "fidelity and courage" though they had neither been mustered nor paid and lacked "regular organization or officers." They "fought bravely and patiently to the end," the general said. He called attention to Forrest's surrender demand as a "threat of indiscriminate slaughter," adding that "an intimation of the same character was made at Union City and afterwards at Columbus." Brayman added, "The shocking manner in which these threats were carried into effect at Fort Pillow proves that the rebel leaders deliberately intended to perpetrate the crimes which were there committed." He was sorry that property belonging to "loyal families" was damaged in the battle of Paducah: "I have no regrets for the losses of those who sympathized with the enemy; who invited and welcomed them." He conceded that many secessionists had sworn the loyalty oath "and wear a disguise of loyalty, but only to enjoy more fully the benefits of trade and safe means of aiding their friends in arms." The general was convinced Forrest would not have raided Paducah were he not invited by pro-Confederate citizens. Thus, he was "satisfied that the retribution which the necessities of war brought upon the city falls far short of that which justice would warrant." He said that on March 27, the Confederates threatened Columbus, adding that he led troops there, but only "slight skirmishing" occurred. Brayman also referred to Tyler's bluff at Columbus on April 13. "No attack was probably intended, but the terms in which the surrender was demanded are significant with the massacre at Fort Pillow. Brayman said when Buford raided Paducah on April 14, he displayed the white flag, as Forrest had done during the battle. Citing a report from Hicks, Brayman said, "the facts show that in nearly every case the flag of truce was sent forward for unlawful purposes" and "depredations committed under its protection."[18]

Brayman's replacement, Brigadier General Henry Prince, ordered civilian hostage holding as another antiguerrilla tactic. Prince evidently came up with the idea after guerrillas captured ten Union soldiers near Mayfield on the night on May 7. Five days later, he ordered Hicks to dispatch mounted men "to arrest some influential rebel sympathizers in the neighborhood in which these guerrillas are maintained and hold them as hostages for the safe return" of the captives to Columbus or Paducah. Prince included a list of southern sympathizers, "some of whom will be sufficient, in all probability." After their arrest, the men "may be paroled for three days." But if the guerrillas did not surrender their prisoners, "confinement will follow" for the hostages.[19]

On May 13, Prince notified Major General Cadwallader C. Washburn in Memphis that he hoped to free the picket guard. But guerrillas were still a deadly peril in rural areas, he explained to the commander of the District of West Tennessee, which included the Purchase. He said anti-Union sentiment in the Purchase was so deep "that large bodies of guerrillas, led by men of respectable families, assemble in the best settled parts." Prince added that on May 11, about sixty guerrillas "killed 3 men"—he did not specify if they were soldiers or civilians—between Baltimore and Dublin. The brigadier also addressed smuggling. He advised Washburn that because Forrest was gone, civilians wanted permission to trade freely, which he was reluctant to grant. Instead, he allowed Hicks in Paducah and Lawrence in Columbus to permit "unconditional Union men" to trade "in a moderate amount of supplies." He suggested that such a policy would encourage Unionists and discourage southern sympathizers. He said there was still considerable smuggling between the Purchase and Tennessee. According to Prince, unrestricted commerce would only increase the smuggling: "When trade is open the worst men toward the Government enjoy the most of it on account of the strength of the anti-unionism, and I believe a genuine Union man is prevented from trading. They break him up."[20]

Meanwhile, Anderson, perhaps the First District's most "genuine Union man," was looking more and more like a Republican. So were Judge Rufus King Williams and John F. Bollinger. The Mayfield trio attended the Unconditional Union Party convention in Louisville on May 26 and got themselves named to the Republican National Convention on June 7–8 in Baltimore. Anderson and Williams were among "prominent speakers" at the gathering. Williams would be an at-large delegate; Anderson and John F. Bolinger were First District delegates. The Republicans were billing the gathering as the National Union convention in hopes of attracting prowar Democrats and southern Unionists who might blanch at the Republican name.[21]

Anderson found himself in a familiar role in familiar surroundings; he had been a Bluegrass State delegate at the 1860 Democratic National Convention in the city. The gathering also named Anderson as the First District National Union elector. At the Louisville convention, Anderson served on the Resolutions Committee, which reported only one resolution of principle, which passed unanimously: "The Union men of Kentucky, in convention assembled, are for the preservation and maintenance of the Union, the supremacy of the National Constitution, and the destruction of the rebellion, without any regard to what these objects may cost." Of course, the implication was that the "cost" would include the end of slavery. Indeed, "a manifest Pro-Lincoln and Anti-Slavery spirit pervaded the body," which comprised 256 men from fifty-six counties. The Unconditional Unionists approved a resolution instructing convention "delegates to cast a unanimous vote for Lincoln."[22]

Again, the irony is inescapable. Anderson, Williams, and Bolinger came from one of the most southern-sympathizing towns in Kentucky, a community where, in late May 1861, a pro-Confederate military alliance with Tennessee, or even regional secession, was seriously discussed. At any rate, Anderson and Judge Williams believed a strong hand was needed to rule the "South Carolina of Kentucky." On June 18, the duo made their case to the president in Washington. They urged Lincoln to reinstate tax assessments on southern sympathizers in their region and to bring back Paine as commander at Paducah. Anderson and Williams might have figured they had some extra leverage with Lincoln; after all, they had just helped renominate him, though that eventuality was a foregone conclusion. The president supported the tax and the return of Paine to the Purchase. "Do both these things for them unless you know some reason to the contrary," he wrote Secretary Stanton. "I personally know Gen. Paine to be a good man, having a West-Point education; but I do not know much of his military ability."[23]

Lincoln did not think much of George B. McClellan's military ability, but the Kentucky Union Democratic convention endorsed him for president and Bramlette for vice president. The May 25 gathering in Louisville brought together 518 men representing sixty-three counties: "The tone of its speakers was decidedly Anti-Lincoln and Pro-slavery. . . . The more denunciatory and defiant of the Administration (not the rebellion) the more were they applauded." The conclave agreed to send S. P. Cope of McCracken County as a First District delegate to the Democratic National Convention in Chicago, set for August 29–31. They chose William Beadles of Graves County as a First District alternate.[24]

Anderson and Williams, Beadles's fellow Graves countians, indeed helped boost Lincoln's renomination. The National Union ticket included pro-Union Democrat Andrew Johnson of Tennessee for vice president. A former congressman and senator, Johnson was the Volunteer State's military governor. By dropping the Republican label and adding a southerner and a Democrat to the ticket, the party of "Lincoln and Liberty" hoped to broaden the president's appeal to a war-weary electorate.

On the other hand, the Democrats hoped to capitalize on war weariness and win the White House with McClellan. George H. Pendleton, an antiwar Ohio Democrat, was "Little Mac's" running mate. McClellan, still a major general, was for continuing the war and restoring the Union but not for ending slavery. The party platform called for an armistice and a negotiated peace settlement with the Confederacy. McClellan repudiated the peace plank, but many people saw him as the antiwar candidate of the antiwar party. Meanwhile, before the decidedly prowar Paine showed up in the Purchase, Washburn was becoming even more provoked by citizens of the region who continued to provide aid and comfort to guerrillas and Confederate raiders. In June, Washburn, in effect, declared economic war: "The people of that disloyal region, Western Ky., will not be allowed to sell their cotton and tobacco, or purchase supplies, until they show some friendship for the U.S. government, by driving out the guerrillas and irregular bands of regular Confederate soldiers who pay them frequent visits."[25]

Lincoln was also alarmed over "the prevalence of Confederate and guerrillas raids" into his home state. So on July 5, he suspended the writ of habeas corpus and declared martial law in Kentucky.[26]

Officers of the Paducah branch of the Union League of America did not comment on Lincoln's action in a letter they sent to Washburn on July 11.

But the missive, signed by president pro tempore William H. Kidd, state representative and league vice president Thomas Barchett, and secretary John Perkins expressed the group's pleasure with the general's order. At the same time, the trio was also happy to hear that "our old and true friend, General Paine," was probably returning to command in Paducah. They complained that "Rebels are doing all the business, and they are reaping all the advantages of trade," but looked to Paine "to obtain relief." Meanwhile, the Union men said "large quantities of goods of all descriptions are going from this post to the interior, and of course the articles find their way into the hands of rebels." Paine, "being somewhat acquainted with the people here, will be able to protect Union men, and give traitors and secret Southern sympathizers their just dues." Kidd, Barchett, and Perkins concluded with a plea: "We have stood by our Union through weal and woe for the past three years of this terrible struggle, and we earnestly hope the military authorities will give us the protection we need and respectfully ask."[27]

On the night of July 17, a group of guerrilla "traitors" got the best of a scouting party of Gregory's home guards in "a sharp and severe contest" at Mayfield Creek near Mayfield. The guerrillas attacked, killing about nine of Gregory's men and wounding several more before the captain ordered a hasty retreat back to Paducah. The month before, Gregory's men became Company A of the Paducah Battalion of the Capital Guards. Many of them, like their captain, were also Graves countians "hunted from their homes because of their attachment to the government."[28]

On July 19, Paine arrived in Paducah. His tenure would represent the high-water mark of the Union crackdown against the Purchase's unregenerate Rebel populace. To the long-suffering Unionist majority, he seemed just the man to "give traitors and secret Southern sympathizers their just dues."[29]

12

A Paine in the Purchase

Brigadier General Eleazer A. Paine's time in the Purchase lasted fewer than three months. Short as the stint was, it became known as Paine's "reign of terror." His successor, Brigadier General Solomon Meredith, eased up on the "South Carolina of Kentucky." But Meredith's carrot was hardly more successful than Paine's stick in making many good Unionists in the Purchase. The seven counties west of the Tennessee River ended the war the way they started, as the state's sole Rebel region.

History is replete with irony. Paine is probably the most hated man in Jackson Purchase history, yet he supposedly looked like Old Hickory, the region's great hero. "He resembled Gen. Jackson more closely than any man I met in the army," recalled Surgeon Willis Danforth, Paine's medical director, in a March 1886 speech to Wisconsin Union veterans. The doctor's address is one of the few favorable accounts of Paine's fifty-one days in the Purchase. When Danforth made his speech, nearly twenty-two years had passed since Paine was commander in far western Kentucky. The doctor recalled that the general and most of his Purchase enemies were dead, but Danforth felt it necessary to defend Paine. "I still believe that his policy and treatment of his country's enemies was righteous altogether," he declared in remarks published in 1891 under the title "How I Came to Be in the Army and General E.A. Paine's Plan of Federal Salvation." While praising Paine, Danforth decried Union commanders who he thought were excessively easy on the Confederates: "It was my opinion then, and is now, there was too much rose water in Halleck's and many of our generals' treatment of rebels."[1]

Doubtless, Danforth's defense of Paine would not have brought forth "amens" from Purchase historians such as Lon Carter Barton, Hall Allen, and Hunter B. Whitesell. The general's return opened "the War's worst chapter for Graves County. . . . His tenure was to be such that it became simply known as the 'Reign of Terror,'" Barton wrote. "During his brief reign, Paine seems to have tried to wreak vengeance for all the blasted hopes of the Federals since the outbreak of the war," Allen opined. "The grossly unwarranted acts of his military establishment would leave scars slow to heal," according to Whitesell.[2]

After the Ohio-born Paine's time in Paducah early in the war, he became a combat commander. His division helped capture New Madrid and Island Number Ten before he was wounded in action at Farmington, Mississippi, near Corinth. Paine recovered and returned to rear-area garrison duty. He took command at Gallatin, Tennessee, close to Nashville, where he allegedly executed more than two hundred guerrillas. But he angered local Union sympathizers by arming African American refugees to help repulse guerrilla attacks and by ordering whites to pay wages to fugitive slaves whom they hired to do work. Paine's strict rule ultimately led his old boss at Paducah to call for his ouster. "Can you not order General Paine to the command of a brigade in the front?" Grant wrote Major General George H. Thomas, commander at Chattanooga, on January 15, 1864. "He is entirely unfit to command a post." Thomas was hardly pro-Paine. "I do not think it is advisable for General Paine to come to the front," Thomas replied. "His rank will entitle him to a division, and if not placed in command according to rank, I should have constant trouble with him." Thomas suggested that the army investigate Paine's behavior and make "his position fixed according to deserts."[3]

Paine was guilty of multiple misdeeds at Gallatin, including murder, according to a *Nashville Dispatch* report the *Journal* published. Paine's vengeance and cruelty knew no bounds, the *Dispatch* said. According to the paper, he even ordered the execution of a fifteen-year-old boy who was accused, falsely, the *Dispatch* declared, of being with some guerrillas who burned a bridge. The Nashville paper suggested that the teen's accuser was "some negro . . . and this was sufficient evidence with Gen. Paine."[4]

At Mayfield, Paine had seventeen-year-old Henry Bascom Hicks shot, according to Barton. He wrote that the lad was one of "at least forty-three persons in the District [who] fell victim to the oppressive commander's firing squad during his fifty-one-day 'reign of terror.'" Yet no records evidently survive to back up claims by Barton or anybody else that Paine was behind wholesale executions, according to Hoskins. "While an argument could be made that the names of the victims were conveniently lost . . . no private letters or diaries, local histories, or newspapers contain a list of the supposed victim's names," she writes. Records detail only eleven executions during Paine's "Reign of Terror." Four men were shot on Paine's order; seven, perhaps including Hicks, were sent to their deaths by Colonel Waters W. McChesney, commander of the 134th Illinois Infantry, Danforth's outfit. According to Paine, McChesney, and Purchase Unionists, all eleven men were guerrillas, including Captain Jim Kesterson, a guerrilla leader who admitted to murdering J. B. Happy and to harassing Union pickets at Paducah and Mayfield. Another man who was executed confessed to shooting pilots on Union transport boats on the Ohio.[5]

Kesterson is all but forgotten. But Hicks is revered in Mayfield, at least by the local Sons of Confederate Veterans. They honor him as a local Sam Davis, the twenty-one-year-old "Boy Hero of the Confederacy." Union soldiers hanged Davis as a spy in Pulaski, Tennessee, in 1863. Union troops shot Hicks as a spy in Mayfield. Execution was the common punishment both sides meted out for espionage.

At any rate, a bronze statue of Davis stands on the Tennessee capitol grounds in Nashville. Hicks's grave, marked by a four-foot stone shaft in Mayfield's Maplewood Cemetery, is a Confederate shrine that is sometimes decorated with small Rebel flags. The Graves County Confederate Veterans Association erected the shaft in 1892. Tilghman-Beauregard Camp No. 1460, Sons of Confederate Veterans, had a stone slab placed over the grave in 1990. The slab repeats a barely legible epitaph on the weatherworn, lichen-dappled stone that claims young Hicks was "shot by order of the Federal tyrant A. E. [*sic*] Paine on the streets of Mayfield, Kentucky."[6]

In his thesis, Barton insists Hicks was innocent but furnishes no evidence. "His crime . . . was that of being a Southern sympathizer and having two brothers in the Confederate army," he writes. Barton quotes Sheriff J. H. Swift's account of Hicks's death. The lawman said the teen met his maker on or about August 30. His epitaph says he died on August 21. It is also unclear whether "the Federal tyrant" ordered McChesney to shoot Hicks or whether the colonel acted on his own. Paine had ordered McChesney and his regiment to occupy Mayfield. In any event, soldiers took Hicks to "the Commander of the Post" about noon. Allegedly, Hicks was denied a last meal. "We have no vittles for a man such as you," the officer supposedly snapped at his captive. After having Hicks handcuffed, he ordered the teen lodged in the county jail to await his 2:00 p.m. execution. At the appointed time, soldiers marched Hicks out and stood him next to his freshly turned grave. Folklore has it that the Yankees made him dig the hole. Hicks supposedly defied his executioners, vowing, "I have got enough nerve to face the music; do not tie my hands, do not blindfold me." They tied a handkerchief over his face anyway, took up their positions, and fired on command; Hicks "fell with his head near the brink of his grave." After the war, Hicks was reburied in Maplewood Cemetery.[7]

While McChesney was a Paine ally, Columbus's commander was not. Colonel Prince sent Grant a long letter accusing Paine of multiple machinations. Prince said he was holding Kesterson for trial when Paine ordered him sent to Paducah and had him shot in public on July 27, "in semblance of an execution, without authority of law or any proper justification." Prince also said Gregory and his home guards, Paine's eager helpers, were further undermining Union efforts to win local hearts and minds. He said on August 2, Paine dispatched Gregory and his "gang" to the Dublin neighborhood, where they seized a man named Bryant. Prince charged that the home guards hustled him to Mayfield, where Gregory "publicly killed him in semblance of an execution, without authority of law or any proper justification."[8]

Further, Prince charged that Paine banished to Canada "quiet and peaceful citizens, who had taken the oath of allegiance." Danforth said the émigrés were "fifty of the most prominent rebel families," most of them from Paducah and Columbus. The group, about forty men, women, and children, arrived in Detroit by train on August 11 after a three-day boat and rail trek from Paducah, according to a sympathetic *Detroit Free Press.* Their escort consisted of a white captain and two dozen African American soldiers from the Eighth Artillery. No doubt, the black troops doubly galled the exiles because they were "former slaves of these masters," Danforth said. The Detroit paper claimed the western Kentuckians "were all made to feel the iron hand of despotism . . . and suffer the tortures of a worse than Siberian exile." The paper claimed they "expressed none but the most loyal sentiments to the Federal government" and protested "that they know not for what reason they were ordered into exile."[9]

The *Journal* argued that Paine erred in banishing the "disloyal citizens . . . with their families." The paper added that "a general fertile in expedients would find the means of thoroughly punishing them at home, instead of sending them abroad in the character of martyrs."[10]

At least some of the "martyrs" were, or had been, well-known Confederate sympathizers, none more so than George B. Moss of Columbus. In April 1861, he and some other local secessionists had sent a letter to Jefferson Davis inviting the Confederate army to take Columbus and Cairo. "We acknowledge no other Union but that of the Confederate states," they pledged. "Horne & Moore" also signed the letter; T. M. Horne, Joe M. Moore, and T. M. Moore were among those banished. Around the same time Moss, Horne, and Moore wrote Davis, their fellow Columbus émigré, W. R. Vance, went to Memphis seeking military help against the Yankees at Cairo. When the Rebels showed up in town, Vance and Moss were among several locals who signed an "open letter" to their fellow Kentuckians explaining why they were glad to see the Confederates. W. G. Malone, driven from Columbus as well, had three sons in the Confederate army, including a major under Forrest. Malone's daughter, Sallie, was twelve when she was banished. She later claimed that she and the others were the only citizens "ever sent beyond the borders of the United States under negro—or military guard." Sallie departed with her parents and five siblings. "Though a minor incident in the great drama of the war," it was a dreadful time for her family, including her father, a "feeble gray haired man," she recalled. In addition, Paine forced Mrs. Robert Woolfolk to leave Paducah. After Union forces arrived in her hometown, also in 1861, her husband—whom Paine had already banned—had stirred the locally famous ruckus by hoisting a Rebel flag over the family home and cheering for Jeff Davis.[11]

Lieutenant Andrew Lucas Hunt of the 134th Illinois Infantry was standing next to Paine when Mrs. Woolfolk, whose three sons reportedly were Rebel soldiers, tearfully begged the general not to send her away. Paine was unmoved, according to Hunt: "The General told her that living or dead she should leave for Canada. . . . I saw her off on the following day." Hunt said eight Woolfolks departed, the family having to abandon its "splendid residence" and its contents, which were guarded by African American troops. "The trip cost some $350 but it all comes out of the rebels who live in the neighborhood."[12]

Danforth also watched the families depart. He said the exiles ended up in Windsor, Ontario, opposite Detroit, and stayed for the rest of the war. The doctor also said he witnessed Kesterson's execution and dismissed Prince's criticism of Paine for summarily shooting the guerrilla leader. "The rebels were very belligerent, and carried on a heavy contraband trade, supplying the enemy with salt, quinine, etc.," said the physician, who was Prince's medical director before holding the same post under Paine. Prince, according to the doctor, was clueless about "the real state of affairs" in the Purchase. Danforth joined Paine's staff after the general ordered the 134th Illinois from Columbus to Paducah, the regiment's last stop before Mayfield. Danforth said that on the same day Paine had Kesterson shot, the general loaned southern-sympathizing J. B. Jacobs an army horse and ordered him to ride to every "rebel commander" in the district and read the general's proclamation: "I have this day shot Captain Kesterson, taken prisoner in guerrilla warfare, and shall shoot in like manner all prisoners so taken, and if I am credibly informed of retaliation being practised on Union men living in my district, I will walk out five of the most prominent citizens of Paducah and shoot them dead for every Union life so taken." Paine gave Jacobs ten days to come back, and he held Jacobs's father and two brothers as hostages to ensure he carried out the general's command. "Jacobs returned on time with the signatures of rebel commanders on the back of the proclamation."[13]

In his speech, Danforth quoted a September 1, 1864, letter he wrote to the *Chicago Tribune* outlining Paine's plan for "federal salvation" in the Purchase. Danforth said that upon Paine's advent, the Purchase "was . . . in a sad plight, guerrillas swarmed along every highway, no Union man's life was safe outside our pickets, and our pickets were in rifle shot of the Ohio and Mississippi from Paducah to Hickman." He claimed "disloyal people and rebels actually grew fat and wealthy in the district; they were bold, defiant and arrogant in their bearing and demands." On the other hand, "Union men were cowed down, desponding and discouraged. In fact, they said and believed, that in order to ensure any favors, it was actually necessary to be a rebel."

Paine revealed his plan soon after he settled into his Paducah headquarters and began receiving "sinners." A half-dozen delegations representing tobacco, cotton, banking, and other financial interests sought audiences with Paine. Though the men of wealth and property probably came to him cap in hand, they might have figured Paine would prove pliable. "In no case was the interest of the delegation represented to be taxed, abridged, or in any way crippled, and upon the favorable reception of it was made to depend the welfare of the Union cause in this district," according to Danforth. His hero was unmoved. Paine told the deputations that "it is a notorious fact that the district is intensely disloyal," adding, "it has caused more trouble to the government than all your tobacco, cotton, banks and business is worth." He said the question was not how much money the men could make or how much tobacco, cotton, or hemp they could grow. "The only question on trial here is: Are you people ready for the federal salvation?" Paine did not mince words: "If so, well, if not, you must die."[14]

Paine proceeded to outline his salvation program. He started with his "first and greatest commandment"—the general would not allow southern sympathizers to "circulate one dollar of capital in all of this land—not a dollar." He explained, "No debt or bill of exchange can be paid without my signature, and I pledge you I will not approve any money transactions of a disloyal man." Every penny a Rebel sympathizer had "shall be placed at the disposal of the Government." Paine warned, "I will teach you that having encouraged this rebellion, having comforted and aided your country's enemies, you must, aye, shall, reap a traitor's reward." He poured it on: "It is now the fourth year of the war, and you rebels have not learned the grand, solemn truth that the life and peace of this great nation are not worth more than the life or pence of an individual. You will never feel it until you are made to feel the want of a nation's defense and support,—made poor that you may become rich—that you may know how to prize strength." Paine kept at it: "Talk about your rights! Why, you have no rights to talk about. A loyal citizen is the only one left with any rights at this time." Paine said his visitors should join the army and permit their slaves to do likewise: "You are all of you able-bodied men, but think yourselves too good to fight, afraid of federal bullets or something else." He told his callers they were "too cowardly to fight" and "too mean and stingy" to give up their slaves to federal recruiting officers. Yet, he added, "you are harping about your rights—that miserable insane idea, 'Southern rights,' Southern aristocracy." Paine wrapped up the first commandment by vowing, "I intend to tie up every dollar of money now in the hands of rebels in this district—every dollar of it, gentlemen."[15]

In his "second commandment" Paine ordered, "all of you notorious rebels get out of your houses and leave my district so that Union men and women may come here to help me redeem this country." Paine said he cared nothing about their tobacco interests or the market value of their slaves or cotton. He said if they were Unionists, then the federal government would protect and defend their financial interests. "Not a man in West Kentucky can point his finger to a single act by which the government ever oppressed him—not one," Paine declared. "If you then rebel against this government so generous, so true and good to you—if you rebel against it how is it that you come to me?" He challenged, "Standing as I do in the field of battle against you rebels, periling my life to redeem my country from the danger into which you have plunged it, do you, can you, be so insane as to suppose that I shall spend a moment's time in guarding your interests in stocks and trade?" Paine said he was in Paducah to offer them "federal salvation, to protect and defend Union men, to show you they are the very salt of the earth, to teach you that the sooner you cluster about them the better it will be for you." Paine reminded his callers that when he was in Paducah in 1861, he had advised them "of the better way, the only way to peace. I told you what would come if you persisted, and now, after three years, I return to you again and find that you have not improved anything except your wealth." In addition, he accused the "rebellious, proud, defiant" betrayers of the Union cause of "actually leading Forrest's army in here and clapping your hands as his murderous fire swept away the life of our nation's defenders." Thus, Paine said, "It is high time that you were made to feel the effects of your disloyalty and I intend that you shall feel them." He swore to shoot every guerrilla his soldiers captured: "If your Southern brethren retaliate by shooting a federal soldier I will walk out five of your rich bankers, brokers and cotton men and make you kneel down and shoot you." He promised to hold "you men of such large influence" responsible for keeping the peace. But he guaranteed that if guerrillas murdered a Union man, "the same fate awaits five of you gentlemen. I have sworn it and it shall be done. I am going to manage this district so that when I am done with it the men and women who remain can come together in the name of the Lord and say that 'we belong to the United States.'"[16]

Danforth was proud of Paine for rebuffing Rebel sympathizers. He "refused to eat with them, refused their proferred hospitality, ate his own bread and butter and sat under his own vine and fig tree." The general "took a straight-forward, high-minded course, never for a moment forgetting that he was the representative of a mighty republic struggling for victory over treason and rebellion."[17]

Paine backed up his tough talk with swift action, declaring what amounted to economic war on southern sympathizers with money and property. On July 20, he forbade all banks in his district—except those in Cairo—to pay out any money or make any transfer except by special permission from the general's headquarters. "This order tied the hands of every business rebel in the district," said Danforth, who quoted from the order in his speech. "He was at liberty to pay debts to Union men only." Three days later, Paine disallowed the payment of rent to all but "landlords and owners who are unswerving, unconditional and undeviating Union persons or corporations." Rent owed to Rebel sympathizers was, starting August 1, to be paid to army quartermasters. "This order substantially furnished the chapter converting all the profits and emoluments of rebel landlords to the United States, opening their eyes to the enormities of their armies and assuring them that they must not ask further protection from a government whose life they were striving to take," Danforth said. Paine took other steps to crimp Rebel purses. He slapped a 25 percent ad valorem tax on all tobacco, cotton, and other goods sold by southern sympathizers. They had to pay up to Major Henry Bartling of the Eighth Artillery, Paducah provost marshal. The revenue raised was to be used "to meet the wants and necessities of Union refugees, from whatever direction, located in this district, and to pay $5,000 to every widow whose husband has been killed in federal service in Western Kentucky," Danforth said.[18]

Hunt, who briefly served on the general's staff, praised Paine and his punitive tax to help Unionists whom the guerrillas burned out. The lieutenant was glad his commander "paid a union woman whose husband had been hung by the rebs for adhering to his union sentiments—a thousand dollars of the fund and told her when she was in a place of safety and wanted more funds he would pay her a thousand more. That's the right kind of doctrine." He liked serving under Paine, whose headquarters were in Judge Campbell's big house. The dwelling occupied handsomely laid-out grounds "full of large fruit and shade trees." Yet Hunt confessed that his Paducah posting would be more enjoyable if he "could only get an introduction to some staunch Union young ladies." Nonetheless, he pledged to "go without any acquaintances before I will be introduced to a sesesh young lady." He said several such ladies lived on Broadway, where Campbell's house stood: "All of them dress in white and red but never the slightest show of blue. I wish the General would issue an order that all the young ladies had to take the oath of allegiance—wouldn't we have lots of amusement!"[19]

Rebecca Eaker, John Eaker's spouse, was anything but amused when Hunt's commanding officer and his staff showed up at her doorstep in Mayfield. Paine invited McChesney. John Eaker was not home, and Rebecca had no choice but to usher her unwelcome guests in the parlor. Paine promptly announced to McChesney that the room would be his headquarters. He told the colonel to let Rebecca and her family stay in the house for ten days. Afterward, the Eakers, including John, if he could be located, were to report to Paine in Paducah. He would "furnish them transportation to New Orleans, and thence to Central America, where they will live hereafter." Before Paine and his entourage left, the general sternly lectured Rebecca. Her husband "has been our enemy; he has done all that he could to destroy the Government of the United States—the Government which has raised him in the lap of luxury, giving him slaves, rich crops, tobacco warehouses—all that his heart could desire, and did he, could he, think that he could raise his two sons and send them out to murder that Government, and yet go unpunished? Is it possible that he could have been so insane?" Paine ordered her to send word to John to report to him forthwith. If he complied, he was welcome to go into exile with his family. She asked Paine to write him. "No, madam, I have no correspondence with rebels, except at the cannon's mouth," the general replied. Paine commanded her to send her son to his father and tell him to pay the Paducah provost marshal "the sum of ten thousand dollars, which is the fine I have levied upon him." The money, Paine told her, "is to go to make up a fund that I am raising from you rebels, from which to pay something toward the support of the widows and orphans your husband has made." The general said half of Eaker's fine was for J. B. Happy's widow. Paine grew even icier: "You know, madam, how that old man was led out in the front yard, across the street there, and *shot dead*! not for having wronged any human being—no, not for this,—but because, and only because, he was unconditionally true to his Government." Rebecca begged Paine not to make her go because she had a sick child in the house. She proposed traveling to friends near Paducah. She had "a daughter living there." Paine was adamant: "Pack your trunks, take all your silver plate, and your linen, bedclothes, all your ready money (except the ten thousand dollars which I fine you)"; she should leave her furniture and "heavy goods" and be gone, he snapped, adding that the federal government would confiscate "all your lands and tobacco, and this will be the end of John Eaker, his estate and family, in the United States." He assured Rebecca that the Eakers would not go alone; he planned to banish one hundred more Graves County families. Paine also advised her that "for every day your husband refuses to report to me after to-day, I shall increase his fine five hundred dollars."[20]

At the same time, Paine decided a fort was needed to protect McChesney and his fifteen-hundred-man garrison, which consisted of the 134th and 136th Illinois Infantry Regiments, a company from the Third Illinois Cavalry Regiment, and part of the Eighth US Colored Heavy Artillery. Too, Paine probably knew that the Graves County seat had suffered numerous bloody guerrilla raids and that Forrest had gone through Mayfield on the way to Paducah. So in early August, Paine ordered the earthen strongpoint built around the courthouse. He conscripted hundreds of citizens from Graves, Hickman, and McCracken Counties, "irrespective of class or sentiment," into "labor battalions" to dig the cannon emplacements and breastworks.[21]

In 1861, armed Confederates had pressed thousands of slaves, overseen by Rebel soldiers, into building their fortifications at Columbus. Now white men had to make the dirt fly, guarded in part by ex-slaves in Union uniforms. Hunt was sent to Mayfield to help supervise the labor. "We have impressed into our service, all the male inhabitants of the town to fortify the courthouse," he said. "They are at work now—have thrown up earth works, barricaded the windows with heavy oak scathing—cut loop holes in the wall—built staging for the men to stand on." The lieutenant claimed only a "very large force" of Rebels backed with artillery could dislodge the Union soldiers from the building. Hunt added that he was in good health but poor spirits: "We are now in a thoroughly rebel town—any thing the men want they take." He said food was in short supply—"no butter—very little milk—hardly enough for coffee at the hotel." Apparently, army hardtack was plentiful. His men pounded it "into crumbs with hammers & hatchets and between stones" before soaking it in water and frying it "in a pan with pork fat."[22]

Later, Hunt wrote his brother about the August 26 execution of a guerrilla named Waters, whom Gregory's men captured about twenty miles from Mayfield: "He had been confined in the jail here—has had a trial or rather hearing. He was a notorious bushwhacker was well known to be one, so General Paine ordered him to be shot." Hunt added that he, Lieutenant Colonel John C. Bigelow, McChesney's second in command, and a chaplain visited the prisoner in his last hours. "He is a most ignorant person—surly and impudent," Hunt claimed. Waters said he was a regular Confederate soldier who had been at Fort Pillow, where he killed a black soldier. He confessed to firing on Union pickets at Paducah but denied he was a guerrilla. The chaplain tried to convince Waters to get right with God, but "he only said that we could do what we wished with him as we had him in our power but you must expect to be avenged if you ever fall in to our hands."[23]

Guards marched the prisoner out of town to a clearing, where Waters's grave had been dug; his coffin rested next to the hole. Hunt said Waters "walked with a firm step" and that when the place of execution was reached, "the Chaplin walked up to him and seemed to pray." After the chaplain and Waters "talked for a while . . . a bandage was tied over his eyes and around his legs—then he cried out so as we could hear him and put up his hands." The execution proceeded after "some men then stepped up and tied his hands behind his back." Ten of Gregory's company formed the firing squad. Hunt said the prisoner was felled by "ten balls passing thru his chest" and that Danforth pronounced him dead. Hunt added that "the gang of sesesh" drafted to build the fortifications was forced to witness the shooting. McChesney warned them, "men, you have been brought out here to see a guerrilla shot—this shall be your fate if you are ever caught harboring guerillas or bushwhackers or if any of you know of the approach or whereabouts of any body of guerrillas and do not inform the federal troops and find it out you shall meet the same fate as this guerrilla." Four "secesh" were ordered to put the body in the coffin and lower it into the grave, "done while we were marching off the field," Hunt said.[24]

Private Hawley V. Needham of the 134th Illinois also witnessed the execution, remarking that the Rebels disparagingly called Gregory's company "the 'Hell Hounds,'" which was, ironically, the Confederates' admiring appellation for King's Rebel cavalry. "It was the first time I ever witnessed the death of any human being," Needham wrote, adding that it was sad that Waters "must appear before God at the judgment with all his hellish crimes to answer for and no hope whatever. But justice does not always sleep and Fort Pillow will not go unavenged for this man was there. How humiliating for a man to commit such crimes and then cannot face the music."[25]

Four days later, Needham watched a second guerrilla, "a young fellow, a mere boy," face the music, but courageously. His execution followed a night punctuated by "a great deal of firing," evidently by guards trying to stop an escape by some of the "Fortification Brigade," Needham's name for the men forced to work on the court square fort. Gregory's company brought in the lad after a shootout with guerrillas in which they slew one of the enemy. "The prisoner was . . . daring and brave to the last degree," Needham wrote. "His bearing was worthy of one who was to die in a better cause."[26]

Needham had seen the graves of other enemy dead when he arrived in Columbus in June. He remembered there was nothing to commemorate the Confederates' "unholy resting places but a mound of earth," musing, "who knows but my fate may be the same?" In any case, the nearby Rebel earthworks impressed him. "What wild country! high hills, deep ravines covered with dense underbrush and cut up with rifle pits and forts and breastwork by the mile," he wrote. "It seems as if, if it was properly garrisoned, that it would be impregnable. How picturesque the scene at my feet turns a deep ravine covered with underbrush here and there is an old stub which looks as if it had been shot off. Beyond is the forest."[27]

Writing from the courthouse cupola in Mayfield on August 12, he disdained Graves County as "the Banner Secession County of the State." Nonetheless, he found "Mayfield . . . quite a pretty place situated in the midst of a fine farming country and possessing a beautiful landscape. The tobacco trade seems to have been the life of the place as it contains two immense Warehouses and not long since another one larger than either of the present ones was burnt down." Even so, he said business was at a virtual standstill: "Stores with the exception of the drugstore are closed and empty."[28]

Below Needham's lofty perch was grim evidence of where another guerrilla had been sent to his reward, but before the private arrived in town. "We are within twenty five or thirty miles of the Tennessee line and in a county abounding with guerrillas," Needham wrote. "There are three shotholes in the walls of the C.H. made by balls after passing though the body of a noted scoundrel. He was captured by the Cavalry only two weeks ago."[29]

On August 15, Needham enjoyed listening to speeches by the Republican-leaning Anderson and from Bolinger. "These men are tried and true and are objects of bitter hatred to the Rebs," Needham wrote. "It was expected that General Paine would be here and make a speech as he had given an invitation to all to come in today and there was a big crowd." Needham added that "many prominent guerrillas" reportedly were in the throng, though Paine failed to appear. Bolinger spoke on the general's behalf, warning that "the people must submit peaceably if they would, forcibly if need be. One hundred rebel families must be banished from the U.S. and the county must pay $250,000." Able-bodied slaves of military age must become soldiers. "Bully for Paine," Needham wrote. "That is my ticket every time."[30]

Paine was not bluffing about conscripting slaves, according to Needham. On August 16, an African American sergeant came into Mayfield with a slave who he said belonged to a Unionist woman: "She appealed to the Pickets but they could not interfere and appealed to us but we could do nothing but report the case which we promised to do, but it was as I expected, of no avail." Later, Needham wrote of "another victim to the Divine institution of slavery," a legless slave. The man's owner had joined the Confederate army; he fled to the woods to avoid going with him. "There his legs became frostbitten so that both legs had to be taken off, one at the knee and one above the ankle. He was obliged to saw one off himself with a knife. The boys have given him considerable money. He is going to Paducah to try and learn the stove makers trade."[31]

Meanwhile, the execution of Kesterson and Paine's threat to show no mercy to guerrillas seemed to have the desired effect. In July and August, Union commanders reported only minor clashes with the ever-elusive marauders, who lost most encounters with the better-armed and more numerous Yankees. Most important, Forrest was nowhere to be found in the Purchase, though he would return to the region one more time before the war ended.[32]

The abolitionist Paine might have relished a chance to fight Forrest, especially after Fort Pillow, but he would not get it. Word of the general's alleged misdeeds in the Purchase reached Governor Bramlette. A conservative Unionist, he was not in the general's corner. On September 2, he wrote Lincoln, charging Paine, Anderson, and Bolinger with corruption and oppression by exiling the "loyal" citizens and taking the émigrés' money and property "for their own private use and gain." Bramlette wanted the banishment lifted and called for the creation of "a military commission composed of good, brave, just, and fearless men" to investigate the Paine-Anderson-Bolinger "system of oppression and plundering."[33]

The next day, Bramlette wrote Lincoln again, protesting that Kentucky was being treated as if were "a rebellious and conquered province" and not a loyal state. He cited the president's martial-law decree, trade restrictions and assessments, and heavy fines arbitrarily levied on citizens. Bramlette singled out western Kentucky, claiming that the people there had "for a long while been the subjects of insult, oppression, and plunder by officers who have been placed to defend and protect them." The governor vowed that while he opposed Lincoln's reelection, his "Unionism is unconditional." Even so, Bramlette, speaking for the majority of Kentucky Unionists, warned, "We are for preserving the rights and liberties of our own race and upholding the character and dignity of our position. We are not willing to sacrifice a single life or emperil the smallest right of free white men for the sake of the negro."[34]

Heretofore, Unionists had no problem with Union commanders lording it over the Purchase, the most diseased part of the "infected" First District. So why did Bramlette now take up for the state's only Rebel region? Surely, he was aware of the outspoken Confederate sympathizers in the group Paine had sent packing to Canada. Could it be that the governor, a Union Democrat, saw their expulsion as a handy pretext to call for the Republican Paine's ouster and also discredit Anderson and Bolinger, who were all but Republicans? In any event, on September 6, Grant ordered Burbridge to fire Paine. His successor would be the North Carolina–born brigadier general Solomon Meredith of Indiana, who would be far more popular with Purchase secesh than his predecessor. Meredith had been severely wounded at the battles of Second Bull Run and Gettysburg.[35]

No doubt, most citizens of the "South Carolina of Kentucky" were glad to see Paine go. Private Needham and Lieutenant Hunt were not. Needham believed Meredith, who took command on September 8, would coddle the Rebels: "instead of carrying out Paine's policy of hunting rebels he takes them and clasps them in his loving embrace. Going to have a love feast. I suppose he is going to feed in the same trough with the lousy Grey Backs and they will all become Union men. Oh! Won't they? Sent them all home to bushwhack as much as they please." In addition, he said Gregory's home guards were so angry over Paine's dismissal that they threatened to disband.[36]

Hunt had nothing but praise for the departing Paine. He described the general as "one of the most pleasant men I know of—he will shake hands with you in the morning when he first comes out on the stoop—sits down asks you to take a chair and will enter into conversation with you very freely." Hunt said Paine conducted post business "personally so as he says he can know what is going on," adding, "I like him very much. Whenever any of the guard salute him, he always takes off his hat." Paine's egalitarian ways also showed in his treatment of African Americans, according to Hunt. "He will give audience to a poor negro woman and listen with all possible attention to her complaint," and "he pays as much attention to the negro soldier who is asking him for a house for his wife and family as he does to the congressman of the district." While Anderson may have admired Paine's egalitarianism, it no doubt irked almost all other whites. Like Bramlette, nearly every Unionist shared the secessionists' belief in white supremacy. Anderson was one of the few white Kentuckians who came to see the Civil War as a crusade to preserve the Union and end slavery. Anderson saw Paine as a worthy ally toward that end.[37]

Consequently, the congressman was quick to protest Paine's removal to Stanton and Lincoln. "General Paine was ordered here by the President to collect assessments on rebel sympathizers," Anderson telegraphed the secretary from Paducah on September 9. "Union men all indorse his policy. If sent away the Union men in this end of the State will all leave. All is lost. Have the order of Grant revoked. Telegraph me." Anderson included a copy of Paine's dismissal order. The next day, Anderson wrote Lincoln that Paine's "removal will destroy all our prospects for success in this end of the State & all I have promised the Union men here turns out to be false." He pledged to "do the best I can no matter who is in command" but besought the president to allow Paine to stay in Paducah for sixty days.[38]

Bramlette soon got his commission of enquiry. Burbridge tapped Brigadier General Speed S. Fry of Danville and Colonel John Mason Brown of Frankfort to go after Paine, Anderson, Bolinger, and their associates. Brown reported to Bramlette that on the evening they arrived in Paducah, Paine decamped with his son, Captain Phelps Paine, who was also the general's assistant adjutant general. The Paines took with them, or ordered to leave, "every clerk who was familiar with the office business of Headquarters." Meredith handed over Captain Paine's office records, but Fry and Brown said they "were so incomplete and irregularly kept, that they proved of little service in the investigation." They added that "many orders, proven to have been issued by Brigadier General Paine," were absent from his books.[39]

Fry and Brown began their report by accusing Paine of often using violent and foul language: "A favorite expression, and frequently made use of, was, 'You are a God damned scoundrel; God damn you, I'll dig a hole and shoot and put you in it.'" He even cursed women, "whose respectability and lady-like manners the entire country could vouch," according to Fry and Brown. A laundry list of worse charges followed. The general, they said, flagrantly abused his power. According to Fry and Brown, he arbitrarily arrested and shot innocent civilians. Too, their report said Paine's catalog of crimes included corruption, extortion, fencing stolen goods, and even countenancing immorality. Colonel Barry had allegedly forced a banker to shell out "$150 in gold to a prostitute whose society the Colonel enjoyed." The commissioners lamented, "It would be endless to enumerate the indignities, wrongs, and outrages that the citizens of Paducah, without distinction of political faith, have endured." Even so, Fry and Brown tried, their report spanning almost nine full pages in the *House Journal.* They also accused Anderson, Bolinger, and others of "corruption, bribery, and malfeasance in office," while adding that Meredith was addressing "complaints . . . as rapidly as possible." Further, Fry and Brown denounced Paine's exile order and claimed the fort at Mayfield was unnecessary. But the duo said they could not accurately determine how many people had faced Paine's firing squads. The general's order books "gave no clue to the matter," nor did guardhouse records. Fry and Brown did report that at Mayfield, McChesney executed seven men. But the investigators confessed they had no way of knowing if they were guilty or innocent. Yet based on "vague and uncertain evidence," they estimated that between five and forty-three people suffered the ultimate punishment while Paine was in command of the Purchase. Fry and Brown were obviously students of history, for they concluded, "The administration of Verres and Warren Hastings may be safely challenged to show a parallel to the fifty-one days of terror and rapine that measured the duration of General Paine's authority."[40]

Perhaps no one was happier at Paine's ouster than editor Prentice of the *Journal.* Fry and Brown's report damning Paine, Anderson, and company had not been made public on September 27 when the *Journal* ran a story about the investigation. Nonetheless, the paper said Paine and his son were still hid-ing out in Illinois, and "all of his subordinate officers also took 'French leave,' knowing their conduct would not bear investigation." Predictably, the paper praised Meredith. "With the feeling of a true soldier, he afforded every facility in his power" to help Fry and Brown in their investigation.[41]

The *Journal* credited Colonel James W. Craddock, commander of the Sixteenth Kentucky Infantry, with exposing Paine's alleged perfidy. Craddock had traveled to the Purchase on "business," and "by close observation he became convinced that Gen. Paine and his subordinates were exercising the iron rule of despots." They "were persecuting and robbing the people under flimsy pretexts, and that the worst corruption prevailed in his office and characterized all of his official acts." Craddock took action, meeting with Burbridge at his headquarters in Lexington and "fully stated the case" against Paine. Burbridge "was loth to believe" Craddock; the colonel swore he was telling the truth. As a result, Burbridge, on September 9, appointed Brown and Fry as commissioners to investigate Paine, the paper said. Craddock was to go along "and assist them in their labors." Though relieved of command, Paine was to remain in Paducah and face the charges against him. Instead, he fled, the *Journal* said.[42]

Paine left a bloody trail behind, according to the Louisville paper, which said that forty-three graves of alleged Paine victims "were counted at Paducah." The *Journal* did not say where the graves were or who counted them. But the paper said that among those put to death "were two men, named Nolin and Taylor, of well-known loyalty, who" somehow offended Paine. The paper claimed to have a statement from Hiram R. Enoch, quartermaster of the 132nd Illinois, in which he said "he heard of four citizens being executed without a shadow of a trial—Kesterson, Taylor, Mathey and Hess." Enoch added that "about the 1st of September," McChesney told him that "he had shot seven men at Mayfield, and had one more in the guardhouse that he intended to execute the next day." McChesney acted under the general's instructions, according to Enoch. He said McChesney admitted he tried none of the men and bragged that one of the prisoners was taken out to be shot, executed, and buried a mere forty-five minutes from the time that he was brought to the colonel's headquarters. The rest of the *Journal* story essentially leveled the same charges against Paine and his associates that Fry and Brown made in their report. Paine, according to the paper, cheated the people and the federal government of "not less than $150,000." The *Journal* also claimed that Bolinger was still at large, but Meredith was making plans to arrest him. Henry Bartling was under close guard in Paducah. McChesney was in Chicago, but Meredith had sent orders to have him apprehended and brought back to Paducah.[43]

On September 28, the *Journal* took dead aim at Anderson. The paper was "not surprised" that Fry and Brown named "the Hon. (how that term is prostituted!) Lucien [*sic*] Anderson . . . among the persons who were 'guilty of corruption and were sharers with General Paine in his swindling transactions.'" The paper dusted off its old charge: Anderson had been elected in 1863 "upon strong conservative pledges" yet "turned abolitionist and voted in all instances for abolition men and abolition measures." Thus, the *Journal* had "known him to be a scoundrel." The paper "felt assured that he was guilty of corruption in that case, and that he could consequently be corrupted in any case, if indeed what is thoroughly corrupt admits of being corrupted." The *Journal* argued that "undoubtedly the corruption just brought to light, including the sharing of the booty of an official robber and swindler, is no worse than the corruption which induced him to prove a base breaker of his plighted faith and the perfidious betrayer of his constituents and the sacred cause of the nation." The paper challenged, "Let the abolition organs, which have hitherto defended him so warmly, defend him hotly now it if suits their worthy purposes." The *Journal* said it had learned that instead of appearing before Fry and Brown, Anderson "skulked away somewhere, and at the last dates was skulking still." The paper guessed "that he can venture to come in. It doesn't seem to us that he needs fear punishment for his crimes." Anderson's "friends in Washington . . . wouldn't like to see so useful a friend martyred. Come in out of the cold Lucien [*sic*]."[44]

Anderson replied in a letter to the *Louisville Daily Union Press,* one of the *Journal*'s "abolition organs," published on October 24. The congressman denied that he shared with the general "any property or any money in any manner, shape, or form." He addressed the executions, singling out Kesterson. Anderson said he knew him; Kesterson was a guerrilla chief who "in the dead of night" had aided in Happy's murder "in front of his own house, in presence of his wife and children. This is one of the citizens shot by order of Gen. Paine, and for which he has incurred the ill will, hatred and denunciation of the Journal." Anderson wrote that local secessionists were as indignant over the execution of Kesterson "as the editors of the Journal are." Rebel sympathizers had threatened to burn Anderson's house and kill him if Kesterson was shot, the congressman claimed, adding that he knew nothing of other alleged executions.[45]

Anderson claimed the *Journal*'s real motive for its "unprovoked and malignant attack on" him at "this particular time" was his vote for Colfax for House speaker. He also said he did go before the commission and answer every question asked him. "I have never, since the rebellion began, skulked from rebels and traitors," Anderson thundered. "A press which is now the slanderer of Union men and Federal officers, the defender of traitors and apologist for guerrillas, will not hesitate to say or do anything." Naturally, the *Journal* returned fire: "The accused parties, before they get through this ugly business, will probably find, unless their abolitionism has the virtue to save them, that they have more persons to deal with than Colonel Craddock and the Editors of the Louisville Journal." The paper asked, "As Anderson proposes to hold us personally responsible for *calling* him a scoundrel, what in the world will he do to the members of the Committee if they *prove* him one?" At the same time, the *Journal* wondered, "but will the Administration permit this matter to go any further than it has gone?" Editor Prentice's paper also jabbed the *Press:* "Our neighbor says that he intends to vote according to his convictions. We wonder whether his friends Paine and Anderson and Bolinger, if convicted, will vote according to *their* convictions?"[46]

In any event, a majority of Anderson's fellow Mayfield citizens—and most Purchase dwellers—must have rejoiced at the hasty departure of his friend Paine. "His removal . . . was hailed with delight by the citizens of the town and surrounding country, many of whom had been subjected to the greatest cruelty on account of their suspected friendship for the Southern cause," Battle, Perrin, and Kniffen wrote.[47]

On the other hand, Hunt defended Paine. In another letter to his mother, he described Meredith as "a very awkward man, six feet five inches tall, not at all handsome looks like Mr. Sherman of the Chicago Ale & Malt Co." Hunt was astonished when Meredith gave a speech to "all the fortification brigade (some 300 sesesh out there) besides all the citizens of the place and all the troops stationed here." Meredith "told the sesesh" that he was sending them all home: "The fort we have been building is to be leveled to the ground, etc. and all horses and mules taken from the sesesh are to be turned over to them again. His policy is just the opposite to that of General Paine." Meredith also said he would keep the 134th Illinois on active service "for 'a week or two'" after the regiment's hundred-day enlistment was up "just to teach us discipline." Meredith faulted McChesney, claiming the colonel had stolen a hogshead of government-owned tobacco, sold it, and pocketed the money. The general also accused the colonel of pilfering a clock and a shotgun, which he had boxed up for shipment to his home in Chicago. McChesney "has been trading in horses, etc. The General has sent for him at Chicago—and he will no doubt have a trial and be dismissed from the service," said Hunt, who conceded it was his duty to accept what today's army calls a "stop loss." The men, on the other hand, were "very angry" at the absent McChesney "and lay the whole blame of our having to stay here for two or three weeks over our time to him. McChesney had better never show his face to the regiment again."

In a later letter to his brother, Hunt was even more critical of Meredith and McChesney. "General Meredith is just the opposite to General Paine—he is a copperhead," Hunt penned. "General Meredith is afraid of hurting a rebel." Hunt again cited Meredith's speech, explaining he had ordered the regiment to remain in Mayfield "so that he could clear up Colonel McChesney's affairs and . . . make soldiers of us—two very silly excuses for keeping us here."[48]

The local "sesesh" might have been glad to see the 134th Illinois go, but they were happy enough at Meredith's advent. He was "an officer of dignity and a true gentleman" whose "conduct was such as to win the confidence and esteem of the people, whom he treated with fairness and courtesy," according to Battle, Perrin, and Kniffen. "His occupancy of Mayfield was the beginning of an era of friendly feeling among all classes." Perhaps nothing better symbolized the change in command than Meredith's decision to abandon the court square fort, which was to local secessionists the very symbol of Paine's alleged misrule. Meredith said it was "useless in case of attack." Instead, Meredith "threw up earthworks on an eminence in the southwest portion of the town, which commanded a wide range of country." Before the war ended, Meredith "planted several batteries on these fortifications." En route to Paducah in March 1864, Forrest had reportedly passed the spot where Meredith had sited his batteries. Meredith evidently suspected that if Forrest returned to the Purchase, then he would travel the same route. The general's work would thus prove a nasty surprise for the raiders. But Meredith's strongpoint went unchallenged to the end of the war. Forrest did come back to the region one more time, riding up from Tennessee to remote, abandoned Fort Heiman, where he briefly wreaked havoc on the Tennessee River.[49]

Paine came and saw but failed to vanquish secessionism in the Purchase with his salvation plan. Despite Meredith's evidently gentler rule, most citizens clung to their Rebel ways. Smugglers still plied their illicit trade with the South. Guerrillas still scourged the countryside where they were harbored, or at least tolerated, by a populace bitterly hostile toward all things Union.

13

Rebel to the End and Beyond

By the fall of 1864, even the most diehard of Purchase secessionists surely knew that Confederate defeat was almost certain. Forrest boosted their spirits again, but only fleetingly, by occupying Fort Heiman in remote southeastern Calloway County and shooting up Yankee boats on the Tennessee River. He soon headed upriver to shell and burn the big Union supply depot at Johnsonville, Tennessee. Like his Paducah raid, Forrest's foray grabbed newspaper headlines but did not change the war's inevitable outcome. Nor did the Purchase vote have any effect on the presidential election. Paine was court-martialed in early 1865 but was acquitted on all but a minor charge; his punishment was a reprimand in general orders. Secessionists—and conservative Unionists—charged that he had literally gotten away with murder. Gradually, the guerrilla warfare that had plagued the Purchase for many months petered out, and spring brought Confederate defeat.

Though Paine was finished in the Purchase, Judge Williams pleaded the general's case in an October 3 letter to the president that mostly focused on the election. Paine "may have done some indefensible things," Williams conceded. But he suspected "the Copperheads have greatly exaggerated" the general's alleged misdeeds. At the same time, Williams far overstated Lincoln's chances in the Bluegrass State: "Let me assure you that our prospects are daily brightening and we have a constant increase in Kentucky." Williams piled on the flattery, too, declaring, "This is a triumph solely attributable to your greatness and goodness, and in some measure a reward to your single devotedness to our nationality." He favorably compared Lincoln to George Washington and to Andrew Jackson, adding, "If impartial history has written that Washington was the father of his Country, this same history shall write Lincoln its preserver." He was right that Lincoln would also go down in history as a hero, alongside Washington. But he was dead wrong about Lincoln and Kentucky in 1864. Nonetheless, the judge added, "Thousands like myself yield you unqualified support, and other thousands will yet do so in Kentucky: that we have great reason to hope and believe Kentucky will go for you in November." He told the president that the McClellan partisans lacked enthusiasm and that "a very large portion of the conservative Union men" really felt they were "not discharging their duty to the Country by" backing the general. Either Williams was just telling Lincoln what he thought the president wanted to hear, or he woefully misunderstood political realities in Kentucky. The state was majority pro-Union, but neither pro-Lincoln nor antislavery.[1]

In an October 17 letter to the president, Anderson also tried to curry Lincoln's favor. The congressman had made three pro-Lincoln speeches in three Purchase counties, in keeping with Meredith's conciliatory policy. Anderson did not mention Paine; he mostly stuck to political prognosticating and military matters. He said the people had listened attentively to his remarks, "and they *profess to be all right* in many places," including his hometown, where he thought "they intend to do right," meaning vote for Lincoln. But the congressman could not resist a backhanded swipe at Meredith, informing the president that Union troops had just been withdrawn from Mayfield, thus leaving the Purchase counties vulnerable to Rebel and guerrilla control. Anderson warned that "unless these Counties are held of course no votes will be polled." Anderson assured Lincoln that Meredith said he would reoccupy Mayfield "in a few days." But, according to the congressman, Meredith said "his forces are not sufficient to hold beyond a doubt the whole of these Counties therefore he desires more troops immediately." Anderson hoped Meredith would get reinforcements and declared, "the whole district shall be canvassed if tis possible to do so, nothing, on my part, shall be wanting." He also hoped Kentucky would "do her duty in this contest," but he confessed, "I am not however sanguine." Should Kentucky go against Lincoln, Anderson said, "it will not be the fault of the *true men* of the state," meaning, of course, men like him.[2]

Lieutenant General Nathan Bedford Forrest of Tennessee was among men anywhere who were the least true to the Union, according to Lucian Anderson. In October 1864, Forrest and his cavalry army rode toward the Purchase for the last time. Paducah was not his target; he aimed to disrupt Yankee shipping on the Tennessee River, a major supply line to Sherman's army marching through Georgia. To that end, Forrest sneaked off to abandoned Fort Heiman and hid artillery batteries at the old earthworks and at Paris Landing, Tennessee, a short distance upriver. "The Federals were in perfect ignorance of this formidable force, so well located to destroy their boats and obstruct the commerce of the river," George wrote. Long gone from Heiman's heights were the troopers of the Fifth Iowa Cavalry Regiment, who had occupied the fort from February 1862, when Fort Henry and nearby Fort Donelson fell, to March 1863. The blue-clad horsemen mostly patrolled, guarded the river, and skirmished with small guerrilla bands. But their bane was a solitary sniper named Jack Hinson, a civilian who waged a one-man war of revenge against the Yankees. According to the story, Hinson started his vendetta because Colonel W. W. Lowe, the regiment's commander, had two of Hinson's sons hanged as bushwhackers. Armed with a deadly accurate rifle that weighed more than seventeen pounds, Hinson would hide in the woods and pick off Yankee soldiers. Or he would build duck blinds from which to shoot boat pilots or other officers on the Tennessee. He filed thirty-six notches on his rifle—each for a man killed—and was never caught. A state historical marker on US Highway 68 in Land Between the Lakes commemorates Hinson's bloody work.[3]

Hinson might have enjoyed sinking Yankee boats, but that pleasure was Forrest's. Early on October 29, his gunners at Fort Heiman made short work of the *Mazeppa.* The steamer, with a pair of barges in tow, was apparently bound for Johnsonville, Tennessee, the big Union supply base that topped Forrest's target list. The shot-up transport managed to land on the Tennessee side of the river, "where she was abandoned by the crew and passengers who fled into the woods," Forrest reported. He added that some of his men fashioned a hawser and pulled the boat over to them. The happy Confederates found the *Mazeppa* laden with "blankets, shoes, clothing, hard bread, &c.," according to their commander. The beleaguered boat also carried a bottle of red whiskey. Brigadier Buford claimed the sauce for himself, good-naturedly chiding his thirsty troops: "Plenty of meat, boys, plenty of hardtack, shoes and clothes—all for the boys, but enough whiskey for the General."[4]

In his report, Forrest did not say who crossed the river to capture the *Mazeppa.* George's book says it was Captain Frank P. Gracey of Hopkinsville, formerly of the Eighth Kentucky, though the captain evidently was from Eddyville. In any event, his willing but unsuccessful helpers were Captain H. Clay Horn and Lieutenant Ed Ross, both of the Third Kentucky. There was no boat at Fort Heiman, so Gracey, Horn, and Ross fashioned "an improvised catamaran." But the craft came apart near shore, dunking the trio. Undaunted, Gracey stripped off his wet clothes, draped his duds and pistols around his neck, flung one arm over one of the parted logs, and with his free arm paddled toward the *Mazeppa.* Gracey forced the skipper to surrender and ordered him to send over a small boat to bring back other Rebel soldiers. Thus "by means of ropes" the Confederates hauled the boat to Fort Heiman. However, the arrival of a trio of Union navy gunboats interrupted the plunder. They opened fire, forcing Forrest's men to scramble for cover. Fearing the Yankees might recapture the *Mazeppa,* Buford ordered the vessel and, apparently, the barges burned.[5]

The next day, it looked like Forrest's gunners would also bag the steamer

Anna, heading downriver. Buford wanted the boat intact, and after the Rebels fired on the *Anna,* the captain agreed to surrender. But it was a ruse. When the ecstatic artillerymen forsook their guns and ran toward the river and their prize, the skipper made a run for it and got away before they could get back to their guns in the fort.[6]

Buford was crestfallen over the *Anna*'s escape. The general supposedly figured booze might be aboard. Crossland recalled that when the steamer headed toward Heiman, "Buford threw his tobacco out and walked down to receive her." But when the *Anna* suddenly made haste for Paducah, "he yelled at the top of his voice, which was almost equal to a lion's, 'Shoot h—l out of her.'"[7]

Forrest's cannon crews did not have long to wait for other victims: the transports *Venus* and *J. W. Cheeseman,* escorted by the gunboat *Undine.* The Rebel batteries disabled the two boats, plus the *J. W. Cheeseman,* which was pushing a pair of barges. The Confederates captured all three boats, but the *Cheeseman* was so badly damaged that Forrest burned it and the two barges. He turned the *Venus* and the *Undine* into his short-lived "Forrest Fleet." The general wanted to use the captured vessels to lure the Yankee gunboats from Johnsonville so his gunners could destroy the depot from across the river. On November 1, Forrest headed toward his objective, his troops moving down the riverbank, his "sailors" floating on the captured boats. The next day, a pair of Union gunboats got the drop on the *Undine,* forcing the Confederates to beach and burn the boat. The *Venus* tried to flee, but the Yankees bagged it, although not for long. On November 4, Forrest shelled Johnsonville from the Tennessee's west bank, heavily damaging the depot and destroying warehouses and several boats and barges moored at the waterfront, including the *Venus.*[8]

Forrest's raid made a minor splash in Yankee newspapers, but the big headlines belonged to Lincoln after November 8, when the voters rewarded the president with a second term. He easily defeated McClellan, who nonetheless carried Kentucky by a wide margin, 64,301 to 27,787. To be sure, Lincoln fared considerably better in his native state than he had in 1860. But his total amounted to just 30.2 percent of the votes cast. Percentage-wise, Kentucky was Lincoln's worst state.[9]

Union authorities had desperately wanted Kentucky in the Lincoln column. Burbridge considered "it of the utmost importance for Kentucky's future that the State should be carried for Mr. Lincoln." The general tried his best to win votes for Lincoln, employing old-fashioned patronage and "honorably" granting favors. "A further stratagem to be worked would be to send into the state claim commissioners to begin settling with" Unionist slave owners whose bondsmen were in the federal forces and have the commissioners "work until after the election, at least." Of course, the implication would be that a vote for Lincoln meant compensation for lost slaves, while a McClellan vote did not. Republican-tilting Reverend Robert J. Breckinridge had a different idea: nobody would get paid "until after the election, and . . . only Lincoln voters would be paid at all." Another incentive was employed: "Only those supporting Lincoln would be given the trade permit, which was required by military authorities to carry on trade." Burbridge also suggested, "With a judicious disposition of the troops the state may be carried for Lincoln." In any event, fifty-four thousand fewer ballots were cast in 1864 than in 1860. The depressed vote also reflected "the great demoralization which prevailed in the state." Military heavy-handedness was not as widespread as it had been in previous elections, but some of the falling off was the result of intimidation by soldiers.[10]

Indeed, in the Purchase, only 4,097 of 13,721 potential voters—less than 30 percent—went to the polls; Calloway County reported no returns. The statewide percentage was 40.5. McClellan managed to edge Lincoln in the Purchase, 2,064 to 2,033. Lincoln carried Fulton, Hickman, Marshall, and McCracken Counties. The Lincoln vote in the Purchase was a huge improvement over 1860, when he managed merely 10 votes in the territory. Yet the presence of Union troops probably boosted the president's total. Also, he ran on the Union ticket, not as a Republican. There were other incentives, according to the *Journal*: "At three different places in the district, Anderson and Bolinger addressed the people and told them, that, if they did not vote for Lincoln, they would be granted no privileges, would not be allowed to trade, their property would be taken, and they would be reduced to beggary and starving conditions." Did Williams and others make similar speeches? Did Union army newspapers at Columbus and Paducah so editorialize for Lincoln?[11]

The Lincoln vote was so small in Kentucky because the president had made the Civil War a conflict to save the Union and destroy slavery. Most Kentuckians were for the Union and slavery. But time was fast running out on the South's peculiar institution. On April 8, 1864, the Republican-controlled Senate mustered the requisite two-thirds majority to approve the Thirteenth Amendment to the constitution, which outlawed slavery. Kentucky's Democratic senators, Garrett Davis and Lazarus W. Powell, voted "no." The Republican House finally overcame Democratic opposition, achieved a two-thirds majority, and concurred with the Senate on January 31, 1865. Anderson and three other Bluegrass State congressmen—William H. Randall, Green Clay Smith, and George H. Yeaman—voted "aye." The remaining five Kentucky representatives voted "nay."[12]

Anderson's vote made him even more of a pariah in the Purchase, where Forrest's Kentucky troops were enjoying what would be their last leave before the war ended. "From the 12th of November to the 27th of December Forrest's men had been constantly marching and fighting, a large part of the time without food for themselves or feed for their horses," George wrote. "The men were exhausted and the horses so jaded that they were useless. It was plain that the men and horses must have some rest before they would be in any sort of condition for service." So Forrest sent them home for twenty days to visit their loved ones and get new clothes and fresh horses. Most of the men were able to bask "in the smiles of their relations and friends." Others kept watch for the Yankees, who were still concentrated at Paducah and Columbus. "They made some demonstration in small force for the purpose of holding the Federals close to their bases, so they would not interfere with those enjoying their vacation," which George said lasted about two weeks.[13]

Evidently, some of the Confederates decided to take a permanent hiatus from fighting Yankees. On February 5, the *Journal* reported that Faulkner's Twelfth Kentucky, "through the vicissitudes of war," was down to a mere 150 men. Quoting the *Cairo News* of February 1, the Louisville paper claimed several of his men had deserted and gone home. Others had crossed Yankee lines and sworn allegiance to the Union, but only to get supplies before returning "to their old friends." Even so, the fight seemed to be going out of the greatly depleted regiment. The Cairo paper said Faulkner's men had "lately bothered no one," except for stealing horses and feed. "In several cases they have swapped old boots and dilapidated hats with the unwilling customers, and at other times they have paid the difference in greenbacks." Too, Faulkner's troops claimed, "they are as bitter against the guerrillas as the Federals and that they will hang them if they fall into their clutches." Yet Faulkner acted like a guerrilla in Blandville on January 29, when he forced a civilian to exchange his coat, hat, and boots with him at the point of a Colt Navy revolver. The Cairo paper suggested that soon Faulkner would take his men south, thus ridding the region "of these young but desperate cavaliers. While they infested the country they had some gay times, always finding themselves present if there was a party given in the neighborhood they infested."[14]

The Rebels' disdain for guerrillas might have been a ruse. On the night of February 7, some Confederate regulars—perhaps part of Forrest's men on leave—showed up at Columbus bearing a flag of truce. They said they wanted to cooperate with the Yankees in fighting guerrillas, the February 12 *Journal* reported, citing a February 11 story in the *Cairo News* that had Colonel Hicks in command at Columbus. Hicks suspected a trick and, "equal to the emergency, at once worked out a plan to gobble the 'Johnnies.'" Hicks heard that about 150 Rebels were camped about a dozen miles east of Columbus, near Clinton. That same night, he ordered Major William N. Lansing and about 150 men of the Fourth Heavy Artillery, acting as infantry, to go get them. Lansing and his little force boarded a train toward Clinton, disembarked about five miles from town, and proceeded cautiously in the darkness. As they neared the camp, the Rebel pickets fired, then "fled in confusion." The Yankees pressed the enemy, who took refuge in "a small fort or stockade" and "opened a vigorous fire." A charge forced the Rebels to quickly decamp in "a grand skeddale." The cannoneers-turned-infantrymen dispatched two Rebels and captured a lieutenant, a sergeant, eleven men, and a dozen "good horses." The rest of the Confederates reached their horses and galloped away. "It was deemed useless to follow them with infantry," the *Journal* explained. "One of the men killed was named Moss, and is said to be well known about Columbus, as is also the Lieutenant, whose name is Welch." The Union side suffered no casualties and was back in Columbus by 7:00 a.m. the next day.[15]

Their leave up, the Purchase Confederates who stayed in the army again forsook their homes, assembling at Clinton, Dukedom, Dresden, and other points in preparation for a southerly move. It would be Faulkner's last rendezvous. At Dresden, the colonel gathered his men, plus some recruits who included two McDougal brothers, one of whom had been a guerrilla leader. Allegedly, Faulkner promised the McDougals that if they would join his regiment, they would not be arrested "or otherwise be molested for any misdoings that might be drawn up against them," George remembered. When Faulkner told the brothers to hand over their weapons, they "commenced firing on the colonel, and did not stop until he was dead." George added that "there seems to have been no effort on the part of Faulkner's men to protect him, owing to the alleged fact that the McDougals had more friends in the regiment than had the colonel." Faulkner, George conceded, "was a courageous, dashing soldier, but for some reason did not seem to be popular with his men."[16]

At least one of the McDougals evidently got his comeuppance in a March skirmish with Union troops. Both he and the captain commanding the federal force died in the gunfight. Union authorities described the slain Yankee officer as "gallant." Fyfe said he "was one of the bravest & most fearless defenders of his county." The dead man was Thomas J. Gregory. Like much of his life, his demise is shrouded in mystery and misinformation. Gregory's battalion had mustered out of federal service on February 12, 1865, yet he was still a captain leading troops. According to *History of Kentucky,* his life ended on March 29 in "a desperate fight" with guerrillas "30 miles from Paducah." The April 4, 1865, *Frankfort Commonwealth* said Gregory died on March 22, identifying him as "Capt. Gregory . . . formerly of the 3d Battalion, Capital Guards." The paper said he had gone guerrilla hunting with a twenty-two-man company "at the solicitations of Gen. Meredith and citizens of Paducah." Gregory encountered McDougal's bunch—fifty-five to sixty strong—at Thomas Hayden's Hickman County home, about "thirty five miles south of Paducah." After detailing five men to guard the horses, Gregory and the rest surrounded the house. The captain broke down the door with the butt of a Spencer carbine, rushed inside, and shot McDougal dead. Gregory "was himself fired upon and instantly killed." His men avenged the captain's death by "wrenching the pistols from the hands of the guerrillas and firing upon them with their own weapons." They dispatched a half dozen of the foe and wounded twenty more, "most of them mortally." The rest of the band got away but forsook "forty horses and sixty guns and pistols, together with a number of blankets, hats caps &c." On the Union side, nobody was wounded, but John Ramsey also perished. Like Gregory, he had been in the Twentieth Kentucky Infantry. "The loss of Capt. Gregory is much lamented," the paper said. "He has proved himself an officer of great ability, both for his fighting and administrative qualities." The *Commonwealth* claimed Gregory "was also a conscientious and accomplished gentleman, and stood firmly by his state and country while most of his friends were seduced into the rebellion." The paper added, "He has suffered greatly from guerrillas by reason of his patriotism, almost all of his property having been destroyed, and a brother and sister murdered by the miscreants." The paper insisted that "he was never actuated by feelings of revenge in his treatment of them" but that "his death was well and terribly avenged by his men." The *Commonwealth* noted that Gregory was a Graves countian and that McDougal was "a great scoundrel, having served four years in the Penitentiary." He had been "the terror of South Western Kentucky and Western Tennessee." Nurse Fyfe mourned Gregory's death. "All much deplore his loss," she wrote home.[17]

Few Paducah citizens were among Fyfe's "all." But most of them probably were glad to see Gregory's friend Paine back in town in February and March to face a court-martial. The *Journal* suspected a whitewash, citing "a letter from a gallant officer at Paducah, who is very familiar with General Paine's case." The letter alleged that Judge Advocate General Holt had sent to Paducah a list of charges on which Paine would be tried. Holt omitted "those two very ugly ones": that Paine had personally ordered the execution of a soldier and a civilian without trial and that the general on "his own authority . . . levied various sums, from $1,000 up to $10,000, upon men and women in Paducah and its vicinity." Holt also left out other charges "that could easily be proved" and left in only those that could be easily refuted, the letter said. Its author also claimed that "the important witnesses for the prosecution are away—*why* he knows not, and that a very strong outside pressure is brought to bear." Further, the letter said Paine's friends were bragging that he "would be reinstated in thirty days and that his enemies will have need to look to themselves." The *Journal* declared that if the correspondent was telling the truth, Paine's "trial, so called, is a cheat, an imposition, a humbug."[18]

Eight days later, the *Journal* went after Holt, again citing the two charges he had allegedly dropped. But first came the praise; the paper had long "thought exceedingly well" of him. Holt "seemed . . . eminently patriotic." But his ardent unionism included "a pretty strong tendency to radicalism." The *Journal* elaborated on the omitted extortion charge, claiming the payoffs were also "the only means of escaping a far severer punishment—probably death." The *Journal* wanted to know why Holt had quashed the two charges but added, "we shall sincerely and heartily rejoice if satisfactory answers can be made to these questions." The paper got off a parting shot: "We expect General Paine's dishonorable dismission from the service but not upon the worst charges proved on him."[19]

Holt's alleged omission aside, Paine faced twenty-five charges, ranging from abuse of power and corruption to extortion and oppression. Paine vehemently denied them all. He claimed he was a victim of the everlasting hostility of Rebel sympathizers that began the day he arrived in Paducah. He said he was forced to deal with hypocrites, perjurers, and traitors, adding that if any place merited martial law it was the Purchase. An attorney before the war, Paine addressed every charge with lawyerly skill and, in the end, was acquitted of all charges save one, publicly denouncing his superior officer, meaning General Halleck. His punishment was a reprimand in general orders, though Stanton did not make public the detailed findings of the court-martial until November 5, 1865, and the secretary left out Paine's "shamefully inadequate sentence," Richard Collins wrote in *History of Kentucky*. Elsewhere in his book, Collins started the anti-Paine ball rolling among historians, accusing the general of "a fifty-one days reign of violence, terror, rapine, extortion, oppression, bribery, and military murders."[20]

Most Purchase historians still demonize Paine, but Dieter Ullrich of Murray State University is not among them. "Paine certainly was no saint, but he was far from the devil," says Ullrich, head of the Forrest C. Pogue Special Collections Library. Ullrich has mined multiple primary sources connected to Paine's Purchase tenure. His research led him to conclude that the local animus toward Paine was largely rooted in the general's staunchly abolitionist views, in his support for the enlistment of African Americans into the Union forces, and in his belief in black equality with whites. Too, Paine made no bones about equating all but unconditional Unionism with treason.[21]

Ullrich points out that Paine remained popular with the staunchest of native Purchase Unionists—starting with Anderson—and the soldiers who served under him. Ullrich also notes that Paine seemed to relish "the headlines he received in the North as being feared and despised by Rebels and southern sympathizers." Yet Ullrich adds that Kentucky's conservative Unionist leadership and press, notably Governor Bramlette and editor George D. Prentice of the *Journal,* set the stage for Paine's downfall and demonization by Collins and subsequent historians: "This image was magnified after the war and became embedded in local culture and in history books. However, the facts have been greatly distorted and the man's name severely and unfairly tarnished. Proof can be seen in his court-martial records and in the diaries and letters from Union soldiers. Many of these documents have only recently come to light, and more will follow as technology opens new avenues to researchers. Like I've told my friends in the Sons of Confederate Veterans—keep an open mind, and search for the truth."[22]

Though Paine was exonerated, his military career ended at Paducah. Following his removal, his status was "awaiting orders" until he finally tendered his resignation, which the army accepted to date from April 5, 1865. He resumed his law practice in Illinois and died in New Jersey in 1882. Paine was sixty-seven.[23]

By the time Paine quit the army, even the most zealous Rebels surely knew the Confederacy would collapse in weeks, if not days. On April 3, Richmond fell to Grant's seemingly unstoppable Union forces. Six days later, Lee gave up to Grant at Appomattox Court House. Other surrenders, large and small, rapidly followed. On April 22, a little over a year after Buford's raid, another Confederate force returned to Paducah, but to capitulate. Four hundred men and officers under the command of Brigadier General Hylan B. Lyon of Eddyville surrendered and swore the loyalty oath, the *Journal* reported. "Gangs of rebel deserters, numbering from twenty to two hundred, daily arrive at the various Federal posts along the lower Ohio and Mississippi and give themselves up and renew their allegiance to the government."[24]

The Second Kentucky Infantry, which included volunteers from Graves and Hickman Counties and was exchanged after its capture at Fort Donelson, fought through the war in the famous Kentucky "Orphan Brigade" of the Army of Tennessee, which Sherman and his Army of the Tennessee—Grant's old command—finally ran to ground near Durham, North Carolina. General Joseph E. Johnston surrendered the Army of Tennessee on April 26. The majority of Purchase Rebels ended up with Forrest, who held out until May 9. He capitulated at Gainesville, Alabama. George wrote: "The end was not unexpected to those who cared to keep up with events. Lee had been crushed by overwhelming numbers; Johnston was being driven from pillar to post, with no more places to fall back upon; the Mississippi and Trans-Mississippi departments had been worn to a frazzle; there was no base of supplies, and in fact no army to supply. The strange thing is that the end did not come sooner."[25]

An untold number of Purchase men who donned Rebel gray or Yankee blue did not come home. How many succumbed to death from battle wounds or disease is almost impossible to say. But several Confederates who survived America's bloodiest conflict became important political leaders and successful business owners and farmers. "For years after the Civil War, a candidate for political office in our part of Kentucky who had not had at least one limb shot off while fighting for the Confederacy might as well have whistled down a rain barrel," Graves County–born Vice President Alben Barkley of Paducah wrote in *That Reminds Me,* his folksy 1954 autobiography.[26]

The first postwar election in Kentucky came in August 1865. The canvass pitted the Conservatives, or Democrats, against the Radicals, who were Republicans. Ex-Confederate soldiers and known or suspected guerrillas and Rebel sympathizers were not yet allowed to vote. Nonetheless, Thomas H. Corbett and Willis R. Bradley, whose pro-Confederate views were hardly a secret, won state house seats from Ballard and Hickman Counties, respectively. Statewide, the Conservatives won a close majority over the Radicals in the state house and senate.[27]

None of the Purchase Unionists elected to the state house and senate in 1863 returned to Frankfort for additional terms. Facing almost certain defeat, Republican Anderson, though he was not charged in connection with Paine's alleged crimes, chose not to run for Congress. His old nemesis Trimble, stumping the district on the Conservative ticket, replaced him. Trimble beat Radical C. D. Bradley of Cadiz, 5,749 to 3,542. But Anderson did not fade into obscurity. In 1882, he and J. N. Beadles, his old Unionist comrade, organized the Bank of Mayfield. Anderson was president and Beadles cashier. Gradually, enmity toward Anderson faded. When he died in 1896 at age seventy-four, the *Mayfield Monitor* remembered the old abolitionist as one of the town's "most noted citizens." The paper was confident that Anderson's "many friends will mourn his death, even though it comes after he lived more than the allotted three score and ten."[28]

Starting in 1871, a raft of Democrats and ex-Rebels from the Purchase followed Trimble to Washington. Edward Crossland of Columbus, a former Seventh Kentucky colonel, served from 1871 to 1875. Andrew R. Boone of Mayfield came next. The Unionist-majority state house had expelled him in 1861 for helping organize Kentucky's rump Rebel government at Russellville.

Oscar Turner of Ballard County, who pushed for Purchase secession from Kentucky in 1861, followed Boone. His tenure stretched to 1885; Turner served as a Democrat and Independent Democrat.

Likewise, Confederate veterans were conspicuous in postwar Purchase delegations in the state legislature. They included state senators G. A. C. Holt, a former colonel of the Third Kentucky; Captain William Lindsey, also of the Third Kentucky; and Major Henry S. Hale, late of the Seventh Kentucky. In addition, Jesse C. Gilbert, who was also booted from the house for going to the Russellville convention, was a senator. So was Henry A. Tyler of Fulton County, late of the Twelfth Kentucky. Too, voters elevated to the house Ervin Anderson, Lucian's secessionist brother, and Francis U. Dodds, a Calloway delegate at the Russellville convention.[29]

Even after the Old Johnnies retired from business, farming, and politics or died, their descendants and admirers did not forget them. Besides the courthouse monuments and cemetery gates, Tilghman got a bronze statue in Paducah, where the city's high school was named for the general's family. Tilghman's home is preserved as a Civil War museum.

Almost a century and a half since the war ended, it is impossible to determine precisely how many Purchase men donned Rebel gray and Yankee blue. But close to 5,000 volunteers from Ballard, Calloway, Fulton, Graves, Hickman, Marshall, and McCracken Counties enlisted in the Confederate forces. In their book *A New History of Kentucky,* historians Lowell H. Harrison and James C. Klotter estimate that between 25,000 and 40,000 Kentuckians were Confederate soldiers. Based on those totals, the seven-county Purchase accounted for between 12.5 and 20 percent of all Rebel volunteers from the state.[30]

In addition, Harrison and Klotter write that Kentucky supplied between 90,000 and 100,000 men to the Union side. From the Purchase, approximately 600 white and 250 African American soldiers served in the Union forces. The numbers are approximations, because in military records, the federal numbers are expressed as enlistments, not as individual soldiers. For example, if a man volunteered for a year's service then signed up for a three-year hitch, he would be counted as two enlistments. Probably the best record of county-by-county enlistment totals is contained in Kentucky inspector and adjutant general D. W. Lindsey's March 1, 1865, report to the legislature on Union enlistments through December 31, 1864. Few troops were raised after that point. In 1865 and 1866, the state published Lindsey's *Report of the Adjutant General of the State of Kentucky, 1861–1865.* The two-volume report contains the names of all Kentuckians, white and African American, who were known to have served in the army or in home guard or militia units. But in most cases, it lists soldiers by unit and place of enlistment. Hence, a soldier from one county might be shown as signing up someplace else. In 1915, the state published Adjutant General J. Tandy Ellis's *Report of the Adjutant General of the State of Kentucky Confederate Volunteers War 1861.* Like Lindsey's report, it is a two-volume work and lists soldiers by unit and place of enlistment, not by county of residence.

Based on available records, Graves and McCracken Counties between them probably contributed about 2,200 volunteers to the Confederacy. Lindsey's 1865 report credits Graves with 156 white and 89 black enlistments. The McCracken totals are 88 whites and 112 African Americans. In terms of troops sent off to war, Marshall was the most closely divided Purchase county. About 500 Marshall men joined the Confederate forces; on the Union side, 221 white and 7 black enlistments were recorded. About 400 Rebels left Fulton County to fight for the Confederates, but only one county resident—Joseph Dougal, a white man—enlisted in the Union ranks. The numbers were almost as lopsided in Hickman County, from which 600 or more men wore Rebel gray. Federal enlistments numbered 11 whites and 5 African Americans. Together, Ballard and Calloway Counties were home to approximately 1,200 Rebels. Ballard had 124 white and 34 black Union enlistments. The Calloway total was 49 whites and 4 African Americans. In every other Kentucky region, Union soldiers outnumbered Confederates to one extent or another. Beyond the Purchase, Rebels significantly outnumbered Yankees in only a handful of counties.[31]

While the Purchase was Kentucky's only Rebel region during the Civil War, most of the rest of the state moved toward the Purchase perspective following the Emancipation Proclamation and the enlistment of African American soldiers, both of which almost every white Kentuckian bitterly opposed. The shift became even more pronounced following Confederate surrender. Coulter famously writes that Kentucky "as was often remarked at the time . . . waited until after the war to secede." Historian Anne E. Marshall writes that "this outward incongruity between the way white Kentuckians entered and participated in the Civil War and the way they remembered it has become one of the great paradoxes of Civil War history." The paradox was not lost on never-say-die Unionists. "The 'Lost Cause' is found again in Kentucky," the *Frankfort Commonwealth* complained. William O. Goodloe, editor of the secessionist-turned-Republican *Lexington Statesman*, cried out in anger, "What [Confederate general] Bragg failed to do in 1862, with his army and banners, the people of Kentucky, five years later, have done; they have given the State over into the hands of those who are and have been the enemies of the Union." Another Republican lamented, "Kentucky is today as effectually in the hands of rebels as if they had every town and city garrisoned by their troops. . . . What is to become of the poor blacks and loyal white men God only knows." African Americans would suffer as second-class citizens for a century; most white Republicans would be marginalized for many years. Kentucky would become the northern border of the white-supremacist Democratic, Jim Crow "Solid South."[32]

Doubtless many visitors to Kentucky—and Kentuckians who do not know their history—get the impression that the Bluegrass State was part and parcel of the Confederacy. Even beyond the Purchase, Confederate memorials sprout from courthouse lawns and other public spaces, even in solidly Unionist Louisville. Rebel battle flags fly over many dwellings, from the humblest to the grandest, even in counties that were firmly pro-Union in 1861–65. From Paducah to Pikeville, too, Confederate flags appear on bumper stickers and novelty front license plates on dozens of cars and trucks. Everywhere in Kentucky, Sons of Confederate Veterans chapters probably far outnumber Sons of Union Veterans (SUV) chapters, or at least these descendants of Kentucky Rebels are more visible than Kentuckians who belong to SUV groups. In some cases, Kentuckians disown their Yankee ancestors. When told he had a staunchly Unionist forebear, a Graves countian declared, "I wouldn't claim him." He was only half joking. Kentucky Civil War reenactors in gray far outnumber those in blue. Had such an imbalance prevailed in 1861, Kentucky would have almost certainly seceded. Despite such ostentatious displays of Confederate symbolism and apparent widespread reverence for the "Lost Cause," the fact remains that the Purchase was the only region of Kentucky where secessionism prevailed in the heyday of real Johnny Rebs and genuine Billy Yanks.

Acknowledgments

Hillary Clinton famously observed that "it takes a village to raise a child." It does with a book, too. Though my byline is on this book, I could not have written it alone. I am indebted to Melinda Hocker Craig, my wife, best friend, and senior English teacher at Mayfield High School, for diligently proofreading the manuscript and to our son, Berry Craig IV, for helping his technologically challenged father use a computer to write a book. I have cited works by several historians, but Alan Bearman, Patricia Ann Hoskins, and Dieter Ullrich merit special mention for their outstanding research, which has helped me present what I hope is a fresh perspective on the Jackson Purchase's unique role in the Civil War. Ullrich, head of the Forrest C. Pogue Special Collections Library at Murray State University, also went well above and beyond the call of his duties in assisting me with my research. I am also grateful to Carol Sickman-Garner for her outstanding copyediting, to LaDonna Hamontree and Cynthia Barnes of the Pogue staff, to Pogue student worker Christie Leith, and to student worker Jackie Reed. Others who came to my aid include Ken Bradshaw, director, and Anita Weathers, interlibrary loan specialist, both at the West Kentucky Community and Technical College Library; Nathan Lynn, Lana Ashley, Jay Hite, Matt Jaeger, and Eileen Smith, all of the McCracken County Public Library; Dena Gschwind of the Graves County Public Library; Molly Kodner of the Missouri Historical Society; David Kirkpatrick of the Kentucky Department of Libraries and Archives; Jackie Penny and Vincent Golden, both of the American Antiquarian Society; Cindy Lynch, manager of Columbus-Belmont State Park; Jennifer Cole of the Filson Historical Society; Jennifer Duplaga of the Kentucky Historical Society; Martha Nell Anderson, of Mayfield, Kentucky; Eli Riveire Warner of the Lexington, Kentucky, Public Library; John Trowbridge of the Kentucky National Guard; Richard Davis of Heath, Kentucky; Thomas Lannom of Portland, Oregon; and Donna D'Angelo of the Murray State University Waterfield Library.

Notes

Introduction

1. Darrell Haug Davis, *The Geography of the Jackson Purchase: A Study of the Distribution and Activities of Man in the Gulf Embayment Area of Western Kentucky* (Frankfort: Kentucky Geological Survey, 1923), 1. In 1861–65, the Purchase consisted of Ballard, Calloway, Fulton, Graves, Hickman, Marshall, and McCracken Counties. The legislature carved Carlisle County from the southern part of Ballard County in 1886. Supposedly, the sweet smell of sizzling bacon and eggs led to the county's creation. Speaker Charles Offutt purportedly promised not to adjourn the state house of representatives for lunch until lawmakers approved the Carlisle County bill. One legislator questioned the necessity of marking off yet another county. The midday repast time was approaching, and Offutt evidently knew the doubting solon was accustomed to eating his main meal at noontime. In any event, the lawmaker supposedly capitulated when Offutt started frying the bacon and eggs on a portable stove he had a page lug into the house chamber. The house promptly voted Carlisle into the commonwealth, and Offutt dismissed legislators for a late feed. See Berry Craig, *True Tales of Old-Time Kentucky Politics: Bombast, Bourbon and Burgoo* (Charleston, S.C.: History Press, 2009), 114.

2. J. H. Battle, W. H. Perrin, and G. C. Kniffen, *Kentucky: A History of the State,* 1st ed. (Louisville and Chicago: F. A. Battey and Co., 1885), 7. Paducah, the region's principal town, was "the Charleston of Kentucky," according to Battle, Perrin, and Kniffen.

3. Hall Allen, "The Reluctant Kentuckians," *Jackson Purchase 150 Years, 1819–1969, Sesquicentennial. Prepared by the Jackson Purchase Historical Society and Published by the Mayfield Messenger, Mayfield, Ky.*, section E, 11. The paper published the bound work in newspaper form. Allen's article was based on speeches he gave to the Filson Club in Louisville and at the Jackson Purchase Historical Society, along with additional material.

4. Ibid.

5. Battle, Perrin, and Kniffen, *Kentucky,* 6–7.

6. Hall Allen also wrote that the idea of Purchase secession and union with West Tennessee surfaced again after the war was over: "In 1873 newspapers at Memphis and other West Tennessee towns started an agitation toward secession, and proposed a state that would contain not only the Jackson Purchase areas of the two states but a section of northern Alabama as well. This time we almost reached immortality in song. I assume that no one in the good year 1968 is a stranger to the so-called popular song, 'Ode to Billie Jo.' It's all about somebody throwing something off the Tallahatchie bridge. For your information, the composer, one Bobbye Gentry has said that whatever you thought was thrown off the bridge probably wasn't so, for Billie Jo was not that kind of girl. Well, this proposed new state would have had as part of its southern boundary, the Tallahatchie River" ("Reluctant Kentuckians," E11).

7. Jasper B. Shannon and Ruth McQuown, *Presidential Politics in Kentucky, 1824–1948: A Compilation of Election Statistics and an Analysis of Political Behavior* (Lexington: Bureau of Government Research, College of Arts and Sciences, University of Kentucky, 1950), 35–36.

8. Henry George, *History of the 3d, 7th, 8th and 12th Kentucky, C.S.A.* (Louisville: Dearing Press, 1911), 175, 182.

9. Davis, *Geography of the Jackson Purchase,* 1.

10. A dearth of primary sources, compared to other parts of Kentucky, makes it difficult to fully flesh out the deep Confederate sentiment that set the region apart from Kentucky, especially in 1861. No copies of the region's newspapers are known to exist. However, the *Louisville Daily Courier,* the state's most important pro-Confederate paper, frequently published excerpts from them. Rare, too, are letters and diaries written by leading secessionists. Also missing are the official minutes of the Mayfield convention, possibly because of subsequent Graves County courthouse fires.

11. See Kendall D. Gott, *Where the South Lost the War: An Analysis of the Fort Henry–Fort Donelson Campaign, February 1862* (Mechanicsburg, Pa.: Stackpole Books, 2003).

12. Lewis Collins and Richard Collins, *History of Kentucky: By the Late Lewis Collins, Judge of the Mason County Court, Revised, Enlarged Four-Fold and Brought Down to the Year 1874, by his son, Richard H. Collins, A.M, LL.B. Embracing Pre-Historic Annals for 331 Years, Outline, and by Counties, Statistics, Antiquities, and Natural Curiosities, Geographical and Geological Descriptions, Sketches of the Court of Appeals, the Churches, Freemasonry, Odd Fellowship, and Internal Improvements, Incidents of Pioneer Life, and Nearly Five Hundred Biographical Sketches of Distinguished Pioneers, Soldiers, Statesmen, Jurists, Lawyers, Surgeons, Divines, Merchants, Historians, Editors, Artists, Etc., Etc.,* 2 vols. (1874; reprint, Berea, Ky.: Kentucke Imprints, 1976), 1: 136, 164.

13. Lowell H. Harrison and James C. Klotter, *A New History of Kentucky* (Lexington: University Press of Kentucky, 1997), 195; Legislative Document, No. 26. "Response of the Adjutant General of Kentucky to a Resolution of Inquiry in Regard to Federal Enrollments in the State, Made to the House of Representatives Wednesday, March 1, 1865" [erroneously published in] *Legislative Document No. 10 Annual Report of the Auditor of Public Accounts, of the State of Kentucky, for the Fiscal Year Ending October 10, 1863* (Frankfort: Wm. E. Hughes, State Printer, 1864), 11; J. Tandy Ellis, *Report of the Adjutant General of the State of Kentucky Confederate Volunteers War, 1861–1865,* 2 vols. (Frankfort: State Journal Company, 1915); Battle, Perrin, and Kniffen, *Kentucky,* 19, 34.

14. Hughie G. Lawson, "Geographical Origins of White Migrants to Trigg and Calloway Counties in the Ante-bellum Period," *Filson Club History Quarterly* 57 (1983): 286–304. However, by 1850, more than 70 percent of Purchase citizens were Kentucky born. See Patricia Ann Hoskins, "'The Old First Is with the South': The Civil War, Reconstruction, and Memory in the Jackson Purchase Region of Kentucky" (PhD diss., Auburn University, 2008), 35–36.

15. Alan Bearman, "'The South Carolina of Kentucky': Religion and Secession in the Jackson Purchase," *Filson Club History Quarterly* 76 (2002): 495–521.

16. Hoskins, "Old First," 48–50, 98–103. Many of Kentucky's leading Unionists owned slaves. Many, too, argued that secession would doom slavery in the state. On May 7, 1861, the *Louisville Daily Journal,* Kentucky's leading pro-Union newspaper, editorialized: "In speaking of the many inevitable consequences of disunion to Kentucky, we have repeatedly mentioned the certain, the unquestionable fact, that, if this State should go out of the United States, thus cutting herself off from the operation of the fugitive slave law, her slaves, learning at once, as they of course would do, the condition of things, would strike by the thousands and tens of thousands for the Indiana, Ohio, and Illinois shores, and none of them would ever be sent back to us. This important truth we have considered, as others have done, self-evident—beyond dispute—palpable to every man of common sense." Also in May 1861 Postmaster General Joseph Holt, an outspoken Kentucky Unionist who would become judge

advocate general of the army in the Lincoln administration, warned that if Kentucky seceded, slavery in the state would "perish away . . . as a ball of snow would melt in a summer's sun." See E. Merton Coulter, *The Civil War and Readjustment in Kentucky* (Chapel Hill: University of North Carolina Press, 1926), 12. South Carolina, Mississippi, Florida, Alabama, Georgia, Louisiana, and Texas seceded before the Civil War began. Virginia, Arkansas, Tennessee, and North Carolina left the Union after the war started. Charles B. Dew, *Apostles of Disunion: Southern Secession Commissioners and the Causes of the Civil War* (Charlottesville: University of Virginia Press, 2001), is a superb study of southern motives for secession that demolishes claims that the South exited the Union over the principle of states' rights and that slavery had little or nothing to do with secession. In *This Mighty Scourge: Perspectives on the Civil War,* James M. McPherson writes that "in the antebellum South, the purpose of asserting state sovereignty was to protect slavery from the potential hostility of a national majority against Southern interests—mainly slavery." McPherson, who earned a Pulitzer Prize for *Battle Cry of Freedom: The Civil War Era,* first published in 1988, quotes Senator Nathaniel Macon of North Carolina in the 1820s, when the issue of slavery's expansion was hotly debated as the central controversy over Missouri statehood: "If Congress can make banks, roads, and canals under the Constitution, they can free any slave in the United States." McPherson added that "John C. Calhoun, the South's leading political philosopher, formulated an elaborate constitutional structure of state's-rights theory to halt any use of federal power that might conceivably be construed at some future time as a precedent to act against slavery. See James M. McPherson, *This Mighty Scourge: Perspectives on the Civil War* (New York: Oxford University Press, 2007), 7.

17. Hoskins, "Old First," 99.

1. Kentucky's South Carolina

1. Jackson defeated the Creek Indians at the Battle of Horseshoe Bend, Alabama, on Mar. 27, 1814. Shelby fought Indians in Lord Dunmore's War of 1774 and battled the British and their Native American allies in the Revolutionary War and the War of 1812. He went down in history as "Old King's Mountain" for helping lead patriot militia to victory over loyalist militia in the Revolutionary War Battle of King's Mountain, South Carolina, on Oct. 7, 1780.

2. Battle, Perrin, and Kniffen, *Kentucky,* 7; John E. Robertson, "Western Kentucky and Paducah in Legend and Lore," *Filson Club History Quarterly* 76 (2002): 186.

3. Battle, Perrin, and Kniffen, *Kentucky,* 3–5.

4. Ibid., 7; Robertson, "Western Kentucky and Paducah," 186–88. As time passed, "Purchase" and "Jackson Purchase" came to refer to the Kentucky section of the territory. The Tennessee portion became "West Tennessee." Robertson debunks an old legend that a "drunken surveyor" accounted for the discrepancy in the boundary of the Purchase and the rest of the state.

5. Battle, Perrin, and Kniffen, *Kentucky,* 46–47; Ted Franklin Belue, quoted in Berry Craig, *Hidden History of Western Kentucky* (Charleston, S.C.: History Press, 2011), 123. Belue's book *The Long Hunt: Death of the Buffalo East of the Mississippi* (Mechanicsburg, Pa.: Stackpole Books, 1996) includes a chapter on barrens. The scarcity of trees prompted Purchase pioneers to name communities for woods or individual trees. Graves County is home to Hickory, originally called Hickory Grove, and Pilot Oak. Brown's Grove and Lynn Grove are in Calloway County. Lone Oak is a Paducah suburb.

6. Lon Carter Barton (Mayfield educator, historian, and author), interview with the author, Apr. 10, 1998.

7. One Purchase stream is intriguingly named Bayou de Chien, French for "Bayou of the Dog," though it is not a swamp. It is a shallow creek that snakes through Graves, Hickman, and Fulton Counties to the Mississippi.

8. Lawson, "Geographical Origins," 286–304.

9. In the Purchase, some civilians had Virginia treasury warrants for land. Revolutionary War veterans, or their heirs or assignees, possessed bounty land warrants given for military service. Records of 242 military claims plus 9,308 "West of the Tennessee River Non-Military patents" are available on the Kentucky Secretary of State's Web site, http://www.sos.ky.gov/admin/land/military/wtrpatents/Pages/default.aspx (accessed Apr. 19, 2014), and in the Kentucky Land Office, which is part of the secretary of state's office. See also Battle, Perrin, and Kniffen, *Kentucky,* 34; Dorothy Jennings and Kerby Jennings, *The Story of Calloway County, 1822–1976* (Murray, Ky.: Murray Democrat Publishing Co., 1980), 19, 24–26; John E. Kleber, ed., *The Kentucky Encyclopedia* (Lexington: University Press of Kentucky, 1992), 428, 663. Murray was named for John L. Murray, a Democrat, who represented western Kentucky's First Congressional District in Congress in 1837–39.

10. Kleber, *Kentucky Encyclopedia,* 152, 427–28. There is no explanation why the spellings of the county and its namesake differ, according to the encyclopedia. The one-sided fight on cold, snowy Jan. 22, 1813, pitted about one thousand Kentuckians, under General James Winchester of Tennessee, against a slightly larger force of Canadian militia and Native Americans, led by General Henry Proctor and Roundhead, a Wyandot chief. The Kentuckians had no artillery; Proctor's three small cannons ultimately routed them. Winchester surrendered, after being led to believe that the American captives would not be harmed. However, "some of the prisoners were killed, and many of the eighty wounded left behind to await transportation [to British-held Detroit] were slaughtered by the Indians," Harrison and Klotter write. "At least four hundred Kentuckians were killed in the battle and its bloody aftermath, and 'Remember the Raisin' became the Kentucky battle cry for the rest of the war." See Harrison and Klotter, *New History,* 91.

11. Before 1818, according to the Kentucky Land Office, much of the mid- to northern parts of the Purchase had been mapped by the metes and bounds system used in the rest of the state and in Virginia. Those patents, which were authorized by treasury warrants, are filed with the Virginia and Old Kentucky Patent Series, available for research on the Kentucky Secretary of State's Web site, http://www.sos.ky.gov/admin/land/Pages/default.aspx (accessed Mar. 23, 2014). Virginia law prohibited the usage of land warrants of any kind in areas belonging to Native Americans in the mid to lower areas of the Purchase. Kentucky honored the military warrants in the Purchase after the region became part of the state.

12. Kleber, *Kentucky Encyclopedia,* 44–45, 70, 360, 384, 427–28, 611, 593, 619. Hickman preserves for posterity the maiden name of the wife of all-but-forgotten G. W. L Marr, a wealthy man who owned the land on which the town was built.

13. Reuben Gold Thwaites, ed., *The Jesuit Relations and Allied Documents Travels and Explorations of the Jesuit Missionaries in New France, 1610–1791,* vol. 59 (New York: Pageant Book Company, 1959), 145; Craig, *Hidden History of Western Kentucky,* 105–7. The Iron Banks Hotel, closed long ago, welcomed travelers for many years on the bluff top above the Columbus Ferry, which shuttled passengers between Columbus and Belmont, Missouri.

14. Thwaites, *Jesuit Relations,* 145, 147; Craig, *Hidden History of Western Kentucky,* 106.

15. Thwaites, *Jesuit Relations,* 147; Craig, *Hidden History* of *Western Kentucky,* 106–7.

16. Kenneth C. Carstens, *George Rogers Clark's Fort Jefferson, 1780–1781: Kentucky's Outpost on the Western Frontier* (Westminster, Md.: Heritage Books, 2005), 1, 144.

17. Kleber, *Kentucky Encyclopedia,* 952.

18. Temple J. Bodley and Samuel M. Wilson, *History of Kentucky,* vol. 1 (Chicago: F. J. Clarke Publishing Co., 1928), 285; Berry Craig, *Hidden History of Kentucky Soldiers* (Charleston, S.C.: History Press, 2011), 14–15.

19. Bodley and Wilson, *History of Kentucky,* 285.

20. Craig, *Hidden History of Kentucky Soldiers,* 15.

21. Battle, Perrin, and Kniffen, *Kentucky,* 230; John Anderson Journal, 1838, in Forrest C. Pogue Special Collections Library, Murray State University, Murray, Ky. Typhus is a bacterial disease spread by lice and rats and is commonly treated with antibiotics, according to the National Institutes of Health.

22. Anderson Journal.

23. Battle, Perrin, and Kniffen, *Kentucky,* 230.

24. Anderson Journal. How Clinton got its name is evidently unknown, but it may have been named for a Captain Clinton who was posted there in 1826. See Kleber, *Kentucky Encyclopedia,* 207.

25. Anderson Journal. Tincture of cantharidin is a chemical compound made from the secretions of the blister beetle and the Spanish fly beetle.

26. Ibid.

27. Ibid. John Anderson would help found Mayfield's First Presbyterian Church.

28. Barataria is evidently Owens Island today. On the Illinois shore, Clark and his soldiers halted at Massac Creek near what is now Fort Massac State Park in Metropolis. In 1778, Clark bloodlessly captured Kaskaskia, Cahokia, and Vincennes, the latter retaken by the British and recaptured by Clark in a brief siege in 1779. See George Rogers Clark, *Col. George Rogers Clark's Sketch of His Campaign in the Illinois in 1778–9* (New York: Arno Press, 1971).

29. Kleber, *Kentucky Encyclopedia,* 197, 705; John E. Robertson, *Paducah: Frontier to the Atomic Age* (Charleston, S.C.: Arcadia Publishing, 2002), 8–9. The city's William Clark Market House Museum is named for the town founder.

30. Lewis Collins, *Historical sketches of Kentucky: Embracing its History, Antiquities, and Natural curiosities, Geographical, Statistical, and Geological Descriptions; with Anecdotes of Pioneer Life, and More Than One Hundred Biographical Sketches of Distinguished Pioneers, Soldiers, Statesmen, Jurists, Lawyers, Divines, Etc.* (1847; rpt., Lexington, Ky.: Henry Clay Press, 1968), 446.

31. *Williams' Paducah Directory, City Guide, and Business Mirror* (Paducah, Ky.: Byers and Clements, 1859), 9. For years, a state historical marker commemorated the "gravesite." It is gone. See William Clark to Meriwether Lewis Clark, Apr. 27, 1827, in William Clark Papers, Missouri Historical Society, St. Louis; Robertson, *Paducah: Frontier,* 10.

32. Fred G. Neuman, *The Story of Paducah (Kentucky)* (Paducah, Ky.: Young Printing Company, 1927), 23–26.

33. Collins and Collins, *History of Kentucky,* 2: 264; Robertson, *Paducah: Frontier,* 20–21.

34. *Williams' Paducah Directory,* 10. The directory claimed Paducah's population was "about 7,000."

35. Carlton J. Corliss, *Main-Line of Mid-America: The Story of the Illinois Central* (New York: Creative Age Press, 1950), 263; Robertson, *Paducah: Frontier,* 23.

36. Corliss, *Main Line,* 264.

37. James H. Lemly, *The Gulf, Mobile & Ohio: A Railroad That Had to Expand or Expire* (Homewood, Ill.: Richard D. Erwin, 1953), 309–10; Collins and Collins, *History of Kentucky,* 2: 264.

38. Kleber, *Kentucky Encyclopedia,* 428; Battle, Perrin, and Kniffen, *Kentucky,* 62.

39. Craig, *Hidden History of Western Kentucky,* 118–20.

40. Ibid. See also Anthony Allen, *Columbus, Kentucky as the Nation's Capital: Legend or Reality?* (Fort Davis, Tex.: River Microstudies, 1993).

41. Collins and Collins, *History of Kentucky,* 2: 263; Battle, Perrin, and Kniffen, *Kentucky,* 43. 63–64; *Richmond Daily Dispatch,* Apr. 19, 1861. Started in 1859, the *Hickman Courier* is one of the oldest newspapers in Kentucky still publishing under the same name.

42. J. G. Randall and David Donald, *The Civil War and Reconstruction,* 2nd ed. (Lexington, Mass.: D. C. Heath and Company, 1969), 228.

43. No candidate won a majority of electoral votes, so the election ended up in the House of Representatives, where Clay had many allies. Clay threw his support to Adams, who made him secretary of state. Angry Jacksonians called it a "corrupt bargain."

44. Shannon and McQuown, *Presidential Politics in Kentucky,* 2–3, 5–6. In 1824, the Jackson Purchase vote was 224 for Jackson and 88 for Clay. In 1828, Jackson beat Adams in the Purchase, 963–138.

45. Ibid., 7–31. The Kansas-Nebraska Act of 1854 shattered Clay's beloved Whig Party. The measure, pushed by Douglas, created the territories of Kansas and Nebraska and allowed settlers to decide whether or not to permit slavery. The act, in effect, overturned the Missouri Compromise of 1820, which forbade slavery north of thirty-six degrees, thirty minutes latitude after the admission of Missouri as a slave state. Kansas and Nebraska were north of thirty-six, thirty. The measure destroyed the Whig Party. Most northern Whigs and a few northern Democrats formed the Republican Party on antislavery principles in 1854. Most southern Whigs became Democrats. Most Kentucky Whigs drifted into the nativist American or "Know-Nothing" Party until it collapsed. Some of them became Democrats, but many Whigs did not and called themselves the "Opposition." Dr. John M. Johnson of Paducah was elected to the state senate on the "Opposition" ticket in 1859.

46. "Diary of Dr. Beeler Is Preserved in Hickman Co.," *Jackson Purchase 150 Years,* section D, 9; Shannon and McQuown, *Presidential Politics in Kentucky,* 26.

47. Shannon and McQuown, *Presidential Politics in Kentucky,* 12, 15, 19, 22.

48. Hoskins, "Old First," 48–49, 98–103.

49. Collins and Collins, *History of Kentucky,* 2: 258–61; Harrison and Klotter, *A New History,* 99; Hoskins, "Old First," 99.

50. Aaron Astor, *Rebels on the Border: Civil War, Emancipation, and the Reconstruction of Kentucky and Missouri* (Baton Rouge: Louisiana State University Press, 2012), 29; Shannon and McQuown, *Presidential Politics in Kentucky,* 35–36.

51. Hoskins, "Old First," 99–101.

52. *Kentucky Slave Narratives: A Folk History of Slavery in Kentucky from Interviews with Former Slaves* (Applewood, Mass: Bedford Books, n.d.), 112. The narratives were drawn from the Federal Writers' Project, part of the Depression-era Works Progress Administration, in 1936–38.

53. Collins and Collins, *History of Kentucky,* 2: 285.

54. Bearman, "'South Carolina of Kentucky,'" 497, 502.

55. Ibid., 505–6, 513. Bearman (503), citing John E. Robertson's *Paducah: 1830–1980, A Sesquicentennial History* (Paducah, Ky.: John E. Robertson, 1980), writes that "only in Paducah is there any evidence that the Catholic and Jewish populations had even the mildest impact upon the 'radical stand on slavery of the Baptists and the Methodists.'" Paducah, Robertson writes, was home to a significant number of Catholics and Jews, many of whom migrated to America from Germany after the failed revolutions of 1848.

56. Ibid., 514.

57. Ibid., 509.

58. Ibid., 516.

59. James M. McPherson, *Battle Cry of Freedom: The Civil War Era* (Oxford and New York: Oxford University Press, 1988), 215; Coulter, *Civil War and Readjustment,* 20–21. In Jan. 1860, Kentucky Democrats met in convention in Frankfort and endorsed popular sovereignty for the Kansas and Nebraska Territories.

60. McPherson, *Battle Cry of Freedom,* 215; Coulter, *Civil War and Readjustment,* 20–21; Collins and Collins, *History of Kentucky,* 1: 84. Douglas's running mate was Herschel V. Johnson of Georgia. Joseph Lane of Oregon was the vice presidential nominee on the Breckinridge ticket. In Kentucky, Breckinridge appeared on the ballot as a "Democrat" and Douglas as an "Independent Democrat." The Southern Democrats also called themselves the "Constitutional Democrats." In defiance of the fugitive slave law, many northern state legislatures passed "personal liberty laws" that prohibited state and local officials and citizens from helping return runaway slaves to their owners.

61. Bell's running mate was Edward Everett of Massachusetts. Lincoln ran with Hannibal Hamlin of Maine.

62. The "Bloody Monday" riot on Aug. 6, 1855, election day, hastened the demise of the Know-Nothings. In the balloting, they claimed the governorship, won a majority of seats in both houses of the state legislature, and took six of the state's ten congressional seats. But in Louisville, where the Know-Nothings also carried the spring municipal elections, Know-Nothing mobs attacked naturalized citizens, mostly German and Irish Catholics, who tried to vote. At least nineteen men were killed, and much property was destroyed. See Kleber, *Kentucky Encyclopedia,* 523–24.

63. Thompson would become one of Paducah's leading secessionists. In 1861, he joined the Confederate Third Kentucky Infantry and became the regiment's colonel. He was killed in the Battle of Paducah on Mar. 25, 1864, leading his troops in a bloody and unsuccessful assault on Union Fort Anderson. In June 1861, Trimble ran for Congress on the Union ticket and lost. His unionism ultimately faded, and he made a second unsuccessful run for Congress in 1863 on an antiwar platform. Trimble finally won in 1865, running as a Democrat, and he served until 1870. Lincoln's election turned Quigley secessionist. See George Quigley Langstaff Jr., *The Life and Times of Quintus Quincy Quigley, 1828–1910: His Personal Journey, 1859–1908* (Paducah, Ky.: Paducah Area Community Foundation, 1999), 49–50; *Louisville Daily Courier,* Sept. 28, 1860; Neuman, *Story of Paducah,* 154; George, *History of the 3d, 7th, 8th and 12th,* 150–51. McCann was born in Ohio, according to the 1860 US census for McCracken County (microfilm in the McCracken County Public Library). He studied law at the University of Chicago in 1860–61. See *Second Annual Catalogue of the University of Chicago. Officers and Students for the Academic Year, 1860–1861* (Chicago: Church, Goodman & Cushing, Book and Job Printers, 1861), 10.

64. Langstaff, *Life and Times,* 53–54.

65. *Louisville Daily Courier,* July 11, 1860. The pro-Breckinridge *Courier* became Kentucky's leading secessionist newspaper. Not until 1975 did Kentucky elect a governor from the Purchase. Governor Julian Carroll, now a state senator from Frankfort, was from the Heath community in McCracken County. Carroll remains the only Purchase governor.

66. Ibid.

67. *Louisville Daily Courier,* July 18, 1860.

68. Ibid.; Battle, Perrin, and Kniffen, *Kentucky,* 28; *Louisville Daily Courier,* July 18, 1860.

69. Goheen was on the bench from 1852 to 1858 and in 1874. See Battle, Perrin, and Kniffen, *Kentucky,* 105; *Louisville Daily Courier,* July 18, 1860.

70. *Herald,* quoted in the *Louisville Daily Courier,* July 11, 1860.

71. Ibid. Born in Trigg County in 1802, Boyd became an ardent secessionist and joined the Confederate Third Kentucky as a quartermaster. His grandfather and father fought in the Revolutionary War. His father served in the state house of representatives from Trigg County, while Linn Boyd, who was born in Nashville in 1800, represented Calloway County. Later, Linn Boyd moved back to Trigg County and got elected to his father's seat. Alfred Boyd represented Calloway, Marshall, and Trigg Counties in the state senate in 1842–46 and was in the army during the Mexican-American War. Linn Boyd went further politically, representing the First Congressional District in 1835–37 and 1839–55. He was speaker of the house in 1851–55. He and Alfred wound up in Paducah, where they owned a general merchandise store. Elected lieutenant governor in 1859, Linn Boyd died before taking office. See Kleber, *Kentucky Encyclopedia,* 108; Collins and Collins, *History of Kentucky,* 2: 543; George, *History of the 3d, 7th, 8th and 12th,* 163.

72. *Louisville Daily Courier,* July 14, 1860; George, *History of the 3d, 7th, 8th, and 12th,* 182. After Lincoln was elected, the *Courier* endorsed secession, and Warren ultimately became a quartermaster in the Confederate Seventh Kentucky Infantry Regiment. Anvil "firing" was a common form of celebrating in the nineteenth-century South and border states. Typically, revelers would use two anvils. One would sit on top of the other, the bottom anvil upside-down. Black powder was packed in the cavity formed by the concave bottoms of the two anvils and a fuse attached to the charge. The blast would produce an ear-splitting boom that would lift the top anvil. A single anvil also could be used, with powder packed under it.

73. *Louisville Daily Courier,* July 17, 1860. The *Southern Yeoman* would also endorse secession. See Battle, Perrin, and Kniffen, *Kentucky,* 53.

74. J. E. Anderson to A. R. Boone, July 22, 1860, typescript, Noble J. Gregory Papers, Pogue Special Collections Library. Williams and lawyer Bolinger sided with Lucian Anderson as Unconditional Unionists. In 1861, Boone was elected to the state house of representatives as a secessionist but was expelled as a traitor to Kentucky. After the war, he returned to the Democratic fold and represented the First District in Congress from 1875 to 1879. See Battle, Perrin, and Kniffen, *Kentucky,* 53, 220, 223; Collins and Collins, *History of Kentucky,* 2: 292.

75. Battle, Perrin, and Kniffen, *Kentucky,* 67; *Louisville Courier,* July 30, 1860. Bullock and *Crescent* editor Len G. Faxon became fiercely secessionist. After Faxon joined the Confederate army, Bullock took over the paper. When the Confederates occupied Columbus in Sept. 1861, Bullock renamed the paper the *Daily Confederate News.* Like Breckinridge, McClarty joined the Confederates. Breckinridge became a general and a Confederate secretary of war. McClarty would serve as a staff officer under Breckinridge.

76. *Louisville Daily Courier,* Aug. 2, 1860.

77. Collins and Collins, *History of Kentucky,* 1: 84; *The Louisville Daily Journal,* Sept. 12, 1860. Edited by George D. Prentice, the *Journal* became Kentucky's most influential pro-Union paper.

78. *Louisville Daily Courier,* Sept. 4, 1860.

79. *Louisville Daily Courier,* Sept. 5, 1860.

80. *Louisville Daily Courier,* Sept. 11, 1860. Hodge and Wadsworth, an ex–state senator, reflected Kentucky's divided loyalties in the Civil War. Hodge became a Confederate general and represented Kentucky's Rebel "government" in the Confederate House of Representatives. Wadsworth became a Union colonel and a US congressman. See Collins and Collins,

History of Kentucky, 1: 111, 353, 2: 547, 582; "Biographical Directory of the United States Congress 1774–Present," http://bioguide.congress.gov/scripts/biodisplay.pl?index=W000015 (accessed Mar. 28, 2014).

81. Langstaff, *Life and Times,* 57.

82. Shannon and McQuown, *Presidential Politics in Kentucky,* 36.

83. William George Pirtle Memoirs, chap. 1, 9, typescript, Filson Historical Society, Louisville, Ky. (Pirtle titled his entries "chapters."); George, *History of the 3d, 7th, 8th and 12th,* 182. Pirtle became a second lieutenant in the Seventh Kentucky Confederate Infantry and survived the war.

84. Letter, Eliza Gregory, Dec. 13, 1860, quoted in Lon Carter Barton, "A History of Graves County, Kentucky" (master's thesis, University of Kentucky, 1960), 97; J. David Hacker, "A Census-Based Count of the Civil War Dead," *Civil War History* 57, no. 4 (Dec. 2011): 307–48. Hacker writes that 752,000 is the most probable number of deaths, but he notes that the figure could be as high as 851,000.

85. Shannon and McQuown, *Presidential Politics in Kentucky,* 36.

86. Coulter, *Civil War and Readjustment,* 22–23; Shannon and McQuown, *Presidential Politics in Kentucky,* 36.

87. Langstaff, *Life and Times,* 58.

88. Ibid., 60.

89. *Journal Of The Called Session Of The House Of Representatives Of The Commonwealth Of Kentucky, Begun And Held In The Town of Frankfort, On Thursday, The Seventeenth Day Of January, In The Year Of our Lord 1861, And Of The Commonwealth The Sixty-Ninth* (Frankfort: John B. Major, State Printer, 1861), 19.

90. Collins and Collins, *History of Kentucky,* 1: 84.

91. *Louisville Daily Courier,* Dec. 14, 1860.

92. *Louisville Daily Courier,* Dec. 27, 1860; Robertson, *Paducah: Frontier,* 54.

93. Langstaff, *Life and Times,* 61–62. Twyman stuck by the Union. Campbell and King endorsed secession. King was elected to the state house of representatives as a secessionist in Aug. 1861 and was expelled for treason. See Collins and Collins, *History of Kentucky,* 2: 594.

94. "The Address of the People of South Carolina, Assembled in Convention, to the People of the Slaveholding States of the United States" (Charleston, S.C.: Evans and Cogswell, Printers to the Convention, 1860), 16; Coulter, *Civil War and Readjustment,* 25–26; Dew, *Apostles of Disunion,* 51–54, 93, 96–98.

95. *Frankfort Tri-Weekly Yeoman,* Jan. 15, 1861.

96. *Louisville Daily Journal,* Jan. 9–10, 1861; Coulter, *Civil War and Readjustment,* 27–28.

97. *Hickman Courier,* quoted in the *Louisville Daily Courier,* Jan. 11, 1861.

98. *Hickman Courier,* quoted in the *Louisville Daily Courier,* Jan. 24, 1861.

99. *Louisville Daily Courier,* Jan. 15, 1861; *Herald,* quoted in the *Louisville Daily Courier,* Jan. 23, 1861.

100. *Louisville Daily Courier,* Jan. 19, 1861. Cadiz is the seat of Trigg County, which borders Calloway and Marshall Counties on the east. In a special June 1861 election, Burnett was sent back to Congress as a secessionist. Later in 1861, he helped recruit the Eighth Kentucky Infantry, presided over the Russellville convention, and became a Confederate congressman and senator from Kentucky. Congress expelled him as a traitor. See Kleber, *Kentucky Encyclopedia,* 144.

101. *Crescent,* quoted in the *Louisville Daily Courier,* Jan. 17, 1861.

102. *Louisville Daily Courier,* Feb. 6, 1861.

103. Edmond S. Meany, *Governors of Washington: Territorial and State* (Seattle: Department of Printing, University of Washington, 1915), 17–19.

104. Ibid., 17; *Louisville Daily Courier,* Feb. 6, 1861; Collins and Collins, *History of Kentucky*, 2: 770.

105. *Louisville Daily Journal,* Jan. 29, 1861.

106. Report by John Eaker and William N. Cargill to Senator John J. Crittenden, Jan. 22, 1861, in the Papers of John Jordan Crittenden, Library of Congress, microfilm copy in the Pogue Special Collections Library, Murray State University.

107. John Eaker to John J. Crittenden and Lazarus W. Powell, Jan. 23, 1861, and R. K. Williams to Crittenden, Jan. 23, 1861, both Crittenden Papers, microfilm, Pogue Library.

108. *Louisville Daily Journal,* Feb. 8, 1861.

109. *Address of the People of South Carolina,* 16.

110. *Louisville Daily Journal,* Aug. 16, 1859.

111. Coulter, *Civil War and Readjustment,* 29.

112. *House Journal,* Jan. 17, 1861, 4–11.

113. R. M. Kelly, "Holding Kentucky for the Union," in *Battles and Leaders of the Civil War, Being for the Most Part Contributions by Union and Confederate Officers. Based Upon "The Century War Series,"* ed. Robert Underwood Johnson and Clarence Clough Buell, of the Editorial Staff of "The Century Magazine," vol. 1 (1887; rpt., South Brunswick, N.Y.: Thomas Yoseloff, 1956), 373.

114. *Louisville Daily Journal,* Aug. 16, 1859; *Journal Of the Called Session Of the Senate Of the Commonwealth of Kentucky, Begun and Held In The Town Of Frankfort, On Thursday The Seventeenth Day of January, In The Year Of Our Lord 1861, And Of The Commonwealth the Sixty-Ninth* (Frankfort: John B. Major, State Printer, 1861), 434. Johnson would be expelled for his role in the Russellville convention.

115. *Louisville Daily Journal,* Aug. 16, 1859; Battle, Perrin, and Kniffen, *Kentucky,* 136; Jenkins and Irvan were elected in 1859; Johnson was elected in 1857. Livingston County adjoins McCracken County and northern Marshall County on the east.

116. *House Journal,* Jan. 17, 1861, 440–42. Coleman's name was not listed among legislators, but the 1860 US Census for Calloway County lists his residence as near Murray. Files in the Forrest C. Pogue Special Collections branch of the Murray State University Library say he was a law partner of Albert P. Thompson, who was from Murray but lived in Paducah in 1861. Thompson apparently practiced law in Paducah and Murray.

117. Ibid., 45–46; Battle, Perrin, and Kniffen, *Kentucky,* 136.

118. *Senate Journal,* Jan. 17, 1861, 64–67.

119. Coulter, *Civil War and Readjustment,* 33–34.

120. Ibid., 34; *Senate Journal,* Jan. 17, 1861, 95–98; *House Journal,* Jan. 17, 1861, 137–40. Cook, Coleman, Goheen, and Husbands voted "aye," and Lannom did not vote.

121. The Unionist delegates were ex-congressmen Joshua F. Bell, James Guthrie, and former governors Charles S. Morehead and Charles A. Wickliffe. James B. Clay, Henry Clay's grandson, represented the Southern Rights side. See *Senate Journal,* Jan. 17, 1861, 156–57, 185–87.

122. *Hickman Courier,* quoted in the *Louisville Daily Courier,* Feb. 6, 1861.

123. *Herald,* quoted in the *Louisville Daily Courier,* Feb. 22, 1861. Johnston became a captain in the Third Kentucky Infantry. See George, *History of the 3d, 7th, 8th and 12th,* 163.

124. *Louisville Daily Courier,* Feb. 22, 1861; *Hickman Courier,* quoted in the *Louisville Daily Courier,* Mar. 7, 1861.

125. *Crescent,* quoted in the *Louisville Daily Courier,* Mar. 14, 1861; *Hickman Courier,* quoted in the *Louisville Daily Courier,* Mar. 7, 1861.

126. Coulter, *Civil War and Readjustment,* 37.

127. B. W. Sharp to Jefferson Davis, Mar. 17, 1861, Letters Received by the Confederate Secretary of War, Feb.–May 1861, National Archives, Washington, D.C., microfilm, Pogue Special Collections. In a postscript, Sharp explained, "We are only about 125 miles removed from Holly Springs Miss."

128. *Louisville Daily Courier,* Mar. 21, 22, 1861. Wickliffe, the nephew and namesake of ex-governor Charles A. Wickliffe, became colonel of the Seventh Kentucky. Wickliffe, the current Ballard County seat, is named for him. Randle was one of Wickliffe's captains. Johnson and Jones were delegates to the Russellville convention. Byers was an assistant commissary of subsistence in the Third Kentucky. See George, *History of the 3d, 7th, 8th and 12th,* 149–50, 182; *Resolution of the [Confederate] Congress [in Kentucky] 1861* (rpt., Lyndon, Ky.: Mull-Wathen Historic Press, 1970), 18–19.

129. *Louisville Daily Courier,* Mar. 21, 1861. State representative George Washington Ewing of Logan County was even more intemperate in his remarks, describing Lincoln as "a n r stealer."

130. Wilson Porter Shortridge, "Kentucky Neutrality in 1861," *Mississippi Valley Historical Review* 9 (Mar. 1923): 293.

131. *Senate Journal,* Jan. 17, 1861, 427–28; *House Journal,* Jan. 17, 1861, 467–75. Senators Jenkins and Johnson voted "aye," and Irvan did not vote. Cook, Goheen, and Lannom voted "aye," and Hamlin and Husbands did not vote.

2. Armies on the Border

1. Langstaff, *Life and Times,* 69.

2. Collins and Collins, *History of Kentucky* 1: 87.

3. Langstaff, *Life and Times,* 69–70.

4. Collins and Collins, *History of Kentucky,* 1: 87.

5. Robert Emmet McDowell, *City of Conflict: Louisville in the Civil War* (Louisville: Louisville Civil War Roundtable, 1962), 26–28; Collins and Collins, *History of Kentucky,* 1: 87–88.

6. *Herald,* quoted in the *Louisville Daily Courier,* Apr. 29, 1861.

7. *The War of the Rebellion: A Compilation of the Official Records of the Union and Confederate Armies* (Washington, D.C.: War Department, 1880–1902) (hereafter *O.R.*), ser. 4, vol. 1, 231–32; Collins and Collins, *History of Kentucky,* 1: 88; Coulter, *Civil War and Readjustment,* 48.

8. *Louisville Daily Courier,* Apr. 29, 1861; Ellis, *Report of the Adjutant General,* 1: 2–35. Taylor was colonel of the regiment and Duncan lieutenant colonel.

9. John M. Lansdens, *A History of the City of Cairo Illinois* (Chicago: R. R. Donnelley and Sons, 1910), 130.

10. *O.R.,* ser. 1, vol. 52, part 2, 61–62. A. J. Barry, "Horne & Moore," and George B. Moss signed the letter. They told Davis that Congressman Burnett would vouch for them.

11. *O.R.,* ser. 1, vol. 52, part 2, 67.

12. *Memphis Daily Appeal,* Apr. 25, 1861.

13. *Memphis Daily Appeal,* Apr. 26, 1861.

14. Fred G. Neuman, *Paducahans in History* (Paducah, Ky.: Young Printing Company, 1922), 50; county by county list of Kentucky State Guard companies in 1861, State Guard

Records, provided by John Trowbridge, command historian, Kentucky National Guard, Frankfort; *Register of the Kentucky State Guard for 1861* (Frankfort: John B. Major, State Printer, 1861), 16. The battalion was organized on Nov. 6, 1860. Tilghman was commissioned on Dec. 3, 1860.

15. *Memphis Daily Appeal,* Apr. 26, 1861; Sharp to L. P. Walker, Apr. 28, 1861, Letters Received by the Confederate Secretary of War, Mar.–May 1861, National Archives.

16. *Louisville Daily Courier,* May 6, 1861.

17. *Louisville Daily Journal,* July 19, 1862.

18. Ibid. Lane and Brown were fiery Kansas abolitionists who were hated in the slave states. Before the Civil War, Lane helped lead antislavery settlers in their fight against proslavery forces in a guerrilla war known as "Bleeding Kansas." Lane's men were known as "Jayhawkers" or "Jayhawks," the latter of which became the nickname of Kansas University sports teams. Brown was executed in 1859 after leading a raid on the US arsenal at Harper's Ferry, Virginia, in an effort to spark a slave revolt, if not an all-out war between North and South that he hoped would end slavery. Kansas was admitted to the Union as a free state in 1861, and Lane became one of the state's first two senators. A fierce Republican, he was also a Union general in the Civil War. In 1858, Senator William H. Seward, a New York Republican, had warned of an "irrepressible conflict between North and South over slavery." He became Lincoln's secretary of state in 1861 and served until 1869. Seward is perhaps best known for arranging the purchase of Alaska from Imperial Russia in 1866, though at the time the deal was ridiculed as "Seward's Folly."

19. Ibid.

20. Langstaff, *Life and Times,* 67.

21. Battle, Perrin, and Kniffen, *Kentucky,* 81–82.

22. *Louisville Daily Journal,* Aug. 20, 1861. The other named converts were A. D. Kingman and Josiah Parker of Fulton County and W. R. Bradley of Hickman County.

23. *Memphis Daily Appeal,* Apr. 26, 1861.

24. *Herald,* quoted in the *Louisville Daily Courier,* May 6, 1861.

25. *O.R.*, ser. 1, vol. 52, part 2, 78.

26. Ibid., 75.

27. Ibid., 81.

28. Ibid., 89–90.

29. Ibid., 93–94.

30. Stanley F. Horn, *Tennesseans in the Civil War* (Nashville: Tennessee Civil War Centennial Commission, 1964), 1: 198–200.

31. *O.R.*, ser. 1, vol. 52, part 2, 94–95. Washington, astride a horse, would appear on the great seal of the Confederacy.

32. Ibid., 95–96.

33. Ibid., 99.

34. Ibid., 99–100.

35. Ibid., 100–103.

36. *Louisville Daily Courier,* May 6, 1861; Coulter, *Civil War and Readjustment,* 66.

37. Coulter, *Civil War and Readjustment,* 66; Frank Moore, ed., *The Rebellion Record: A Diary of American Events with Documents, Narratives, Illustrative Incidents, Poetry, Etc.,* 12 vols. (New York: G.P. Putnam, 1861), 1: 194–95.

38. Coulter, *Civil War and Readjustment,* 54; Collins and Collins, *History of Kentucky,* 1: 88.

39. *Frankfort Daily Commonwealth,* May 17, 1861; Shannon and McQuown, *Presidential Politics in Kentucky,* 36.

40. *Louisville Daily Journal,* Aug. 20, 1861.

41. *Herald,* quoted in the *Galveston Civilian and Gazette Weekly,* May 28, 1861.

42. *Journal Of The Called Session Of The House Of Representatives Of The Commonwealth Of Kentucky, Begun And Held In The Town Of Frankfort, On Monday The Sixth Day Of May, In The Year Of Our Lord 1861, And Of The Commonwealth The Sixty-Ninth* (Frankfort: John B. Major State Printer, 1861), 8.

43. *Journal Of The Called Session Of The Senate Of The Commonwealth Of Kentucky, Begun And Held In The Town Of Frankfort, On Monday The Sixth Day Of May, In The Year Of Our Lord 1861, And Of The Commonwealth The Sixty-Ninth* (Frankfort: John B. Major State Printer, 1861), 18, 129; Moore, *Rebellion Record,* 1: 329.

44. *Herald,* quoted in the *Richmond Daily Dispatch,* May 14, 1861.

45. County by county list, Trowbridge records; John A. Boyd, "Intimidation, Conspiracy, Provocation and Intrigue: The Militias of Kentucky, 1859–1861," *Army History* (Fall 2008): 13.

46. *House Journal,* May 6, 1861, 91–94; Collins and Collins, *History of Kentucky,* 1: 90–91.

47. *Senate Journal,* May 6, 1861, 143–45.

48. Coulter, *Civil War and Readjustment,* 86–87; *House Journal,* May 6, 1861, 177–78; *Senate Journal,* May 6, 1861, 123.

3. The Mayfield Convention

1. See Berry Craig, "The Jackson Purchase Considers Secession: The 1861 Mayfield Convention," *Register of the Kentucky Historical Society* 99 (2001): 339–61.

2. *Lexington Kentucky Statesman,* June 7, 1861. Besides the Purchase counties, the First District consisted of Caldwell, Crittenden, Hopkins, Livingston, Lyon, Trigg, Union, and Webster Counties.

3. A copy of Carr's speech is in the Carr Family Papers, Pogue Special Collections.

4. *Louisville Daily Journal,* May 21, 1861; "Biographical Directory of the United States Congress 1774–Present," http://bioguide.congress.gov/scripts/biodisplay.pl?index=T000425 (accessed Sept. 28, 2013).

5. Ibid.

6. Ibid. See also D. Trabue Davis, *Story of Mayfield through a Century, 1823–1923* (Paducah: Billings Printing Co., 1923), 57.

7. *Louisville Daily Journal,* July 19, 1862; Battle, Perrin, and Kniffen, *Kentucky,* 52–53; Taliaferro P. Shaffner, ed., *The Kentucky State Register, for the Year 1847* (Louisville: Morton & Griswold, 1847), 88.

8. *Louisville Daily Journal,* July 19, 1862.

9. Ibid.; McPherson, *Battle Cry of Freedom,* 291.

10. *Louisville Daily Journal,* July 19, 1862.

11. *Louisville Daily Journal,* May 24, 1861.

12. *Louisville Daily Journal,* May 18, 1861.

13. *Louisville Daily Journal,* May 22, 1861.

14. Ibid.; Horn, *Tennesseans in the Civil War,* 184–86; John Berrien Lindsley, *Military Annals of Tennessee, Confederate* (Nashville: J. M. Lindsley and Company, 1886), 332.

15. *Louisville Daily Journal,* May 28, 1861.

16. *Louisville Daily Journal,* May 29, 1861.

17. *Louisville Daily Journal,* May 30, 1861.

18. *Louisville Daily Journal,* May 30, 1861.

19. *New York Times,* June 1, 1861. The May 28 *Louisville Daily Journal* also reported that "three secession papers" in the First District, including the *Paducah Herald,* "have just died." The result, according to the *Journal,* "will be a great falling off in the amount of lying in that part of the State. 'Dead men,' they say, 'tell no tales,' and dead papers tell no—stories."

20. David C. Mearns, ed., *The Lincoln Papers* (Garden City, N.Y.: Doubleday and Company, 1948), 2: 625.

21. *Louisville Daily Journal,* June 6, 1861.

22. Ibid.; Edmond S. Meany, "Richard Dickinson Gholson," *Washington Historical Quarterly* 8 (1917): 180–82.

23. *Louisville Daily Journal,* June 6, 1861; *Statesman,* June 11, 1861; *Yeoman,* June 11, 1861; Collins and Collins, *History of Kentucky,* 2: 731.

24. *Louisville Daily Journal,* June 6, 1861, Aug. 20, 1861. Austin might have been Hugh Rice Austin. See Craig, "Jackson Purchase Considers Secession," 350; *Confederate Veteran* 32 (1924): 75.

25. *Louisville Daily Journal,* June 6, 1861.

26. Ibid.

27. Ibid.

28. *Louisville Daily Courier,* June 5, 1861.

29. *Louisville Daily Journal,* June 6, 1861; Collins and Collins, *History of Kentucky,* 2: 490, 736.

30. *Louisville Daily Journal,* June 6, 1861.

31. *Tri-Weekly Kentucky Yeoman,* June 11, 1861.

32. Ibid.

33. Ibid.

34. Ibid.

35. Ibid.

36. Ibid.

37. Ibid.

38. Ibid.

39. Ibid.

40. Ibid.

41. Ibid.

42. Ibid.

43. Ibid.

44. *Kentucky Statesman,* June 11, 1861.

45. Ibid.

46. Ibid.

47. Ibid.

48. Ibid.

49. Ibid.

50. Ibid.

51. Ibid.

52. Ibid.

53. Ibid.

54. Carr speech, Carr Family Papers.

55. Others from the Mayfield convention who participated in the Russellville convention included Coffee, Kingman, Cobb, Machen, Gilbert, Matthewson, Alexander, Wooldridge, and Boone. See *Resolution of the [Confederate] Congress [in Kentucky]* (rpt., Lyndon, Ky.: Mull-Wathen Historic Press, 1970), 17–19.

4. Flag Snatching and Gun Grabbing

1. Coulter, *Civil War and Readjustment,* 98.

2. *Louisville Daily Courier,* June 17, 1861; county by county list, Trowbridge records; Ezra J. Warner, *Generals in Blue: Lives of the Union Commanders* (Baton Rouge: Louisiana State University Press, 1964), 385–86.

3. *Louisville Daily Courier,* June 17, 1861.

4. Boyd, "Intimidation," 13.

5. *Louisville Courier,* June 17, 1861.

6. Mary E. Kellogg, comp. and pub., *Army Life of an Illinois Soldier Including a Day by Day Record of Sherman's March to the Sea Letters and Diary of the Late Charles W. Wills* (Washington, D.C.: Globe Printing Company, 1906), 18–19.

7. Ibid.

8. *Louisville Daily Courier,* June 15, 1861.

9. Berry Craig, *Hidden History of Kentucky in the Civil War* (Charleston, S.C.: History Press, 2010), 15.

10. William Howard Russell, *My Diary North and South* (Boston: T. O. H. P. Burnham, 1863), 329.

11. Ibid., 327–28.

12. Ibid., 332, 335–36.

13. Craig, *Hidden History of Kentucky in the Civil War,* 15; Russell, *My Diary,* 335.

14. Craig, *Hidden History of Kentucky in the Civil War,* 15; Russell, *My Diary,* 336.

15. Craig, *Hidden History of Kentucky in the Civil War,* 15; Russell, *My Diary,* 336.

16. Craig, *Hidden History of Kentucky in the Civil War,* 15; Russell, *My Diary,* 336.

17. Robert McNutt McElroy, *Kentucky in the Nation's History* (New York: Moffat and Yard, 1909), 533–34.

18. *O.R.,* ser. 4, vol. 1, 376–78.

19. *Louisville Daily Courier,* May 6, 1861; *Louisville Daily Journal,* Aug. 9, 1861; Collins and Collins, *History of Kentucky,* 1: 92.

20. *Herald,* quoted in the *Daily Louisville Democrat,* July 3, 1861. Edited by John H. Harney, the paper strongly supported the Union cause. Machen, from Lyon County, was an outspoken secessionist. Tennessee voters rejected secession in Feb. 1861. But in June, the voters ratified secession by close to the margin the *Herald* cited.

21. *Louisville Daily Journal,* Aug. 9, 1861; Shannon and McQuown, *Presidential Politics in Kentucky,* 35–36.

22. *Louisville Daily Journal,* Aug. 9, 1861; Shannon and McQuown, *Presidential Politics in Kentucky,* 35–36.

23. Shannon and McQuown, *Presidential Politics in Kentucky,* 35–36; *Louisville Daily Courier,* June 26, 28, 1861; *Louisville Daily Journal,* Aug. 9, 1861. If other towns or counties put the Union or secession question to the voters, there is evidently no record of it.

24. *Louisville Daily Courier,* June 28, 1861.

25. *Louisville Daily Journal,* Aug. 9, 1861; Shannon and McQuown, *Presidential Politics in Kentucky,* 35–36.

26. Collins and Collins, *History of Kentucky,* 1: 92.

27. Samuel Paine Ridgway to Jennie Stanfield, June 25, 1861, in possession of Hugh and Evelyn Williams of Mayfield, Ky. Ridgway's words are per the original. Samuel and Jennie were married on June 15, 1865. See also Battle, Perrin, and Kniffen, *Kentucky.*

28. Horn, *Tennesseans in the Civil War,* 1: 205; Ed Gleeson, *Illinois Rebels: A Civil War Unit History of G Company Fifteenth Tennessee Regiment Volunteer Infantry* (Carmel: Guild Press of Indiana, 1966), 10–12; Horn, *Tennesseans in the Civil War,* 1: 219.

29. *Louisville Daily Courier,* July 10, 1861.

30. *Louisville Daily Journal,* July 23, 1861. John A. Sauner was mayor.

31. *Louisville Daily Journal,* July 23, 1861; *Report of the Military Board of Kentucky Made to the General Assembly, September 10, 1861* (Frankfort, Ky.: Jno. B. Major, State Printer, 1861), 9–10; county by county list, Trowbridge records.

32. *Report of the Military Board,* 16–17.

33. Ibid., 17.

34. *Louisville Daily Journal,* July 23, 1861.

35. *Report of the Military Board,* 15–16.

36. Ibid., 15.

37. *Louisville Courier,* July 26, 1861.

38. A Tennessee State Historical Society marker on US Highway 79 East denotes the site of Camp Boone. See *O.R.,* ser. 1, vol. 4, 373–74, 378; *Louisville Daily Journal,* July 29, 1861; George, *History of the 3d, 7th, 8th and 12th,* 163; Battle, Perrin, and Kniffen, *Kentucky,* 107. George spells Cargill's name as "Cargell." Stone was a first lieutenant, but Battle, Perrin, and Kniffen have him as a captain, adding that he was killed at Shiloh.

39. *Report of the Military Board,* 10–11.

40. George, *History of the 3d, 7th, 8th and 12th,* 19; Ellis, *Report of the Adjutant General,* 1: 84–143. Company F, commanded by Captain Hylan B. Lyon of Eddyville, was detached and ultimately became the famed Cobb's Battery of the Kentucky Orphan Brigade, commanded by Captain Robert Cobb of Eddyville, an ancestor of Paducah-born writer and humorist Irvin S. Cobb. In 1931, the United Daughters of the Confederacy had a stone marker erected to Cobb's Battery. It still stands near Kuttawa, on Lake Barkley. See Craig, *Hidden History of Kentucky in the Civil War,* 114–16. Lyon became a Confederate general. In 1864, a second Company F, mostly Ballard countians, was added to the regiment.

41. Ben L. Bassham, *Ten Months in the "Orphan Brigade": Conrad Wise Chapman's Civil War Memoir* (Kent, Ohio: Kent State University Press, 1999), 38.

42. Samuel Paine Ridgway to Jennie Stanfield, July 14, 1861, in possession of Hugh and Evelyn Williams of Mayfield, Ky.

43. Samuel Paine Ridgway to Jennie Stanfield, July 21, 1861, in possession of Hugh and Evelyn Williams of Mayfield, Ky.

44. Ibid.; county by county list, Trowbridge records; Thompson, *History of the Orphan Brigade,* 395–96. According to Battle, Perrin, and Kniffen (*Kentucky,* 56), Slayden's outfit was one of the first—if not the first—company raised in Graves County in the Civil War. It included about ninety men.

45. Horn, *Tennesseans in the Civil War,* 1: 220–22; Lizzie Lowe Fuller, "History of Camp Beauregard Graves County Kentucky," compiled in 1932, typescript in possession of Hugh and Evelyn Williams of Mayfield, Ky., 6; Barton, interview, Apr. 10, 1998; Battle, Perrin, and Kniffen, *Kentucky,* 42.

46. Battle, Perrin, and Kniffen, *Kentucky,* 42.

5. Politics, Pirates, and More Purchase Perfidy

1. Thomas L. Connelly, *Army of the Heartland* (Baton Rouge: Louisiana State University Press, 1967), 46; *Memphis Daily Appeal,* Aug. 6, 1861.

2. *Louisville Daily Courier,* Aug. 10, 1861.

3. *O.R.*, ser. 1, vol. 4, 376.

4. *Louisville Courier,* Aug. 6, 1861; *O.R.*, ser. 1, vol. 4, 379.

5. *O.R.*, ser. 1, vol. 52, part 2, 126–27.

6. *O.R.*, ser. 1, vol. 4, 381.

7. Ibid.

8. Collins and Collins, *History of Kentucky,* 1: 92; Coulter, *Civil War and Readjustment,* 97; *Louisville Daily Journal,* Sept. 7, 1861. The *Journal* reported the official state returns, which included 5 votes for Garrard in Hickman County and no votes for Barrick or Terry. But the *Louisville Daily Courier* of Aug. 16, 1861, said Terry received 211 votes in Hickman County, where "only one or two precincts" voted in the state treasurer's race.

9. *New York Times,* Aug. 10, 1861.

10. Jackson, a native of Fleming County, Kentucky, was the prime mover in creating a rump, Rebel government for the "Show Me State" in the autumn of 1861. The Unionist legislature deposed him. Dubious and short-lived as the Confederate government was—it collapsed when Union forces gained control of most of Missouri—the Confederates "admitted" Missouri as their thirteenth state, with Jackson as governor. At about the same time, Breckinridge became a Rebel general (and secretary of war just before Confederate defeat in 1865), and Burnett played a key role in forming a bogus Confederate government for Kentucky. Like the Missouri government, it did not represent majority opinion, had no legal standing, and fell apart after Union forces occupied most of the Bluegrass State. Nonetheless, Kentucky became the thirteenth Confederate "state."

11. *New York Times,* Aug. 14, 1861.

12. Samuel Paine Ridgway to Jennie Stanfield, n.d., in possession of Hugh and Evelyn Williams of Mayfield, Ky.

13. Given Campbell to Bettie Campbell, Aug. 10, 1861, Southern Historical Collection, University of North Carolina, Chapel Hill, http://blogs.lib.unc.edu/civilwar/index.php/2011/08/10/10-august-1861-kentucky-has-elected-a-large-majority-of-union-men-to-her-legislature/ (accessed Apr. 19, 2014.) Campbell ended up a cavalry officer and was part of Jefferson Davis's personal escort during his flight from Richmond in 1865. He wrote an account of the trek titled "Memorandum of a journal, kept daily during the last march of Jefferson Davis." Many of Campbell's men were from Trigg County. Secessionist G. W. Barbour, a leader of the Mayfield convention, beat Unionist D. W. McGoodwin, 674–219; see *Louisville Daily Courier,* Aug. 17, 1861.

14. *Louisville Daily Courier,* Aug. 10, 16, 1861; *Louisville Weekly Courier,* Aug. 24, 1861; *Louisville Daily Journal,* Sept. 7, 1861.

15. *Louisville Daily Courier,* Aug. 10, 16, 1861; *Louisville Daily Journal,* Sept. 7, 1861.

16. *Louisville Daily Journal,* Aug. 3, 12, 1861.

17. *Daily Louisville Democrat,* Aug. 13, 1861; *Louisville Daily Courier,* Aug. 7, 1861. A *Chicago Times* reporter wrote the Aug. 7 story.

18. *Louisville Weekly Courier,* Aug. 24, 1861.

19. *Louisville Daily Journal,* Aug. 15, 1861. Stone's wooden house still stands in Milburn.

20. *Louisville Daily Journal,* Aug. 22, 1861.

21. *Louisville Daily Journal,* Aug. 17, 1861.

22. Ibid.

23. *Louisville Daily Journal,* Aug. 3, 1861.

24. *Louisville Daily Journal,* Aug. 20, 1861.

25. Ibid.

26. *Louisville Daily Journal,* Aug. 20, 3, 1861.

27. *Louisville Daily Courier,* Aug. 9, 1861; *Louisville Daily Journal,* Aug. 10, 17, 20, 1861. Cargill was apparently First Lieutenant W. M. Cargill of Company E, Third Kentucky. See George, *History of the 3d, 7th, 8th and 12th,* 167.

28. *Louisville Daily Journal,* Aug. 20, 1861.

29. Ibid.

30. Ibid.

31. Ibid.

32. Coulter, *Civil War and Readjustment,* 101–4. Nelson had been largely responsible for convincing Lincoln to ship five thousand muskets into Kentucky for arming home guard companies. The weapons were dubbed "the Lincoln Guns." In Sept. 1861, he was made a brigadier general in the army. Promoted to major general in 1862, he survived unscathed the battles of Shiloh, Tennessee, and Corinth, Mississippi, but was wounded in the battle of Richmond, Kentucky. He was assassinated by Brigadier General Jefferson Davis in Louisville on Sept. 27, 1862, following an altercation between the two officers.

33. *Louisville Daily Courier,* Aug. 26, 1861.

34. Coulter, *Civil War and Readjustment,* 113–14.

35. *Louisville Daily Democrat,* Aug. 22, 1861.

36. *Louisville Daily Journal,* Sept. 5, 1861. In Greek mythology, Thersites was a dim-witted, crude, and obscene soldier in the Trojan War.

37. *Louisville Daily Courier,* Sept. 7, 1861; *Resolution of the [Confederate] Congress [in Kentucky],* 18. Vallandigham and Bright were leaders of the antiwar, anti-Lincoln, southern-sympathizing northern Democrats dubbed "Copperheads" by Republicans and prowar northern Democrats. In 1863, a military tribunal found Vallandigham guilty of treason, and he was banished to the Confederacy. He went to Canada and, in absentia, ran for governor of Ohio and lost. He returned to Ohio in 1864 and continued to criticize the president and the war. The Senate expelled Bright for treason in 1862.

38. *O.R.,* ser. 1, vol. 4, 176–78.

39. *Louisville Daily Courier,* Aug. 28, 1861.

40. *Louisville Daily Journal,* Aug. 30, 1861.

41. *O.R.,* ser. 1, vol. 4, 176–77.

42. *Frankfort Tri-Weekly Yeoman,* quoted in the *Louisville Daily Courier,* Aug. 26, 1861; *Memphis Daily Appeal,* Aug. 24, 1861.

43. *Louisville Daily Courier,* Aug. 21, 1861.

44. *Louisville Daily Journal,* Aug. 29, 1861.

45. *Journal Of The Senate Of The Commonwealth of Kentucky, Begun And Held In The Town Of Frankfort On Thursday The Second Day of September, In The Year Of Our Lord 1861, And Of The Commonwealth The Sixty-Ninth* (Frankfort: John B. Major, State Printer, 1861), 46–49. Johnson identified the captives as Watson and Stoveall. A Ballard County man named Carter was also apprehended at Norfolk, Missouri, opposite Island Number One. He, too, was released. See *Louisville Daily Courier,* Aug. 28, 1861; Collins and Collins, *History of Kentucky,* 1: 93.

46. *O.R.,* ser. 1, vol. 3, 141–42, 151.

47. *Appeal,* Sept. 4, 1861.

48. *O.R.,* ser. 1, vol. 4, 179–80, vol. 3, 148; Coulter, *Civil War and Readjustment,* 108; Nathaniel Cheairs Hughes and Roy P. Stonesifer, *The Life and Wars of Gideon J. Pillow* (Chapel Hill: University of North Carolina Press, 1993), 194.

49. *O.R.,* ser. 1, vol. 3, 152.

50. *Memphis Daily Appeal,* Sept. 4, 1861. A gallinipper is a mosquito.

51. Ulysses S. Grant, *Personal Memoirs of Ulysses S. Grant* (1885; rpt., New York: Charles A. Webster, 1994), 114; *O.R.,* ser. 1, vol. 3, 150.

52. *O.R.,* ser. 1, vol. 4, 197.

6. "Abolition Invaders" and Rebel Deliverers

1. Nathaniel Cheairs Hughes Jr., *The Battle of Belmont: Grant Strikes South* (Chapel Hill: University of North Carolina Press, 1991), 5; Neuman, *Story of Paducah,* 147; *O.R.,* ser. 1, vol. 4, 197.

2. *O.R.,* ser. 1, vol. 4, 197; *Louisville Courier,* Sept. 12, 1861, excerpt from the *Cincinnati Enquirer;* Neuman, *Story of Paducah,* 147.

3. Neuman, *Story of Paducah,* 147.

4. Neuman, *Story of Paducah,* 147–48; *O.R.,* ser. 1, vol. 4, 197; *Louisville Courier,* Sept. 12, 1861, excerpt from the *Cincinnati Enquirer.*

5. Pirtle Memoirs, chap. 6.

6. *O.R.,* ser. 1, vol. 3, 197; George Henry Preble, rear admiral, US Navy, *History of the Flag of the United States of America and of the Naval and Yacht-Club Signals, Seals, and Arms, and Principal National Songs of the United States, with a Chronicle of the Symbols, Standards, Banners, and Flags of Ancient and Modern Nations* (Boston: A. Williams and Company, 1880), 476.

7. Neuman, *Story of Paducah,* 150–51.

8. Encouraged by Pillow, Polk made a belated attempt to drive Grant from Paducah by sending a force under Brigadier General Frank Cheatham from Columbus. But Cheatham got no farther than Mayfield. Grant was convinced that Polk was content to stay put and fortify Columbus. See Hughes, *Battle of Belmont,* 5; *O.R.,* ser. 1, vol. 4, 197.

9. *O.R.,* ser. 1, vol. 4, 181–84.

10. John Milton Hubbard, *Notes of a Private* (Memphis: E. H. Clarke and Brother, 1909), 11–12; *Appeal,* Sept. 12, 1861.

11. *Senate Journal,* Sept. 2, 1861, 80–81; *O.R.,* ser. 1, vol. 4, 185.

12. *O.R.,* ser. 1, vol. 4, 185–87.

13. Hughes, *Battle of Belmont,* 5.

14. *Louisville Daily Courier,* Sept. 11–12, 1861; Coulter, *Civil War and Readjustment,* 113–14. Coulter notes that some members of the Peace Convention would become leaders of Kentucky's rump Confederate government. They included Kentucky's first and second Confederate "governors": George W. Johnson of Scott County and Richard Hawes of Bourbon County. All of the Purchase delegation except Irvan would help organize the Rebel "government" at Russellville in Nov. 1861.

15. *Senate Journal,* Sept. 2, 1861, 85–87, 92, 97.

16. *House Journal,* Sept. 2, 1861, 81–84.

17. *Senate Journal,* Sept. 2, 1861, 99–100; *House Journal,* Sept. 2, 1861, 1014.

18. *Senate Journal,* Sept. 2, 1861, 130–33; *House Journal,* Sept. 2, 1861, 153–60.

19. *O.R.,* ser. 1, vol. 4, 180.

20. Ibid., 181.

21. *Appeal,* Sept. 18, 1861. The signers were W. J. N. Welborn, George B. Moss, Joseph Kennedy, William Henderson, J. M. Strickland, W. R. Bradley, John Jackson, J. M. Robinson, J. P. Gray, W. Harper, C. S. Harper, R. M. Spillman, R. Jackson, C. C. Jackson, E. J. [*sic*] Bullock, and W. R. Vance.

22. John Paine Ridgway to Jennie Stanfield, Sept. 7, 1861, Historical Records Survey Transcription Unit, Division of Women's and Professionals Project, Works Projects Administration (Nashville: 1939), transcribed in Steven Birchfield, *Civil War Letters, Volume One: West Tennessee* (Melber, Ky.: Simmons Historical Publishing, 1995), 20.

23. *New York Times,* Sept. 12, 1861.

24. *Louisville Courier,* Sept. 12, 1861, excerpt from the *Cincinnati Enquirer.*

25. *O.R.,* ser. 1, vol. 52, 190; Neuman, *Story of Paducah,* 148.

26. Diary of Aaron Loder Mastin, 2, typescript on the Jackson Purchase Historical Society's Web site, http://www.jacksonpurchasehistory.org/wp-content/uploads/2011/04/Mastin-Diary.pdf (accessed Apr. 6, 2014).

27. Warner, *Generals in Blue,* 455; *Nashville Daily Union,* quoted in *Appeal,* Sept. 14, 1861.

28. *Appeal,* Sept. 18, 1861, excerpt from the *St. Louis Daily Missouri Republican.*

29. *Appeal,* Oct. 18, 1861.

30. Paducah Civil War Hospital File, Special Collections, McCracken County Public Library, Paducah, Ky.; Mastin diary.

31. Leland R. Johnson, *The Falls City Engineers: A History of the Louisville District Corps of Engineers United States Army* (Louisville, Ky.: Louisville District Corps of Engineers, 1974), 107; Mastin diary, 4; Collins and Collins, *History of Kentucky,* 1: 96.

32. *Times,* Sept. 28, 1861.

33. *Harper's Weekly,* Oct. 26, 1861; Johnson, *Falls City Engineers,* 107. Johnson writes that the bridge's length across the main channel was 3,900 feet. Adding the width of the island and the bridge section between the island and the Kentucky shore, the span was nearly a mile long, a length record unsurpassed as late as 1975.

34. *Harper's Weekly,* Oct. 26, 1861.

35. *Appeal,* Oct. 26, 1861.

36. *Times,* Nov. 1, 1861.

37. Ibid.

38. Kellogg, *Army Life of an Illinois Soldier,* 29.

39. Pirtle Memoirs, chap. 6, 10.

40. John Kelly Ross Jr., "'Columbus Scrapbook': Articles on Local and Civil War History" (bound typescript, n.d.), Pogue Special Collections, 31–32.

41. William H. Mulligan Jr., "African American Troops in Far West Kentucky during the Civil War: Recruitment and Service of the Fourth U.S. Heavy Artillery (Colored)," typescript of speech given at Fort Donelson National Military Park, Dover, Tenn., Feb. 25, 2012, 9. Mulligan, a history professor at Murray State University, was instrumental in getting signs erected at Columbus-Belmont State Park highlighting the role of African American troops at Columbus. See Hughes, *Battle of Belmont,* 36–38; Ross, "'Columbus Scrapbook,'" 1–2. Hughes writes that the "Lady Polk" was a Whitworth rifle. Ross writes that the cannon was an experimental 6.4-inch Anderson rifle manufactured at the Tredegar Iron Works in Richmond, Virginia, in 1861. According to Ross, the monster weighed about fifteen thousand pounds. The barrel was a shade over ten feet long and was nearly three feet wide at the breech.

42. Dr. William M. Polk, "General Polk and the Battle of Belmont," in *Battles and Lead-*

ers of the Civil War (rpt., New York: Thomas Yoseloff, 1956), 348. A Confederate captain and the general's son, Polk explained that to provide the Columbus gunners a clear field of fire, the Confederates cut trees "for some distance" around the camp and tangled the fallen timber into "an abatis capable of obstructing the advance of an enemy." See Ross, "'Columbus Scrapbook,'" 27–28; Hughes, *Battle of Belmont,* 37.

43. Ross, "'Columbus Scrapbook,'" 26.

44. Alice Henderson Phipps Memoirs, Pogue Special Collections.

45. Pirtle Memoirs, chap. 7, 11; George, *History of the 3d, 7th, 8th and 12th,* 29. No trace of the campsite remains.

46. George, *History of the 3d, 7th, 8th and 12th,* 27, 182; Ellis, *Report of the Adjutant General,* 1: 26; Battle, Perrin, and Kniffen, *Kentucky,* 19, 32–34, 42, 55–57, 69–70, 81–85, 102, 107.

47. *Columbus (Ky.) Daily Confederate News,* Oct. 24, 1861, quoted in the *Louisville Courier,* Oct. 26, 1861, in Ross, "'Columbus Scrapbook,'" 6. Having been shut down as treasonous by federal authorities after Union troops entered Louisville, the *Courier* went to Bowling Green and resumed publishing there.

48. *Daily Confederate News,* Nov. 1, 1861. Typically, Confederates referred to Republicans as "Black Republicans." In calling them "Red Republicans," Bullock may have been likening them to the French Red Republicans of the Revolution of 1848, which toppled King Louis Philippe.

49. *O.R.*, ser. 1, vol. 4, 432–33; Dieter C. Ullrich, "Confederate Operations in the Jackson Purchase: Camp Beauregard, Kentucky," *Filson Club History Quarterly* 76, no. 4 (2002): 462.

50. Phillip M. Shelton, "Camp Beauregard Graves County, Kentucky," *Register of the Kentucky Historical Society* 61, no. 3 (Apr. 1963): 150; Fuller, "History of Camp Beauregard," 3, 6–7, 9, 17.

51. Connelly, *Army of the Heartland,* 19, 78–79; John A. Eisterhold, "Fort Heiman: Forgotten Fortress," *West Tennessee Historical Society Papers* 28 (1974): 44.

52. *O.R.*, ser. 1, vol. 7, 738–39.

53. *O.R.*, ser. 1, vol. 7, 728; Battle, Perrin, and Kniffen, *Kentucky,* 33, 56, 85; George, *History of the 3d, 7th, 8th and 12th,* 158–59; Fuller, "History of Camp Beauregard," 6. King's battalion was afterward merged into the First Confederate Cavalry and later the Sixth Confederate Cavalry. The *O.R.* says King's battalion consisted of 351 men, present and absent (Ellis, *Report of the Adjutant General,* 2: 328–30; Horn, *Tennesseans in the Civil War,* 1: 244).

54. *House Journal,* Sept. 2, 1861, 184, 193.

55. *Louisville Daily Journal,* Oct. 24, 1861.

56. Coulter, *Civil War and Readjustment,* 137.

57. *Resolution of the [Confederate] Congress [in Kentucky],* 17–19. Other Purchase delegates included A. D. Kingman, W. I. Lunsford, and R. B. Alexander, all of Fulton County; W. Towsley of Ballard County; P. S. Hamlin, T. M. Jones, Alexander Wesson, Francis W. Dodds, W. T. Mathes, C. A. Duncan, A. J. Holland, H. L. Gilmer, and J. F. Bell, all of Calloway County; H. M. Rose, I. A. Pirtle, I. D. Scaff, and John Ridgway, all of Graves County; and William G. Bullitt and H. H. Huston of McCracken County. See Coulter, *Civil War and Readjustment,* 138.

58. *Resolutions of the [Confederate] Congress,* 13–14; *O.R.*, ser. 4, vol. 1, 741.

59. Dew, *Apostles of Disunion,* 11–13.

60. *Resolutions of the [Confederate] Congress,* 14–17; *O.R.*, ser. 4, vol. 1, 741–43; Coulter, *Civil War and Readjustment,* 138.

61. Coulter, *Civil War and Readjustment,* 138; Ezra J. Warner and W. Buck Yearns, *Biographical Register of the Confederate Congress* (Baton Rouge: Louisiana State University Press, 1975), 220, 291; Lowell H. Harrison, "George W. Johnson and Richard Hawes: The Governors of Confederate Kentucky," *Register of the Kentucky Historical Society* 79 (1981): 15. Missouri also had a bogus Confederate government that led to the Show Me State's "admission" as the Confederacy's twelfth "state" on Nov. 28, 1861.

62. Caleb S. Jones to "My dear children," typescript, Pogue Special Collections.

63. Ibid.

64. *Memphis Daily Appeal,* Oct. 18, 1861, citing the *Nashville Patriot.* Crittenden emerged as the strongest pro-Union county in the western Pennyrile region. When the war started, Yeiser's Unionism made him "unpopular with the masses in his vicinity," according to Battle, Perrin, and Kniffen, *Kentucky,* 332.

65. Excerpt from the *Daily Confederate News,* in the *Louisville Daily Courier,* Oct. 29, 1861. Federal authorities closed down the *Courier* after Union troops occupied Louisville. To avoid arrest, editor Walter N. Haldeman escaped to Bowling Green, where he resumed publication.

66. *Louisville Daily Journal,* Nov. 5, 1861.

67. H. Levin, ed., *Lawyers and Lawmakers of Kentucky* (Chicago: Lewis Publishing Company, 1897), 94.

68. D. W. Lindsey, *Report of the Adjutant General of the State of Kentucky* (Frankfort: John H. Harney, Public Printer, 1866), 2: 54–56. The Yankee Marshall countians, like the Rebel Marshall men in the Third and Seventh Kentucky, Confederate, would receive their baptism of fire at Shiloh. See Battle, Perrin, and Kniffen, *Kentucky,* 107, 341.

69. Grant, *Personal Memoirs,* 117–23. Some residents of Vicksburg, Mississippi, have claimed that the Civil War's first shots were fired in their town, at the *Tyler.* Before it was the USS *Tyler,* the vessel was the *A. O. Tyler,* a civilian steamer. When the New Orleans–bound *A. O. Tyler* passed Vicksburg on Jan. 13, 1861, militia soldiers guarding the town opened fire, stopped the steamer, searched it, and let it go, according to a state historical marker in Vicksburg. The marker hedges on the "first shots" claim: "The firing on the *Tyler,* just four days after Mississippi's secession, was one of the first shots of the Civil War." The metal plaque also explains that the Union navy converted the boat into the USS *Tyler,* a "timberclad gunboat."

70. Grant, *Personal Memoirs,* 122–23; Hughes, *Battle of Belmont,* 174. In terms of personal danger, the battle of Belmont "was about as bad a spot as Grant got into in all the war," Bruce Catton writes in *Grant Moves South.* "As the bullets whined about his ears he gave way, suddenly, to a desperate thought of home: what would become of Julia and the children, if he should be killed here? For a moment the thought possessed him with power, and far away in their home in Galena Julia Grant, going to her bedroom to rest after some household task or other, suddenly saw a distant but mysterious vision: Grant mounted and in the field, gazing at her with a peculiar intensity. When they met a few days later, they found that his odd experience had come to her at the moment when Grant, all alone on his horse, was the target for concentrated rifle fire, and was thinking of his wife and children; and they both felt it was the depth of his feeling that projected this strange vision into the house at Galena." See Bruce Catton, *Grant Moves South* (Boston and Toronto: Little, Brown and Company, 1960), 78–79.

71. George, *History of the 3d, 7th, 8th and 12th,* 27.

72. Pirtle Memoirs, chap. 10, 12.

73. *Louisville Daily Journal,* Nov. 11, 1861.

74. *Resolutions of the [Confederate] Congress,* 18.

75. *Louisville Daily Journal,* Nov. 20, 1861.

76. *Louisville Daily Journal,* Nov. 25, 1861.

77. *O.R.,* ser. 1, vol. 4, 302.

78. Neuman, *Story of Paducah,* 149–50; *New York Times,* Dec. 8, 1861. Wallace is more famous for writing the novel *Ben Hur: A Tale of the Christ,* published in 1880. The Tilghman-Woolfolk house is a Civil War museum.

79. *New York Times,* Dec. 8, 1861.

80. Ibid.

81. *Louisville Daily Journal,* Dec. 12, 1861; Westin A. Goodspeed, *A History of Tennessee from the Earliest Times to the Present* (1886; rpt., Nashville: Charles and Randy Elder, Booksellers, 1973), 534.

82. *New York Times,* Dec. 4, 1861; Warner and Yearns, *Biographical Register,* 38–39.

83. Battle, Perrin, and Kniffen, *Kentucky,* 116; *House Journal,* Sept. 2, 1861, 531, 545–47. The House also expelled Representative John M. Elliott of Floyd and Johnson Counties, George W. Ewing of Logan County, and Merritt. Merritt was also at the Russellville convention. See *Resolutions of the [Confederate] Congress,* 17–19.

84. Craig, *Hidden History of Kentucky in the Civil War,* 39–40. The Market House Museum in Paducah has a special exhibit about Sister Mary Lucy.

85. Hughes, *Battle of Belmont,* 190.

7. Gibraltar Crumbles

1. Collins and Collins, *History of Kentucky,* 1: 99; *Kentucky Secretary of State Elections Register, 1855–1872,* Kentucky Department for Library and Archives, Frankfort, 278. Two other candidates received eighteen votes, including one vote in Calloway County, where Casey topped Trimble 41–0. Casey bested Trimble 140–4 in Graves County, but Trimble triumphed in Marshall, 22–0.

2. *Louisville Daily Journal,* Nov. 20, 1861; *Evansville Journal,* quoted in the *Louisville Daily Journal,* Jan. 25, 1862. The letter was signed "A REFUGEE from the First District."

3. Harrison, "George W. Johnson and Richard Hawes," 22; Warner and Yearns, *Biographical Register,* 291, 295. Ex-congressman William E. Simms of Paris was the other senator. John J. Crittenden unseated Simms in the special June 20 congressional election. Machen was a grandfather of Zelda Fitzgerald, wife of the famous novelist F. Scott Fitzgerald.

4. *Senate Journal,* Sept. 2, 1861, 378–79, 402–5. Seven more Southern Rights members of the legislature resigned or were expelled. Representatives J. S. Barlow of Barren County and J. C. Lindsey of Carroll County resigned. Senator Cissell also resigned. Representatives Vincent Ashe of Anderson County and David May of Pike and Letcher Counties were also expelled. See Collins and Collins, *History of Kentucky,* 2: 34, 36, 39, 43, 109, 118, 237, 292, 342, 479, 481, 543, 594, 670, 679, 731; Thomas A. Duke to Abraham Lincoln, July 6, 1863, Lincoln Papers, Library of Congress, http://memory.loc.gov/cgi-bin/query/P?mal:1:./temp/~ammem_DJsY:: (accessed Apr. 7, 2014).

5. *Louisville Daily Journal,* Jan. 25, 1862.

6. *Louisville Daily Journal,* Jan. 28, 1861; Ellis, *Report of the Adjutant General,* 2: 408.

7. *Louisville Daily Journal,* Jan. 28, 1861.

8. Berry Craig, "Henry C. Burnett, Champion of Southern Rights," *Register of the Kentucky Historical Society* 77 (1979): 266–74.

9. *New York Times,* Jan. 27, 1862; Craig, *Hidden History of Kentucky in the Civil War,* 43–44.

10. *O.R.*, ser, 1, vol. 7, 625. Grant said he also captured General Bushrod R. Johnson, around twenty thousand stand of arms, forty-eight artillery pieces, seventeen large guns, and between two thousand and four thousand horses, plus "large quantities of commissary stores"; see Catton, *Grant Moves South,* 177; Mastin diary, 5–8.

11. Hughes, *Battle of Belmont,* 39.

12. Ross, "'Columbus Scrapbook,'" 61; George, *History of the 3d, 7th, 8th and 12th,* 28.

13. *New York Times,* Feb. 23, 1862.

14. Craig, *Hidden History of Kentucky in the Civil War,* 36; *Cairo City Weekly Gazette,* Feb. 13, 1862, quoted in Ross, "'Columbus Scrapbook,'" 2.

15. *Confederate News,* Jan. 3, 1862, photocopy at Columbus-Belmont State Park; see also *Hickman County Gazette, 100th Anniversary Edition,* Apr. 30, 1953. Bullock went to Richmond, Virginia, and stayed until 1864, when he came back to Columbus. See Battle, Perrin, and Kniffen, *Kentucky,* 249.

16. *New York Times,* Mar. 9, 1862; *O.R.*, ser. 1, vol. 7, 437.

17. *New York Times,* Mar. 9, 1861.

18. *New York Times,* Mar. 9, 1862.

19. Ibid.

20. Ibid.

21. Ibid.

22. Junius Henry Browne, *Four Years in Secessia: Adventures Within and Beyond the Union Lines Embracing a Great Variety of Facts, Incidents and Romance of the War* (Hartford, Conn.: O. D. Case and Co., 1865), 89–92.

23. *O.R.*, ser. 1, vol. 7, 436–37.

24. Ibid., 437.

25. *Federal Scout,* Mar. 11, 1862, photocopy at Columbus-Belmont State Park; Ross, "'Columbus Scrapbook,'" 165–66, 182–84.

26. *O.R.*, ser. 1, vol. 7, 438.

27. *Harper's Weekly,* Mar. 29, 1862.

28. Samuel Paine Ridgway to Jennie Stanfield, Feb. 24, 1862, in possession of Hugh and Evelyn Williams of Mayfield, Ky.

29. Pirtle Memoirs, chap. 13, 14; George, *History of the 3d, 7th, 8th and 12th,* 30–31.

30. Barton, interview, Apr. 10, 1998; Ullrich, "Confederate Operations," 463, 486; Fuller, "History of Camp Beauregard," 3.

31. Ullrich, "Confederate Operations," 465, 474–75; Fuller, "History of Camp Beauregard," 21–22.

32. Ullrich, "Confederate Operations," 486, 489–92; Fuller, "History of Camp Beauregard," 1–2.

8. Yankee Occupation

1. *Louisville Daily Journal,* Apr. 9, 1862.

2. Daniel E. Sutherland, *A Savage Conflict: The Decisive Role of Guerrillas in the Civil War* (Chapel Hill: University of North Carolina Press, 2009), ix–xi; *O.R.*, ser. 3, vol. 3, 157. While Sutherland's book is comprehensive and provides an excellent overview of guerrilla warfare, it does not examine such fighting in the Jackson Purchase. Hoskins, on the other hand, devotes a great deal of her dissertation to Purchase guerrillas and Union efforts to combat them ("Old First").

3. *Louisville Daily Journal,* Apr. 7, 1862. Depoyster's son and brother were Confederate

soldiers. In 1862, his wife drowned at Cairo while coming home from a visit to their son at Camp Douglas, Illinois, a Union prisoner-of-war facility. Depoyster died in 1863 at age fifty-one. See Battle, Perrin, and Kniffen, *Kentucky,* 120.

4. *Louisville Daily Journal,* Apr. 17, 1862.

5. *Louisville Daily Journal,* May 10, 1862.

6. Collins and Collins, *History of Kentucky*; Neuman, *Paducahans in History,* 69.

7. Coulter, *Civil War and Readjustment,* 151; Collins and Collins, *History of Kentucky,* 1: 104–5.

8. Coulter, *Civil War and Readjustment,* 216.

9. Ibid.

10. Ibid., 217–18.

11. *Louisville Daily Journal,* June 10, 1862.

12. *Louisville Daily Journal,* July 1, 1862.

13. *Louisville Daily Journal,* July 8, 1862.

14. *Louisville Daily Journal,* July 9, 1862.

15. See Paducah Civil War Hospital File, Special Collections Section, McCracken County Public Library, Paducah; Neuman, *Story of Paducah,* 193.

16. *Kentucky Secretary of State Elections Register, 1855–1872,* 261, 279; *Louisville Daily Journal,* Aug. 12, 1862.

17. Collins and Collins, *History of Kentucky,* 2: 39, 109, 292, 342, 542, 594.

18. Battle, Perrin, and Kniffen, *Kentucky,* 19; Captain Thomas Speed, *The Union Regiments of Kentucky Published Under the Auspices of the Union Soldiers and Sailors Monument Association* (Louisville, Ky.: Courier-Journal Job Printing Co., 1897), 192–94, 201. Owens was killed, evidently in action, on Sept. 23, 1863, according to Lindsey, *Report of the Adjutant General,* 1: 225.

19. Coulter, *Civil War and Readjustment,* 160.

20. Benjamin Quarles, *The Negro in the Civil War* (Boston: Little, Brown & Co., 1969), 144–45; Abraham Lincoln, "Message of Appeal to Border-State Representatives in Favor of Compensated Emancipation," July 12, 1862, at *The American Presidency Project,* by Gerhard Peters and John T. Woolley, http://www.presidency.ucsb.edu/ws/?pid=584 (accessed Apr. 21, 2014); Jacob F. Lee, "'The Union as It Was and the Constitution as It Is': Unionism and Emancipation in Civil War Kentucky" (master's thesis, University of Louisville, 2007), 19.

21. *Louisville Daily Journal,* Oct. 29, 1862.

22. Speed, *Union Regiments of Kentucky,* 259–60, 262; Battle, Perrin, and Kniffen, *Kentucky,* 56, 107.

23. Jonathan D. Sarna, *When General Grant Expelled the Jews* (Schocken, N.Y.: Nextbook, 2012), 3–7.

24. *O.R.*, ser. 1, vol. 16, part 2, 424; Sarna, *When General Grant Expelled,* xi, 7. Sarna quotes the order in the *O.R.,* but he notes that there were three other versions of the order with slightly different wording.

25. Sarna, *When General Grant Expelled,* x, 3–7.

26. Ibid., 3–23. Grant spent the rest of his life regretting and atoning for General Orders No. 11. When he was president, Grant was eager to prove he was not anti-Semitic. He named more Jews to public office than had any previous president. He offered unprecedented support for persecuted Jews in Imperial Russia and Romania. He "apologized for the order publicly, and repented of it privately." Over and over, "partly as a result of his enlarged vision of what it meant to be an American and partly in order to live down General Orders No. 11,

Grant consciously worked to assist Jews and secure them equality." Grant rejected a constitutional amendment declaring the United States a "Christian nation": "During his administration, Jews achieved a heightened status on the national scene. Judaism won recognition (at least from him) as a faith coequal to Protestantism and Catholicism." Still, the order ate at him, especially when he was around Jews. Grant did not mention the order in his memoirs, but "he gloried in the fact that, on his deathbed, Jews numbered among those who visited with him and prayed for his recovery" (ibid., xi–xv).

9. Traitors Beware

1. Coulter, *Civil War and Readjustment,* 161–65.

2. *Louisville Daily Journal,* Jan. 1, 1863. All three were abolitionist Republican congressmen—Lovejoy from Illinois, Julian from Indiana, and Bingham from Ohio.

3. Langstaff, *Life and Times,* 74.

4. *Louisville Daily Journal,* Nov. 25, 1861, Jan. 14, 1863; Fuller, "History of Camp Beauregard," 17.

5. *Louisville Daily Journal,* Jan. 14, 1863.

6. Ibid.

7. *Louisville Daily Journal,* Jan. 31, 1863.

8. Coulter, *Civil War and Readjustment,* 170.

9. Ibid., 170–75.

10. *Louisville Daily Journal,* Mar. 7, 19, 1863.

11. *Louisville Daily Journal,* Mar. 14, 1863.

12. *Louisville Daily Journal,* Mar. 18, 1863.

13. *Louisville Daily Journal,* Mar. 19–20, 1863.

14. Ellis, *Report of the Adjutant General,* 2: 142; George, *History of the 3d, 7th, 8th and 12th,* 68–69; county by county list, Trowbridge records.

15. Coulter, *Civil War and Readjustment,* 163–64; Astor, *Rebels on the Border,* 108–9.

16. Craig, *Hidden History of Kentucky in the Civil War,* 105–9.

17. Mulligan, "African American Troops," 10–12.

18. Marion B. Lucas, *A History of Kentucky Blacks from Slavery to Segregation, 1760–1891* (Frankfort: Kentucky Historical Society, 1992), 1: 150.

19. Mulligan, "African American Troops," 13.

20. Lucas, *History of Kentucky Blacks,* 1: 148–49; Mulligan, "African American Troops," 12–13.

21. Coulter, *Civil War and Readjustment,* 197; Steven A. Channing, *Kentucky: A Bicentennial History* (New York: W. W. Norton and Company, 1977), 131.

22. Ann E. Marshall, *Creating a Confederate Kentucky: The Lost Cause and Civil War Memory in a Border State* (Chapel Hill: University of North Carolina Press, 2010), 27–28.

23. Mulligan, "African American Troops," 8. Camp Nelson was named for Brigadier General William O. "Bull" Nelson of Maysville, who was shot and killed by Brigadier General Jefferson C. Davis of Indiana in an 1862 argument at the old Galt House Hotel in Louisville.

24. Mulligan, "African American Troops," 14; *O.R.,* ser. 3, vol. 3, 1115, 1189–91, ser. 1, vol. 39, part 1, 857–58.

25. Speed, *Union Regiments of Kentucky,* 235, 242–44, 263–64; Battle, Perrin, and Kniffen, *Kentucky,* 85, 107, 330.

26. Langstaff, *Life and Times,* 78. "Vanlandigham" was Representative Clement L. Vallandingham of Ohio, a bitter foe of Lincoln, the war, and abolitionism.

27. *Louisville Daily Journal,* June 4, 1863.

28. Ibid. Ervin Anderson's great-great-granddaughter Martha Nell Anderson lives in Lucian Anderson's house, the oldest dwelling in Mayfield.

29. *O.R.,* ser. 1, vol. 24, part 3, 74.

30. Ross, "'Columbus Scrapbook,'" 140. Fort Halleck was named for General Halleck.

31. Laura Smith Haviland, *A Woman's Life-Work: Labors and Experiences of Laura S. Haviland* (Cincinnati: Walden & Stowe, 1882), 270–71; Ross, "'Columbus Scrapbook,'" 207.

32. Haviland, *Woman's Life-Work,* 271; Ross, "'Columbus Scrapbook,'" 174–75.

33. Haviland, *Woman's Life-Work,* 271–72.

34. Ibid., 272–73. Haviland does not state Moss's first name, but he may have been related to James W. Moss of Hickman County, who raised Company A of the Confederate First Kentucky Infantry and ended up colonel of the Second Kentucky Infantry Regiment.

35. Ibid., 273–78.

36. Ross, "'Columbus Scrapbook,'" 125–26.

37. Coulter, *Civil War and Readjustment,* 177–78; *O.R.,* ser. 1, vol. 23, part 2, 572.

38. *O.R.,* ser. 1, vol. 23, part 2, 570.

39. Thomas A. Duke to Abraham Lincoln, July 6, 1863, Lincoln Papers, http://memory.loc.gov/cgi-bin/query/P?mal:1:./temp/~ammem_bLNJ:: (accessed Apr. 10, 2014). The other candidates were N. N. Cowgill, Thomas Owens, and R. B. J. Twyman.

40. *O.R.,* ser. 1, vol. 23, part 2, 570–71.

41. Ibid., 568–69. In 1857, Waring, an engineer, supervised the drainage of wetlands that became New York's Central Park. After the war, he designed a sewer system for Memphis.

42. Ibid., 589.

43. *Columbus War Eagle,* Aug. 3, 1863, quoted in Ross, "'Columbus Scrapbook,'" 175–76.

44. *Kentucky Secretary of State Elections Register, 1855–1872,* 311–14, 327; Collins and Collins, *History of Kentucky,* 1: 127–28. Boone, Carroll, and Trimble Counties elected "No-men-or-money" representatives.

45. *Kentucky Secretary of State Elections Register, 1855–1872,* 261, 311–13, 327. Cowgill got 18 votes, Owens 166, and Twyman 11.

46. *Evansville Journal,* quoted in the *Louisville Daily Journal,* Jan. 25, 1862.

47. Collins and Collins, *History of Kentucky,* 2: 39, 109, 292, 543, 594, 731; *Kentucky Secretary of State Elections Register, 1855–1872,* 336–37; Battle, Perrin, and Kniffen, *Kentucky,* 106.

48. *Kentucky Secretary of State Elections Register, 1855–1872,* 261, 311–13, 327.

10. The Battle of Paducah

1. *Louisville Daily Journal,* Aug. 3, 1863.

2. *Louisville Daily Journal,* Nov. 11, 1863.

3. *New York Times,* Nov. 15, 1863. George does not list a "Major Newsome" on the rolls of the Twelfth Kentucky in *History of the 3d, 7th, 8th and 12th.* See pp. 175–81.

4. *Louisville Daily Journal,* Dec. 30, 1863.

5. *Louisville Daily Journal,* Nov. 9, 1863.

6. John T. Hubbell and James W. Geary, eds., *Biographical Dictionary of the Union: Northern Leaders of the Civil War* (Westport, Conn.: Greenwood Press, 1995), 8; *Louisville Daily Journal,* Jan. 14, 1864.

7. *Louisville Daily Journal,* Jan. 14, 1864.

8. Hoskins, "Old First," 202; *Louisville Daily Journal,* Nov. 2, 1863.

9. *War Eagle,* Dec. 12, 1863, photocopy at Columbus-Belmont State Park; *New York Times,* Dec. 24, 1863.

10. Coulter, *Civil War and Readjustment,* 220; Lucian Anderson to Salmon P. Chase, Jan. 29, 1864, Lincoln Papers, http://memory.loc.gov/cgi-bin/query/P?mal:2:./temp/~ammem_66z2:: (accessed Aug. 22, 2013).

11. *The Congressional Globe, The Official Proceedings of Congress, Published by John C. Rives,* 38th Congress, 1st session, 384, 456–59; "Biographical Directory of the United States Congress, 1774–Present, http://bioguide.congress.gov/scripts/biodisplay.pl?index=A000152 (accessed Apr. 11, 2015).

12. Hubbell and Geary, *Biographical Dictionary,* 8.

13. Coulter, *Civil War and Readjustment,* 197–98.

14. Mulligan, "African American Troops," 3; Coulter, *Civil War and Readjustment,* 197; John David Smith, "The Recruitment of Negro Soldiers in Kentucky," *Register of the Kentucky Historical Society* 72 (1974): 374–75; *O.R.,* ser. 3, vol. 4, 429–30.

15. Astor, *Rebels on the Border,* 128; *O.R.,* ser. 3, vol. 4, 429; Warner, *Generals in Blue,* 502; Ira Berlin, *Freedom: A Documentary History of Emancipation, 1861–1867,* series 2, book 1, *The Black Military Experience* (Cambridge and New York: Cambridge University Press, 1982), 255; *O.R.,* ser. 1, vol. 32, part 3, 157, part 1, 548; Janet B. Hewett, ed., *Supplement to the Official Records of the Union and Confederate Armies, Part II, Record of Events,* vol. 77, serial no. 89 (Wilmington, N.C.: Broadfoot Publishing Company, 1998), 212.

16. Collins and Collins, *History of Kentucky,* 1: 132.

17. Moore, *Rebellion Record,* 8: 468–69.

18. *O.R.*, ser. 1, vol. 32, part 1, 417.

19. *Louisville Daily Journal,* Feb. 29, 1864.

20. *O.R.*, ser. 1, vol. 32, part 1, 485, 492–94.

21. *Louisville Daily Journal,* Mar. 1, 1864.

22. *Congressional Globe,* 38th Congress, 1st session, appendix, 98–99.

23. Ibid., 99.

24. Ibid., 99; Neuman, *Story of Paducah,* 154.

25. *Congressional Globe,* 38th Congress, 1st session, appendix, 99–10; *Louisville Daily Journal,* July 19, 1862.

26. *Congressional Globe,* 38th Congress, 1st session, appendix, 100–103.

27. *O.R.*, ser. 1, vol. 32, part 1, 628, and part 3, 131.

28. George, *History of the 3d, 7th, 8th and 12th,* 74–75.

29. Pirtle Memoirs, chap. 43, 51–53.

30. George, *History of the 3d, 7th, 8th and 12th,* 75–76.

31. Moore, *Rebellion Record,* 8: 499–500.

32. Ibid.; George, *History of the 3d, 7th, 8th and 12th,* 75–76.

33. George, *History of the 3d, 7th, 8th and 12th,* 76; Craig, *Hidden History of Western Kentucky,* 130–32; Neuman, *Story of Paducah,* 152–53.

34. Moore, *Rebellion Record,* 8: 505, 506; Battle, Perrin, and Kniffen, *Kentucky,* 83; *New York Times,* Apr. 1, 1864; Neuman, *Story of Paducah,* 152–53; J. V. Grief, "Forrest's Raid on Paducah," *Confederate Veteran* 5 (May 1897): 212. The *Times* and Battle, Perrin, and Kniffen have Hayes in the Fifteenth Kentucky Cavalry, but that regiment mustered out in 1863. The fort's defenders included the Sixteenth Kentucky Cavalry.

35. Brian Steel Wills, *The Confederacy's Greatest Cavalryman: Nathan Bedford Forrest* (Lawrence: University Press of Kansas, 1992), 176; John Allan Wyeth, *Life of General Nathan*

Bedford Forrest (New York: Harper & Brothers, 1899), 330. "Supposing that the charge had been ordered by General Forrest, and being too far away from my regiment to join it in time, I asked permission to accompany him in this assault," Tyler said, according to Wyeth. See Grief, "Forrest's Raid," 213.

36. George, *History of the 3d, 7th, 8th and 12th,* 76–77; Pirtle Memoirs, chap. 44.

37. *O.R.,* ser. 1, vol. 32, part 3, 153.

38. Neuman, *Story of Paducah,* 151; *O.R.,* ser. 1, vol. 32, part 1, 547.

39. *Chicago Times,* quoted in the *New York Times,* Apr. 1, 1864.

40. *O.R.,* ser. 1, vol. 32, part 1, 547.

41. Ibid., 547–48.

42. Ibid., 548–49; *Chicago Daily Tribune,* quoted in the *New York Times,* Apr. 1, 1864.

43. Jennie Fyfe to "Dear Ones in H_____," Mar. 31, 1861, and Jennie Fyfe to "My Darling Matie," Apr. 6, 1864, photocopies in McCracken County Public Library, Fyfe Family Collection, Property of Bentley Library, University of Michigan, copyright by Bentley Library, University of Michigan.

44. *O.R.,* ser. 1, vol. 32, part 1, 607; clipping from *Paris Post,* Mar. 14, 1872, in possession of Thomas Lannom; George, *History of the 3d, 7th, 8th and 12th,* 79–83.

45. Moore, *Rebellion Record,* 8: 503, 510.

46. Robertson, *Paducah: Frontier to the Atomic Age,* 49–50; *New York Times,* Apr. 1, 1864. Forrest and his apologists—then and now—claimed there was no massacre. But James M. McPherson writes in *Battle Cry of Freedom* (748) that "some of [Forrest's] . . . men had murdered black soldiers after they surrendered." In a footnote, McPherson adds, "Although formerly disputed by southerners, the truth of a massacre of several dozen black prisoners and some whites—along with their commander Major William F. Bradford, who was captured and subsequently shot 'while attempting to escape'—is now well established and generally accepted." He says that "summaries and analyses of the evidence" may be found in Robert Selph Henry's *"First with the Most" Forrest* (Indianapolis, 1944), 248–69; Albert Castel's "The Fort Pillow Massacre: A Fresh Examination of the Evidence," *Civil War History* 4 (1958): 37–50; and John Cimprich and Robert C. Mainfort Jr.'s "Fort Pillow Revisited: New Evidence about an Old Controversy," *Civil War History* 28 (1982): 293–306.

47. Ronald K. Huch, "Fort Pillow Massacre: The Aftermath of Paducah," *Illinois State Historical Society Journal* 66 (Spring 1973): 67–70. In *Confederacy's Greatest Cavalryman,* Wills writes that at Fort Pillow, Forrest had "the opportunity to expose the fallacy of placing guns in the hands of blacks by demonstrating their inferiority as soldiers. In his attitudes toward the . . . fort's garrison, Forrest exposed his deepest prejudices. As a white Southerner, he considered the white Southerners [Union soldiers] in Fort Pillow to be traitors and examples of humanity at its worst. To Forrest, it was such 'renegade Tennesseans' who violated the norms of warfare and civilization. They were the cold-blooded savages who waged war on civilians, tortured prisoners, and compounded their sins by fighting beside former slaves. And the black troops were little better. They were deluded miscreants, coerced from the fields by their new masters. But their current behavior, as misguided as it might be, could not be tolerated. Bedford Forrest's past experience with black Southerners led him to develop several generalizations. He could not think of such people as people and certainly refused to take them seriously as soldiers. Black Southerners were commodities to be bought and sold and made to work, not human beings who might wish to control their lives by carrying weapons and wearing uniforms. That they carried weapons and wore uniforms could only be attributed to interference from Northern whites, who threatened what many Southern whites saw as the proper social order." See pp. 180–81.

48. *Louisville Daily Journal,* Mar. 29, 1864.

49. *Louisville Daily Journal,* Mar. 31, 1864; Moore, *Rebellion Record,* 8: 500.

50. *Louisville Daily Journal,* Mar. 31, 1864. Grierson is most famous for his 1863 raid from La Grange, Tennessee, through Confederate territory in Mississippi all the way to Union-held Baton Rouge, Louisiana. Grierson led seventeen hundred Illinois and Iowa horsemen on the foray, which lasted from Apr. 17 to May 2. He engaged Rebel forces numerous times, wrecked two railroads, and destroyed vast amounts of enemy property. See Warner, *Generals in Blue,* 190.

51. *Louisville Daily Journal,* Mar. 31, 1864; Moore, *Rebellion Record,* 8: 506.

52. *Louisville Daily Journal,* Mar. 31, 1864.

53. Ibid.

54. Ibid.

55. Neuman, *Story of Paducah,* 154.

56. *New York Times,* Apr. 1, 1864; Moore, *Rebellion Record,* 8: 501.

57. *New York Times,* Apr. 1, 1864.

58. Neuman, *Story of Paducah,* 150–54.

59. Neuman, *Paducahans in History,* 65–66; George, *History of the 3d, 7th, 8th and 12th,* 78. The Hougoumont Chateau was the famous walled farmhouse the British defended against Napoleon at the Battle of Waterloo, Belgium, in 1815. Neuman writes that after the war, several people asked the federal government to reimburse them for the destruction of their homes: "A known Union man succeeded in having Congress pass a bill aiding the losers, but President U. S. Grant vetoed the measure as a bad precedent to set, declaring with Colonel Hicks that the usages of war made burning of property a line of defense."

60. Neuman, *Story of Paducah,* 155.

61. Speed, *Union Regiments of Kentucky,* 235, 242–44; Lindsey, *Report of the Adjutant General,* 1: 403.

11. Still Disloyal

1. Pryor may have been one of the men who came to take the state guard weapons in July 1861 but turned back. See George, *History of the 3d, 7th, 8th and 12th,* 78–79.

2. *Cairo News,* quoted in the *Evansville Daily Journal,* Aug. 12, 1864, and the *Louisville Daily Journal,* Aug. 16, 1864. The story said the younger Gregory brother died in a skirmish but furnished no other details. Also, the paper referred to the captain as "Jim Gregory."

3. *Louisville Daily Journal,* Sept. 18, 1862; Lindsey, *Report of the Adjutant General,* 1: 54–55, 765, 825–26.

4. George, *History of the 3d, 7th, 8th and 12th,* 79. L. S. Slayden was captain of Company D, Second Kentucky Confederate Infantry.

5. Ibid., 79–80.

6. Ibid., 80.

7. Ibid.

8. Ibid., 79–81. Crossland does not say what happened to Pryor, Burns, or Front.

9. Pirtle Memoirs, chap. 43, 53, chap. 44, 53; George, *History of the 3d, 7th, 8th and 12th,* 78; Ellis, *Report of the Adjutant General,* 1: 332–35. According to Ellis, James G. Pirtle was "severely wounded by fragment of shell at the battle of Shiloh, Apr. 6, 1862, and permanently disabled; first man wounded in regiment."

10. Pirtle Memoirs; chap. 43, 55, chap. 44, 55, chap. 45, 55–56; George, *History of the 3d, 7th, 8th and 12th,* 182.

11. George, *History of the 3d, 7th, 8th and 12th,* 78; *O.R.,* ser. 1, vol. 32, part 1, 553; Wills, *Battle from the Start,* 178–79.

12. *New York Times,* Apr. 14, 1864.

13. *O.R.,* ser. 1, vol. 32, part 1, 549–50.

14. George, *History of the 3d, 7th, 8th and 12th,* 179.

15. *O.R.,* ser. 1, vol. 32, 550; Pirtle Memoirs, chap. 45.

16. *Louisville Daily Journal,* Apr. 23, 1864.

17. *Louisville Daily Journal,* May 3, 1864.

18. *O.R.,* ser. 1, vol. 32, 508–12.

19. *O.R.,* ser. 1, vol. 39, part 2, 24.

20. Ibid., 26.

21. McPherson, *Battle Cry of Freedom,* 716.

22. *New York Times,* May 29, 1864; *Louisville Daily Journal,* May 26, 1864.

23. Roy P. Basler, Marion Dolores Pratt, and Lloyd A. Dunlap, eds., *The Collected Works of Abraham Lincoln,* vol. 7 (New Brunswick, N.J.: Rutgers University Press, 1953), 400.

24. *New York Times,* May 29, 1864; *Louisville Daily Journal,* May 26, 1864.

25. Collins and Collins, *History of Kentu*cky, 1: 134.

26. Ibid., 1: 135.

27. Ibid., 1: 135; *O.R.,* ser. 1, vol. 39, part 2, 171.

28. *Louisville Daily Journal,* July 23, 1864; Lindsey, *Report of the Adjutant General,* 1: 54–55, 765, 825–26.

29. *O.R.,* ser. 1, vol. 39, part 2, 171.

12. A Paine in the Purchase

1. Willis Danforth, "How I Came to Be in the Army and General E. A. Paine's Plan of Federal Salvation," in *War Papers Read Before the Commandery of the State of Wisconsin, Loyal Legion of the United States,* vol. 1 (Milwaukee: Burdick, Armitage, & Allen, 1891), 331, 339.

2. Barton, "History of Graves County," 109, 111; Hall Allen, *Center of Conflict: A Factual Story of the War between the States in Western Kentucky and Tennessee* (Paducah, Ky.: Paducah Sun-Democrat, 1961), 130. Allen drew some of his book from *The Civil War and Readjustment in Kentucky,* though without attributing Coulter. "During his short day of authority, Paine seems to have tried to reek vengeance for all the blasted hopes of the Federals during the previous three years," Coulter writes. See *Civil War and Readjustment,* 221. See also Hunter B. Whitesell, "Military Operations in the Jackson Purchase," *Register of the Kentucky Historical Society* 63, no. 4, part 3 (1965): 329.

3. Sutherland, *Savage Conflict,* 223; *O.R.,* ser. 1, vol. 32, part 2, 103.

4. *Nashville Dispatch,* quoted in *Louisville Daily Journal,* Nov. 1, 1864.

5. Barton, "History of Graves County," 115–16. According to Battle, Perrin, and Kniffen's *Kentucky,* Paine executed sixty-one people, "many of them entirely innocent." See p. 56. See also Hoskins, "Old First," 217–18. Hoskins's dissertation is an excellent and balanced account of Paine's time in Paducah and his subsequent court-martial. See esp. pp. 201–20.

6. Craig, *Hidden History of Kentucky in the Civil War,* 94–95.

7. Barton, "History of Graves County," 115–16; Craig, *Hidden History of Kentucky in the Civil War,* 96.

8. *O.R.,* ser. 1, vol. 39, part 2, 261.

9. Danforth, "How I Came to Be in the Army," 331; *Detroit Free Press,* Aug. 11, 1864. In *Paducah: Frontier to the Atomic Age,* Robertson names the exiles: from Columbus James P.

Walker, Burn M. Walker, Joe M. Moore, T. M. Moore, T. M. Horne, Mrs. Josephine Overall, William McKeene Hubbard, Judge W. R. Vance, Robert E. Cook, James Morton, George B. Moss, Charles Rickee, John Glenn, and W. G. Malone and his wife and six children, twenty-one in all; from Paducah Mrs. Robert Woolfolk and six children, Mrs. Rollston, Kate Saunders, Mrs. Joe Sam Hobbs, Robert Shanklin, and others, totaling eighteen to twenty. See p. 54.

10. *Louisville Daily Journal,* Aug. 15, 1864.

11. Robertson, *Paducah: Frontier to the Atomic Age,* 54; *O.R.*, ser. 1, vol. 52, part 2, 61–62; *Appeal,* Apr. 25, Sept. 18, 1861; Patrick, *Three Years with Wallace's Zouaves,* 60–61; *Times,* Dec. 8, 1861; Sallie Malone Brevard, "A Reminiscence of the War," photocopy, Columbus-Belmont State Park; George, *History of the 3d, 7th, 8th and 12th,* 175; *Louisville Daily Journal,* Aug. 12, 1864. The paper listed the exiles: "From Paducah, Mrs. Robert Woolfolk and family, eight persons; Mr. Woolfolk was banished to Canada two weeks since by Gen. Paine; Mrs. Hobbs, Mrs. Melrouse and sister; Robert Shanklin, from Columbus; Mrs. Dowell, Mr. Malone, George B. Moore, Pembroke Walker, James Morton, Burns Walker, Judge Vance, N. Cook, McKean Hubbard."

12. Andrew Lucas Hunt to "My dear Parents," Aug. 14, 1864, Andrew Lucas Hunt Papers, Southern Historical Collection, University of North Carolina, Chapel Hill (MS#3225), typescript in Pogue Special Collections.

13. Danforth, "How I Came to Be in the Army," 330–31.

14. Ibid., 333.

15. Ibid., 333–34.

16. Ibid., 334–35.

17. Ibid., 336.

18. Ibid., 336–38.

19. Hunt to "My dear Mother," Aug. 12, 1864; Hunt to "My dear Parents," Aug. 14, 1864.

20. Frazar Kirkland, *The Pictorial Book of Anecdotes and Incidents of the War of the Rebellion, Civil, Military, Naval and Domestic* (Hartford, Conn.: Hartford Publishing Co., 1867), 122–23.

21. Battle, Perrin, and Kniffen, *Kentucky,* 56; Barton, "History of Graves County," 117.

22. Andrew Lucas Hunt to "My dear Mother," Aug. 19, 1864, Hunt Papers.

23. Andrew Lucas Hunt to "My dear Willie" (his brother), Aug. 25, 1864, Hunt Papers.

24. Ibid.

25. "Journal of Private Hawley V. Needham, 134th Illinois Volunteer Infantry Regiment, Company G," 18–19, typescript in Pogue Special Collections.

26. Ibid., 18–20.

27. Ibid., 3.

28. Ibid., 13.

29. Ibid.

30. Ibid., 15.

31. Ibid., 16–17.

32. *O.R.*, ser. 1, vol. 39, part 1, 365–66, 463, part 2, 268, 346–47.

33. *Journal of the Adjourned Session of the House of Representatives of the Commonwealth of Kentucky Begun and Held in the Town of Frankfort, on Monday, the Seventh Day of December, in the Year of Our Lord 1863 and of the Commonwealth the Seventy-Second* (Frankfort: George D. Prentice, State Printer, 1865), 31.

34. *O.R.*, ser. 3, vol. 4, 688–89.

35. *O.R.*, ser. 1, vol. 39, part 2, 349; Warner, *Generals in Blue*, 319–20.

36. "Journal of Private Hawley V. Needham," 22–23; Collins and Collins, *History of Kentucky,* 1: 1864.

37. Hunt to "My dear Mother," Aug. 14, 1864.

38. Ibid.; Lucian Anderson to Abraham Lincoln, Sept. 10, 1864, Lincoln Papers, http://memory.loc.gov/cgi-bin/ampage?collId=mal&fileName=mal1/361/3611800/malpage.db&recNum=2&tempFile=./temp/~ammem_H8mg&filecode=mal&next_filecode=mal&prev_filecode=mal&itemnum=3&ndocs=100 (accessed Apr. 18, 2014).

39. *Journal of the Adjourned Session of the House*, 32.

40. Ibid., 31–40. Verres was a famously corrupt and cruel Roman governor of Sicily. Hastings was accused of similar machinations while he served as the first British governor-general of India.

41. *Louisville Daily Journal,* Sept. 27, 1864.

42. Ibid.

43. Ibid.

44. *Louisville Daily Journal,* Sept. 28, 1864.

45. *Louisville Daily Union Press,* Oct. 24, 1864.

46. Ibid.; *Louisville Weekly Journal*, Nov. 1, 1864.

47. Battle, Perrin, and Kniffen, *Kentucky,* 56.

48. Andrew Lucas Hunt to "My dear Mother," Sept. 14, 1864, and Andrew Lucas Hunt to "My dear Willie" (his brother), Sept. 16, 1864, both Hunt Papers.

49. Andrew Lucas Hunt to "My dear Mother," Sept. 14, 1864; D. Trabue Davis, *Story of Mayfield*, 15–16. The fortifications were actually an earthen mound with a flat top. The steep banks survive at the intersection of Tenth and Walnut Streets.

13. Rebel to the End and Beyond

1. Rufus King Williams to Abraham Lincoln, Oct. 3, 1864, Lincoln Papers, http://memory.loc.gov/cgi-bin/query/r?ammem/mal:@field(DOCID+@lit(d3695000)) (accessed Aug. 26, 2013).

2. Lucian Anderson to Abraham Lincoln, Oct. 17, 1864, Lincoln Papers, http://memory.loc.gov/cgi-bin/ampage?collId=mal&fileName=mal1/373/3730000/malpage.db&recNum=1&tempFile=./temp/~ammem_EgZr&filecode=mal&next_filecode=mal&prev_filecode=mal&itemnum=5&ndocs=100 (accessed Apr. 17, 2014).

3. Eisterhold, "Fort Heiman," 49–50; George, *History of the 3d, 7th, 8th and 12th,* 128.

4. *O.R.*, ser. 1, vol. 39, part 1, 870; Eisterhold, "Fort Heiman," 52.

5. George, *History of the 3d, 7th, 8th and 12th,* 128; *O.R.*, ser. 1, vol. 39, part 1, 870. Forrest reported that the *Anna* sank en route to Paducah.

6. Eisterhold, "Fort Heiman," 52; *O.R.*, ser. 1, vol. 39, part 1, 870. Forrest reported that his gunners so badly shot up the *Anna* that it sank en route to Paducah.

7. *O.R.,* ser. 1, vol. 39, part 1, 860, 870; George, *History of the 3d, 7th, 8th and 12th,* 129.

8. *O.R.*, ser. 1, vol. 39, part 1, 870–71; George, *History of the 3d, 7th, 8th and 12th,* 129; Wyeth, *Life of General Nathan Bedford Forrest,* 520–29; Allen, *Center of Conflict,* 142–44.

9. Shannon and McQuown, *Presidential Politics in Kentucky,* 37–40.

10. Coulter, *Civil War and Readjustment,* 185–87.

11. Shannon and McQuown, *Presidential Politics in Kentucky,* 37–40; *Louisville Daily Journal*, Sept. 27, 1864.

12. *Congressional Globe,* 38th Congress, 2nd session, 531. They were representatives Henry Grider, Aaron Harding, Robert Mallory, Brutus J. Clay, and William Henry Wadsworth.

13. George, *History of the 3d, 7th, 8th and 12th,* 139.

14. *Louisville Daily Journal,* Feb. 5, 1865.

15. *Louisville Daily Journal,* Feb. 13, 1864.

16. George, *History of the 3d, 7th, 8th and 12th,* 139.

17. Collins and Collins, *History of Kentucky,* 1: 158; Lindsey, *Report of the Adjutant General,* 2: 325–26, 765; Jennie Fyfe to "My Dearest Nell," Mar. 23, 1865, Fyfe Collection; *Frankfort Commonwealth,* Apr. 4, 1865.

18. *Louisville Daily Journal,* Mar. 2, 1865.

19. *Louisville Daily Journal,* Mar. 10, 1865.

20. E. A. Paine Court Martial Papers, Pogue Special Collections. The library bought the collection, which consists of photocopied records, from the National Archives and Records Administration. The documents were part of Record Group 153: Records of the Judge Advocate General's Office (Army), Entry 15: Court Martial Case Files, 1809–1894, File no. MM-1609, Boxes 1032–1033. See also Collins and Collins, *History of Kentucky,* 1: 136, 157, 164.

21. Dieter Ullrich, interview with the author, Feb. 15, 2013.

22. Ibid.

23. Warner, *Generals in Blue,* 355–56.

24. *Louisville Daily Journal,* Apr. 27, 1865.

25. George, *History of the 3d, 7th, 8th and 12th Kentucky,* 143.

26. Alben W. Barkley, *That Reminds Me* (Garden City, N.Y.: Doubleday & Company, 1954), 34.

27. Collins and Collins, *History of Kentucky,* 2: 39, 342; Coulter, *Civil War and Readjustment,* 273, 282. Some sources say the Conservatives and Radicals were tied in the state senate.

28. Collins and Collins, *History of Kentucky,* 1: 163; Battle, Perrin, and Kniffen, *Kentucky,* 220, 222; *Mayfield Weekly Monitor,* Oct. 19, 1898.

29. Collins and Collins, *History of Kentucky,* 2: 109, 281, 292, 342.

30. Harrison and Klotter, *New History,* 195.

31. Ibid.; Battle, Perrin, and Kniffen, *Kentucky,* 42; Legislative Document, No. 26, 11; Lindsey, *Report of the Adjutant General,* 1: 255–56, 338–51, 293–403, 2: 54–57. The Confederate totals are estimations based on Ellis, *Report of the Adjutant General,* 1: 14–22, 38–43, 54–59, 84–143, 332–75, 386–89, 2: 98–143. Battle, Perrin, and Kniffen's *Kentucky* offers some insight into the ratio of Confederate to Union volunteers from the Purchase. For example, the book says Ballard County furnished "fully 400 men" to the Confederate army and "about one fourth that number" to the Union Army (19). Approximately 800 Calloway countians put on Rebel gray, and "fully 200 men" donned Yankee blue, according to the book (34). The historians list companies by county origin, but not always accurately. For example, on p. 56, the book says Company G of the Third Kentucky, commanded by Captain C. C. Edwards, was from Graves County. On p. 107, it says Edwards's company was from Marshall County. The counties where Rebels were significantly more numerous than Yankees included Trigg, Lyon, Caldwell, Livingston, Union, Webster, and Henderson in the Pennyrile; Trimble, Carroll, and Owen in northern Kentucky; Bourbon, Clark, Scott, and Woodford in the Bluegrass; and Wolfe and Morgan in the mountains.

32. Coulter, *Civil War and Readjustment,* vii; Marshall, *Creating a Confederate Kentucky,* 2; Harrison and Klotter, *New History,* 241–42.

Bibliography

Archives

John Anderson diary. Forrest C. Pogue Special Collections Library, Murray State University, Murray, Ky.

Martha Nell Anderson. Private collection, Mayfield, Ky.

Given Campbell Papers. Southern Historical Collection, University of North Carolina, Chapel Hill.

Carr Family Papers. Forrest C. Pogue Special Collections Library, Murray State University, Murray, Ky.

William Clark Papers. Missouri Historical Society, St. Louis.

John J. Crittenden Papers. Library of Congress, Washington, D.C.

Filson Historical Society, Louisville, Ky.

Fyfe Family Collection. Bentley Library, University of Michigan, Ann Arbor.

Noble J. Gregory Papers. Forrest C. Pogue Special Collections Library, Murray State University, Murray, Ky.

Andrew Lucas Hunt Papers. Southern Historical Collection, University of North Carolina, Chapel Hill.

Lincoln Papers. Library of Congress, Washington, D.C.

Michael Mastin. Private collection, McKinney, Tex.

Paducah Civil War Hospital File. Special Collections, McCracken County Public Library, Paducah, Ky.

Forrest C. Pogue Special Collections Library. Murray State University Library, Murray, Ky.

Records of the Judge Advocate General's Office (Army). National Archives and Records Administration, Washington, D.C.

State Guard Records. John Trowbridge, command historian. Kentucky National Guard, Frankfort.

Hugh Williams and Evelyn Williams. Private collection, Mayfield, Ky.

Interviews

Lon Carter Barton. Interview with the author. April 10, 1998.

Dieter Ullrich. Interview with the author. February 15, 2013.

Newspapers and Periodicals

Cairo City Weekly Gazette

Cairo Times

Chicago Daily Tribune

Chicago Times

Cincinnati Daily Gazette

Cincinnati Enquirer

Columbus Crescent
Columbus Daily Confederate News
Columbus Federal Scout
Columbus War Eagle
Congressional Globe
Daily Louisville Democrat
Detroit Free Press
Evansville Journal
Frankfort Tri-Weekly Yeoman
Galveston Civilian and Gazette Weekly
Harper's Weekly
Hickman Courier
Lexington Daily Kentucky Statesman
Louisville Daily Courier
Louisville Daily Journal
Louisville Daily Union Press
Louisville Weekly Courier
Mayfield Southern Yeoman
Mayfield Weekly Monitor
Memphis Daily Appeal
Nashville Daily Union
Nashville Dispatch
New Orleans Daily Delta
New York Times
Paducah Herald
Richmond Daily Dispatch
St. Louis Daily Missouri Republican
St. Louis Republican

Primary Sources

"The Address of the People of South Carolina, Assembled in Convention, to the People of the Slaveholding States of the United States." Charleston, S.C.: Evans & Cogswell, Printers to the Convention, 1860.

Adjourned Session Of 1863–4, Of The House of Representatives Of The Commonwealth Of Kentucky, Begun And Held In The Town Of Frankfort, On Monday, The Seventh Day Of December, In The Year Of Our Lord 1865, And Of The Commonwealth The Seventy-Second. Frankfort, Ky.: State Printing Office, George D. Prentice, State Printer, 1865.

Barkley, Alben W. *That Reminds Me.* Garden City, N.Y.: Doubleday & Company, 1954.

Basler, Roy P., Marion Dolores Pratt, and Lloyd A. Dunlap, eds. *The Collected Works of Abraham Lincoln.* Vol. 7. New Brunswick, N.J.: Rutgers University Press, 1953.

Bassham, Ben L. *Ten Months in the "Orphan Brigade": Conrad Wise Chapman's Civil War Memoir.* Kent, Ohio: Kent State University Press, 1999.

Brevard, Sallie Malone. "A Reminiscence of the War." Photocopy. Columbus-Belmont State Park.

Browne, Junius Henry. *Four Years in Secessia: Adventures Within and Beyond the Union Lines Embracing a Great Variety of Facts, Incidents and Romance of the War.* Hartford, Conn.: O. D. Case and Co., 1865.

Clark, George Rogers. *Col. George Rogers Clark's Sketch of His Campaign in the Illinois in 1778–9.* New York: Arno Press, 1971.

Danforth, Willis. "How I Came to Be in the Army and General E. A. Paine's Plan of Federal Salvation." In *War Papers Read Before the Commandery of the State of Wisconsin, Loyal Legion of the United States, Volume I.* Milwaukee: Burdick, Armitage, & Allen, 1891.

Ellis, J. Tandy. *Report of the Adjutant General of the State of Kentucky Confederate Volunteers War, 1861–1865.* 2 vols. Frankfort: State Journal Company, 1915.

George, Henry. *History of the 3d, 7th, 8th and 12th Kentucky, C.S.A.* Louisville: Dearing Press, 1911.

Grant, Ulysses S. *Personal Memoirs of Ulysses S. Grant.* 1885. Vol. 1. Reprint, New York: Charles A. Webster, 1994.

Grief, J. V. "Forrest's Raid on Paducah." *Confederate Veteran* 5 (May 1897).

Haviland, Laura Smith. *A Woman's Life-Work: Labors and Experiences of Laura S. Haviland.* Cincinnati: Walden & Stowe, 1882.

Hewett, Janet B., ed. *Supplement to the Official Records of the Union and Confederate Armies, Part II, Record of Events.* Vol. 77, serial no. 89. Wilmington, N.C.: Broadfoot Publishing Company, 1998.

Hubbard, John Milton. *Notes of a Private.* Memphis: E. H. Clarke and Brother, 1909.

Hughes, Nathaniel Cheairs, Jr. *The Battle of Belmont: Grant Strikes South.* Chapel Hill: University of North Carolina Press, 1991.

Journal of the Adjourned Session of the House of Representatives of the Commonwealth of Kentucky Begun and Held in the Town of Frankfort, on Monday, the Seventh Day of December, in the Year of Our Lord 1863 and of the Commonwealth the Seventy-Second. Frankfort: George D. Prentice, State Printer, 1865.

Journal Of The Called Session Of The House Of Representatives Of The Commonwealth Of Kentucky, Begun And Held In The Town Of Frankfort, On Monday The Sixth Day Of May, In The Year Of Our Lord 1861, And Of The Commonwealth The Sixty-Ninth. Frankfort: John B. Major State Printer, 1861.

Journal Of The Called Session Of The House of Representatives of the Commonwealth of Kentucky, Begun and Held In The Town of Frankfort, on Thursday, The Seventeenth Day Of January, In The Year Of Our Lord 1861, And Of The Commonwealth The Sixty-Ninth. Frankfort: John B. Major, State Printer, 1861.

Journal Of The Called Session Of The Senate Of The Commonwealth Of Kentucky, Begun And Held In The Town Of Frankfort, On Monday The Sixth Day Of May, In The Year Of Our Lord 1861, And Of The Commonwealth The Sixty-Ninth. Frankfort: John B. Major State Printer, 1861.

Journal Of The Senate Of The Commonwealth of Kentucky, Begun And Held In The Town Of Frankfort On Thursday The Second Day of September, In The Year Of Our Lord 1861, And Of The Commonwealth The Sixty-Ninth. Frankfort: John B. Major, State Printer, 1861.

Journal Of the Called Session Of the Senate Of the Commonwealth of Kentucky, Begun and Held In The Town Of Frankfort, On Thursday The Seventeenth Day of January, In The Year Of Our Lord 1861, And Of The Commonwealth the Sixty-Ninth. Frankfort: John B. Major, State Printer, 1861.

Kellogg, Mary E., compiler and publisher. *Army Life of an Illinois Soldier Including a Day by Day Record of Sherman's March to the Sea Letters and Diary of the Late Charles W. Wills.* Washington, D.C.: Globe Printing Company, 1906.

Kelly, R. M. "Holding Kentucky for the Union." In *Battles and Leaders of the Civil War, Being for the Most Part Contributions by Union and Confederate Officers. Based Upon "The Century War Series."* Edited by Robert Underwood Johnson and Clarence Clough Buell, of the Editorial Staff of "The Century Magazine." Vol. 1. 1887. Reprint, South Brunswick, N.Y.: Thomas Yoseloff, 1956.

Kentucky Secretary of State Elections Register, 1855–1872. Kentucky Department for Libraries and Archives, Frankfort, Ky.

Kentucky Slave Narratives: A Folk History of Slavery in Kentucky from Interviews with Former Slaves. Applewood, Mass: Bedford Books, n.d.

Kirkland, Frazar. *The Pictorial Book of Anecdotes and Incidents of the War of the Rebellion, Civil, Military, Naval and Domestic.* Hartford, Conn.: Hartford Publishing Co., 1867.

Langstaff, George Quigley, Jr. *The Life and Times of Quintus Quincy Quigley, 1828–1910: His Personal Journey, 1858–1908.* Paducah, Ky.: Paducah Area Community Foundation, 1999.

Legislative Document, No. 26. "Response of the Adjutant General of Kentucky to a Resolution of Inquiry in Regard to Federal Enrollments in the State, Made to the House of Representatives Wednesday, March 1, 1865." Frankfort: George D. Prentice, State Printer, 1865.

Lincoln, Abraham. "Message of Appeal to Border-State Representatives in Favor of Compensated Emancipation." July 12, 1862. *The American Presidency Project,* by Gerhard Peters and John T. Wooley. http://www.presidency.ucsb.edu/ws/?pid=584.

Lindsey, D. W. *Report of the Adjutant General of the State of Kentucky.* 2 vols. Frankfort: John H. Harney, Public Printer, 1866.

Mearns, David C., ed. *The Lincoln Papers.* 2 vols. Garden City, N.Y.: Doubleday and Company, 1948.

Moore, Frank, ed. *The Rebellion Record: A Diary of American Events with Documents, Narratives, Illustrative Incidents, Poetry, Etc.* 12 vols. New York: G. P. Putnam, 1861.

Phillips, Christopher. *The Civil War in the Border South.* Santa Barbara, Denver, and Oxford: Praeger, 2013.

Preble, George Henry. *History of the Flag of the United States of America and of the Naval and Yacht-Club Signals, Seals, and Arms, and Principal National Songs of the United States, with a Chronicle of the Symbols, Standards, Banners, and Flags of Ancient and Modern Nations.* Boston: A. Williams and Company, 1880.

Register of the Kentucky State Guard for 1861. Frankfort: John B. Major, State Printer, 1861.

Report of the Military Board of Kentucky Made to the General Assembly, September 10, 1861. Frankfort, Ky.: Jno. B. Major, State Printer, 1861.

Resolution of the [Confederate] Congress [in Kentucky] 1861. Reprint, Lyndon, Ky.: Mull-Wathen Historic Press, 1970.

Russell, William Howard. *My Diary North and South.* Boston: T. O. H. P. Burnham, 1863.

Speed, Captain Thomas. *The Union Regiments of Kentucky Published Under the Auspices of the Union Soldiers and Sailors Monument Association.* Louisville, Ky.: Courier-Journal Job Printing Co., 1897.

Thompson, Ed Porter. *History of the Orphan Brigade.* Louisville, Ky.: Lewis N. Thompson, 1898.

Thwaites, Reuben Gold, ed. *The Jesuit Relations and Allied Documents Travels and Explorations of the Jesuit Missionaries in New France, 1610–1791.* Vol. 59. New York: Pageant Book Company, 1959.

Shaffner, Taliaferro P., ed. *The Kentucky State Register, for the Year 1847.* Louisville: Morton & Griswold, 1847.

Wallace, Lew. *An Autobiography.* New York: Harper & Brothers, 1906.

The War of the Rebellion: A Compilation of the Official Records of the Union and Confederate Armies. Washington, D.C.: War Department, 1880–1902.

Williams' Paducah Directory, City Guide, and Business Mirror. Paducah, Ky.: Byers and Clements, 1859.

Wyeth, John Allan. *Life of General Nathan Bedford Forrest.* New York: Harper & Brothers, 1899.

Secondary Sources

Allen, Anthony. *Columbus, Kentucky as the Nation's Capital: Legend or Reality?* Fort Davis, Tex.: River Microstudies, 1993.

Allen, Hall. *Center of Conflict: A Factual Story of the War between the States in Western Kentucky and Tennessee.* Paducah, Ky.: Paducah Sun-Democrat, 1961.

———. "The Reluctant Kentuckians." *Jackson Purchase 150 Years, 1819–1969, Sesquicentennial. Prepared by the Jackson Purchase Historical Society and Published by the Mayfield Messenger, Mayfield, Ky.* 1969.

Astor, Aaron. *Rebels on the Border: Civil War, Emancipation, and the Reconstruction of Kentucky and Missouri.* Baton Rouge: Louisiana State University Press, 2012.

Barton, Lon Carter. "A History of Graves County, Kentucky." Master's thesis, University of Kentucky, 1960.

Battle, J. H., W. H. Perrin, and G. C. Kniffen. *Kentucky: A History of the State.* 1st ed. Louisville and Chicago: F. A. Battey and Co., 1885.

Bearman, Alan. "'The South Carolina of Kentucky': Religion and Secession in the Jackson Purchase." *Filson Club History Quarterly* 76 (2002).

Belue, Ted Franklin. *The Long Hunt: Death of the Buffalo East of the Mississippi.* Mechanicsburg, Pa.: Stackpole Books, 1996.

Berlin, Ira. *Freedom: A Documentary History of Emancipation, 1861–1867.* Series 2, book 1, *The Black Military Experience.* Cambridge and New York: Cambridge University Press, 1982.

Birchfield, Steven. *Civil War Letters.* Volume One: *West Tennessee.* Melber, Ky.: Simmons Historical Publishing, 1995.

Bodley, Temple J., and Samuel M. Wilson. *History of Kentucky.* Vol. 1. Chicago: F. J. Clarke Publishing Co., 1928.

Boyd, John A. "Intimidation, Conspiracy, Provocation and Intrigue: The Militias of Kentucky, 1859–1861." *Army History* (Fall 2008).

Carstens, Kenneth C. *George Rogers Clark's Fort Jefferson, 1780–1781: Kentucky's Outpost on the Western Frontier.* Westminster, Md.: Heritage Books, 2005.

Catton, Bruce. *Grant Moves South.* Boston and Toronto: Little, Brown and Company, 1960.

Channing, Steven A. *Kentucky: A Bicentennial History.* New York: W. W. Norton and Company, 1977.

Collins, Lewis. *Historical sketches of Kentucky: Embracing its History, Antiquities, and Natural curiosities, Geographical, Statistical, and Geological Descriptions; with Anecdotes of Pioneer Life, and More Than One Hundred Biographical Sketches of Distinguished Pioneers, Soldiers, Statesmen, Jurists, Lawyers, Divines, Etc.* 1847. Reprint, Lexington, Ky.: Henry Clay Press, 1968.

Collins, Lewis, and Richard Collins. *History of Kentucky: By the Late Lewis Collins, Judge of the Mason County Court, Revised, Enlarged Four-Fold and Brought Down to the Year 1874, by his son, Richard H. Collins, A.M, LL.B. Embracing Pre-Historic Annals for 331 Years, Outline, and by Counties, Statistics, Antiquities, and Natural Curiosities, Geographical and Geological Descriptions, Sketches of the Court of Appeals, the Churches, Freemasonry, Odd Fellowship, and Internal Improvements, Incidents of Pioneer Life, and Nearly Five Hundred Biographical Sketches of Distinguished Pioneers, Soldiers, Statesmen, Jurists, Lawyers, Surgeons, Divines, Merchants, Historians, Editors, Artists, Etc., Etc.* 2 vols. 1874. Reprint, Berea, Ky.: Kentucke Imprints, 1976.

Connelly, Thomas L. *Army of the Heartland.* Baton Rouge: Louisiana State University Press, 1967.

Corliss, Carlton J. *Main-Line of Mid-America: The Story of the Illinois Central.* New York: Creative Age Press, 1950.

Coulter, E. Merton. *The Civil War and Readjustment in Kentucky.* Chapel Hill: University of North Carolina Press, 1926.

Craig, Berry. "Henry C. Burnett, Champion of Southern Rights." *Register of the Kentucky Historical Society* 77 (1979).

———. *Hidden History of Kentucky in the Civil War.* Charleston, S.C.: History Press, 2010.

———. *Hidden History of Kentucky Soldiers.* Charleston, S.C.: History Press, 2011.

———. *Hidden History of Western Kentucky.* Charleston, S.C.: History Press, 2011.

———. "The Jackson Purchase Considers Secession: The 1861 Mayfield Convention." *Register of the Kentucky Historical Society* 99 (2001).

———. *True Tales of Old-Time Kentucky Politics: Bombast, Bourbon and Burgoo.* Charleston, S.C.: History Press, 2009.

Davis, Darrell Haug. *The Geography of the Jackson Purchase: A Study of the Distri-*

bution and Activities of Man in the Gulf Embayment Area of Western Kentucky. Frankfort: Kentucky Geological Survey, 1923.

Davis, D. Trabue. *The Story of Mayfield through a Century, 1823–1923.* Paducah: Billings and Company, 1923.

Dew, Charles B. *Apostles of Disunion: Southern Secession Commissioners and the Causes of the Civil War.* Charlottesville: University of Virginia Press, 2001.

Eisterhold, John A. "Fort Heiman: Forgotten Fortress." *West Tennessee Historical Society Papers* 28 (1974).

Gleeson, Ed. *Illinois Rebels: A Civil War Unit History of G Company Fifteenth Tennessee Regiment Volunteer Infantry.* Carmel: Guild Press of Indiana, 1966.

Goodspeed, Westin A. *A History of Tennessee from the Earliest Times to the Present.* 1886. Reprint, Nashville: Charles and Randy Elder, Booksellers, 1973.

Gott, Kendall D. *Where the South Lost the War: An Analysis of the Fort Henry–Fort Donelson Campaign, February 1862.* Mechanicsburg, Pa.: Stackpole Books, 2003.

Hacker, David. "A Census-Based Count of the Civil War Dead." *Civil War History* 57, no. 4 (December 2011).

Harrison, Lowell H. "George W. Johnson and Richard Hawes: The Governors of Confederate Kentucky." *Register of the Kentucky Historical Society* 79 (1981).

Harrison, Lowell H., and James C. Klotter. *A New History of Kentucky.* Lexington: University Press of Kentucky, 1997.

Horn, Stanley F. *Tennesseans in the Civil War.* 2 vols. Nashville: Tennessee Civil War Centennial Commission, 1964.

Hoskins, Patricia Ann. "'The Old First Is with the South': The Civil War, Reconstruction, and Memory in the Jackson Purchase Region of Kentucky." PhD diss., Auburn University, 2008.

Hubbell, John T., and James W. Geary, ed. *Biographical Dictionary of the Union: Northern Leaders of the Civil War.* Westport, Conn.: Greenwood Press, 1995.

Huch, Ronald K. "Fort Pillow Massacre: The Aftermath of Paducah." *Illinois State Historical Society Journal* 66 (Spring 1973).

Jennings, Dorothy, and Kerby Jennings. *The Story of Calloway County, 1822–1976.* Murray, Ky.: Murray Democrat Publishing Co., 1980.

Johnson, Leland R. *The Falls City Engineers: A History of the Louisville District Corps of Engineers United States Army.* Louisville, Ky.: Louisville District Corps of Engineers, 1974.

Kleber, John E., ed. *The Kentucky Encyclopedia.* Lexington: University Press of Kentucky, 1992.

Lansden, John M. *A History of the City of Cairo, Illinois.* Chicago: R. R. Donnelley and Sons, 1910.

Lawson, Hughie G. "Geographical Origins of White Migrants to Trigg and Calloway Counties in the Ante-bellum Period." *Filson Club History Quarterly* 57 (1983).

Lee, Jacob F. "'The Union as It Was and the Constitution as It Is': Unionism and Emancipation in Civil War Kentucky." Master's thesis, University of Louisville, 2007.

Lemly, James H. *The Gulf, Mobile & Ohio: A Railroad That Had to Expand or Expire.* Homewood, Ill.: Richard D. Erwin, 1953.

Levin, H., ed. *Lawyers and Lawmakers of Kentucky.* Chicago: Lewis Publishing Company, 1897.

Lindsley, John Berrien. *Military Annals of Tennessee, Confederate.* Nashville: J. M. Lindsley and Company, 1886.

Lucas, Marion B. *A History of Kentucky Blacks from Slavery to Segregation, 1760–1891.* 2 vols. Frankfort: Kentucky Historical Society, 1992.

Marshall, Ann E. *Creating a Confederate Kentucky: The Lost Cause and Civil War Memory in a Border State.* Chapel Hill: University of North Carolina Press, 2010.

McDowell, Robert Emmet. *City of Conflict: Louisville in the Civil War.* Louisville: Louisville Civil War Roundtable, 1962.

McElroy, Robert McNutt. *Kentucky in the Nation's History.* New York: Moffat and Yard, 1909.

McPherson, James M. *Battle Cry of Freedom: The Civil War Era.* Oxford and New York: Oxford University Press, 1988.

———. *This Mighty Scourge: Perspectives on the Civil War.* New York: Oxford University Press, 2007.

Meany, Edmond S. *Governors of Washington: Territorial and State.* Seattle: Department of Printing, University of Washington, 1915.

———. "Richard Dickinson Gholson." *Washington Historical Quarterly* 8 (1917).

Mulligan, William H., Jr. "African American Troops in Far West Kentucky during the Civil War: Recruitment and Service of the Fourth U.S. Heavy Artillery (Colored)." Typescript of speech given at Fort Donelson National Military Park, Dover, Tenn., February 25, 2012.

Neuman, Fred G. *Paducahans in History.* Paducah, Ky.: Young Printing Company, 1922.

———. *The Story of Paducah (Kentucky).* Paducah, Ky.: Young Printing Company, 1927.

Patrick, Jeffrey L., ed. *Three Years with Wallace's Zouaves: The Civil War Memoirs of Thomas Wise Durham.* Macon, Ga.: Mercer University Press, 2003.

Polk, Dr. William M. "General Polk and the Battle of Belmont." In *Battles and Leaders of the Civil War.* Reprint, New York: Thomas Yoseloff, 1956.

Quarles, Benjamin. *The Negro in the Civil War.* Boston: Little, Brown & Co., 1969.

Randall, J. G., and David Donald. *The Civil War and Reconstruction.* 2nd. ed. Lexington, Mass.: D. C. Heath and Company, 1969.

Robertson, John E. *Paducah: 1830–1980, A Sesquicentennial History.* Paducah, Ky.: John E. Robertson, 1980.

———. *Paducah: Frontier to the Atomic Age.* Charleston, S.C.: Arcadia Publishing, 2002.

———. "Western Kentucky and Paducah in Legend and Lore." *Filson Club History Quarterly* 76 (2002).

Sarna, Jonathan D. *When General Grant Expelled the Jews.* Schocken, N.Y.: Nextbook, 2012.

Shannon, Jasper B., and Ruth McQuown. *Presidential Politics in Kentucky, 1824–*

1948: A Compilation of Election Statistics and an Analysis of Political Behavior. Lexington: Bureau of Government Research, College of Arts and Sciences, University of Kentucky, 1950.

Shelton, Phillip M. "Camp Beauregard Graves County, Kentucky." *Register of the Kentucky Historical Society* 61, no. 3 (April 1963).

Shortridge, Wilson Porter. "Kentucky Neutrality in 1861." *Mississippi Valley Historical Review* 9 (March 1923).

Smith, John David. "The Recruitment of Negro Soldiers in Kentucky." *Register of the Kentucky Historical Society* 72 (1974).

Stickles, Arndt M. *Simon Bolivar Buckner: Borderland Knight.* Chapel Hill: University of North Carolina Press, 1910.

Sutherland, Daniel E. *A Savage Conflict The Decisive Role of Guerrillas in the Civil War.* Chapel Hill: University of North Carolina Press, 2009.

Ullrich, Dieter C. "Confederate Operations in the Jackson Purchase: Camp Beauregard, Kentucky." *Filson Club History Quarterly* 76, no. 4 (2002).

Warner, Ezra J. *Generals in Blue: Lives of the Union Commanders.* Baton Rouge: Louisiana State University Press, 1964.

Warner, Ezra J., and W. Buck Yearns. *Biographical Register of the Confederate Congress.* Baton Rouge: Louisiana State University Press, 1975.

Whitesell, Hunter B. "Military Operations in the Jackson Purchase." *Register of the Kentucky Historical Society* 63, no. 4. part 3 (1965).

Wills, Brian Steel. *The Confederacy's Greatest Cavalryman: Nathan Bedford Forrest.* Lawrence: University Press of Kansas, 1992.

Index